PENGUIN CLASSICS

THE DIVINE COMEDY VOL. III: PARADISE

DANTE ALIGHIERI was born in Florence in 1265 and belonged to a noble but impoverished family. He followed a normal course of studies, possibly attending University in Bologna, and when he was about twenty he married Gemma Donati, by whom he had several children. He had first met Bice Portinati, whom he called Beatrice, in 1274, and when she died in 1290, he sought distraction by studying philosophy and theology and by writing *La Vita Nuova*. During this time he became involved in the strife between the Guelfs and the Ghibellines; he became a prominent White Guelf, and when the Black Guelfs came to power in 1302, Dante, during an absence from Florence, was condemned to exile. He took refuge first in Verona, and after wandering from place to place—as far as Paris and even, some have said, to Oxford—he settled in Ravenna. While there he completed *The Divine Comedy*, which he began in about 1308. Dante died in Ravenna in 1321.

MARK MUSA is a graduate of Rutgers University (B.A., 1956), the University of Florence (Fulbright, 1956–58), and the Johns Hopkins University (M.A., 1959; Ph.D., 1961). He is a former Guggenheim fellow and the author of a number of books and articles. Best known for his translations of the Italian classics (Dante, Petrarch, Boccaccio, Machiavelli, and the poetry of the Middle Ages) as well as his Dante criticism, he holds the title of Distinguished Professor of French and Italian and is Director of the Center for Italian Studies at Indiana University. He translated and edited *The Divine Comedy, Vol. I: Inferno* and *Vol. II: Purgatory*, and translated and edited with Peter Bondanella *The Portable Machiavelli*, and, most recently, translated and edited *The Portable Dante*, all published by Penguin Books.

DANTE ALIGHIERI
THE DIVINE COMEDY
VOLUME III

PARADISE

TRANSLATED WITH AN INTRODUCTION,
NOTES, AND COMMENTARY BY
MARK MUSA

PENGUIN BOOKS

PENGUIN BOOKS
Published by the Penguin Group
Penguin Books USA Inc.,
375 Hudson Street, New York, New York 10014, U.S.A.
Penguin Books Ltd, 27 Wrights Lane,
London W8 5TZ, England
Penguin Books Australia Ltd, Ringwood,
Victoria, Australia
Penguin Books Canada Ltd, 10 Alcorn Avenue,
Toronto, Ontario, Canada M4V 3B2
Penguin Books (N.Z.) Ltd, 182–190 Wairau Road,
Auckland 10, New Zealand

Penguin Books Ltd, Registered Offices:
Harmondsworth, Middlesex, England

This translation first published in the United States of America by
Indiana University Press 1984
Pubished with a new Introduction
and a Glossary and Index of Persons and Places
in Penguin Classics 1986
Published simultaneously in Canada

13   15   14

LIBRARY OF CONGRESS CATALOGING IN PUBLICATION DATA
Dante Alighieri, 1265–1321.
Paradise.
(The divine comedy / Dante Alighieri; v. 3)
(Penguin classics)
Translation of Paradiso.
Bibliography: p.
Includes index.
1. Heaven — Poetry.   I. Musa, Mark.   II. Title.
III. Series: Dante Alighieri, 1265–1321. Divina
commedia. English (Harmondsworth, Middlesex); v. 3.
IV. Series: Penguin classics.
PQ4315.M8   1984 vol. 3   [PQ4315.4]   851'.1   85-28461
ISBN 0 14 04.4443 2

Printed in the United States of America
Set in CRT Garamond

For Bruno, my father

ACKNOWLEDGMENTS

Thank you, Tom Bergin, my very dear friend, for your careful reading of the second version of this translation and for the times you caught me not keeping time to the music.

Thanks to my student and research assistant Lisa Holekamp, who was so helpful with the notes, to Cliff Marcus for helping out with the glossary, and to Sandy Claxon, who typed and retyped the many drafts of this translation.

Special thanks to my friend Francesco Mazzoni, President of the Società Dantesca in Florence, who made this past year in Florence such a happy and profitable one for me by giving me free run of the fine collection of Dante books in the Palagio dell'Arte della Lana as well as the cooperation of his staff: Gabriella Pomaro and Martino Marchi. This made it possible for me to polish the translation and complete the notes with ease and joy.

And, of course, to all those students over the years who taught me to read the Poem.

CONTENTS

INTRODUCTION TO
THE *PARADISE*

The Divine Comedy is one man's vision of the state of souls after death written with the purpose of saving all mankind. It is both man's attempt to communicate with God and an allegory depicting how Everyman, represented by the protagonist or Pilgrim, wins reward or punishment in the afterlife while still living in this life, by exercising his free will to do good or evil. The *Inferno* treats the state of souls of the wicked who are condemned to the pains of Hell. The *Purgatory* deals with the learning of what is good through a spiritual process of purification that is painful yet pleasing, since someday this pain will come to an end. It is a place of moral growth and progress, the realm in which we learn how earthly love becomes divine. The *Paradise* reveals the great beauty of virtue seen in the rewards awaiting God's Blest. The main action of the *Paradise* is concerned with how man's soul, as it contemplates the making of God's universe, rises by stages in order to arrive at an understanding of the One creator of that universe. To see the universe as One is the final goal of the journey, and the movement of the journey is from fragmentation to unity. What the Pilgrim sees in the cantos of the lower heavens, in fact, is all in preparation for his vision in the highest heaven, the Empyrean, where he will see the redeemed, united with their bodies, as they will be after the Last Judgment. The cantos of the lower heavens are the steps of knowledge leading to Perfect Vision and union with God.

The Inferno exists as a concrete place somewhere below the surface of the earth. The Purgatory is a mountain that rises high above the sphere of water and has a definite, explained origin. But where is Paradise? Of what does it consist? No matter how primitive or simple medieval science, and especially astronomy, may appear to us today, it did have its own solid, rational system based on deductive reasoning, and within this system it functioned perfectly. According to Dante's Ptolemaic astronomy the universe is geocentric: the earth is at the center of the universe and the planets revolve around it. Constructing the physical universe of his poem on the Ptolemaic system, then, Dante has nine concentric crystalline spheres composed of ethereal substance. Contained within this substance and carried along within these spheres are the heavenly bodies. They are, in ascending order from the earth, the moon, Mercury, Venus, the sun, Mars, Jupiter, Saturn, and the Fixed Stars or Constellations. The ninth sphere, or Primum Mobile, is the outer boundary of the universe at the edge of space; it is empty and is described by Dante in terms of pure motion. It is the largest and fastest of the spheres, containing and communicating its movement to the eight heavens below it. Enclosing all of these nine spheres is the tenth one of immeasurable size: the Empyrean, the realm of pure spirit and perfect peace, spaceless and motionless. It is here that the souls of the Blest dwell with God and His angels.

It is God who gives the Primum Mobile its motion, and it is the Primum Mobile that imparts motion to the spheres below it. Each of the nine spheres is governed by its own spiritual intelligence or hierarchy of angels, and the combined force of these angelic intelligences over all the spheres is what is known in Dante's world as Nature. Between the realm of brute matter and the angels is man with his immortal soul. Man is beckoned by the spheres which circle around and above him reflecting God's creation. They invite his contemplation. This is the setting for man's return to God, for his drama of salvation.

Canto I of the *Paradise* serves as the overture to the great musical which follows. All of the major themes, movements, structures, images, and symbols appear in some way or another in the opening canto. The Almighty, "The One Who moves all things," is present as soon as the *Paradise* begins in line 1. The Empyrean, "His brightest shining heaven" (4), where the final action of this part of the *Comedy* will take place, is introduced as early as possible as if to stress the circular movement of the *Paradise* before the movement itself starts. This is followed immediately by the "incommunicability" topos: "no man ... has wit or skill to tell about" (5–6), a theme which will return again and again in the course of the journey and will reach its final "irresolution" in the closing canto of the poem. The concept of "intellect," "goal," and "desire" is introduced in the third tercet. All the joy that will fill the thirty-three cantos of the *Paradise* resounds in line 33: "a new joy in the joyous Delphic god." The symbolic geometry which begins to reveal itself once the Pilgrim and his guide pass beyond that heavenly region upon which the earth still casts its shadow is clearly present in lines 38–39: "the place which joins/four circles with three crosses . . ." Beatrice's all important "eyes," the "sun," and even the "eagle" which will be so brilliantly developed in later cantos are all in tercet 46–48. We are also given a glimpse of all "the eternal spheres" (65) which the Pilgrim will soon visit. The idea of Beatrice as "mother" and the Pilgrim as "child" (101–102) often returns in the course of the journey. There is also the concept of "order" and "form" (104–105). The "bow" (119 and 125) will appear a number of times during the journey, especially in the earlier cantos. The words "intellect and love" are joined in line 120. The Pilgrim's "eagerness to learn" (83), all the light, the "blazing sparks of light" (59), the sound, "strains of harmony" (77–78), and motion that will fill the rest of the *Paradise* are born here in the opening canto.

Let us take a quick look at one of these themes introduced in the opening canto, the one I have called symbolic geometry, and briefly trace its development in the *Paradise*. Dante describes the time of year that he made his ascent to Paradise in terms of four circles and three crosses as a vernal equinox which was thought to be a propitious time of year. The four and three represent another reminder of the seven virtues (four cardinal and three theological) that were shining at the beginning of the ascent of the Mountain of Purgatory (the four stars in *Purgatory* I, 23, and the three torches later on in VIII, 89). Circles and crosses, as the reader will see, are shapes that will be developed in the course of the journey through the Paradise. The action in the sphere of the sun, for example, (cantos X–XIII) is built on the figure of the circle and the sphere of Mars (cantos XIV–XVII), whose action takes place all within the confines of an immense cross. The circle, as I try to point out in my notes, is the dominating figure in the *Paradise,* and Dante makes the circle work for him in a number of ways. There are times when he will even imitate the shape of the circle with his words. At the end of the poem three circles become contained in one, as the pattern running through the Paradise reaches its culmination. A stunning example of this circularity which Dante used to reflect perfection and trinity and in which language is imitating concept is shown in Canto XIV, 28–30:

> That One and Two and Three which never ends
>   and ever reigns in Three and Two and One,
>   uncircumscribed and circumscribing all.

There are several other examples in this canto of the same technique. This type of geometrical imagery is particularly evident in the central cantos of the *Paradise* where the circle gives way to the linear cross. In Canto XIV again, we see movement conveyed in terms of the horizontal and vertical lines of a cross in verses 109–111:

> From top to base, across from arm to arm
>   bright lights were moving, sparkling brilliantly
>   as they would meet and pass each other's glow.

As theology gives way to politics, so the circular becomes the linear. We find this shift in verses 100–102 of Canto XIV:

> so, constellated in the depths of Mars,
>   these rays of light crossed in the holy sign
>   which quadrants make when joining in a circle.

The straight line will become the circle again towards the end of the Poem. In Canto XXX, 88–90, as the Pilgrim's eyes drink in the river of light emanating from the Empyrean, a miraculous change takes place:

> no sooner had the eaves of my eyes drunk
>   within those waters, than the river turned
>   from its straight course to a circumference.

And from this image we move to the concept of God as both center and circumference of the same circle a few tercets later (103–105):

> in figure of a circle this light spreads,
>   and is so vast that its circumference
>   would be too loose a belt to bind the sun.

All this is leading, of course, to the final vision of the Godhead in Canto XXXIII, 115-117, where three circles with three colors are seen clearly all within the same circumference:

> Within Its depthless clarity of substance
> I saw the Great Light shine into three circles
> in three clear colors bound in one same space

And finally, the Pilgrim becomes the geometer whose wish to square the circle (an impossible task) is granted him—though only for a brief moment. With the circle squared the poem comes to an end in the perfect, powerful balance of the closing three verses:

> but, like a wheel in perfect balance turning,
> I felt my will and my desire impelled
>
> by the Love that moves the sun and the other stars.

Some of the difficulty the reader of the *Paradise* encounters can be reduced to the one important word which Dante invents to describe his unusual condition in Canto I when he looks into Beatrice's eyes that are gazing straight into the sun. He invents the verb *trasumanar* ("transhumanize"):

> Gazing at her, I felt myself becoming
> what Glaucus had become tasting the herb
> that made him like the other sea-gods there.
>
> "Transhumanize"—it cannot be explained
> *per verba,* so let this example serve
> until God's grace grants the experience.
>
> (67-72)

The Pilgrim is undergoing a miraculous inner transformation in preparation for his approach to Paradise. He is, in a sense, becoming divine in order to be accepted by all those divine souls who occupy God's immense sea which he is about to enter. He is entering a state beyond mortal explication, one that cannot be explained *per verba* ("with words"). What the poet is saying in the above tercets is that the image of Glaucus and the sea-gods is the best he can do to explain his miraculous adventure and that those who are deserving will have to wait until they die to understand the true experience of sanctification.

Dante cannot ground his Paradise in the concrete things of the living world as he did in the *Inferno* and *Purgatory*. The souls of the Blest in *Paradise* will be lights, splendors, and sparks that dance and whirl about; they will assume diverse shapes, and speak to the Pilgrim in symbols and signs. The Poet will have to invent more words for other occasions (as he did the verb *trasumanar*), in order to articulate things that cannot possibly be seen by the human eye. The eyes that have been "transhumanized" must learn to read a new and different language.

It was the medieval view that God's creation is the symbol through which He reveals himself and at the same time remains hidden. And that is why Dante bases his imagery to describe what cannot be described on the temporal. Dante makes the visible world of the *Paradise* accessible to the reader by means of light, sound, and motion. Never does he use a simile or any other rhetorical device as mere decoration. There is always a relationship between word and reality. For example, when a cluster of stylistic elements are found in a canto (or in a group of cantos), they are there in imitation of the meaning conveyed therein. It is the subject and meaning, the conceptual, that dictates the course of the structural or stylistic setup. It is Dante imitating God's universe with language.

Contained in the opening tercet of the *Paradise* we find not only the general theme of the entire canticle clearly announced but also the two fundamental structures or movements operating throughout, which are expressed by the two verbs of line 2: "penetrates" and "reflecting" (the Italian is "penetra e risplende"). God's glory, grace, or light pours down from above and in turn is brought back up to Him. As the cantos of the *Paradise* progress there is also a gradual increase in the use of verbs of expanding growth and ones with connotations of the intensity of light. The stress is on "more and more"—more light, more brilliance—all leading to more understanding as the Pilgrim's vision increases. Dante will double words, triple them (for example, line 63 of Canto XI in the original reads: "poscia di di in di l'amo più forte") and limit a line to exactly three words. He invents words (many of them with the prefix *in*) with the intention of intensifying light, sound, and motion—as well as reflecting the general movement and goal of the *Paradise*. I will quote just two of the many examples of the "more and more" technique. In Canto XXIII, 82–84 (the italics are mine):

> just so I saw there hosts of countless *splendors*
> struck from above by *ardent rays* of love,
> but could not see the source of such a *blaze*.

and in Canto XXVIII, 16–18:

> I saw a point that *radiated light*
> *so piercing* that the eyes its *brightness strikes*
> are forced to shut from such *intensity*.

No time has passed between the end of the *Purgatory* and the beginning of the *Paradise*. The Pilgrim Dante and his spiritual guide Beatrice are standing as they were at the end of the *Purgatory* in the Earthly Paradise. It is noon, and they are probably still surrounded by those seven maidens who symbolize the four moral virtues and three theological ones. Matilda and Statius, who were a part of the scene at the top of the mountain of Purgatory, are no longer present. The mystical rivers of Lethe and Eunoë have been crossed, the one erasing the memory of sin, the other restoring the remembrance of good deeds. The Pilgrim is now, as the closing verse of *Purgatory* tells us, "eager to rise, now ready for the stars."

Beatrice explains how God is the goal that every creature seeks. The universe is made in his image; it is stamped with the likeness of Divine Wisdom, and its beauty depends on its order. She explains the law of love. God or Love, the beginning and end, moves everything, and everything, through Love, moves back to him. According to their diverse instincts, God moves all things to their natural end. All nature is subject to God's law. Now that the Pilgrim is purified and "ready for the stars," Beatrice tells him that his ascent is as natural and inevitable and as much a part of the order of things as a river that must rush down a high mountain or as a flame that must burn upward. The Pilgrim *must* rise now to his natural end, the natural goal of full, perfect, and eternal happiness. God has ordered it so.

In the first nine cantos of the *Paradise* (containing the first three heavens of Paradise) there is an emphasis on the doctrine of derivation, how from the one comes the many, an expansion of the opening tercet of the *Paradise*. There is also emphasis on man's place in society in relation to his spiritual status. Society involves diversity of function, which implies mankind's different gifts and abilities, and this difference among men is the ultimate cause of the diversity of the stars and, of course, of the spots on the moon. By the time the reader reaches the end of Canto IX, which marks the close of the first major division of the *Paradise,* he should realize that the long discussion of moon spots occupying most of Canto II, and about which the modern reader of the poem may feel Beatrice is making too big a to-do, is, in fact, a prefiguration of the structure of Paradise itself as well as a poetic point of reference for many of the themes running through the *Paradise* as a whole.

The souls Dante encounters on his way up to the Empyrean represent, by means of the sphere in which they appear to him, the visible signs of the degree of grace that they have attained in relation to the capacity they have been given. This Dante would not have been able to ascertain in his final vision of the Rose in the Empyrean because of the intensity of the vision. What is symbolized in the vision of the Rose is the equality with which every blessed soul experiences God's grace regardless of its capacity. The important theme in the *Paradise* of the varying capacities of souls for containing the grace of God is also intimately connected to the discussion of the moon spots in Canto II. The explanation of the varying ability of the moon's composition to absorb the *virtú* or power distributed by the order of the Cherubim angels is a foreshadowing in physical or scientific terms of the varying capacities of the blessed souls for assimilating the grace of God. The moon spots, then, are the result of the diverse ways in which divine virtue, originating in the Empyrean, passing through the Primum Mobile, and from there filtering down through the spheres below by means of the angelic Intelligences, joins with the body of the moon.

Not everyone in Paradise is equally blessed. God bestows his grace in different degrees according to his own pleasure, and blessedness is a matter of grace. Depending on the amount of grace given through divine predestination, men's visions of God will differ, but it is upon each soul's vision of God that its happiness depends. Though each soul enjoys a different degree of bliss, each is perfectly happy, since it knows it is enjoying bliss to its full capacity which has been ordained by the will of God. The degree of bliss enjoyed by the soul in

Heaven, then, is not dependent entirely on how one led his life on earth, but more on the mystery of predestination. This is the answer the Pilgrim will hear from a number of the souls in Paradise.

In *Paradise* III, Piccarda, in reply to the Pilgrim's question as to whether the happiness of the souls there in the lowest sphere of the moon is not tinged with the desire for a higher place in God's Heaven, says:

"Brother, the virtue of our heavenly love,
tempers our will and makes us want no more
than what we have—we thirst for this alone.

If we desired to be higher up,
then our desires would not be in accord
with His will Who assigns us to this sphere;

think carefully what love is and you'll see
such discord has no place within these rounds,
since to be here is to exist in Love.

Indeed, the essence of this blessèd state
is to dwell here within His holy will,
so that there is no will but one with His;

the order of our rank from height to height
throughout this realm is pleasing to the realm,
as to that King Who wills us to His will.

In His will is our peace—it is the sea
in which all things are drawn that it itself
creates or which the work of Nature makes."
                                                    (70-87)

Just as Beatrice had explained in the preceding canto, centered around the discussion of the moon spots, that each sphere takes in an amount of Divine Light that is in proportion to its capacity to receive it, so, in the same way, does each individual soul enjoy the bliss of the highest realm in accordance with its capacity.

While still in the first sphere, that of the moon, the Pilgrim is given another piece of important information concerning the workings of Paradise. In Canto IV, Beatrice, answering one of the Pilgrim's unspoken questions, explains:

Not the most Godlike of the Seraphim,
  not Moses, Samuel, whichever John
  you choose—I tell you—not Mary herself

has been assigned to any other heaven
  than that of these shades you have just seen here,
  and each one's bliss is equally eternal;

all lend their beauty to the Highest Sphere,
  sharing one same sweet life to the degree
  that they feel the eternal breath of God.

These souls appeared here not because this sphere
  has been allotted them, but as a sign
  of their less great degree of blessedness.

(28–39)

The souls, then, that appear to the Pilgrim are not really there. They are projections of their true selves which exist only in the Empyrean, the spaceless heaven of God which is their true home. The spheres serve only to point out certain distinctions or qualities the souls had shown during their life on earth. It is as though God were projecting their images down onto eight crystalline screens for the benefit of the Pilgrim's mortal condition. It is the only way he, as a man making the voyage in the flesh, can be instructed and learn. His condition does not allow him to see things as they truly are; he will see and feel in this realm in a way unknown to him in the previous ones. The Pilgrim, in fact, is not even certain that he is making this final part of the journey with his body (I, 73–75). The faces of the souls he sees are faint images of light, and gradually, the higher up we go, the more the image fades and the emphasis is on the light itself. What he cannot learn directly must be taught him through analogy involving the senses. In *Paradise* XXX, 76–81, Beatrice explains the symbolic nature of what the Pilgrim has seen so far in his journey through Paradise. Talking about the flowing light in the shape of a stream which the Pilgrim has just seen, she explains:

> ... "The stream, the jewels you see
> leap in and out of it, the smiling blooms
> are all prefigurations of their truth.

> These things are not imperfect in themselves;
> the defect, rather, lies within your sight,
> as yet not strong enough to reach such heights."

This stream from which Beatrice invites the Pilgrim to drink is the last of God's projections of reality prefiguring truth.

The first three heavens of the *Paradise* may be thought of as corresponding to the first nine cantos of the *Purgatory,* or to that section known as the Antepurgatory, the place of late repentants, those still tainted with human defects or the shadows of our world. In fact, the Pilgrim in his journey through the first three heavens meets souls who reveal themselves through shadows of inconstancy (the moon), worldly ambition (Mercury), and earthly love (Venus). In the sphere of the moon, Beatrice explains the limits of human perception in her long discourse concerning the spots on the moon. In the second sphere of Mercury, the Emperor Justinian (who speaks for the entire canto) gives the history of the Empire, while Beatrice in the next canto (VII) explains the meaning of the Redemption, and in so doing more light is shed for the Pilgrim, especially regarding some of the events that took place in the mysterious garden at the top of the mountain of Purgatory. In the third sphere of Venus, one of the souls (Charles Martel of the renowned Anjou family) expounds the doctrine of heredity, and the Pilgrim learns that the reason why many men go astray in the world is that they are not encouraged to follow their inherent character or nature.

In the first three spheres of the *Paradise* the Pilgrim meets some souls that he knew in life—as was also true in the Antepurgatory—but this no longer happens once he leaves the sphere of Venus and enters that of the sun. In these first nine cantos the Pilgrim has relatively little to say compared to Beatrice and the souls that come to greet him in these lower spheres.

With Canto X the poet makes a new start, stressing the division he would make between cantos I–IX and what is to follow. The emphasis in this new section is immediately evident in the opening two tercets of Canto X, the many and the one, the trinity and the unity of God:

> Looking upon His Son with all that love
> which each of them breathes forth eternally,
> that uncreated, ineffable first One,

> has fashioned all that moves in mind and space
> in such sublime proportions that no one
> can see it and not feel His Presence there.

Some critics believe that all the doctrine espoused in the *Paradise* falls in either the opening tercet of the canticle itself or the first two tercets of the new beginning in Canto X.

Once the Pilgrim is past the sphere of Venus and into the spheres of the sun, Mars, Jupiter, and Saturn, the individual souls who speak to him have become parts of larger symbols. The theologians and wise teachers of the sphere of the sun appear in the form of a circle (the symbol of perfection as well as Divinity), those of Mars in a great glowing cross, the souls of Jupiter in an amazing eagle, and those of Saturn as lights that perform around an immense golden ladder.

The heavens are moved by different angelic orders reflecting the Trinity. The sign of the Trinity, like God Himself, seems to be everywhere in the poem. We even saw it in the *Inferno,* not only in the inscription above the Gate of Hell (*Inf.* III, 1–9) but in the presentation of Lucifer in terms of a mock trinity at the bottom of Hell in the final canto. Other manifestations of it in the lower regions could be cited. We saw the Trinity in the Three Advents of Christ as well as in the three dreams of the *Purgatory* (see Introduction to *Purgatory,* pp. xix–xxiii), but most of all we see it here in the third and final realm of *The Divine Comedy.*

The first three spheres are governed by a triad of angels who contemplate God in terms of the Holy Spirit. The next three spheres ascending (sun, Mars and Jupiter) are ruled by that triad of angels who contemplate God in terms of God the Son. Saturn, the Fixed Stars, and the Primum Mobile, the final spheres encased by the Empyrean, are governed by the highest triad of angels, who contemplate God as the Father.

The sphere of Saturn represents a transition point between the six lower spheres and those above in Heaven's hierarchy. No mention is made of entering this sphere, the heaven of the contemplatives. Beatrice simply announces that they are there in the "Seventh Light" (XXI, 13). It is the active life that prepares man for the life of contemplation, and the just rulers of the sphere directly below, not men but shapes of golden lights that sing and fly like a flock of birds, represent the highest level of the active life. It is in that sphere that the

Pilgrim beholds the divine and mystical origin of the Empire and the concept of Justice in relation to it. In the sphere of Saturn the Pilgrim sees a ladder of gold, representing the perfection of the contemplative life, that stretches upward farther than his eye can see. There is no singing or dancing in this sphere as there was in others, since there is no smile from Beatrice. There is, however, a mysterious burst of thunder made by the spirits, and the Pilgrim is terrified by it. It is through contemplation that man begins to enter the mysteries of Paradise, and for this reason Beatrice suggests that her ward follow the souls up the golden ladder. Suddenly they are all swept up the ladder, and the Pilgrim finds himself in the eighth heaven of the Fixed Stars in his own sign of Gemini. From there he looks down upon the seven spheres of the planets, down through to the puny planet of earth, and he smiles at its relative worth and littleness.

The sphere of the Fixed Stars recalls the Earthly Paradise at the top of the mountain of Purgatory. There the Pilgrim was witness to the scene of man's fall, while here in the highest visible region of the celestial world the work of man's redemption is revealed to him. The souls of the Elect who appeared to the Pilgrim separately in the spheres he traveled through now appear all together with numerous other souls in the eighth sphere, which filters its divine influence down through the planets. It is in this heaven that Adam himself appears and instructs the Pilgrim on the Fall. It is here that the Pilgrim will take examinations on Faith, Hope, and Charity, the three theological virtues that are essential for the attainment of the Beatific Vision, and that will allow him to rise closer to God's glory. Just before ascending to the ninth sphere, the Primum Mobile, the Pilgrim takes a last look back at the earth and goes into another one of his protests against the corruption of the Church which he had done at other transitional points in the *Paradise*.

The Primum Mobile is the swiftest-moving heaven, and with its movement it directs the daily revolutions of all the other spheres below it. Nature, which is the first principle of motion and rest, has its starting point from this sphere, which is bounded only by the love and light of the Empyrean beyond it. Here Beatrice talks about the heavens and the lack of orderly government on earth which refuses to follow divine order. The Seraphim angels turn this ninth sphere, where both motion and time have their origin, and they shed their virtue down upon the Universe. In the eighth sphere, Dante witnessed the Humanity of Christ and His relation to His mother and the saints; here he discusses the relation between God and His angels. Here the Pilgrim sees God as a minute point of light first reflected in the eyes of Beatrice and then in reality. The light is the symbol for Divine unity as well as the immateriality of the Divine. From that point comes all the spiritual light that penetrates all of creation. In the ninth sphere the movement begun with the opening tercet of the *Paradise* reverses. The pouring down of Divine light through the universe is reversed and the movement now strongly pulls back to God. This we see in that point of light reflected in Beatrice's eyes surrounded by nine whirling circles, the smallest of which spins the fastest in this miraculous vision instead of the slowest as it would in reality.

Beatrice and the Pilgrim reach the Empyrean, the place of pure light and man's perfect happiness. In his ascension through the nine lower heavens the Pilgrim has witnessed as much of God's glory and divinity as is allowed any living man; now he will receive the reward of such contemplation. The light of this realm is so strong that the Pilgrim suffers temporary blindness. His sight returns, and with it a new way of seeing things. He is in a state of ecstasy which man can achieve only in the highest stage of contemplation and with the special grace of God. He will witness the glory and the joy of God's angels and saints in the Rose of Paradise.

Just as Virgil leads to Matilda in the Earthly Paradise, as human reason or natural philosophy leads man to the blessedness of the active life, so Beatrice, or Divine Wisdom, leads man to the blessedness of eternal life represented in the vision of God's countenance. While Beatrice can lead the Pilgrim to God she can do nothing to actually reveal Him. This can be done only through contemplation and grace. It is for this reason that St. Bernard takes Beatrice's place at the end of the poem. Beatrice in her role of Theology is no longer needed in the Empyrean; here the Highest Truth is revealed through intuition, which is the knowledge of invisible things.

Let us pause for a moment and review briefly Beatrice's purpose in *The Divine Comedy.* Her role in the poem is to lead Dante the Pilgrim, who stands for all of us, to the blessedness of eternal life and the vision of God, to which man in his own natural power cannot approach.

Beatrice, the lady with whom Dante the Pilgrim is so much in love throughout *The Divine Comedy,* is first of all the glorified but real woman the poet loved when she lived on earth. It is only later that she functions as a symbol. The Beatrice who makes her first appearance in the poem in Canto II of the *Inferno* (which should be thought of as the opening canto of the *Inferno*, since Canto I is an introduction to the entire poem) is full of tenderness and pity as she implores Virgil to help her friend who is lost in the "dark wood" to find salvation. Here the figure of Beatrice is veiled in the atmosphere of the *Vita nuova*. There are strong courtly overtones filling Canto II of the *Inferno*. However, when we see Beatrice again in cantos XXX and XXXI of the *Purgatory*, while certain events from the *Vita nuova* are specifically referred to, the atmosphere has changed and Beatrice has become a dominating figure. She is severe and pitiless toward the protagonist in order that he feel true repentance and become worthy of crossing the river Lethe and rising into Heaven. Then in the closing canto of the *Purgatory* Beatrice makes her final symbolic change when she heads a procession with the seven virtues holding their torches, and proceeds to explain the allegorical meaning of the pageant in the previous canto. Here she is more than just that lady in the *Vita nuova;* she has taken on the meaning Dante had in mind for her in its final chapter. She is now *Sapentia;* she is all the wisdom God has revealed to man which allows him to return to his Creator, and this aspect of Beatrice will remain throughout the journey through Paradise. But it is the real woman, and not Divine Wisdom, who in the final canto of the poem takes her seat among the Blest (*Par.* XXXIII, 38). Her role as guide has ended, and she turns her ward over to St. Bernard, who prepares the Pilgrim for the final vision. Truth must now be seen through grace and contemplation. It is through the intercession of Mary Mother of God that the Pilgrim will be allowed to complete his vision, and it is for this reason that Beatrice before returning to her seat in the third circle of the heavenly Rose drops her allegorical role once they reach the Empyrean and puts her ward in the hands of St. Bernard. Beatrice in her allegorical role prepares man for the kind of contemplation he must practice in this realm.

It would be wrong, however, to read Beatrice exclusively or consistently as a symbol. The Beatrice of *The Divine Comedy* is the same flesh-and-blood woman as the Beatrice of the *Vita nuova*. She is the same mediator between the things of this world and those of the next. To read Beatrice as a symbol, and only as a symbol, is to risk missing much of her lyric beauty. Beatrice in the *Paradise* grows more and more beautiful and her smile, eyes, and face grow brighter as she moves higher from sphere to sphere with the Pilgrim, who seems to fall more and more in love as she reveals her beauty through the truths she expounds. She who is brilliant in her holiness and beautiful in her wisdom shares her light with her lover in the upward flight to God. Her beauty is proportionate to the truth she conveys in her words to the Pilgrim. It is in those often long monologues, which the modern reader of the poem may find tedious, that Beatrice's beauty shines forth as she sheds her light on that Truth which can only fill the Pilgrim with joy, because with her every discourse or explanation he is approaching the very Source of her light and beauty. The lady's face shines with God's glory. She articulates that glory in human terms of wisdom to her lover:

> Such was the flowing of the holy stream
> that pours down from the Fountain of All Truth
> that it now laid both of my doubts to rest.

> "Beloved of the First Love, lady divine,"
> I said then, "you whose words bathe me in warmth,
> wakening me to life again, the depth

> of my deep love is not profound enough
> to find the thanks your graciousness deserves—

> (IV, 115–122)

It is true that the Pilgrim also receives enlightenment from a number of blessed souls who talk to him in the different spheres, but what he does learn from them is, in one way or another, mediated by Beatrice, who will ask a question or encourage her ward to do so.

While the Beatrice of the *Paradise* is the same Beatrice the poet wrote about in his *Vita nuova,* there is a difference between the two. In *Paradise,* though we often find her preaching, she appears as a more human figure. In the *Vita nuova* she never speaks, she gives no explanations. She is simply there as a figure signifying truth. She is a nine, a three, a number in a poem. Her beauty is cold, because the light she sheds upon her lover from her place in Heaven has no real effect on him. He does not understand it; he is not ready to receive it, and that is why the *Vita nuova* ends as abruptly as it does and why, in a sense, it ends in failure. Not until the *Paradise* does the Pilgrim truly learn to love his lady. And it is for this reason that Beatrice, though she may well speak on weighty subjects in order to reveal

God's truths, is more human, more beautiful, more radiant and tender than she has ever been before. Beatrice's beauty in the *Paradise* is in her words. It reveals itself through her arguments.

The journey of the Pilgrim through *Paradise* takes place between two impressive images which occur at the beginning and end of the canticle. These images are stated and restated, developed and modified, reduced and magnified as they stretch and weave their way into the fine lacework of the *Paradise*. The two images are, of course, the one presented by the opening tercet of the *Paradise*:

> The glory of the One Who moves all things
> penetrates all the universe, reflecting
> in one part more and in another less.

and the one contained in the closing lines of the poem:

> At this point power failed high fantasy
> but, like a wheel in perfect balance turning,
> I felt my will and my desire impelled
>
> by the Love that moves the sun and the other stars.

The glory that shines down from the Empyrean reflects on the souls; those reflections fill the spheres which fill in turn the Pilgrim with their knowledge for his greater understanding as he approaches the Light itself. They teach him by means of light, motion, and music, and by symbol as they shape messages for him in some of the spheres, and dance in unending circles to the triune rhythm of One, Two, Three in others. There are spirits who literally radiate truth for him, others sing it to him in miraculous strains, and in the sphere of the sun the learned spirits, in order to convey their message, turn into lovely dancing maidens for him and then at the close of the canto into a great clock that stikes with the most sensual (and sexual) tones in the entire poem. Each sphere conveys its message in a different way, and the poet never seems to perform the same artistic miracle twice. The *Paradise* may be the most difficult of the three parts of the poem for the reader to understand and appreciate (Dante is well aware of this and warns his reader at the beginning of Canto II that it is not going to be easy traveling in this realm), but it certainly is the most "artistic."

It is in Canto XXVII that the reader will begin to feel the shift in the poem's movement from down to up, at the point when all the souls in the sphere of the Fixed Stars return to the Empyrean. This change of perspective is subtly introduced in lines 67-72 in what may be called an inverted snowstorm image:

> As frozen vapors flake and start to snow
> down through our air during the time of year
> the horn of heaven's goat touches the sun,
>
> so I saw all of Heaven's ether glow
> with rising snowflakes of triumphant souls
> of all those who had sojourned with us there.

The spirits are moving upward, thereby reversing the normal direction of the snowflakes. The snow of souls is falling up toward God, from Whose point of view the image is born. There are other inversion images in this canto and the ones that follow. There is an outstanding example of this in the next canto in tercet 127-129 of XXVIII as Beatrice is bringing to a close her explanation of the perfect correspondence between the heavenly spheres and the angelic orders which govern them:

> And all of the angelic ranks gaze upward,
> as downward they prevail upon the rest,
> so while each draws the next, all draw toward God.

While both movements join in this tercet the stress is on the upward.

In the final canto of the poem the movement started in the very first tercet of the *Paradise* is entirely reversed. The light of God's glory penetrating the universe and reflecting in the many parts of that universe (the division of the One into its parts) is here once and for all gathered back up again and returned to the One. This reversal reaches its climax when the Pilgrim gazing into the "Eternal Light" says of it:

> I saw how it contains within its depths
> all things bound in a single book by love
> of which creation is the scattered leaves:
>
> how substance, accident, and their relation
> were fused in such a way that what I now
> describe is but a glimmer of that Light.

I know I saw the universal form,
    the fusion of all things, for I can feel,
    while speaking now, my heart leap up in joy.
                              (XXXIII, 85-93)

The idea of reversal or the return of the parts to the One is even re-
flected in the "surrealistic" tercet that immediately follows, a tercet
in which the "ineffability" or "incommunicability" theme intro-
duced in Canto I reaches its climax. This is the last of the sea-voyage
images in *The Divine Comedy*, and it is a stunning one:

One instant brings me more forgetfulness
    than five and twenty centuries brought the quest
    that stunned Neptune when he saw Argo's keel.
                              (94-96)

On the literal level Dante uses this image to convey how remote his
experience seemed in time even a moment after it happened. He is
saying that the journey of the Argo, the first ship ever to sail the seas
2,500 years ago, is more easily remembered today than is his moment
of vision, though he has just experienced it. On another level the
language and the structure of this tercet is suggesting that the num-
ber 2,500 is being reduced to a one. This is, of course, only one level
upon which this tercet functions (see XXXIII, note 94-96).

The return to Unity continues through the final canto. It is clearly
there in lines 103-104 ("because the good which is the goal of will is
all collected there . . .") and again in 117 ("in three clear colors
bound in one same space") as the poet strains to recall his moment
of ecstasy when he looked deep into the light of God. And suddenly
the Pilgrim sees and understands the dual nature of God. With this
"flash of understanding" the two major forces of the *Paradise* are re-
solved in its final lines, in which the descending and reascending
themes join to form a circle:

At this point power failed high fantasy
    but, like a wheel in perfect balance turning,
    I felt my will and my desire impelled

by the Love that moves the sun and the other stars.

A circle that is a wheel revolving in its perfect balance is how the
Pilgrim Poet's will and desire seem to be impelled by Love (God) at

the moment *The Divine Comedy* closes. Into these closing verses the poet manages to recall with key words the major movements and basic concepts not only of the *Paradise* but also of the entire *Divine Comedy*. The "high fantasy," referring literally to that faculty of the poet which is capable of receiving images, is now filled to capacity and he can see no deeper, and as a result it fails. Also contained in these two words is the concept of "fantasy" in the sense of creative ability: that capacity which made the actual creation and writing of the poem possible. The reader will not be long into his reading of the *Paradise* before he realizes the importance of the nouns "power" (*possa*) and "wheel" (*rota*), "sun" (*sole*) and "stars" (*stelle*), and the verbs "turning" (*volgea*) and "impelled" (*è mossa*), as well as the concepts and their ramifications of "perfect balance" (*igualmente*) and the all-important interconnections of "my will and my desire" (*il mio disio e'l velle*). All this is in relation to the most significant word in our world and that of the poem: Love (*l'amor*). It is the agent that set the action of the poem into motion at the beginning of the *Inferno* as much as it is the receiver or object of that same action here at the close of the *Paradise*. And, of course, we know Who Love is: God (*Deus est caritas*). All the lines of the *Comedy* terminate and start in this word; it is the alpha and omega of the poem.

Dante, when he wrote the closing line for his poem, must have had in the back of his mind those three motifs or poetic techniques that gave birth to so much of the fundamental imagery of the *Paradise* and that define its miraculous message: light, motion, and music. In this line

l'amor che move il sole e l'altre stelle.

(by the Love that moves the sun and the other stars.)

there is the light of the "sun" positioned in the middle of the verse itself, and because of its centralization its light illuminates all parts of the verse equally—in fact, there are twelve letters on one side of "il sole" and thirteen following it. There is also the verb "move" which defines its own action, and the word "stelle" in closing position which reflects the central light of the "sun" and gives it back. What is most impressive, however, is the music of this line. Its rhythm seems to be imitating the perfectly balanced turning wheel of the preceding verse as the endecasyllabic Italian line comes to a definite stop after "sole" in order for the voice to pick up the "e" immediately following, which must be pronounced. I have tried to render this balanced spinning movement by breaking the iambic pentameter of the closing line in English for the first and only time in the *Paradise* with two balancing anapests: one at the beginning (bў thĕ Lóve) and one at the end that leads up to the stars (añd thĕ óthĕr stárs). It is the music of the spheres (contained in the word "stars"), a sense of peace and tranquillity, man as one with God and creation, that the author of *The Divine Comedy* wishes to leave his reader.

The word "stars," the last word of the poem, glows with a number of meanings which *The Divine Comedy* itself has given it in the course of the journey. The sun is another star, as the last verse surely implies through the use of the word "other," and we know that the sun is the symbol for God—this is clear from the first canto of the *Inferno*, and the stars stand for all the heavens. It is through the sphere of the Fixed Stars, immediately below the Primum Mobile, that God's grace is filtered down through the lower spheres, finally reaching the material universe—that is what Canto II concerning the spots on the moon is all about. The stars, then, are the link between God and His creation. They are His eyes set in the outermost limits of the physical universe:

> O Triune Light which sparkles in one star
> upon their sight, Fulfiller of full joy!
> look down upon us in our tempest here!
> (XXXI, 28–30)

They are the constant reminder to mankind of his connection to his Maker. Through them we see God from our earth. Through them God touches us. Through them Dante connects the three distinct parts of his miraculous poem, the *Inferno*, the *Purgatory*, and the *Paradise*, into a single unity which is *The Divine Comedy*.

M.M.
May 1985
Florence, Italy

a. articulus

Aen. *Aeneid* (Virgil)

Consol. philos. *Consolatio philosophiae* (Boethius)

Conv. *Convivio* (Dante Alighieri)

Cron. *Chronicles* (Villani)

De civ. Dei *Ad Marcellinum De civitate Dei contra paganos* (Augustine)

De doct. Chris. *De doctrina Christiana* (Augustine)

De mon. *De monarchia* (Dante Alighieri)

De vulg. eloqu. *De vulgari eloquentia* (Dante Alighieri)

E.D. Enciclopedia Dantesca

Eclog. *Eclogues* (Virgil)

Epist. *Epistolae* (Dante Alighieri)

Eth. Nicom. *Ethica Nicomachea* (Aristotle)

Etym. *Etymologiarum Libri XX* or *Origines* (Isidore of Seville)

Hist. *Historiarum adversum paganos libri septem* (Orosius)

Inf. *Inferno* (Dante Alighieri)

lect. lectio

Metam. *Metamorphoses* (Ovid)

Metaphys. *Metaphysica* (Aristotle)

Meteor. *Meteorologica* (Aristotle)

Moral. *Moralium libri, sive Expositio in librum b. Iob* (Gregory I)

Par. *Paradiso* (Dante Alighieri)

Phars. *Pharsalia* (Lucan)

Purg. *Purgatorio* (Dante Alighieri)

q. quaestio

resp. respondeo

Summa theol. *Summa theologica* (Thomas Aquinas)

suppl. supplementum

CANTO I

AFTER STATING THAT God's glory shines throughout the universe, Dante informs us that he has been to Paradise, and has seen things so extraordinary that he cannot possibly hope to tell about them. Nevertheless, he determines to make this final song his crowning achievement as a poet, and he calls on both the Muses and Apollo for inspiration as he focuses on his journey heavenward. At noon on the spring equinox, Dante, still in the Earthly Paradise, sees Beatrice gazing into the sun, and he imitates her gaze. In so doing, he becomes aware of an extraordinary brightness, as though God had placed in the heavens a second sun, and feels himself being "transhumanized" in preparation for his experience of Paradise. He then finds himself soaring heavenward through God's grace, although he is uncertain whether it is his soul or his corporeal self that rises. As Dante and Beatrice pass out of the earth's atmosphere into the sphere of fire that lies above it, Dante hears the music of the spheres. This music fills him with wonderment and perplexity, but before he can question Beatrice about it, she explains to him the teleological order of the universe, and how it is only natural that, having been purified, he should now rise heavenward.

The glory of the One Who moves all things
    penetrates all the universe, reflecting
    in one part more and in another less.   *3*

I have been in His brightest shining heaven
    and seen such things that no man, once returned
    from there, has wit or skill to tell about;   *6*

for when our intellect draws near its goal
    and fathoms to the depths of its desire,
    the memory is powerless to follow;   *9*

but still, as much of Heaven's holy realm
    as I could store and treasure in my mind
    shall now become the subject of my song.   *12*

O great Apollo, for this final task,
    make me a vessel worthy to receive
    your genius and the longed-for laurel crown.   *15*

Thus far I have addressed my prayers to one
   peak of Parnassus; now I need them both
   to move into this heavenly arena.   18

Enter my breast, breathe into me as high
   a strain as that which vanquished Marsyas
   the time you drew him from his body's sheath.   21

O Power Divine, but lend me of yourself
   so much as will make clear at least the shadow
   of that high realm imprinted on my mind,   24

and you shall see me at your chosen tree,
   crowning myself with those green leaves of which
   my theme and you yourself will make me worthy.   27

So seldom, Father, are they plucked to crown
   the triumph of a Caesar or a Poet
   (the shame, the fault of mortal man's desires!)   30

that when a man yearns to achieve that goal,
   then the Peneian frond should surely breed
   a new joy in the joyous Delphic god.   33

From one small spark can come a mighty blaze:
   so after me, perhaps, a better voice
   may rise in prayer and win Cyrrha's response.   36

The lamp that lights the world rises for man
   at different points, but from the place which joins
   four circles with three crosses, it ascends   39

upon a happier course with happier stars
   conjoined, and in this way it warms and seals
   the earthly wax closer to its own likeness.   42

This glad union had made it morning there
   and evening here: our hemisphere was dark,
   while all the mountain bathed in white, when I   45

saw Beatrice turned round, facing left,
   her eyes raised to the sun—no eagle ever
   could stare so fixed and straight into such light!   48

As one descending ray of light will cause
   a second one to rise back up again,
   just as a pilgrim yearns to go back home,   51

so, like a ray, her act poured through my eyes
   into my mind and gave rise to my own:
   I stared straight at the sun as no man could.   53

In that place first created for mankind
   much more is granted to the human senses
   than ever was allowed them here on earth.   57

I could not look for long, but my eyes saw
   the sun enclosed in blazing sparks of light
   like molten iron as it pours from the fire.   60

And suddenly it was as if one day
   shone on the next—as if the One Who Could
   had decked the heavens with a second sun.   63

And Beatrice stood there, her eyes fixed
   on the eternal spheres, entranced, and now
   my eyes, withdrawn from high, were fixed on her.   66

Gazing at her, I felt myself becoming
   what Glaucus had become tasting the herb
   that made him like the other sea-gods there.   69

"Transhumanize"—it cannot be explained
   per verba, so let this example serve
   until God's grace grants the experience.   72

Whether it was the last created part
   of me alone that rose, O Sovereign Love,
   You know Whose light it was that lifted me.   75

When the great sphere that spins, yearning for You
   eternally, captured my mind with strains
   of harmony tempered and tuned by You,   78

I saw a great expanse of heaven ablaze
   with the sun's flames: not all the rains and rivers
   on earth could ever make a lake so wide.   81

The revelation of this light, this sound,
   inflamed me with such eagerness to learn
   their cause, as I had never felt before;   84

and she who saw me as I saw myself,
   ready to calm my agitated mind,
   began to speak before I asked my question: 87

"You have yourself to blame for burdening
    your mind with misconceptions that prevent
    from seeing clearly what you might have seen.

You may think you are still on earth, but lightning
    never sped downward from its home as quick
    as you are now ascending to your own."   93

As easily did these few and smiling words
    release me from my first perplexity
    than was my mind ensnared by yet another,   96

and I said: "Though I rest content concerning
    one great wonder of mine, I wonder now
    how I can rise through these light bodies here."   99

She sighed with pity when she heard my question
    and looked at me the way a mother might
    hearing her child in his delirium: 102

"Among all things, however disparate,
    there reigns an order, and this gives the form
    that makes the universe resemble God,"   105

she said; "therein God's higher creatures see
    the imprint of Eternal Excellence—
    that goal for which the system is created,   108

and in this order all created things,
    according to their bent, maintain their place,
    disposed in proper distance from their Source;   111

therefore, they move, all to a different port,
    across the vast ocean of being, and each
    endowed with its own instinct as its guide.   114

This is what carries fire toward the moon,
    this is the moving force in mortal hearts,
    this is what binds the earth and makes it one.   117

Not only living creatures void of reason
    prove the impelling strength of instinct's bow,
    but also those with intellect and love.   120

The Providence that regulates the whole
    becalms forever with its radiance
    the heaven wherein revolves the swiftest sphere;   123

to there, to that predestined place, we soar,
  propelled there by the power of that bow
  which always shoots straight to its Happy Mark.   126

But, it is true that just as form sometimes
  may not reflect the artist's true intent,
  the matter being deaf to the appeal,   129

just so, God's creature, even though impelled
  toward the true goal, having the power to swerve,
  may sometimes go astray along his course;   132

and just as fire can be seen as falling
  down from a cloud, so too man's primal drive,
  twisted by false desire, may bring him down.   135

You should, in all truth, be no more amazed
  at your flight up than at the sight of water
  that rushes down a mountain to its base.   138

If you, free as you are of every weight,
  had stayed below, then that would be as strange
  as living flame on earth remaining still.   141

And then she turned her gaze up toward the heavens.

NOTES

1 — 12

In the opening verses of this canto Dante states the general
terms of his ascent into Paradise, and thereby creates a kind of
prologue to the rest of the canticle. The tone is one of reverence
and wonderment, in accordance with the subject matter to be
treated. Several elements which are central to Dante's experience
in Paradise are contained in this prologue, beginning with the
notion of God as Prime Mover, or First Cause, Whose light is
received by each part of the universe, according to its capacity.
Also introduced here are images of light, sound, and motion, all
of which are essential factors in the poet's journey. Of them, light
is the most important, and thus is mentioned before the others.
Within the symbolic structure of the poem, the light, sound,
and motion images are joined to the intellectual, emotional, and
mystical aspects of the poet's experience, which involves the ac-

quisition of true vision or understanding of the nature of beatitude, one of the sublime mysteries of Divine Love.

The ineffability topos, which recurs throughout the canticle, is also presented in these verses: the poet expresses his doubts about his ability to recall, and then to describe, what he has witnessed. It is also important to note that this canto begins with a reminiscence of the poem's ending, namely Dante's ascent into God's highest heaven. Thus, the narrative is circular rather than linear, and is in harmony with the structure of its setting. Moreover, by making his account retrospective, and not simultaneous with the action it portrays, Dante emphasizes the difficulty of his poetic task and heightens the effect of pathos connected with it.

2 – 3. *and shines / in one part more and in another less:* The light of God shines more in one part and less in another according to the greater or lesser capacity of each thing to contain it. This was a fundamental concept of scholastic philosophy, and Dante stresses the idea in his *Convivio* (III, vii, 2) as well as in his letter to Can Grande (*Epist.* XIII).

In my translation of the opening tercet of the *Paradise* I wanted to be as close to the original as possible. A more interpretive rendering of verses 1 – 3 would have been the following:

> The glory of the One Who moves all things
>   shines through the universe and is reflected
>   by all things in proportion to their merit.

But verse 3 is so simple in the Italian; and only as the reader gets further and further into the poem will verse 3 be able to support the other meaning. For example, much of the next canto, which treats the spots on the moon, serves as a gloss for verse 3.

4. *His brightest shining heaven:* The Empyrean, the uppermost sphere, is the abode of God and all the Blest. The blessed spirits will also manifest themselves to the Pilgrim during his journey upward throughout the lower spheres. The souls appear in these various spheres in order to illustrate to the Pilgrim the degree of heavenly bliss which each of them enjoys.

6. *has wit or skill to tell about:* This is a topos used throughout the *Paradise:* that of inexpressibility.

7 – 9. *when our intellect draws near its goal / and fathoms . . . its desire:* The "goal" and the "desire" of the intellect are the journey's

end, or vision and understanding of God. Thomas Aquinas, discussing the question of man's beatitude consisting in the vision of the Divine Essence, answers (see Gardner [1970], pp. 2 – 4):

The last and perfect happiness of man cannot be otherwise than in the vision of the Divine Essence. In evidence of this statement two points are to be considered: first, that man is not perfectly happy so long as there remains anything for him to desire and seek; secondly, that the perfection of every power is determined by the nature of its object. Now the object of the intellect is the essence of a thing: hence, the intellect attains to perfection so far as it knows the essence of what is before it. And therefore, when a man knows an effect, and knows that it has a cause, there is in him an outstanding desire of knowing the essence of the cause. If, therefore, a human intellect knows the essence of a created effect without knowing anything about God beyond the fact of His existence, the perfection of that intellect does not yet adequately reach the First Cause, but the intellect has an outstanding natural desire of searching into the said Cause: hence, it is not yet perfectly happy. For perfect happiness, therefore, it is necessary that the intellect shall reach as far as the very essence of the First Cause.

Gardner adds: "This beatitude of man belongs, therefore, to the intellectual faculty, since by no activity of sense can man be united to this uncreated Good. And so Dante's Paradise is the beatitude of the intellect in joyful possession of absolute Truth, the supreme bliss which is reached in the Empyrean Heaven of pure light."

13–36

Dante follows his prologue with an invocation to Apollo and the Muses. In the *Inferno* (II,7) and the *Purgatory* (I, 8), Dante calls upon the Muses to provide inspiration for his poetic endeavors. Here, however, as he enters Paradise, he seeks divine guidance and therefore invokes the aid of Apollo, God of Poetry, in addition to that of the Muses. Apollo is also associated with theology, and with the sun, both of which suggest that the Poet seeks inspiration of the highest kind for the task at hand.

15. *the longed-for laurel crown:* Dante prays here that in this, the final portion of the *Comedy*, his poetic talents will reach their apex. The laurel wreath, symbol of victory and achievement, was awarded to poets and conquerors. Apollo held the laurel in special regard because it was the tree into which the wood nymph

Daphne was transformed. Ovid (*Metam.* I, 452 – 567) relates how Cupid, taking revenge for a taunt, shot an arrow of desire into Apollo, and one of aversion into Daphne. Desperate over Apollo's pursuit of her, Daphne prayed to her father, the river-god Peneus, and was changed into a laurel tree.

16 – 17. *I have addressed my prayers to one / peak of Parnassus:* Mount Parnassus, as Lucan tells us in his *Pharsalia* (III, 173), has two peaks. Dante assigns one of these, Nisa, to the Muses, and the other, Cyrrha, to Apollo, God of Poetry. Cyrrha is also the name of a town in Phocis, near Delphi on the Gulf of Corinth. Delphi was the seat of the oracle of Apollo. Thus, the names Cyrrha and Delphi are closely linked to the god Apollo and are often used in connection with him. (See also Isidore of Seville, *Origines* XIV, 8.)

18. *this heavenly arena:* By using the word "arena" (*l'aringo*), Dante suggests a place of struggle or combat, and by extension, the difficulty of the material he will deal with in his *Paradise*. And the *Paradise* is the battleground for theology which emerges triumphantly in all its glory. This "heavenly arena" also prepares us for the unusual image in the next tercet (see note 20 – 21).

20 – 21. *a strain as that which vanquished Marsyas:* Marsyas, a satyr of Phrygia, found a flute which Minerva had discarded because it distorted her features as she played. Upon discovering that the flute emitted beautiful sounds of its own accord, Marsyas challenged Apollo to a music-making contest, with the condition that the winner could do whatever he wished with his unsuccessful rival. The Muses, judges of the contest, awarded the victory to Apollo, who sang and played the cithara or lyre. Apollo decided that Marsyas should be punished for his presumption by being tied to a tree and then pulled out of his skin while still alive. The gruesome account of this can be found in Ovid's *Metamorphoses* (VI, 382 – 900).

In mentioning this incident as part of his invocation to Apollo, Dante prays that he be given the power to perform as wonderfully as Apollo did when he vanquished Marsyas. Dante could also be asking here to be lifted out of himself in the sense of having his mind freed from his body, as well as his poetic abilities from all limitations, to enable him to describe his experiences in Paradise. See also *Purgatory* I, 11 – 12 and note.

25. *your chosen tree:* This is the laurel (see above, n. 15).

26. *crowning myself with those green leaves:* Here and in verses 1–9 of *Paradise* XXV are the only places in the *Comedy* where the Poet makes explicit his hope that the great poem will win him the poet's crown of laurel. Dante never doubted that he was a great poet.

28–33

Dante expresses regret that the reward for excellence in poetry or in war exploits (both of which are symbolized by the laurel wreath) is so rarely deserved by mortal man; indeed, such reward is seldom even sought after. When it is desired, however, Apollo should take great pleasure at the unusual fact and rejoice.

32. *Peneian frond:* The laurel, here named for Daphne's father, the river-god Peneus.

33. *joyous Delphic god:* This is Apollo, who had a temple and an oracle at Delphi below Mount Parnassus.

36. *and win Cyrrha's response:* Cyrrha is the peak of Mount Parnassus associated with Apollo. Here, the peak stands for the god himself as Dante speculates that should his efforts find favor with Apollo, "a better voice" (literally, "better voices," 35) than his own may subsequently be encouraged to write on the same lofty subject and to invoke the God of Poetry and gain response from him. Not everyone is in agreement on how this tercet should be interpreted. Toffanin, for one, sees these "better voices" as those of the blessed souls in Heaven as well as Beatrice's praying for the success of the Poet's mission.

37–42. *The lamp that lights the world . . . four circles with three crosses:* With this reference Dante refers to the time and season during which he, as Pilgrim, took his journey through Paradise, as he had done earlier in the *Inferno* (II, 1–5) and *Purgatory* (I, 13; 115–117). The "different points" (38) are the various points on the celestial horizon where the "lamp" or sun rises at different times of the year. The "place which joins / four circles with three crosses" (38–39) is the point at which the sun rises in the vernal or spring equinox (night and day of equal duration)—March 21. The "four circles" are the equinoctial colure, the celestial horizon, the celestial equator, and the ecliptic; the "three crosses" are formed at the point where the four circles intersect.

When the sun rises at this point, it is in the constellation of

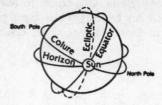

Aries, and this position was thought to be a particularly favorable one, because the sun was held to be in Aries (from March 21 through April 20) when God created the universe (see *Inf.* I, 37 – 40). According to early commentators, the four circles and three crosses symbolized the four cardinal and three theological virtues (respectively Prudence, Fortitude, Temperance, and Justice; Faith, Hope, and Charity). Thus, when the sun was at its spring equinox, the two groups of virtues were symbolically conjoined, and the sun was thought to work its most favorable influence upon the world at this time, molding "the earthly wax closer to its own likeness" (42).

Symbolically, the spring equinox is the ideal time for Dante's ascent to Paradise; the three crosses formed by the intersection of the celestial circles bring to mind both the Cross and the Trinity, and the conjunction of cardinal and theological virtues indicates a time propitious for salvation, when the sun, as Divine Illumination, shines upon the earth. But see also the explanation given by Baldacci.

43 – 44. *This glad union had made it morning there / and evening here:* At noon on the day of the spring equinox, the northern hemisphere would theoretically be in darkness while the southern hemisphere would be filled with light. Thus, "morning there" refers to the southern hemisphere, which includes the Mountain of Purgatory, Eden, and the hemisphere of water where Dante found himself illumined by God's light; "evening here" refers to the hemisphere of land, the place to which the Poet has returned following his journey to Paradise—it is the place of ignorance, sin, and worldly cares from which he now writes.

The reader will remember that the Pilgrim's journey through Hell begins in the evening, while that of Purgatory takes place at dawn. Now we know that the journey through Paradise will start at high noon.

46. *Beatrice turned round, facing left:* Now Beatrice, who with the Pilgrim had been facing east, turns left to face the noonday sun. Virgil had made a similar movement earlier in the *Purgatory* (XIII, 13 – 15), when he turned to look up and stare at the sun.

In order to keep the rhythm of the line, Beatrice's name should always be pronounced as double trochees: *Bé-ă-trí-cĕ,* four syllables with the first and third accented.

47 – 48. *no eagle ever / could stare so fixed:* Beatrice's ability to look directly into the sun is compared with that of the eagle, which, according to medieval histories, possessed this remarkable power to withstand the sun's rays. St. Augustine (*Tract in Joan.* XXXVI) tells how the parent eagle takes its young up in its talons, and turns their eyes to the sun to test them. Those eaglets which are unable to tolerate the light are not true offspring, and they are dropped from the parent's talons to perish. Benvenuto connects the eagle, lord of its realm, to theology, queen of her realm.

49 – 53. *And one descending ray of light:* Dante follows Beatrice's example, receiving strength from her. He compares his act to the natural inclination of a reflected ray of light to bounce back to its source, or to the yearning of a pilgrim to return to his own home. Implicit in these comparisons is the undeniable impulse of the soul to return to its place of origin, a journey which Dante the Pilgrim is now making symbolically: the journey of the mind to God.

There is disagreement as to the interpretation of verse 51: "as a pilgrim yearns to go back home." Chimenz (pp. 626 – 27) complicates things by turning the "pilgrim" of verse 51 into a young falcon. If Beatrice is like the eagle, I suggest we let the Pilgrim be a pilgrim.

54. *In that place first created for mankind:* Dante is still in the Garden of Eden. Having attained to the state of Adam before the Fall as a result of his purification, the Pilgrim experiences a heightening of perceptions; consequently he can gaze directly into the sun. Pasquazi (pp. 214 – 15), on the other hand, takes "that place" to be the Empyrean.

58 – 59. *my eyes saw / the sun enclosed in blazing sparks:* With this verse Dante the Pilgrim, though he is not aware of it yet, has started his journey upward to the heavens (see n. 61 – 63).

61 – 63. it was as if one day / shone on the next: Without knowing it, Dante has begun to rise from the Earthly Paradise, through the sphere of air, and is now approaching the sphere of fire, which was thought to encircle the earth at some distance between the sphere of air and that of the moon (Fig. 2). As he rises toward the sun, he is surrounded by light that grows brighter and brighter, as though a second sun were shining on him. The Pilgrim is in the process of receiving God's Divine Grace, the grace which will allow him to make the final part of his journey.

The Earth Surrounded by Air and Fire

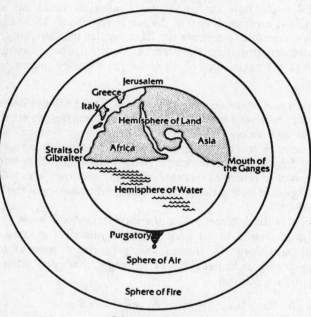

67 – 69. I felt myself becoming / what Glaucus had become: Glaucus, a fisherman, noticed that his catch revived and jumped back into the sea after being placed upon a certain herb. He ate some of the herb and was transformed into a sea-god, as Ovid relates (*Metam.* XIII, 898 – 968). The Pilgrim is being compared to Glaucus, for, as he looks at Beatrice, who still gazes toward the sun, he too begins to undergo a transformation—the miraculous inner transformation that will prepare him to approach Paradise. The Pilgrim, then, must become divine, in a sense, in order to be accepted by the sea of blessed souls he is about to enter. This is all in preparation for the opening word of the next tercet: "Transhumanize" (*Trasumanar*).

70. *"Transhumanize":* Dante the Pilgrim becomes "transhumanized," and enters a state beyond mortal explication, a state that cannot be explained with words (*per verba*). This transformation, associated with the miraculous change of Glaucus from fisherman to sea-god, is prefigured by the earlier reference in this canto to the laurel crown and Daphne, and is then later recalled by the appearance of Jason, transformed into a plowman (*Par.* II, 16–18). The wondrous change in Dante's condition is explained by the fact of his purification, which has taken place in the Earthly Paradise. In his new state, he is to ascend through Paradise and gradually acquire understanding of Divine Love. Thus he already enjoys a condition far beyond mortal limitations, and in this sense he has become superhuman. Dante has crossed an essential threshold: what he is about to experience during the rest of his journey must by its very nature exceed the intellectual grasp of mortals. To those who are deserving, the experience of sanctification will come only after death (72). For the present, the Poet can only approximate his extraordinary adventure by calling up the example of Glaucus.

73–75. *Whether it was the last created part:* In the *Purgatory* (XXV, 67–75), Statius had explained to the Pilgrim that God breathes the soul into the body after everything else is formed. Here, unable to explain his "transhumanization" with any precision, Dante implies that he is confused as to whether he rose body and soul to Paradise or whether his soul alone rose. He knows only that God's grace has wrought a wonderful transformation in him as he approaches Paradise. Bosco feels that while Dante never explicitly states that his was an ascent of the soul and body, he did have the possibility in mind. It would be possible to ascend in body since the body is now so rarified that the duality between body and soul has disappeared. Dante is as elusive as St. Paul who also did not reveal whether or not his body rose with him to Heaven (2 Cor. 12).

76–78. *When the great sphere:* The "great sphere" here is the Primum Mobile, outermost and swiftest of all the revolving heavens and boundary of the material universe. The "desire" motivating its spinning motion is the eagerness of all parts of the material universe to come into contact with all parts of God's own heaven, the Empyrean. Hence the motion of the Primum Mobile, itself the response to this "desire," is transmitted to all spheres within the boundary of the material universe. As they moved, these spheres were thought by Pythagoras, and refuted by Aristotle (*De coelo* II, 9), to emit a kind of music or harmony resulting both from their ceaseless motion and their concentric relationship to one another. This music of the spheres was thought to be pleasant and perpetual, and Pythagoras posited that humans generally did not hear it because they had become thoroughly inured to it. In verse 78, Dante pictures God as the source and controller of this music. The *Somnium scipionis* is most likely Dante's source for this theory. The work was well known in the Middle Ages through the commentary of Macrobius. (See Cicero's *De re publica* VI, xviii, 18–19.)

79–81. *I saw a great expanse of heaven ablaze:* Dante believed that beyond the earth's sphere of air there was another sphere of fire, beyond which was Paradise. He has by now risen into this fiery realm. For a different interpretation see Nardi (1967), pp. 86–88.

85–87. *and she . . . began to speak before I asked my quesiton:* Not only Beatrice but all the souls in Paradise can read the Pilgrim's mind, and often through the course of his journey souls will resolve his doubts before he expresses them. This happens from time to time in the *Purgatory* but never in the *Inferno*. For Virgil's ability to read the Pilgrim's mind, see Musa (1977), pp. 149–52.

91–93. *but lightning / never sped:* Lightning was thought to emanate from the sphere of fire and to travel downward to earth. More quickly than lightning, Dante is rising to Paradise, his own home, from whence his soul came.

Beatrice, who reads Dante's mind, sees his wonderment at the blaze of light surrounding him and explains that it is due to the fact that he is now rising from the earth, up through the sphere of fire, toward Paradise. The reference to lightning is actually a reverse comparison: just as lightning speeds down to earth from its true "home" in the sphere of fire, Dante speeds upward from the earth to his real home in heaven.

99. *How I can rise through these light bodies here":* Dante is passing through the regions or "spheres" of air, then fire, which surround the earth. Although he has previously expressed doubt about which part of him is rising, body or soul, or both, at this point he seems to be thinking of himself as corporeal, since he is apparently defying the laws of physics as his weighty body rises above lighter matter (see *Par.* II, 34–42). But the question whether or not Dante is actually rising through the heavens in his body is never answered in the poem, although the spirits do recognize that he is mortal.

101. *the way a mother might:* The maternal aspect of Beatrice, which will show forth on a number of occasions in the course of the *Paradise,* begins here with this image of the concerned and indulgent mother looking upon her feverish child in his helpless, unknowing delirium. (See also *Par.* XXII, 4–6.) This very human picture of Beatrice stands in elegant contrast to the first of a number of different explanations of the workings and order of God's cosmos. Her explanation will occupy the rest of this canto, except for the final closing verse (142).

103–42

In this section of the canto Beatrice explains to the Pilgrim how it is that he is able to ascend from the earth to Paradise, and in so doing she does much more than answer his question. All things are, according to Beatrice, teleologically ordered, and it is in terms of this order that the form of the material universe is cast in the image of God. The parts of the universe are hierarchically positioned in relation to God; those *most perfect* are closest to Him, and those *least perfect* are furthest away. Each part seeks by instinct its proper position in the hierarchy, moving in response to a kind of "attraction" or "desire" toward its destined place. Man, having been fashioned in God's likeness and redeemed by Christ, has Paradise as his ultimate station in God's order. However, "just as form sometimes may not reflect the artist's true intent" (127–28), so man can (potentially) become so burdened with sin that the journey heavenward becomes impossible. Beatrice remarks that since Dante has been purified, his elevation toward Paradise should not seem at all unnatural to him, as he is moving toward his proper position in God's order.

106. *"therein:* Within "the form" (104) which is the governing principle "that makes the universe resemble God" (105).

God's higher creatures are all those rational and intellectual beings, including mankind, the angels, and the spirits of the Blest.

109. *all created things:* Even inanimate things are included in the system, not only men and angels.

115-18. *This is what . . . binds the earth and makes it one:* Instinct, or natural inclination, causes all created things to move toward their determined end, and thereby provides the order and cohesion that exist in the world. This principle applies to inanimate things (earth, fire, water), as well as to all living creatures, even those which are "void of reason" (118).

116. *fire toward the moon:* On earth the natural tendency of fire is to burn upward, toward the sphere of fire and the heavens above it.

119. *instinct's bow:* Dante makes frequent and effective use of the bow image in this part of his poem (see also *Par.* II, 22-24). Here, it evokes the notion of impetus; later, it is used to suggest great speed. Dante introduces all of his major themes and images to be developed throughout the poem here in Canto I of the *Paradise.* He did this most effectively in an earlier work, the *Vita nuova.* For a discussion of this narrative technique see Musa (1974, pp. 89-91).

120. *those with intellect and love:* I.e., all rational beings who possess both intelligence and love—in the sense of free will or choice (see *Purg.* VII, 91-102). If man's rational power exercises its will and resists its natural inclination, the result is sin. See note 133-35.

123. *the heaven wherein revolves the swiftest sphere:* The Primum Mobile is the heavenly sphere that spins the fastest and gives the other spheres contained within it their respective motions. And the Primum Mobile itself is contained within the Empyrean, the infinite space of peace in which God dwells.

124. *to there, to that predestined place:* To the Empyrean.

125-26. *that bow / which always shoots straight to its Happy Mark:* Continuing the archery image of verse 119, God becomes the Archer Who aims mankind (through natural instinct or love) at Himself, the "Happy Mark" (126).

127 – 29. *just as form . . . may not reflect the artist's true intent:* The Poet implies here that the intention of the artist (which is always good) is not always fully realized in the object he creates, because the material he uses is not always as good as it should be. The material is "deaf" to the artist's "appeal" (129) or "true intent" (128). The fault rests with the material, then, and never with the artist. The image has shifted from archery to art, and will, in the next tercet, return to archery.

133 – 35. *and just as fire can be seen as falling:* Just as lightning falls to earth from heaven (Dante has already stated the natural inclination of fire to rise), so man—with awareness of universal Good and inclination to seek it—exercises his free will and often pursues a course in favor of an apparent good. By moving against the Divine Will, and toward a false end, man falls into sin. As Dante has witnessed in Hell and Purgatory, such a breach of Divine law causes suffering in accordance with the extent of the transgression.

136 – 41. *You should, in all truth, be no more amazed:* Once again Dante emphasizes that natural inclination is the force which guides the purified soul toward its true home in Heaven, just as fire rises from the earth, and water rushes to lower ground.

142. *And then she turned her gaze up toward the heavens:* Beatrice was looking at her ward while lecturing him on the workings of God's cosmos. She is finished now. There are no more problems. It is only natural now that the Pilgrim rise with her to Heaven. All this is implied in this framing final verse which dramatically pictures Beatrice fixed in her gaze toward the heavens, pointing the way to Paradise. And this narrative frame of verse 142 will remain fixed until verse 22 of the next canto, where we find Beatrice in exactly the same position and the Pilgrim staring at her. What happens between these two verses that stop the action of the poem is the most unusual "Address to the Reader" in the entire poem.

CANTO II

NOW ON THE threshold of the first heavenly sphere, that of the moon, Dante warns all those who have followed him as far as this stage in his account of the eternal realms that they must either be prepared, spiritually and intellectually, to learn of the delights of Paradise, or they should turn back. Having invoked Minerva, Apollo, and the nine Muses, and having begun to prepare himself for anticipated wonders, Dante ascends with Beatrice toward Paradise. When they reach the first of the heavenly bodies, the sphere of the moon, and are "taken" into it, Dante asks Beatrice what causes the markings on the moon that are visible from earth. After asking Dante to tell what he believes to be the cause of the spots on the moon, and then demonstrating the errors in his reasoning, Beatrice finally explains the true cause to him, and in doing so illuminates the nature of Divine Power, and of the heavens.

All you who in your wish to hear my words
　　have followed thus far in your little boat
　　behind my ship that singing sails these waters,　　　　　3

go back now while you still can see your shores;
　　do not attempt the deep: it well could be
　　that losing me, you would be lost yourselves.　　　　　6

I set my course for waters never travelled;
　　Minerva fills my sails, Apollo steers,
　　and all nine Muses point the Bears to me.　　　　　9

Those few of you who from your youth have raised
　　your eager mouths in search of angels' bread
　　on which man feeds here, always hungering,　　　　　12

you may, indeed, allow your boat to sail
　　the high seas in the furrow of my wake
　　ahead of parted waters that flow back.　　　　　15

Those heroes who once crossed the deep to Colchis,
　　and saw their Jason put behind a plow,
　　were not amazed as much as you will be.　　　　　18

By that innate and never-ending thirst
    for God's own realm we sped up just as fast
    as human eyes can rise to meet the skies.   *21*

My gaze on Beatrice, hers on Heaven,
    in less time than an arrow strikes the mark,
    flies through the air, loosed from its catch, I found   *24*

myself in some place where a wondrous thing
    absorbed all of my mind, and then my lady,
    from whom I could not keep my thirst to know,   *27*

turned toward me as joyful as her beauty:
    "Direct your mind and gratitude," she said,
    "to God, who raised us up to His first star."   *30*

We seemed to be enveloped in a cloud
    as brilliant, hard, and polished as a diamond
    struck by a ray of sunlight. That eternal,   *33*

celestial pearl took us into itself,
    receiving us as water takes in light,
    its indivisibility intact.   *36*

If I was body (on earth we cannot think,
    in terms of solid form within a solid,
    as we must here, since body enters body),   *39*

then so much more should longing burn in us
    to see that Being in Whom we can behold
    the union of God's nature with our own.   *42*

Once there we shall behold what we hold true
    through faith, not proven but self-evident:
    a primal truth, incontrovertible.   *45*

I said, "My lady, all my adoration,
    all my humility is gratitude
    to Him Who raised me from the mortal world.   *48*

But tell me what the dark spots are which, seen
    from earth along the surface of this body,
    lead men to make up stories about Cain?"   *51*

She smiled a little, then she answered me:
    "That human judgment must reach false conclusions
    when no key is provided by our senses,   *54*

this surely should be no surprise to you,
  since, as you know, even when the senses guide,
  reason's wing-span sometimes can be short.

But tell me what you think the cause might be."
  And I: "The differences we see from earth,
  I think, are caused by different densities."   60

She said, then: "I am certain you shall see
  that your beliefs are deeply steeped in error.
  Now listen to my counter-arguments: 63

Heaven's eighth sphere is lit by many lamps
  all of which shine with great diversity
  both in their quality and quantity.   66

If rare and dense alone produced all this,
  one single virtue would be in them all
  in more or less or equal distribution;   69

but these show different qualities, the fruits
  of diverse active principles of which
  your reasoning would demolish all but one.   72

Moreover, if the cause of those dark marks
  were density alone, this planet's substance
  would either be in certain parts translucent,   75

or else there would be simple alternation
  of dense and rare like lean and fat in meat,
  or, in a book, as pages alternate.   78

Yet if the first were true, the moon could not
  fully block out the sun: in an eclipse
  some light would shine through the transparencies—   81

but it does not. So now let us examine
  the second case, and if I prove it wrong,
  then your opinion will be falsified.   84

Well, then, if this rare matter does not spread
  all the way through, this means there is a point
  at which some denser matter blocks its way,   87

and it would be from there that the sun's rays
  would be bent back, as color is reflected
  back from a glass concealing lead behind it.   90

Now, you could say that though there is reflection,
    the ray is dimmer there than other spots,
    since it reflects across a greater reach.   *93*

But you can rid yourself of this objection,
    if you are willing, by experiment,
    the source which fills the rivers of man's art: *96*

Set up three mirrors so that two of them
    are equidistant from you, and the third
    between them, farther out in front of you;   *99*

as you stand facing them, have someone place
    a light behind you which strikes all of them
    and which reflects from them back to your sight.   *102*

Although the light seen farthest off is not
    as great in size as are the other two,
    you will observe its brilliance is the same.   *105*

Now, as the substance of the snow gives up
    the whiteness and the coldness it once had,
    beneath the piercing rays of a bright sun,   *108*

so is your intellect stripped clear, and I
    will now reveal a truth so radiant
    that it will sparkle for you like a star.   *111*

Within the highest Heaven of God's peace
    revolves a body in whose power lies
    the essence of all things contained therein.   *114*

The next sphere which is lit with myriad eyes
    divides this essence into many types,
    distinct from it and yet contained in it.   *117*

The other spheres, by various differences
    direct their own distinctive qualities
    to their own ends and fruitful operations.   *120*

These universal organs, you now see,
    proceed from grade to grade, receiving power
    from those above, acting on those below.   *123*

And now, mark well the path that I take up
    to reach the truth you seek, so that henceforth
    you will know how to take the ford alone.   *126*

The power and motion of the sacred spheres
  must by the blessed movers be inspired
  just as the hammer's art is by the smith.   *129*

That heaven whose beauty shines with countless lamps
  from the deep mind that turns it takes its stamp
  and of that image makes itself the seal;   *132*

and as the soul within your living dust
  diffuses through your body's different parts,
  adapted to its various faculties,   *135*

just so does this Intelligence unfold
  its bounty which the stars have multiplied
  while turning ever in its unity.   *138*

Different virtues mingle differently
  with each rich stellar body that they quicken,
  even as the soul within you blends with you.   *141*

True to the glad nature from which it flows,
  this blended virtue shines throughout that body,
  as happiness shines forth through living eyes,   *144*

and from this virtue, not from dense and rare,
  derive those differences of light we see:
  this is the formal principle that gives,   *147*

according to its virtue, dark and light."

NOTES

1 – 18

   This unusual prelude and "Address to the Reader" are rem-
iniscent of the opening of the *Purgatory* (I, 1–6), where Dante
compares his genius to a little boat, navigating strange waters.
There, as in the *Inferno* (II, 7), he appealed to the Muses to guide
him in his journey. Here the Poet also invokes Minerva and
Apollo, and his little boat becomes a more substantial ship, the
better to navigate the vast sea of the heavens and Paradise. It is
the reader who now occupies the little boat, and Dante recom-
mends careful attention lest the little boat stray from the wake of
the Poet's ship, for its course represents the true way to knowl-
edge and vision of God. Thus, just as Dante once enjoyed the

guidance of Virgil, and now benefits from the assistance of Beatrice, in his own turn he provides guidance to the reader, but only if that reader is spiritually and intellectually prepared to follow his difficult course. (See also *Purg.* II, 25 – 45; XXIX, 37; and XXX, 58.) On the navigational metaphor see Curtius (pp. 128 – 29).

7. *I set my course for waters never travelled:* The words "waters never travelled" most likely refer to the material his poem will be treating: the difficult doctrinal questions never dealt with before in poetry. It is also true that Dante was the first poet to attempt a detailed description of Paradise.

8 – 9. *Minerva fills my sails, Apollo steers:* In his unprecedented enterprise, Dante is guided by Minerva, Goddess of Wisdom, Apollo, God of Poetry (see *Par.* I, n. 13), and all nine Muses. They are to direct Dante's "ship" (or poetic craft) to the summit of human knowledge and artistic ingenuity. *Point the Bears to me:* The constellations Ursa Major and Ursa Minor (the Big Bear and the Little Bear) by which sailors steered.

11. *in search of angels' bread:* The bread of angels is the knowledge of God, or wisdom. As long as man's knowledge of God is incomplete, which it must be as long as he is alive and not in heaven, he must remain unsatiated. The yearning which results is part of the natural inclination discussed in Canto I.

13 – 15. *you may, indeed, allow your boat to sail:* Those who have given much time to the pursuit of Divine Knowledge ("angels' bread") are welcome to follow in their boat as Dante navigates the "high seas" of the Paradise, but they must be sure to pay close attention to his words ("the furrow of my wake," 14), very close attention, otherwise they will lose track of him in the "parted waters that flow back."

16 – 18. *Those heroes who once crossed the deep to Colchis:* The Argonauts, who journeyed with Jason, their leader, to obtain the Golden Fleece from King Æetes of Colchis. One of the tasks that Jason had to perform before obtaining the Fleece was to plow a field with two wild, fire-breathing bulls with horns of iron and feet of bronze, then plant serpent's teeth from which armed men would grow. (See *Metam.* VII, 104 – 22.) What Dante is probably saying here is that his journey through the heavens to reach God

(his own quest for the Fleece) will amaze his readers more than the feats of Jason amazed the Argonauts.

19. *By that innate and never-ending thirst:* This natural and insatiable thirst is the desire to know God. It is the innate aspiration of the soul, similar to the natural longing for God described by Beatrice in the final portion of the previous canto (*Par.* I, 115–20; 136–41). Here, as before, the desire for the sight of God serves as the impetus for Dante's rapid rise toward Paradise. (See also *Purg.* XXI, 1.)

21. *as human eyes can rise to meet the skies:* The image is one of extremely rapid movement, nearly instantaneous and imperceptible. In Canto I (*Par.* I, 91–93) the Pilgrim's rapid ascent was compared to a flash of lightning.

22–24. *My gaze on Beatrice:* Dante and Beatrice have just risen to the moon. The preceding speed image of a glance upward (20–21) is now reinforced by that of an arrow leaving the bow and flying to its mark. However, Dante reverses the sequence in the image by mentioning first the arrow's arrival at its target, then its flight through the air, and finally its release from the bow. The three parts of the action occur so fast as to appear simultaneous to the human eye; in analyzing the threefold structure of the event, the mind reverses the order by focusing first on the most recent part: arrival at the mark or the arrow's having already hit the target. Dante makes frequent use of the bow image, but not always in quite the same way. In the preceding canto (*Par.* I, 119; 125–26) for instance, it was used in connection with the discussion of instinct, not to emphasize speed.

For the importance of verse 22 in relation to narrative technique see note 142 of the preceding canto.

25. *a wondrous thing:* Dante is filled with awe by the physical appearance of the moon.

30. *His first star:* The moon. It is the closest star or planet (for Dante these terms are interchangeable) to the earth and the first approached by the traveller and Beatrice as they rise toward Paradise. See Figure 3.

31–39. *We seemed to be enveloped in a cloud:* Using the concrete images of a diamond and a pearl, Dante recounts his impressions as he and Beatrice enter the moon and find themselves engulfed

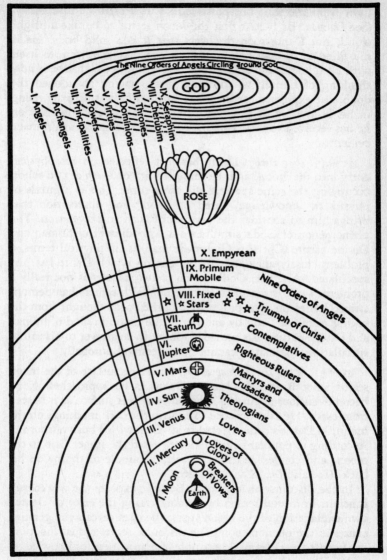

in bright light. Dante thought that the moon not only received light from the sun, but possessed its own intrinsic luminosity. (See *De mon.* III iv.) At first the moon seems to be like a bright cloud, but Dante soon discovers that it is a solid body. He is mystified as to how one solid body can take another into itself with both bodies remaining intact. It would seem that he is now thinking of himself as corporeal mass, having abandoned the doubts he expressed earlier about whether he was actually rising in his body (*Par.* I, 70–75; 97–99). The special dispensation he has received to visit Paradise as a mortal being is again made evident.

41–45. *that Being:* Dante has just reflected on his physical entry into the moon, and the impossibility on earth of two solids' occupying the same space at the same time. This is a puzzle of physics, a "knowledge" based on reason and observation that brings him to consider the mystery of faith and revelation. The phenomenon of God's simultaneous embodiment of human and Divine nature (Christ is God made man) is, in physical terms, a problem closely analogous to the one on which Dante has just speculated. And yet, God's fusion of two natures is not really a problem, for it is meant to be taken on faith rather than demonstrated by reason. The progression of the Poet's thought from the taking in of one body by another to the union in God of human and Divine natures has provided him with an answer to his initial speculation: the matter cannot be understood rationally.

49–51. *what the dark spots are:* Since the surface of the moon seems smooth and flawless to Dante as he approaches it, he becomes curious about the appearance of this surface as it is seen from earth. He asks Beatrice to explain the dark markings on the moon, in Dante's time referred to as "Cain with a bush of thorns." According to popular belief, God relegated the sinner Cain to the moon, and condemned him to carry a bundle of thorns on his back. (See also *Inf.* XX, 124–26.)

In the discourse that follows, Beatrice exposes the weaknesses inherent in mortal reason by demonstrating the error of Dante's own explanation of the moon spots; she then reveals the genuine causes of the phenomenon. The discourse serves a dual function: it presents a paradigmatic example of man's quest for knowledge, which Dante thought to be innate, and it develops the idea of a heaven characterized by differentiation: as the various portions of the moon reflect variously the light of the sun, so all of creation reflects variously the unvarying powers of God (see Sayers, p. 69).

56–58. *even when the senses guide:* As Beatrice points out here, even with his senses to guide him, man frequently makes errors of reason. She now invites Dante to explain the existence of the moon spots, and having no sensory evidence from which to reason, it is not surprising that Dante comes up with an incorrect hypothesis.

59–60. *The differences we see from earth:* Dante argues that the substance of the moon must be of varying density. Where it is most dense, the sun's light is reflected, and where it is least dense, the sun's light shines through without reflecting, causing darkened patches to appear to those viewing the moon on earth. This same opinion, which follows Averroës, is expressed by Dante in his *Convivio* (II, xiii, 9). (See also *Par.* XXII, 139ff.) In the speech that follows, through the mouth of Beatrice, Dante puts forth a revised theory about the moon spots. He clearly had changed his mind about this (as well as other matters) since writing the *Convivio*. On the doctrine of the moon spots see Nardi (pp. 3–39).

64. *Heaven's eighth sphere:* The sphere of the fixed stars in which the different constellations are found. It is located between the Primum Mobile (the ninth sphere) and the sphere of Saturn (the seventh sphere). See Figure 3.

65–69. *great diversity / both in their quality and quantity:* The fixed stars, like the substance of the moon, show varying degrees of brilliance. These variations are not just a matter of relative intensity; they derive also from the very nature, or quality, of the light shed. The constellations were held to possess diverse powers which influenced the universe below in many different ways. Thus, the degree (quantity) of influence, combined with the particular power (quality) at work, would produce a specific effect. The influence of the fixed stars is discussed more fully as Dante's journey progresses.

70–71. *the fruits / of diverse active principles:* According to scholastic philosophy, two types of principles operate in all bodies. First, there exists the material principle, or the basic fact of substance, which is the same in all bodies. Second, there is the active, or formal, principle, which determines species and potentiality. There are many different active principles at work in the universe. They originate with God, the Prime Mover, and are passed down by Him to the highest sphere, the Primum Mobile. Having thus received the power, or "virtue," to direct the movement of the universe below, and to bestow form upon matter, the Primum Mobile distributes the virtue differently among the stars, each of which, in its turn, sends forth its special, distinctive power, acting on the spheres below. Thus, the diversity that exists on earth, within the moon, and among the fixed stars, is ultimately connected to one source.

The weakness in Dante's theory about density of matter is that it excludes the possibility of distinctive qualities, or diverse virtues from diverse active principles. It admits only the simple, single fact of density/rarity.

73–78. *if the cause of those dark marks:* Beatrice here describes what the substance of the moon would be like if it were, as Dante has suggested, composed of dense and rare matter. First, she states that the moon could have random translucent, or thin, areas. Next, she suggests that the moon's substance might show the kind of differentiation, or "alternation," found in meat, with layers of fat and lean. This comparison is reinforced by another concrete image used by Beatrice to evoke the idea of alternation and layering: that of the book. In Dante's time, books were written on parchment or vellum, which was produced from animal skins. Even after the skins were prepared to receive writing, they still showed a definite "hair" side, with the follicles, and an equally obvious "flesh" side, which was paler in color and smoother in texture. In a parchment quire, the pages were arranged so that when the book lay open, the left and right leaves were both either hair side or flesh side. (What an association: a thick steak and a medieval manuscript!)

In the verses that follow, Beatrice proceeds to disprove the notions she has just put forth.

79–81. *Yet if the first were true:* In refuting Dante's idea about dense and rare matter, Beatrice first states that the moon cannot have outright transparent spots, passing completely through the lunar mass, for then the sun's light would penetrate these during a solar eclipse, and the resulting phenomenon would be visible from earth.

82 – 90. *So now let us examine:* Beatrice's response to the second possible arrangement of dense and rare matter (in strata that reflect light of varying intensity, depending upon the depth of the rare strata and the distance involved) is in the form of an experiment.

94 – 105. *But you can rid yourself of this objection:* To illustrate the point she has just made about reflection, Beatrice here proposes that Dante perform an experiment, since human knowledge is acquired through demonstration (see Fig. 4).

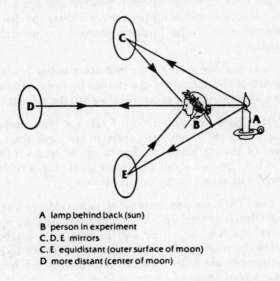

A lamp behind back (sun)
B person in experiment
C. D. E mirrors
C. E equidistant (outer surface of moon)
D more distant (center of moon)

109 – 11. *so is your intellect stripped clear:* Beatrice has completed her refutation of Dante's ideas about the moon's markings, and in so doing has purged his mind of its human error on the subject. The Poet, freed now from false suppositions, is prepared to have the truth revealed to him.

112. *within the highest Heaven of God's peace:* The place is the motionless Empyrean, or God's abode. Within it the Primum Mobile revolves from which the essence of the heavenly spheres, the earth, and each created thing is derived. (See also *Conv.* II, xiv, 15 – 16.)

115 – 17. *The next sphere which is lit with myriad eyes:* This is the next sphere down, contained within the Primum Mobile, that of the fixed stars. In this sphere occurs the first stage of differentiating and distributing the essence or "quality" which derives from God. Though distinct from Him, the differentiated "quality" nevertheless is contained in God because He envelops all of creation and exists everywhere in it.

118 – 20. *the other spheres:* These are the planetary spheres that lie within and beneath the Primum Mobile and the sphere of the fixed stars. The various secondary causes and effects within each sphere are determined by its own powers and operations, the primary cause of each having been derived from the distribution and differentiation of that "quality," essence, or "power" derived from God.

122 – 23. *receiving power / from those above, acting on those below:* The essence of the universe is determined by the double action of receiving and giving that takes place within the spheres.

124 – 26. *mark well the path that I take up:* Here, Beatrice exhorts Dante to pay careful attention to the next stage, or the expansion of her argument, so that he might retain it for application to his question about the moon spots. He is to "take the ford alone" and draw conclusions of his own.

127 – 29. *The power and motion of the sacred spheres:* The angelic orders or "Intelligences" impress upon their assigned spheres a distinctive "quality" or virtue and motion, just as the smith determines the motion of his hammer and hence the form of his art. The spheres are called "sacred" because they are incorruptible, having been created directly by God.

130 – 32. *That heaven whose beauty:* Beatrice's speech now returns to the sphere of the fixed stars ("the myriad eyes" of verse 115) with which her argument began. She has explained that it is this sphere which first differentiates and distributes "quality"; she now adds that it derives its own form or "quality" from its assigned angelic intelligence ("the deep mind that turns it," 131), the Cherubim.

133 – 48. *as the soul within your living dust:* Beatrice now completes her explanation. The essence of existence, which is undifferentiated in God, becomes diverse as it is reflected and passed down through the sphere of the fixed stars. When this essence,

or light, encounters a heavenly body, it mixes with that body in a special way, just as happiness "shines forth through living eyes" (144). In the same way that the soul distributes its power throughout the body, where it becomes differentiated according to the nature of the receiving part or faculty, the undifferentiated power of God, when it is distributed through the spheres, becomes differentiated in the stars and planets as it combines with the qualities inherent in them. This produces a "blended virtue" (143) that causes each body to emit light in accordance with its individual qualities and its degree of excellence. Each star or planet, then, both receives and gives forth light. The light varies from sphere to sphere, as well as within one body, as the example of the moon has illustrated. Thus, the moon's markings are not the result of dense and rare matter, as Dante had supposed when he allowed his reason to follow his senses: what is distributed through the spheres is not one quality, more or less, but different blendings. It is the power of the Divine and Angelic Intelligences in conjunction with the stars that produces the dark and light markings on the moon. This discussion brings the reader back to reflect on the opening tercet of the *Paradise:*

The glory of the One Who moves all things
    penetrates all the universe and shines
    in one part more and in another less.

So much of the *Paradise* will serve as a gloss to this glorious opening.

CANTO III

DANTE, NOW REALIZING the folly of his ideas about the markings on the moon and appreciating Beatrice's wisdom, is about to acknowledge his errors when he sees before him pale, nebulous faces. Thinking them to be reflections, he turns around, but sees nothing. Beatrice, smiling at his mistake, informs Dante that the faces belong to those who made vows to God and broke them. Although they have a place with God in His realm, the Empyrean, these souls occupy the lowest position in the hierarchy of Paradise, and they appear to Dante in the lowest of the heavenly spheres, that of the moon. Beatrice urges Dante to speak with them and listen well to what they have to say, as they are filled, to the extent of their capacity, with the light of God. One of the souls, Piccarda Donati, explains that she was forced to leave the convent and marry, thus breaking her religious vows. In response to Dante's question about the desire of souls to attain a higher place in the hierarchy of Paradise, Piccarda talks about the perfected volition possessed by the Blest, and about the teleological order inherent in Paradise. Piccarda points out the soul of the Empress Constance, and recounts the circumstances of Constance's life on earth. As Piccarda finishes speaking, the faces begin to recede, growing fainter and fainter, and Dante turns his eyes back to the brilliance of Beatrice.

The sun that once warmed my young heart with love
   had now revealed with proofs and arguments
   the beauty in the face of what is true,   *3*

and I, to show that I had understood
   my error and her wisdom, raised my head
   just high enough to meet her eyes and speak,   *6*

when there, before my eyes, appeared a vision,
   absorbing my attention so completely
   that all thoughts of confessing left my mind.   *9*

As faint an image as comes back to us
   of our own face reflected in a smooth
   transparent pane of glass or in a clear   *12*

and tranquil pool whose shallow still remains
    in sight—so pale, our pupils could as soon
    make out a pearl upon a milk-white brow—   15

such faces I saw there, eager to speak;
    I had made the opposite mistake to that
    which kindled love in one man for his pool.   18

The moment I became aware of them,
    believing that they were reflected forms,
    I turned around to find out whose they were,   21

and saw no one. I looked around again
    into the radiance of my sweet guide
    whose sacred eyes were glowing as she smiled.   24

"You should not be surprised to see me smile
    at your naive reaction," she announced,
    "you do not trust the evidence you see;   27

you turn away to stare at emptiness:
    these are real substances that you behold,
    appearing here because they broke their vows.   30

Speak to them, listen, trust in what they say,
    for they are filled with the true light of God
    that gives them peace and does not let them err." 33

I turned, then, to that shade who seemed to be
    the most intent to speak, and I began,
    moved by an overwhelming urge, to say   36

"O well-created soul who, in the rays
    of endless life, enjoy that sweetness which,
    till truly tasted, never can be known,   39

how happy it would make me if you were
    so gracious as to tell me who you are
    and of your fate." Gladly, with smiling eyes,   42

she said: "The love in us no more rejects
    a just request than does the love in Him
    Who wills His court to be like Love Himself.   45

I was a virgin sister in the world;
    if you search deep into your memory,
    you will remember me—though now I am   48

more beautiful by far—I am Piccarda.
　　You see me here among these other blest,
　　blest, all of us, within the slowest sphere.　　　　51

Our own desires that are stirred alone
　　in the desires of the Holy Ghost
　　rejoice conforming to His ordering.　　　　54

Our station which appears so lowly here
　　has been assigned because we failed our vows
　　to some degree and gave less than we pledged."　　　57

I said: "Your faces shine so wondrously
　　with something undescribably divine,
　　transforming them beyond the memory,　　　　60

and so I was not quick remembering;
　　but now with what your words have just revealed,
　　I find it easy to recall your face.　　　　63

But tell me: all you souls so happy here,
　　do you yearn for a higher post in Heaven,
　　to see more, to become more loved by Him?"　　　66

She gently smiled, as did the other shades;
　　then came her words so full of happiness,
　　she seemed to glow with the first fire of love:　　　69

"Brother, the virtue of our heavenly love,
　　tempers our will and makes us want no more
　　than what we have—we thirst for this alone.　　　72

If we desired to be higher up,
　　then our desires would not be in accord
　　with His will Who assigns us to this sphere;　　　75

think carefully what love is and you'll see
　　such discord has no place within these rounds,
　　since to be here is to exist in Love.　　　78

Indeed, the essence of this blessèd state
　　is to dwell here within His holy will,
　　so that there is no will but one with His;　　　81

the order of our rank from height to height
　　throughout this realm is pleasing to the realm,
　　as to that King Who wills us to His will.　　　84

In His will is our peace—it is the sea
  in which all things are drawn that it itself
  creates or which the work of Nature makes."   87

Then it was clear to me that every where
  of Heaven is Paradise, though there the light
  of Grace Supreme does not shine equally.   90

As happens when we find we've had our fill
  of one food but still crave another kind,
  while giving thanks for this, we ask for that,   93

so did my words and gestures beg to know
  about the cloth through which she had not drawn
  the shuttle of her incompleted vow.   96

"A perfect life, great virtue have enshrined
  a lady high above," she said, "whose rule
  decides the cloak and veil of some on earth,   99

who wish, till death, to wake and sleep beside
  that Bridegroom Who accepts all vows of love
  conforming to his pleasure. From the world   102

I fled, as a young girl, to follow her,
  and in her habit's rule I closed myself,
  and pledged to always follow in her practice.   105

Then men, acquainted less with love than hate,
  took me by force away from that sweet fold,
  and God, alone, knows what my life became!   108

This other radiance, here to my right,
  who shows herself to you as she shines full
  with all the light of our low sphere, well knows   111

from her own life what my own words can mean.
  She was a sister, too; from her head, too,
  they ripped the shadow of our holy veil.   114

But even when forced back into the world
  against her will, against her sacred vows,
  she always wore the veil over her heart.   117

She is the light of the great Empress Constance
  who, wed to Swabia's second gust of wind,
  bore him the third and final gust of power.   120

These words she spoke, and then she started *"Ave,
Maria"* to sing and, singing, disappeared
as something sinking in deep waters fades,   *123*

and I, who had been fixed upon her form
until she vanished, turned and set my eyes
upon the greater mark of my desire—   *126*

in Beatrice I was all absorbed—
but her light flashed so deep into my eyes
I could not bear the sight, and so at first   *129*

I found it difficult to question her.

NOTES

1 – 3. *The sun that once warmed:* The "sun" here is Beatrice, who
as a young woman had awakened love in Dante. This same young
woman with whom he had fallen in love when she and he were
only nine years old, as he tells in Chapter II of his *Vita nuova*,
has, in the previous canto, just refuted the Pilgrim's theories
about the markings on the moon's surface and proved their true
cause to him. The echoes of the *Vita nuova* and the loving warmth
in the opening verse of this canto prepare the way by setting the
tone for the main character in this canto, a woman.

9. *thoughts of confessing:* This pertains to the Pilgrim's acknowl-
edgment that his ideas about the moon's markings were
erroneous.

10 – 18

Dante quickly forgets about his intention to confess his
error, for he is suddenly distracted by a strange and marvelous
sight. He sees before him what appear to be faces, so pale and
shadowlike that they look as if they were dim reflections in a
pane of glass, or perhaps in clear, shallow water. The contrast
between such reflected images and their medium is extremely
negligible; by comparison, the contrast between a pearl and the
"milk-white brow" against which it is worn would be obvious.
Dante's use of the pearl image here is more subtle and
complex than is at first apparent. In a literal sense, it could be
seen as a concrete reference to a type of medieval headdress, worn
by upper-class women, that has a piece (known as a frontlet, and

sometimes garnished with pearls) worn against the forehead (see Wilcox for descriptions of such headdress). One must also recall that the pearl is also synonymous with the moon itself; Dante has already referred to it as "That eternal, / celestial pearl" in the preceding canto (*Par.* II, 33 – 34). Thus, a kind of reversal occurs in the metaphor: the faces, set against the pearl of the moon, are paler than the pearl worn against the pale forehead of a lady.

17 – 22. *I made the opposite mistake:* He makes the mistake of assuming that the faces are reflections rather than real faces. Thus, his error contrasts with that of Narcissus, who mistook his reflection in a fountain for an actual being and became enamored of it. (See *Metam.* III, 407 – 510.) Just as Narcissus was too credulous—he looked and loved before knowing what he saw— so the Pilgrim is too quick to believe what his senses tell him about the images before him (perhaps his mind has not yet entirely left the discussion of the preceding canto, in which the question of reflected light was treated). Thus, relying on physical perception rather than spiritual awareness, Dante accepts the apparitions as reflections, and turns around to seek their source. What he finds, in contrast to the position of the light in the experiment in Canto II, is nothing.

23 – 24. *the radiance of my sweet guide . . . glowing as she smiled:* Beatrice in this canto, unlike the cold, doctrinal figure that she cuts in the preceding canto, is presented in the lyrical warmth of the opening verse with its reminiscences of the *Vita nuova.* Verses 23 – 24 manage to present Beatrice in both her worldly and her heavenly role.

25. *"You should not be surprised:* Beatrice corrects Dante's misapprehension about the limitations of mortal, earthbound perception and the appearance of the faces, reminding him again of the importance of faith and trust.

29 – 30. *these are real substances:* The faces are of those who on earth made a vow to God and then either broke or neglected it. They enjoy the lowest degree of excellence in the hierarchy of Paradise, as their appearance in the sphere of the moon indicates, for it is the closest planet to the earth and the farthest from the Empyrean in which God dwells. The sphere of the moon, then, is the place for the Inconstant, the moon itself being a symbol of inconstancy. The members of this group to which the Pilgrim is

introduced are nuns who were forced to leave their cloisters and contract political marriages, thus breaking their religious vows. This sphere, of course, is not reserved only for nuns who broke their vows but rather for all those in general who were inconstant.

The words "appearing here" in verse 30 are intentionally ambiguous: are we to think that this is the permanent home of these blessed souls? This question provides much of the material for the next canto (see *Par.* IV, 28–63, where the question is answered). The souls of the Elect, we will learn, are all located in the Empyrean where God dwells; they appear (or are reflected images of themselves) in the various spheres in order to show the Pilgrim their different degrees of beatitude.

43–45. *"The love in us:* In stating that the love in her is not capable of rejecting any just request, the soul associates herself with God's love, which pervades all of Paradise. Having become perfected, each soul in Paradise is an embodiment of Divine Love, and in this respect, God's court (the Blest, who surround Him) is like God Himself.

49. *I am Piccarda:* The soul is Piccarda Donati, kinswoman of Dante's wife, sister of Dante's friend Forese (see *Purg.* XXIII, 48) and of Corso, the infamous war leader and contributor to Dante's banishment. While still a young woman, she entered the convent of the Franciscan order of St. Clare in Florence. Her brother Corso, in need of a political alliance, invaded the convent with his followers, taking Piccarda from it and forcing her to wed Rossellino della Tosa. Thus she was compelled to break her religious vows. Sometime after her marriage, Piccarda became ill and died (the date of her death is not known, but verse 108 would suggest she did not die soon after her marriage), and one legend has it that she was blessed with a sickness which necessitated the preservation of her virginity. Here, her face is so transformed by the joy of beatitude that Dante does not recognize her at first.

51. *the slowest sphere:* The sphere of the moon, being the innermost of the nine concentric spheres, and the furthest from the Empyrean, moves the slowest, since the speed of each sphere is in direct proportion to its proximity to God. Speed, like intensity and quality of light, is an indication of their share of Divine Love.

65 – 66. *do you yearn for a higher post in heaven:* Dante's question arises from the fact that the souls of the Inconstant appear to him in the lowest sphere of Heaven. (We are reminded of the shades in Limbo [*Inf.* IV], for whom no hope of ascendancy exists, but who yearn constantly for a change in their condition.) At this point in his journey, the Pilgrim has not yet learned that all the Blest are inhabitants of the Empyrean, and that they appear to him in the sphere that best symbolizes their earthly inclinations.

67. *She gently smiled, as did the other shades:* Benvenuto is probably correct in explaining this "smile" in terms of "de simplicitate quaerentis": Piccarda and the other souls around her, then, would be smiling at the Pilgrim's naive question.

69. *she seemed to glow with the first fire of love:* There are two possible interpretations for this verse: (1) Piccarda's happiness at that moment was like that of a woman who has just fallen in love for the first time, or (2) Piccarda was so happy that she seems to glow with the light of God (or the Holy Ghost). The verse, I feel, is intentionally ambiguous, and my translation allows for both interpretations.

70 – 78. *the virtue of our heavenly love:* As Beatrice stated in Canto II, each heaven takes in an amount of Divine Light that is in proportion to its capacity to receive it. In the same way, each individual soul enjoys the bliss of the highest realm, in accordance with its capacity. Thus, the Blest are all content, wherever they are in the hierarchy of Paradise. For Piccarda to desire to be elsewhere would be impossible, since such a desire would spring from an imperfect will and a lack of knowledge of the teleological character of the Divine Order.

82 – 84. *The order of our rank:* The order imposed upon the realm of Paradise is pleasing to its inhabitants because it represents the will of God. Every place in Heaven is Paradise, and the various degrees of blessedness are part of a harmonious unity that rejoices in its own concord and contentment.

85 – 87. *In His will is our peace:* Everything, according to its nature, is attracted by the power of Divine Love and wishes to put itself in harmony with the Divine Will, the source from which all things come. I wonder if Dante the Poet might have wanted his reader to think of another lady in his poem at this point (there are so few in the *Comedy*). Just as Piccarda is the first

woman to speak in the *Paradise*, so Francesca da Rimini is the first (and only) woman to speak in the *Inferno*. Compare Francesca's words (*Inf.* V, 97 – 99) with this tercet. See also Singleton (p. 70).

88 – 90. *every where / of Heaven is Paradise:* Once again our mind is brought back to the opening tercet of the *Paradise*, which itself both surrounds and is contained in everything it begins.

91 – 96. *As happens when we find:* Dante's curiosity about the aspirations of the souls has now been satisfied by Piccarda's explanation of how each soul enjoys its full complement of contentment in Paradise. Yet, even as he expresses his gratitude to Piccarda, he finds that her words have aroused in him the desire to know the circumstances of her life, and how she has come to appear in this sphere of Heaven. To illustrate his state of mind at this moment, Dante constructs a double metaphor. First, he compares his satisfaction and curiosity, which are operating in him simultaneously, to the experience of being between courses in a meal: while savoring the course just completed, the diner looks forward with great anticipation to what is to come in the next. However, instead of carrying this metaphor to the point at which the eager diner requests and receives satisfaction by being served the next course, Dante drops the metaphor in favor of another, that of the weaver's shuttle and loom. Though the shift seems abrupt, the second metaphor does complement and complete the first. In a general sense, both metaphors are drawn from the same context: that of domestic life. Furthermore, though the weaving image is applied specifically to the circumstance of an unrealized vow (which is likened to an unfinished tapestry), it can also be extended and applied to the fact that Piccarda is to satisfy Dante's curiosity by telling her story. The activities of weaving and storytelling were closely associated in medieval tradition. Therefore, though the "final thread" of her past vow must remain unwoven, she does draw through the last thread of her narrative to Dante. The shift is not as sharp as it was from meat to manuscript in the preceding canto on the moon spots (see *Par.* II, 76 – 78).

98. *a lady high above:* The reference is to St. Clare, founder of the Franciscan Order of the Poor Clares, who inspired Piccarda to enter the religious life. Chiara Sciffi (b. Assisi 1194, d. 1253) was a noblewoman of wealth and beauty who, with St. Francis, founded in 1212 the first Franciscan convent for women. The order was confirmed by Pope Gregory IX in 1247. She was canonized by Pope Alexander IV in 1255. The order that bears her name was noted for its austerity.

101. *that Bridegroom:* The true bridegroom is Christ, as opposed to the earthly bridegroom for whom Piccarda was forced to break her vows.

106 – 108. *Then men:* This is an allusion to Piccarda's brother, Corso Donati (see n. 49).

109. *This other radiance:* Piccarda refers to another face (who will be named in 118), that of the Empress Constance (1154 – 1198). Herself heiress to the Norman house of Tancred, and thus to the crown of Naples and Sicily, she was the wife of Henry VI, son of the Emperor Frederick Barbarossa, and the mother of Frederick II. She is referred to by Manfred, who describes himself as her grandson (*Purg.* III, 113). It was thought in Dante's time that she had once been a nun, and had been forcibly taken from her convent to wed Henry VI. Their marriage took place in 1185, when Henry was 22 and Constance about 32, and their son was born nine years later.

114. *they ripped the shadow of our holy veil:* The "shadow" of Constance's veil must be seen in connection with verse 117: in forcing her to leave the convent they may well have ripped the veil from her head, but it was only the "shadow" of her veil that they were able to remove, because "she always wore the veil over her heart" (117) from the time she was forced to leave the convent until her death.

118. *the great Empress Constance:* See note 109.

119 – 20. *wed to Swabia's second gust of wind:* Swabia was a duchy in southwestern Germany, extending from the Rhenish provinces to Switzerland and from Burgundy and Lorraine to Bavaria. Dante refers to three Swabian princes, and calls them "gusts" of wind, perhaps because of the violence and brevity of their rule. The first "gust" was Frederick Barbarossa, father-in-law of the Empress Constance; the second was Henry VI, Constance's husband; the third and final "gust" was Constance's son, Frederick II, last of the line and, according to Dante (*Conv.* IV, iii, 6), last of the Roman emperors.

121 – 23. *she started* "Ave / Maria" *to sing and, singing, disappeared:* In the original this tercet reads:

Così parlommi, e poi cominciò *"Ave,*
Maria" cantando, e cantando vanio
come per acqua cupa cosa grave.

The splitting of the "Ave, Maria" and the repetition of the word *cantando* with its stretched-out echoing sound serve to slow down the action of the tercet as these mellifluous words, so close to each other in verse 122, separate and begin to disappear retaining, as it were, only the sound of the "*c*" in verse 123 ("come . . . cupa cosa . . .") which in itself is imitation of action: the rhythm of the stressed and unstressed syllables gives the picture of an object of substance slowly disappearing, by degrees, from our sight. And with "cantando, e cantando" there is a recall of the reflection motif which dominates earlier in the canto (see especially 10 – 24).

126. *the greater mark of my desire:* Having watched the face of the Empress Constance grow fainter as it drew away, Dante now turns to Beatrice and is dazzled by her appearance, which has become brighter and will continue to become ever brighter as she and the Pilgrim move higher into Paradise.

CANTO IV

HAVING LISTENED TO Piccarda talk about herself and the Empress Constance, the Pilgrim becomes plagued with two doubts and is unable to decide which question to ask first. His dilemma is solved by Beatrice, who knows his thoughts and poses the questions for him. Teacher and guide that she is, she answers first the more "poisonous" (theologically speaking) of the questions—whether or not Plato was correct in believing that each soul returns to the star from which it came. Then, in turning to the second question, why Divine Justice lessened the degree of merit of the souls in this sphere, she discourses on the nature of the Will, by distinguishing between the Absolute Will, which always longs for God, and the Conditioned Will, which bends according to circumstances. Piccarda and Constance are assigned to the sphere of the moon, not for corruption of the Absolute Will, but for that Will which bowed to external circumstances. Apparently still in sympathy with those who have broken their vows, Dante wishes to know if it is possible to compensate for this transgression in some way. The answer is found in the next canto.

Between two equal equidistant foods
   a man, though free to choose, would starve to death
   before he put his teeth in either one.   3

So would a lamb between the ravenings
   of two fierce wolves be caught in fear of both,
   so would a dog stand fixed between two does.   6

If, then, I stood there mute, drawn equally
   by my two doubts, I merit neither blame
   nor praise—the victim of necessity.   9

I did not speak, but written on my face
   was my desire, all of my questioning
   more vividly than words could have expressed.   12

Then Beatrice did what Daniel did
   when he appeased Nebuchadnezzar's wrath
   that drove him to such unjust cruelty.   15

She said: "I see how you are torn between
  your two desires, so that your eagerness
  is choking itself into speechlessness.   18

You think: 'But if my will for good remains
  unchanged, how can another's violent act
  lessen the measure of my just deserts?'   21

There is a second doubt that gives you pause:
  that after death all souls seem to return
  each to his star, as Plato's word affirms.   24

These are the questions that have equal weight,
  contending with your will to know; I first
  shall treat the one that is more poisonous.   27

Not the most Godlike of the Seraphim,
  not Moses, Samuel, whichever John
  you choose—I tell you—not Mary herself   30

has been assigned to any other heaven
  than that of these shades you have just seen here,
  and each one's bliss is equally eternal;   33

all lend their beauty to the Highest Sphere,
  sharing one same sweet life to the degree
  that they feel the eternal breath of God.   36

These souls appeared here not because this sphere
  has been allotted them, but as a sign
  of their less great degree of blessedness.   39

I speak as one must speak to minds like yours
  which apprehend only from sense perception
  what later it makes fit for intellection.   42

For this same reason Scripture condescends
  to your intelligence, attributing
  with other meaning, hands and feet to God;   45

and Holy Church presents to you archangels
  with human features: Gabriel and Michael
  and that one who made Tobit see again.   48

If what Timaeus says about the souls
  in Heaven is to be taken literally,
  it contradicts the truth we witness here: 51

44 / CANTO IV

he says the soul returns to its own star
from which, he thinks, it once had been cut off
when Nature sent it to substantial form.   54

Perhaps his words were not meant to be heard
exactly as they sound, but make a claim
deserving the respect of every man.   57

If he means that the honor and the blame
of each sphere's influence returns to it,
his arrow, then, has hit upon some truth.   60

This principle, misunderstood, once led
the world astray when they bestowed on planets
such names as Jove and Mercury and Mars.   63

The other doubt that still perturbs your mind
is not as poisonous, for all its malice
could never make you wander from my side.   66

That in the eyes of mortal men our justice
appears to be unjust is proof of faith,
not of heretical iniquity.   69

But since this truth is such that your own powers
can understand its meaning easily,
I shall explain it to you, as you wish.   72

Now, if the one who suffers violence
contributes nothing to the violent act,
he cannot be excused on that account;   75

for will, if it will not, cannot be quenched
but does as nature does within a flame,
though violence force it down a thousand times.   78

The will abets the force when it gives in
even a little bit; this their will did,
for they could have gone back into the cloister.   81

Had they been able to maintain their will
intact, like that of Lawrence on the grid,
and Mucius cruel to his own hand in fire—   84

it would have forced them back, once they were free,
back to the path from which they had been drawn.
But such firm will as this is seldom found.   87

If you have truly taken in my words,
    you see how they have quashed the argument
    that never would have ceased to plague your mind.   *90*

But now another pass that must be crossed
    opens before your eyes, and by yourself
    you would collapse before you could get through.   *93*

I certainly have led you to believe
    that these souls cannot lie, for they exist
    forever in the sight of Primal Truth;   *96*

but then you heard Piccarda say that Constance
    had never lost devotion to the veil;
    this must have seemed to contradict my words.   *99*

Often, my brother, it occurs that men
    against their will, to avoid a greater risk,
    have done that which should never have been done;   *102*

so Alcmeon, moved by his father's prayer,
    killed his own mother: so as not to fail
    in piety, he was pitilessly cruel.   *105*

You understand, when things like this occur,
    how will and violence can mix to cause
    offenses that can never be condoned.   *108*

Absolute Will does not consent to wrong,
    but it consents in so far as it fears,
    if it draw back, to fall into worse trouble.   *111*

And so, Piccarda, in her explanation
    was speaking of Absolute Will, and I
    about the other; both of us spoke truth."   *114*

Such was the flowing of the holy stream
    that pours down from the Fountain of All Truth
    that it now laid both of my doubts to rest.   *117*

"Beloved of the First Love, lady divine,"
    I said then, "you whose words bathe me in warmth,
    wakening me to life again, the depth   *120*

of my deep love is not profound enough
    to find the thanks your graciousness deserves—
    may He Who knows and sees all be my answer.   *123*

I see man's mind cannot be satisfied
    unless it be illumined by that Truth
    beyond which there exists no other truth.   126

Within that Truth, once man's mind reaches it,
    it rests like a wild beast within its den.
    And it can reach it—if not, all desire   129

is vain! So at the foot of truth, like shoots,
    our doubts spring up; this is a natural force
    urging us to the top from height to height.   132

And this gives me the courage that I need,
    my lady, in all reverence, to ask
    about a truth that is not clear to me: 135

would it be possible for those who break
    their vows to compensate with such good deeds
    that they would not weigh short upon your scales?"   138

Then Beatrice looked at me, her eyes
    sparkling with love and burning so divine,
    my strength of sight surrendered to her power—   141

with eyes cast down, I was about to faint.

NOTES

1–9

Piccarda's words to Dante in Canto III have aroused in him
two doubts or questions. One revolves around the idea that al-
though Piccarda and Constance broke their vows against their
will, they are penalized nonetheless for vow-breaking by being
accorded a lesser degree of excellence in the hierarchy of Paradise.
The other doubt stems from Piccarda's remark that she and
Constance have been assigned to the moon. Taken literally, this
would appear to confirm Plato's assertion that, at death, we go
back into the planets from which we came.

Dante is paralyzed by these doubts, and transfixed between
them. Both are equally strong and pressing; hence, he cannot
decide which one should be dealt with first. His predicament in
these opening verses is likened first to that of a man forced to
choose between two equidistant and equally appealing dishes,
then to that of a lamb caught between two equally frightening

wolves, and finally to a deerhound between two equidistant does. In such a situation, the man would starve before deciding what to eat; the lamb would be killed before deciding how to escape; and the dog would be without prey, the does having escaped while he decided which one to attack.

This imaginary dilemma was a popular medieval logical exercise, though it can be traced as far back as Aristotle (*De coelo* II, 13, 295b). Perhaps the most widely enduring form of the dilemma is that known as the paradox of Buridan's ass: an ass, finding itself between two equidistant and identical bundles of hay, would starve to death before deciding which one to eat. This was thought to have been formulated by the French philosopher and dynamics expert Jean Buridan, who became Rector of the University of Paris soon after Dante's death, though no trace of the paradox exists in his writings. The problem is also treated by St. Thomas in his discussion of the will. The opponent's argument (which St. Thomas refutes) holds that the will does not enjoy the freedom to move of its own accord; it acts, according to the argument, "de necessitate," obeying the strongest impulse, or motive. When perfect balance exists between two motives, the will is deprived of its power to move, and is thus paralyzed. As St. Thomas puts it,

> If any two things are absolutely equal, a man is not moved to the one thing more than to the other; just as a starving man, if he has food equally appetizing in different directions and at an equal distance, is not moved to the one more than to the other. [*Summa theol.* I – II, q. 13, a.6]

Cf. also *Metam.* V, 164 – 66:

> Just like a tiger when, maddened by hunger, it hears the lowing of two herds in different valleys, and does not know in which direction to rush, but would like to charge both ways at once, so Perseus hesitated whether to attack to the right or to the left.

The same dilemma could be said to apply to Piccarda's situation in life, caught between the prospect of death and that of marriage. When confronted with this choice, she was forced to break her religious vows.

9. *the victim of necessity:* The necessity is that referred to by St. Thomas in his discussion of will (see note 1 – 9, above). Dante finds that *both* of his questions exert upon him the motive force

of necessity, and this is why he is caught, helplessly, between them. Only when man activates his free will is he liable to be blamed or praised.

13. *Then Beatrice did what Daniel did:* As is related in the Book of Daniel (2:1–46), Daniel described and interpreted a dream that had plagued Nebuchadnezzar, when not one of the sages of Babylon had been able to do this. Before receiving Daniel's interpretation, Nebuchadnezzar had been so incensed at the sages' inability to recount and interpret his dream that he ordered them all to be executed. Daniel appeased his wrath.

Just as Daniel described and elucidated Nebuchadnezzar's troublesome dream, Beatrice discerns the two doubts that perplex Dante, and explains them.

19–21. *if my will for good remains:* In these verses, Beatrice articulates one of Dante's doubts (see n. 1–9 above): if Piccarda wished to keep her vow, how then could her brother's violent insistence that she marry lessen her merit? It is interesting to note that Beatrice, as she reads the Pilgrim's mind, expresses his question for him in the first person singular.

22–24. *a second doubt:* Here, the other doubt is presented (see n. 1–9 above). Dante wonders about the truth in the platonic idea that at death the soul goes back to the star (planet) from which it came. The idea appears in the *Timaeus* (41, 42), which Dante knew only indirectly, either through a translation or via St. Augustine or Albertus Magnus (cf. *Conv.* IV, xxi, 2).

In his discussion of creation and the soul, Plato depicts the Creator as a kind of mixer, who began by blending the elements and "the soul of the universe" in a cup. Next,

he divided the whole mixture into souls equal in number to the stars, and assigned each soul to a star. . . . He who loved well during his appointed time was to return and dwell in his native star, and there he would have a blessed and congenial existence. But if he failed in attaining this, at the second birth he would pass into a woman, and if, when in that state of being, he did not desist from evil, he would continually be changed into some brute who resembled the evil nature which he had acquired, and would not cease from his toils and transformations until . . . [he] returned to the form of his first and better state." (Benjamin Jowett, trans.)

The platonic idea runs counter to Christian doctrine by contradicting the role of the Creator as the Bestower of Free Will. In the sixth century, the Council of Constantinople pronounced heretical a number of theories similar to the platonic doctrine, and declared that every soul was created by God at the birth of its body.

25 – 63

The second of Dante's doubts, says Beatrice, is the more "poisonous," in that a grave theological error underlies it. Beatrice goes on to explain to Dante that there is one Paradise, in which all the souls of the Blest reside after death. Within this single Paradise, the souls appear at different levels or stations, not because a particular planet or sphere has been arbitrarily assigned to them or because they "came from" a particular planet, but because the notion of various spheres is a symbolic indication of the various degrees of blessedness in the souls. Beatrice here does not deny that celestial bodies and patterns influence human life; what she denies is that they determine an individual soul's whereabouts in the eternal life.

29 – 30. *whichever John / you choose:* John the Baptist or John the Evangelist.

30. *not Mary herself:* And that's about as high as you can go!

33. *each one's bliss is equally eternal:* Beatrice asserts that all souls in Paradise exist in the one and only Heaven (the Empyrean) and that all are there eternally. This, the Pilgrim will see for himself at the end of the poem.

37 – 39. *These souls appeared here:* The souls in Paradise appear in a particular level or station according to their degree of blessedness and not because of any platonic affinity between the soul and the sphere.

40 – 42. *I speak as one must speak to minds like yours:* Theological truths (and indeed, any abstraction) can be understood most readily by signs which pass through the senses to play in the imagination, leaving images which can be intellectually considered, and by symbolic language, which conveys concepts in terms of images, which can then be pondered. Beatrice develops this idea (upheld by Aristotle and the Scholastics) in the following two tercets by giving examples of spiritual essences symbolically rendered in human form.

48. *that one who made Tobit see again:* This is the archangel Raphael, who instructed Tobit's son Tobias to cover his father's eyes with a certain substance, saying that when he peeled it off, Tobit's sight would be restored (Tob. 11:1 – 15).

49. *If what Timaeus says about the souls:* Timaeus is the name of the principle interlocutor in Plato's dialogue called the *Timaeus* (see note 22 – 24). The *Timaeus* is somewhat obscure because Plato made no attempt to explicate or justify the ideas therein. This stems in part from his belief that sense perception and the resulting data could not lead to knowledge, and therefore he did not couch his ideas in imagistic representations. Therefore, his words must be taken literally, at face value. By contrast, the teachings of the Church, as Beatrice has already pointed out, depend upon image and symbol to convey their truths, thus addressing man's intellect by first appealing to his senses. According to St. Thomas (*Summa theol.* I, q. I, a.9):

> It befits Holy Scripture to teach divine and Spiritual things under the similitude of corporeal things. For God provides for all creatures according to the nature of each. But it is natural to man to come to things of the intellect through things apprehended by the senses; because all our knowledge has its beginning from sense. Hence in Holy Scripture spiritual things are fittingly conveyed to us under metaphors of corporeal things.

52 – 63. *he says the soul:* Beatrice presents here two possible ways to understand Plato's remarks in the *Timaeus* on the nature of the soul. One is totally out of harmony with Christian theology, and the other is acceptable. The first is a literal reading (see n. 1 – 9, n. 27), the second an attempt to understand Plato symbolically. If Plato meant that the planets have some influence on human life then he was not, according to Beatrice, altogether wrong. The concept of influence is, however, not entirely clear in this context, as can be seen from the Roman attempt to equate planets with divinities, which involved the belief that a planet exercised the special influence of the god after which it was named (61 – 63). Hence, the planet Venus was associated with love, Mars with war, etc.

64 – 69

"The other doubt" (concerning Divine Justice) which Piccarda's words have left in Dante is not as "poisonous" as the one just resolved, for it arises from a misunderstanding of the nature of Will, rather than from an intrinsically heretical proposition. As such, it does not lead him away from the teachings of the Church, away from Beatrice's "side" (66).

68. *is proof of faith:* To question Divine Justice is to admit the existence of the Almighty: if mortal man did not believe in the perfection of God's wisdom, then he would not be disturbed by the apparent lack of that perfection in the judgment that has placed Piccarda and the other souls in this sphere.

76–81. *for will, if it will not, cannot be quenched:* Just as fire displays a natural inclination to rise in spite of the winds that cause momentary deviation from the upward path, so does man's will, when it remains firm, refuse to yield to external force. For Piccarda and Constance, who broke their religious vows because of violence done them by others, there always remained the possibility of returning to the cloister: once the outside force was removed, the will should have regained its rightful direction.

83. *Lawrence:* St. Lawrence, a supposed native of Huesca in Spain, was a deacon of the Church of Rome at the time of Valerian. He was grilled alive on an iron grid in 258 for his refusal to disclose the hiding place of Church treasures entrusted to him by Pope Sixtus II. When asked for them, he had brought forth a group of sick and poor people, designating them as the true "treasures" of the Church. Even while roasting, St. Lawrence did not reveal the whereabouts of the treasures; in fact, it is said that he mocked his tormentors by asking them to turn his body so that it might be roasted on the other side.

84. *Mucius:* Gaius Mucius Scaevola ("left-handed") was a Roman citizen who attempted to kill the Etruscan King Porsena during the latter's siege of Rome in the late sixth century B.C. When he stabbed Porsena's secretary by mistake, Mucius was condemned to be burned alive. He thereupon stuck his right hand into a nearby sacrificial fire, and held it there without flinching. Porsena was so impressed by this display of fortitude that he spared Mucius' life. (See also *Conv.* IV, v, 13 and *De mon.* II, v, 14).

89–90. *the argument / that never:* The argument that would have continued to torment the Pilgrim's mind had Beatrice not destroyed it refers to the apparent injustice on God's part in placing Piccarda and Constance where He did. The argument is the one stated by Beatrice as she expressed the Pilgrim's first doubt for him in verses 19 − 21.

91 − 114

In these lines, Beatrice brings up another difficulty (again she reads the Pilgrim's mind) and prepares Dante for her discourse on the nature of Will, in which she explains the difference between Absolute Will and Conditioned Will. She begins by pointing out that Piccarda's words about Constance's devotion to the veil are only in apparent contradiction with her own statement about the flawed will that prevented these souls from returning to the cloister. As she goes on to show, Piccarda was referring to Absolute or general Will, while Beatrice was speaking about the Conditioned Will, or the will that is tempered by circumstances (*voluntas secundum quid*). The same distinction is made by both Aristotle (*Eth, Nicom.* III, I, 1110ª) and St. Thomas (*Summa theol.* I − II q. vi, a.4 − 6).

103 − 105. *Alcmeon:* He was the son of Amphiaraus the seer and Eriphyle. Amphiaraus foresaw that he would die during the Theban expedition, and hid so as not to have to join it. Eriphyle betrayed him. Before he died, he demanded that Alcmeon avenge him by slaying Eriphyle. Thus, out of obligation to and pity for his father, he killed his mother. Alcmeon's act here is presented as an example of Conditioned Will, will consenting reluctantly to evil out of a sense of fear or false obligation. (See also *Purg.* XII, 49 − 51.)

106 − 108. *You understand, when things like this occur:* Beatrice is saying that whenever, in order to escape danger (see 101 − 102), a person does something he should not do—when his will bends to the violence of another ("how will and violence can mix")—the result is offensive to God, or sin.

109 − 11. *Absolute Will does not consent to wrong:* Will in the absolute sense (Absolute Will) never consents to doing wrong; it is only in a relative sense that it consents (Conditioned Will); that is, it gives in or draws back in fear that if it does not it will be in greater danger ("fall into worse trouble").

112 − 14. *And so, Piccarda, in her explanation:* When Piccarda stated that in her heart Constance remained true to her vows, she

meant that her Absolute Will still honored the contract with God, but that her Conditioned Will, perceiving the only choice to be between death and marriage, consented to break the vows. The apparent contradiction between Piccarda's words and those of Beatrice has now been resolved.

124–32

Man's desire for knowledge is innate. No man can be intellectually satisfied until he attains ultimate knowledge, the Truth that is God. It is natural that doubts should spring up in the minds of men who have not yet attained this knowledge, as means of forcing them to resolve perplexity after perplexity until finally the truth is understood. Once this becomes the case, once the mind knows God's truth, then it rests in this knowledge just as a wild animal rests in the peace of its lair.

128. *it rests like a wild beast within its den:* This is a daring and powerful simile: man's mind is like a wild beast and the knowledge of God's truth is his den.

129–30. *all desire / is vain:* It was a basic concept of scholastic philosophy that nothing in the universe is without a goal or purpose. Man's innate desire to know God must be satisfied, for God would never have put such a desire in man's mind if it could not be satisfied. (See *Summa theol.* I, q. 12, a. 1.)

131–32. *a natural force / urging us to the top:* What is presented in these verses is an overall picture of the Pilgrim's action in the Poem: as one question after another is answered for the Pilgrim, as one doubt after another is resolved, he will move from heaven to heaven ("from height to height") until finally he will reach God ("the top").

136–38. *would it be possible for those who break / their vows:* This question results in Beatrice's exposition of the nature of vows, which begins Canto V. Dante has apprehended the truth which replaced his two doubts, and uses his understanding to formulate yet another question. Thus, Dante's ability to express another doubt is justified by the preceding verses in which the process of acquisition of True Knowledge has been described.

CANTO V

BEATRICE EXPLAINS TO the Pilgrim that a vow is a freely made sacrifice of one's own free will to God, and since free will was God's most precious gift to His creatures, what could possibly be substituted for it? But since the Church from time to time does free the individual from his vow, she finds it necessary to explain further. While a person can never take back from God the sacrifice he has made to Him of his free will, he can change the substance of his vow on two conditions: that he have the consent of the Church and that the substitution made be of greater value than the original promise. Beatrice then addresses all mankind, warning them not to take their vows lightly, to think carefully before making them, and to use the Scriptures and ecclesiastical authority as guides. Then, in silence, she turns her eyes on high, and the Pilgrim, still with questions to ask, dares not speak. In the meantime they ascend with great speed to the second sphere, the heaven of Mercury, which shines more brightly with the happiness of Beatrice as she enters the planet. Countless lights appear to the Pilgrim, one of whom he asks two questions: who it is and why it is in this particular heaven. The light of this soul closed tightly in its own light answers, as the closing verse of this canto says, "the way in which the following canto chants."

"If, in the warmth of love, you see me glow
   with light the world below has never seen,
   stunning the power of your mortal sight,   3

you should not be amazed, for it proceeds
   from perfect vision which, the more it sees,
   the more it moves to reach the good perceived.   6

I can see how into your mind already
   there shines Eternal Light which, of Itself,
   once it is seen, forever kindles love;   9

and should some other thing seduce man's love,
   it can be only some trace of this Light,
   misapprehended, shining through that thing.   12

You wish to know if for a broken vow
    one can make compensation of the kind
    that makes the soul secure from litigation."   15

These were the words with which my Beatrice
    began this canto, then without delay
    continued with her sacred explication: 18

"The greatest gift that our bounteous Lord
    bestowed as the Creator, in creating,
    the gift He cherishes the most, the one   21

most like Himself, was freedom of the will.
    All creatures with intelligence, and they
    alone, were so endowed both then and now.   24

Such reasoning as this should make it clear
    how sacred is the vow when it is made
    with God consenting to your own consent;   27

when, therefore, God and man have sealed the pact,
    this treasure, then, of which I speak becomes
    the sacrifice the free will wills itself.   30

What compensation can you offer, then?
    Can you use well what is no longer yours?
    You cannot do good works with ill-got gains.   33

So far, the main point should be clear to you,
    but since the Church grants dispensations here,
    which seems to contradict the truth I spoke,   36

you must sit at the table yet awhile
    because the food that you have taken in
    is tough and takes time to assimilate.   39

Open your mind to what I shall reveal
    and seal it in, for to have understood
    and not retained, as knowledge does not count.   42

The essence of this sacrifice depends
    on two things: first, the promised act itself,
    and next, the solemn nature of the pact.   45

The latter cannot be annulled except
    by its fulfillment; and it was of this
    I spoke in such precise terms earlier.   48

Thus, it was mandatory for the Jews
  to sacrifice, but they could, as you know,
  substitute one offering for another.   51

This may be called the substance of the vow,
  and may be such that no real fault occur
  if the one substance take the other's place. 54

But let no one assume by his own choice
  responsibility for substitution;
  be sure the white and yellow keys have turned. 57

And any change must be considered vain
  if the new matter not contain the old,
  as six exceeds and holds the number four.   60

There are, however, certain things once sworn
  that by their value can tip every scale:
  for these no substitution can be made.   63

Let no man take his vow too lightly. Keep
  your word! But, do not make a blind, rash oath
  as Jephthah did in his first offering—   66

better if he had said, 'My vow was wrong,'
  than do far worse by keeping it. No less
  insensate was that great war-chief, the Greek 69

whose Iphigenia mourned her loveliness,
  and made the wise as well as simple weep
  to hear the tale of such a grievous rite.   72

Christians, beware of rushing into vows.
  Do not be like a feather in the wind,
  or think that every water washes clean!   75

You have the Testaments, the Old and New;
  as guide you have the Shepherd of the church:
  they should be all you need to save your soul. 78

If evil greed incites you otherwise,
  be men, not senseless sheep, lest any Jew
  among you point his finger out of scorn!   81

Do not be like the lamb who turns away
  from its own mother's milk, capriciously
  playing a silly game to its own harm!"   84

As I have written, so spoke Beatrice.
  Then full of yearning she turned to that height
  where all the universe is quickened most.   87

Her stillness, her transfigured countenance
  imposed silence upon my eager mind,
  already stirred with new questions to ask;   90

and like an arrow that has struck the mark
  before the bow-string stops its quivering,
  we soared into the second realm, and there,   93

I saw my lady so caught up in joy
  as she went into that new heaven's glow,
  the planet shone with more than its own light.   96

And if the star changed then and seemed to smile,
  imagine what took place in me, a man
  whose nature is transmutability.   99

As in the clear, still water of a pond
  the fish are lured toward something fallen in,
  as if they knew it was their food—so, here,   102

I saw more than a thousand splendors move
  toward us, and in each one I heard the cry:
  "Behold one more who will increase our love."   105

And as they came nearer to us, the joy
  of each soul there was rendered visible
  in the clear luminance with which it shone.   108

Imagine, Reader, if I were to stop
  right here without describing what came next,
  how keenly you would crave to hear the rest—   111

and you will surely understand how keen
  I was to learn from them all they could tell
  about themselves as soon as they appeared.   114

"O bliss-born soul, to whom God grants the grace
  to see the thrones of the eternal triumph
  before abandoning the war of life,   117

the light of God that shines throughout the heavens
  is lit in us, and so, if you desire
  enlightenment, ask to your heart's content."   120

So spoke one holy soul, and Beatrice
    was quick to urge me: "Speak, and have no fear,
    confide in them, as if they were all gods!"   *123*

"I see how you have made yourself a nest
    of your own light and how those rays of light
    pour from your eyes that dazzle when you smile,   *126*

but who you are, I do not know, or why,
    O worthy soul, you are assigned this sphere
    which with another's rays is veiled to man."   *129*

These were the words I spoke into the glow
    that had addressed me; whereupon it shone,
    this time with light far brighter than before.   *132*

Just as the sun, when its increasing rays
    have broken through dense vapors, hides itself
    within the very excess of its light—   *135*

even so, in its own glowing jubilance
    that holy figure hid itself from me,
    and so enraptured wrapt, it answered me   *138*

the way in which the following canto chants.

NOTES

1–6. *If, in the warmth of love, you see me glow:* In the course of
the ascent through the heavenly spheres, Beatrice becomes more
beautiful and, in a literal sense, more radiant. The brightness of
the light that emanates from her increases as her joy is amplified.
The love with which Beatrice glows has nothing to do with
earthly emotion; rather, it is the love that comes from perfected
vision. A soul with this kind of vision is naturally inclined toward
the Good (perfect love) it perceives. Thus Beatrice's radiance and
her movement in the direction of the desired Good are the result
of her ability to understand and partake of that Good. It is with
this light that she becomes more radiant at the close of the
preceding canto, so dazzling the Pilgrim.

7–9. *I can see how into your mind:* As Dante's journey pro-
gresses, his understanding and his ability to know God increase.

The "Eternal Light" is the light of God, which enkindles love and spiritual illumination in Dante's soul.

10–12. *and should some other thing seduce man's love:* The light of God is Goodness, total and complete, and it shines in all created things. If man's love should become fixed on some earthly object, it is because this object contains something of God's light, and as such becomes appealing. When confronted with something partaking of this Goodness, the unenlightened soul is incapable of distinguishing between the Goodness itself and that which has a part of that Goodness within it, and therefore is attracted by a trivial good. Virgil defines this misapprehension at the center of the *Divine Comedy* (*Purg.* XVI, 85–93), and later explains how man's pursuit or rejection of an unworthy object depends upon the exercise of his free will (*Purg.* XVIII, 40–75). See also *Purg.* XXX, 130–31.

13–15. *You wish to know:* Beatrice here restates the question which the Pilgrim had expressed toward the close of the preceding canto (*Par.* IV, 136–38).

16–18. *the words with which my Beatrice / began this canto:* In his poem Dante continually balances two kinds of time and personae: Dante the Poet reminds us occasionally that he is writing of an event that has already taken place; Dante the Pilgrim moves in an immediate time, the time of the Poem. In this tercet Dante seems to be combining the separate times and reminds us, by making direct reference to "this canto," of the aesthetic of the journey. A similarly "self-conscious" reference will occur in the last verse (139) when the poet speaks of "the next canto." Beatrice, while being present with the Pilgrim, seems to step out of the immediate time of the journey to join Dante the Poet in composing his poem. Most commentators refer to this tercet as "superfluous." See Beall on these verses and addresses to the reader in general.

23. *All creatures with intelligence:* Only angels and men, the highest of creatures, receive the gift of free will from God (cf. *Purg.* XVI, 67–81). This is the beginning of the discourse which Virgil (in *Purg.* XVIII, 73–75) had predicted Beatrice would make.

24. *both then and now:* God gave his creatures the gift of free

will when he first created them ("then"), which He continued to bestow on them even after the Fall of Adam ("now").

26–30

God's greatest gift to man is freedom of the will. When man directs this freedom toward fulfillment of a pact made with God, God's gift (the will) becomes transformed into a sacrifice, or a gift given back to God, in perfect reciprocity.

27. *with God consenting:* God does not accept all vows, as will be explained later (see n. 64–72).

31–33. *What compensation can you offer:* When one breaks or fails to honor a pact made with God, no real recompense is possible, because in making such a pact one has given up one's free will. Just as freedom of the will is God's greatest gift to man, so man's direction of his will toward God is his greatest gift to God. Accordingly, when man breaks his vow, his sacrifice, and thereby loses the capacity to direct his will toward God, he has taken back the greatest gift he had to offer; any other would be of considerably less value. Furthermore, there is no real (or better) use for this gift, once man has attempted to recall it from God, for there is no higher purpose for man's will than its total dedication to God.

35. *The Church grants dispensations:* Beatrice points out an apparent contradiction to what she has just stated about the inviolability of vows made to God: in certain cases, the Holy Church allows the interruption of vows. In the tercets that follow, Beatrice explains how such a release can be possible, and why it is acceptable.

41–42. *for to have understood / and not retained:* Dante is here urged to come to a personal understanding of what he has been told, and cautioned that if he fails to do this, the information will slip away. Just as the mere action of taking in food does not guarantee digestion and absorption, so the simple act of hearing Beatrice's words is not in itself sufficient for comprehension and assimilation as knowledge.

43–48. *The essence of this sacrifice depends:* Two things are involved in the taking of a vow, whereby an individual offers his free will to God. The first of these is the substance of the vow (e.g., virginity, abstinence, poverty), or that which the individual promises to accomplish. The second is the nature of the vow, or the fact that the individual has abdicated his free will and contracted to keep faith with God. This second component cannot be discharged save through complete fulfillment, and cannot be declared void without obliteration of the pact and eventual revocation of one's gift to God. And this is what he spoke of "in such precise terms earlier" (48) in the tercet 31 – 33.

49 – 51. *it was mandatory for the Jews:* This law, handed down to Moses from God, is explicitly stated in Leviticus 27. While it was possible for substitute offerings to be made, the Jews were bound by the Mosaic law to make the substitutions as one-fifth above the value of the original gifts.

55 – 57. *But let no one assume by his own choice:* Although the fact of the individual's contract with God and the orientation of will which accompanies this contract cannot be changed in the context of the vow, the substance of the contract, or the promised thing itself, may be changed by the individual without obliterating the contract. One cannot, however, substitute one thing freely for another, but must obtain a dispensation granted through priestly authority. As Beatrice states in verse 57, one must "be sure the white and yellow keys have turned." The "white" or silver key here symbolizes the priest's capacity to judge the legitimacy of one's desire to be released from a vow, and the "yellow" or gold key symbolizes the power to effect a release (See *Purg.* IX, 117 – 29).

58 – 63. *any change must be considered vain:* The thing promised, the substance of the vow, cannot be replaced by a lesser, more easily accomplished, thing. Metaphorically, the new promised thing must contain and go beyond the old, just as the number 6 contains and exceeds the number 4 (see above, n. 49 – 51). In certain vows, however, the substance is of such high worth that no substitution is possible. This was the case with the religious vows of Piccarda and Constance. As Beatrice has pointed out, in such religious vows, the gift is the free will, which is unsurpassed in nature and therefore irreplaceable.

64 – 72

Beatrice now cites two examples in which the substance of the vow was very poorly chosen, without due consideration for its meaning and consequences. In such cases, she points out, it would have been better to break the vow, and thereby avoid the needless sacrifice of two innocent people. See *Summa theol.* II – II, q. 88, a. 10.

66. *Jephthah:* He was a judge of Israel (ca. 1143 – 1137 B.C.) who fought the Ammonites and promised God that if he should be victorious, he would sacrifice to Him the first living creature that should come out of his house to greet him after the battle. As he approached his house, his daughter ran out the door (Judg. 11:30 – 40).

69 – 72. *the Greek / whose Iphigenia:* Beatrice's second example of a rashly taken vow is from classical antiquity rather than from the Bible. Agamemnon displeased Diana by killing a stag favored by her. In consequence, she stilled the winds, so that Agamemnon's army could not sail against Troy. Calchas, Agamemnon's seer, advised him to sacrifice his daughter Iphigenia to appease Diana. According to various accounts, he killed her and thereby obtained favorable winds (as presented in Aeschylus' *Oresteia*), or was making ready to kill her when she was miraculously replaced by a stag on the sacrificial block (as described in Euripides' *Iphigenia in Aulis*). See *Aen.* II, 116 – 19 and *Metam.* XII, 24 – 34; XIII, 181 ff.

73 – 75. *Christians, beware:* In the preceding verses, the gravity of vows made to God has been emphasized, and the consequences of rashly made vows have been decried. These verses contain a strong exhortation to Christians against rushing into vows at the slightest pretext ("like a feather in the wind"). There is no easy absolution for unfaithfulness to vows: a few drops of holy water cannot free man of the burden of his obligations. Verse 75, "or think that every water washes clean," can also mean, "do not think that with a vow you can wash away your sins."

76 – 78. *You have the Testaments:* A Christian is not obligated to make vows in order to ensure his salvation. He has Scriptural precedent to guide him, as well as the Church; he has only to resist faulty motivation, which leads to hasty decisions.

79 – 81. *If evil greed incites you otherwise:* The "evil greed" according to some early commentators of the *Comedy* refers either to the greed of the religious orders in general or, in particular, to that of the Friars of St. Anthony, a religious order that contrived to release men from their vows for a small fee. Beatrice will return

to this argument later on in the Poem (see *Par.* XXIX 118–26). The word "otherwise" in verse 79 must be understood in relationship to the preceding tercet (76–78). I understand the tercet to mean: if something other than the Bible or the Church offers you another means of saving your soul, such as corrupt friars ("evil greed") who incite you to make vows from which they can release you for a fee, do not follow their advice ("be men, not senseless sheep").

Verses 80–81 imply that a Jew can deride the Christian for seeking an easy absolution, especially since the Jew, with only the Old Testament to guide him, still manages to keep his vows.

82–84. *Do not be like the lamb:* Beatrice has just warned Christians against becoming "senseless sheep" (81); she now extends the figure by condemning the foolish lamb that leaves its mother and her milk (the guidance of the Church).

85. *As I have written, so spoke Beatrice:* There are two other places in this canto where the same insistence on preciseness occurs: verses 16–17 and verse 139, the closing verse of the canto. This didactic technique underscores both the reality of the journey (Dante the scribe writing precisely what Beatrice tells him) as well as the importance which Dante himself placed on the seriousness of the vow made to God and the breaking of it.

87. *where all the universe is quickened most:* Beatrice looks up to the Empyrean, the place where God dwells and the source of all light. The fact that Beatrice once again directs her eyes to the highest heaven signals the continuation of the Pilgrim's ascent. The Pilgrim and his guide are about to move upward and into the next sphere, which is Mercury.

91–93. *and like an arrow:* The Pilgrim and Beatrice now soar toward the sphere of Mercury with extreme rapidity. The speed of their ascent is compared to that of an arrow, that hits its mark even as the bowstring continues to vibrate. This image recalls the one used earlier in the *Paradise* (II, 22–25) to describe the ascent to the moon. (Dante has also used the bow/arrow image to represent the power of instinct in all created things. (See Par. I, 118–20 and 124–26.)

94–96. *I saw my lady so caught up in joy:* Beatrice is bathed in the light of Mercury, brilliant literally because of its proximity to the sun and allegorically because of its closeness to the realm of God. Beatrice radiates with so much joy that her presence in the planet increases the brilliant light already there.

97—99. *And if the star changed:* Dante often uses the word "star" to mean "planet." The heavens are, of course, immutable. If Mercury responded noticeably to Beatrice's radiance, then the Pilgrim's reaction, the response of a changing and changeable creature, must have been unimaginably strong.

100—105

Similar adjectives ("clear, still") were used to describe the faces of the souls who appeared to the Pilgrim in the sphere he has just left (see *Par.* III, 11). They appeared to him as pale reflections in a pond, and Piccarda, representing the Blest in the moon, takes her leave from the Pilgrim (see *Par.* III, 121—23 and note) as she sings the *Ave Maria* and fades away as an object that has weight fades slowly, gradually sinking out of sight. The opposite, it might be said, is the case here. Again making use of "the clear, still water of a pond" Dante introduces the second group of the Blest he meets in the second sphere of the heavens. But the waters of this pond serve to introduce an image quite different in its movement from that in the previous sphere. Though we are not told explicitly until the next canto (*Par.* VI, 112—14), the fish in this pond are the souls of those who in their earthly lives sought fame and honor, and the splendid rush of "more than a thousand" of these fishlike souls, attracted to the Pilgrim who, as it were, has "fallen" into their pond of Mercury, seems an apt reflection of their earthly ways. And when they take their leave of the Pilgrim at the beginning of Canto VII (4—9) there is nothing slow or fading about their departure, nor do they sing as they disappear from sight: they whirl at great speed to their own music and like speeding sparks they shoot off into space!

105. *"Behold one more who will increase our love":* While in Purgatory (*Purg.* XV, 49—78) the Pilgrim learned that the amount of love in Paradise increases in proportion to the number of souls that are there to be loved. The majority of commentators take this verse cried out by the fishlike souls to mean that by answering the Pilgrim's questions (which they are already aware of, being able to read them in the mind of God), the power of their love will be increased (and this seems to be the case in the

following cantos). I find most attractive, however, the theory that with this verse the souls of the Blest here in the sphere of Mercury are welcoming Dante the Poet who will after his death on earth join them in this same sphere of Heaven where those who sought honor and fame while on earth now dwell (see *Par.* VI, 112–14).

106–108. *the joy / . . . the clear luminance:* Light and joy are related to each other throughout Dante's *Paradise.*

115–20. *"O bliss-born soul:* One of the souls addresses the Pilgrim. Recognizing that what he sees before him is a living man with corporeal substance (probably), the soul joyfully offers to tell the Pilgrim all about the souls here ("if you desire / enlightenment, ask to your heart's content").

123. *confide in them, as if they were all gods":* This verse, which at first reading may sound blasphemous, is nonetheless in keeping with Christian doctrine: since the souls of the Blest participate in the truth of God Who is the fountain of all truth, they are like him, as Thomas Aquinas, for one, will attest to (*Summa theol.* I, q. 13, a.9).

124–25. *you have made yourself a nest / of your own light:* The concept of the soul nestling in its own light will be imitated in the language of the last two verses of the canto, which in the Italian read:

e così *chiusa chiusa* mi rispuose
nel modo che 'l seguente *canto canta.* (138–39)

Light over light, the tightness of the nestling soul, light within light, is imitated by the doubling of the same word (exactly the same word in verse 138 and almost the same word in the following verse) with nothing separating them. The brilliance of light here invites the reader as the canto comes to a close, to remember also the "stunning" (3) with which this canto opens!

129. *which with another's rays is veiled to man:* Mercury is so close to the sun that it is usually obscured by it, and therefore is seldom visible from earth.

133–39

Just as the view of Mercury is obscured by the greater brilliance of the sun (128–29), in the same way the very mass of the sun is lost in the light that emanates from it. In fact, the only time the sun can be looked upon directly by mortal eyes is when it is shrouded in "vapors" (see *Purg.* XXX, 25 – 27). Dante compares the brilliance of the sun with the light that now radiates from the jubilant soul who has just addressed him. From this point on in the journey the human features of the souls in Paradise will be completely hidden by their own light from the eyes of the Pilgrim, who catches his last glimpse of a human feature in verse 126 where he mentions the "eyes that dazzle when you smile."

Who this dazzling soul is we are not told until the next canto. Nevertheless, the preparations (especially 123 – 39) to bring him on stage are indeed formidable.

139. *the way in which the following canto chants:* Here we have the third of the major didactic breaks in the narrative of this canto, the first coming in verses 16 – 17 and the second in verse 85 (see the notes to these verses). The repetition of the Italian *canto canta* ("canto chants") would seem to me to be dictated by the *chiusa chiusa* ("enraptured wrapt") of the preceding verse—all of which is in imitation of the action of this as yet unidentified soul (see n. 124 – 25).

CANTO VI

THIS SOUL, IN answer to the Pilgrim's first question, iden-
tifies himself as Justinian, Emperor of the Eastern Roman Empire
in the sixth century, famous for his compilation of Roman law
which became known as the Justinian Code. He then states that
the very nature of his answer, in which he made mention of the
Roman Eagle, necessitates a digression, and begins to give the
long history of the Empire in terms of its "sacred standard," so
worthy of reverence. The story of the Eagle starts with the first
kings of Rome and the Republic, continuing through to the age
of the Empire. He concludes his historical digression with an
invective against the Guelphs and the Ghibellines, accusing both
parties of defiling the Eagle in different ways. Now ready to
answer the Pilgrim's second question, Justinian says that in the
sphere of Mercury are those souls of the Blest who were too
concerned with their own fame and earthly glory which, as a
result, lessened their degree of beatitude. Nonetheless, they are
perfectly happy with their degree of blessedness because they
know that their reward is in perfect accord with their merit. The
light of Justinian speaks from beginning to end of this canto
without interruption. He concludes by making reference to a
certain Romeo of Villeneuve, who proves to be a figure similar to
Dante the Poet in a number of ways.

"Once Constantine reversed the eagle's flight,
    against the course of Heaven which it pursued
    behind that warrior who wed Lavinia,   3

one hundred and one hundred years and more
    the bird of God remained on Europe's edge
    close to the mountains whence it first arose;   6

there, shadowed by its sacred wings, it ruled
    over the world, passing from hand to hand,
    and changing thus, alighted on my own.   9

Caesar I was, Justinian I remain
    who, by the will of the First Love I feel,
    purged all the laws of excess and of shame.   12

Before I had assumed this task I thought
    that Christ had but one nature and no more,
    and I was satisfied with this belief;   *15*

but blessed Agapetus, he who was
    supreme shepherd of God, directed me
    with his enlightened words to the true faith;   *18*

I trusted him, and what he knew by faith
    I now see clear, as clear as you can see
    all contradictions are both true and false.   *21*

And once I was in step with Holy Church,
    God in his grace inspired me to assume
    that task to which I gave all of myself: *24*

To my Belisarius I gave my arms,
    for God's right hand so guided his, I knew
    it was a sign for me to rest from war.   *27*

With this your first question is answered now,
    but I have answered it in such a way
    that I am forced to add on something more   *30*

to make it plain to you how little cause
    have those who move against the sacred standard,
    be it the ones who claim it or disdain it.   *33*

Behold what courage consecrated it,
    the courage which began with that first hour
    when Pallas died to give it its first realm.   *36*

You know that for three hundred years and more
    it stayed in Alba Longa till, at last,
    the three fought with the three to make it theirs.   *39*

And you know what it did through seven kings,
    from Sabine rape up to Lucretia's woe,
    as it grew conquering its neighbor's lands,   *42*

and you know what it did, borne by the illustrious
    Romans against Brennus, against King Pyrrhus,
    against many a prince and government.   *45*

Torquatus, then, and Quintius (so named
    for his rough curls), the Decii and the Fabii,
    all, won the glory I am glad to honor.   *48*

It brought low all of that Arabian pride
  that followed Hannibal across the Alps
  from which you, River Po, make your descent.   51

Under the eagle triumphed in their youth
  Scipio and Pompey, and it showed its wrath
  against that hill beneath which you were born.   54

Then, when the time came that all Heaven willed
  to bring the world to its own harmony
  Caesar, at Rome's behest, laid hold of it.   57

What it did, then, from Var to Rhine, the Seine,
  Isère and Loire beheld and every vale
  whose waters flow to fill the river Rhone.   60

Then what it wrought, when from Ravenna's shore
  it soared the Rubicon, was such a flight
  no tongue can tell or pen can write about.   63

It turned to lead its armies into Spain;
  then toward Dyrrachium, and struck Pharsalia
  so fiercely that the hot Nile felt the blow.   66

Antandros and Simois, whence it first soared,
  it saw again, and Hector's grave, and then,
  again it sprang to flight—the worse for Ptolemy.   69

On Juba, next, it struck like lightning, then,
  again it turned round to attack your West
  in answer to the blast of Pompey's horn.   72

And what it did with its succeeding chief,
  Brutus and Cassius wail about in Hell;
  it made Modena and Perugia grieve.   75

For that, still weeps the tragic Cleopatra,
  who, fleeing from its conquest, finally clasped
  the black and sudden viper to her breast.   78

With him it reached the shore of the Red Sea;
  with him it ushered in a world-wide peace
  that kept the gates of Janus' temple locked.   81

But what this banner, the cause of my words,
  had done before and what it yet would do
  throughout the realm it conquered—all of this   84

appear as dim and paltry deeds, if we
　　but see it with clear eyes and honest heart
　　as it appears in the third Caesar's hand,　　　　　　　87

because the living Justice that inspires me
　　granted it, in the hand of whom I speak,
　　the glory of the vengeance of His wrath.　　　　　　90

Now marvel at what I shall add to this:
　　later, it sped with Titus to avenge
　　the vengeance taken for the ancient sin;　　　　　　93

Lombard fangs bit into Holy Church,
　　and under those same wings came marching forth
　　victorious Charlemagne to rescue her.　　　　　　96

Now you can judge those men that I accused
　　when speaking earlier, and judge their crimes
　　which are the cause of all your present woes.　　　　99

Against the public standard one group sets
　　the yellow lilies; one claims it for its
　　own party flag—and who knows which is worse?　　102

Let them, those Ghibellines, let them connive
　　under some other sign, for those who sever
　　justice from it are not true followers!　　　　　　105

Let not the new Charles trust his Guelphs to tear
　　the banner down! But let him fear those claws
　　that ripped the hides off mightier lions than he.　　108

Many a time a father's sinful deeds
　　are wept for by his sons: let Charles not think
　　his lilies can replace the bird of God.　　　　　　111

This little star is made more beautiful
　　by valiant souls whose zealous deeds on earth
　　were prompted by desire for lasting fame:　　　　114

the more desire tending toward that goal
　　thus deviating from true love, the less
　　intensely burn the rays that rise toward heaven.　117

To see the perfect balance we have here
　　between reward and merit gives us joy:
　　for we see each commensurate with each.　　　　120

And thus, we feel the sweetness of True Justice
   so much alive in us our will cannot
   be warped and made to turn to bitterness.   *123*

Disparate voices blend into sweet tones;
   so, in our heavenly life, the disparate ranks
   produce sweet harmony among these spheres.   *126*

Within this pearl there also radiates
   the radiance of Romeo who accomplished
   fair, noble deeds that went unrecompensed;   *129*

those Provençals who worked against him, though,
   will not laugh last: he who resents the good
   done by another, walks an evil road.   *132*

Four daughters had Count Raymond Berenger,
   each one of them a queen, thanks to Romeo,
   this man of lowly birth, this pilgrim-soul;   *135*

but when those envious tongues convinced his lord
   that he should call this just man to account,
   this man who had rendered him twelve for ten,   *138*

Romeo, proudly, old and poor, departed.
   And could the world know what was in his heart
   as he went begging, door to door, his bread—   *141*

though praised today, he would be praised still more."

NOTES

1. *"Once Constantine reversed the eagle's flight:* The Emperor Constantine (born ca. A.D. 288) ruled from 306 to 337. He was supposedly converted to Christianity in 312, but was not actually baptized until shortly before his death in 337. In 324, he moved the seat of the Roman Empire from Rome to Byzantium. The city was renamed Constantinople, and in 330 was formally dedicated as the new Christian Rome. Thus, the Imperial Eagle, standard and symbol of the Empire, was moved eastward to the new capital, in a direction counter to the westward course of the sun in the heavens.

3. *that warrior:* The reference is to Aeneas, who came from Troy west to Latium (Italy) where he married Lavinia, daughter

of the Latian king (see *Inf.* IV, 125 – 26), and in so doing founded the line of the Roman Empire. Lavinia, then, is the mother of the Roman race. In symbolically bringing the Eagle to Latium, Aeneas moved in accordance with the east-west course of the heavens, and with implicit celestial justification. Constantine's relocation to Byzantium is set by Dante in wrongful contradiction to this.

4. *one hundred and one hundred years and more:* Between the time of the removal of the seat of the Empire to Byzantium (A.D. 330), and the accession of Justinian (527) and the reconquest of Italy by his generals, less than 200 years passed. But it has been suggested that Dante was probably following the chronology set forth by Brunetto Latini in his *Trésor,* who incorrectly sets the dates at 333 and 539, thus making this period of time more than 200 years, as the verse requires.

5. *the bird of God:* The Eagle is the symbol of the Empire as ordained by God.

6 – 9. *close to the mountains . . . alighted on my own:* The Eagle remained in Constantinople, not very far from the mountains of Troas, the Troad (territory of Troy) and the point from which Aeneas had begun his journey to Latium. While in Constantinople it was passed from one imperial ruler to another, until it came down to Justinian, who established the seat of his rule at Ravenna. This move was understood by Dante as the divinely ordained reinstatement of the Imperial Eagle in Western Europe.

10. *Caesar I was, Justinian I remain:* The speaker here is Justinian, born at Illyricum in A.D. 483, Emperor of Constantinople from 527 – 565, and the renowned codifier of Roman law. Justinian here symbolizes the majesty of Rome, and Dante has chosen him to narrate the history of Rome from its foundation to the time of Charlemagne.
    Although Justinian was "Caesar" on earth, in heaven he bears only his Christian name. Notice how he introduces himself *into* the history of the Eagle which he is recounting. While Justinian is the only speaker in this canto, the fact remains that the main character in the story is the Eagle.

12. *purged all the laws of excess and of shame:* Soon after Justinian became Emperor, he organized a commission of jurists to collect all the valid edicts of the Roman Emperors since Hadrian. This

collection became the *Codex Justinianus* in 529. The following year Justinian organized another commission to cull and revise these edicts, which resulted in the 50-volume *Digesta*, or *Pandectae*.

14–15. *that Christ had but one nature:* Before his conversion by Agapetus I, Pope from 535–536, Justinian adhered to the Eutychian or Monophysite heresy, according to which Christ was thought to exist only in his divine nature, rather than as God-made-man. This piece of information concerning the heresy of Justinian, according to the historians, is false. Again, Dante's source was probably Brunetto Latini's *Trésor* (I, 87, 5).

19–21. *I trusted him:* In describing how he came to reject his belief about the nature of Christ and accept that of Agapetus, Justinian invites the Pilgrim to appreciate this enlightenment by appealing not to his faith at this point in the journey, but to his intellect. He states that the true faith is as self-evident and incontrovertible for him as the law of contradictories must be for the Pilgrim. (In Aristotelian logic, a contradiction consists of two propositions, one affirming an idea and another denying it. It is impossible for both propositions to be true at the same time, in the same way. At any given moment, only one can be true; the other *must* be false.)

25. *Belisarius:* Belisarius (ca. 505–565) was a general under Justinian, who was responsible for the overthrow of the Vandals in North Africa and for the conquering of the Ostrogoths. The latter victory restored Italy to the Empire, and enabled Justinian to establish himself in Ravenna. Belisarius was repaid rather harshly for his forty years of service to Justinian. When nearly sixty, he was accused of conspiring against the Emperor, and held under house arrest. After eight months, however, he was cleared of the charges. Dante may have been unaware of this aspect of the relationship between Justinian and his general, since the Medieval Chroniclers such as Villani make no mention of the Emperor's ingratitude.

28. *With this your first question is answered:* In the preceding canto (*Par.* V, 127) the Pilgrim asked this soul to identify himself. Justinian, who is a very orderly soul, as we shall see as the canto proceeds, has answered that question, and now he proposes to continue his speech with an account of the history of the Empire.

33. *be it the ones who claim it or disdain it:* The Ghibellines, who supported the Empire, retained the imperial standard as their own, but not necessarily because they supported the ideal of the Empire. The Guelphs, who supported the French emperor and the papal party, attempted to suppress the imperial standard and replace it with their own. Disapproval is here expressed for *both* groups.

34. *Behold what courage consecrated it:* The word for "courage" in the original is *virtù*. For other possible meanings of this word see Mariotti (pp. 383 – 85).

36. *when Pallas died:* Pallas was the son of Evander, a Greek who had established a kingdom at Latium, the present site of Rome. Evander and Pallas joined Aeneas in his fight against Turnus, and in Aeneas' victory Pallas was killed. Since the land won by Aeneas included Pallas' inheritance from Evander, the victory provided the Imperial Eagle with its first kingly state. (See *Aen.* X, 479ff. and XII, 887 – 952.)

37 – 39. *You know that for three hundred years and more:* Aeneas established the Eagle in Latium, but after his death, his son Ascanius moved it to Alba Longa. There it remained for more than 300 years, until, during the reign of Tullus Hostilius (670 – 638 B.C.), the three Curiatii of Alba fought with the three Roman Horatii to determine which city would claim it. In the course of the fight, two of the Horatii were killed; however, the third managed to defeat all three Curiatii. In the end, the city of Alba Longa was destroyed, never to be rebuilt, and the Imperial Eagle was restored to Rome.

40 – 42. *And you know what it did through seven kings:* After being expelled from Alba, Romulus established a base on one of the seven hills (the Palatine) and recruited a band to raid the Sabines so as to obtain wives. From the resulting settlement, the kingdom of Rome grew through a succession of seven kings who regularly annexed the lands of their neighbors. After this Sextus, son of the last King, Tarquinius Superbus, violated Lucretia, who subsequently killed herself. The Roman people then overthrew Sextus and established the Republic in 510 B.C.

43 – 45. *what it did:* The Eagle was carried to numerous victories during the Republic. Brennus was the leader of the Gauls, who were defeated after invading the Empire and besieging the

Capitol in 390 B.C. Pyrrhus, king of Epirus, aided Greek invaders in their war against the Romans and was defeated with them at Beneventum in 275 B.C.

By means of enjambement in verses 43–44 ("illustrious / Romans") and the insistence on the word "against" used three times (twice in verse 44 and once in 45) the Poet underscores the sweeping course and persistent victories of the Eagle.

46. *Torquatus . . . Quintius:* Titus Manlius Torquatus was dictator twice (in 353 and 349 B.C.), and consul three times (in 347, 344, and 340 B.C.), and led numerous Roman victories. Lucius Quintius Cincinnatus (whose surname, from the Latin *cincinnus,* means "curly" or "shaggy-haired") was summoned from his farm to become dictator and lead the Roman army against the Aequians in 458 B.C.

47. *the Decii and the Fabii:* The Decii were a famous Roman family whose leaders died in the service of Rome for three successive generations (father, son, and grandson, all called Publius Decius Mus). The Fabii, another prominent family, produced a number of well-known Romans, including Fabius Maximus Cunctator ("Delayer"), who was consul five times (233–209 B.C.), and famous for the strategy of delay which he employed in a losing effort against Hannibal at the battle of Lake Trasimene.

49. *that Arabian pride:* The reference (an anachronistic one) is to the Carthaginians, whose territory was occupied by the Arabs in Dante's time.

50. *that followed Hannibal across the Alps:* Hannibal (247–ca. 183 B.C.), the famous Carthaginian general, campaigned in Spain during the Second Punic War, and then crossed the Alps into Italy in 218 B.C. After four years of successful fighting there, he moved into Africa, where, in 202 B.C., he was defeated at Zama by Scipio Africanus the Elder.

51. *from which you, River Po, make your descent:* The source of the Po River is at Monte Viso in the Piedmont Alps.

53. *Scipio and Pompey:* The great Roman general Scipio Africanus the Elder (ca. 235 B.C. – ca. 183 B.C.) won fame by saving his father's life in battle against Hannibal at Ticinus in 218 B.C. Scipio was at that time about 17 years old. While in his twenties he defeated Hannibal's forces in Spain, and at 31 he invaded

Africa. In 202 he earned his decisive victory over Hannibal in Africa. Twice elected consul and much celebrated for his exploits, Scipio nevertheless spent the last years of his life in exile from Rome, having been accused of taking bribes.

Pompey—Gnaeus Pompeius Magnus (106–48 B.C.) was one of Sulla's most effective generals. He was responsible for victories in the African campaign against the faction led by Marius. In 70 B.C. he was made consul along with Crassus; with Julius Caesar and Crassus, he became part of the first triumvirate in 59 B.C. After being elected consul for a second time in 55 B.C., Pompey became engaged in a struggle for power with Julius Caesar, which culminated in the Civil War of 49 B.C. He was finally defeated by Caesar the next year at the Battle of Pharsalia in Thessaly. He fled to Egypt where he was murdered by order of the ministers of King Ptolemy XII.

54. *that hill:* This is the hill of Fiesole, which overlooks Florence. According to medieval accounts, the famous Roman conspirator Catiline took refuge there, and there he was defeated by Roman forces sent out under the authority of Cicero, then consul (62 B.C.). Fiesole is said to have been destroyed during the battle.

It is interesting to note how, all of a sudden, Justinian indirectly brings Dante into his story: "that hill beneath which *you* were born."

58–60. *from Var to Rhine, the Seine, / Isère and Loire:* These lines refer to campaigns of Julius Caesar during the Gallic Wars. The Var River bounded Gaul on the east, the Rhine in the north. Within these boundaries, the rivers Seine and Loire, along with the tributaries of the Rhone, including the Isère, "beheld" Caesar's triumphs.

61–63. *what it wrought:* In Caesar's time, the Rubicon, a small river in northern Italy, marked the boundary between Italy and Cisalpine Gaul. By crossing it to get from Ravenna to Rimini in 49 B.C. without permission of his Senate, Caesar precipitated the civil war against Pompey.

64–66. *It turned to lead its armies into Spain:* During this same year, 49 B.C., Caesar defeated Pompey's lieutenants in Spain. In 48 B.C. he fought Pompey in Dyrrachium (now Durrës, on the Adriatic) and finally defeated him at Pharsalia in Thessaly. After this, Pompey fled to Egypt, where Ptolemy had him killed.

67. *Antandros and Simois:* Antandros is a coastal town near Troy, and the Simois is a nearby river. When he brought the Eagle to Latium, Aeneas sailed from Antandros. After Pompey's death Caesar visited Troy, thus occasioning a symbolic visit of the Eagle to its homeland.

68. *Hector's grave:* The great Trojan hero, who was slain by Achilles, was buried at Troy after the siege.

69. *again it sprang to flight—the worse for Ptolemy:* Ptolemy XII was king of Egypt from 51–47 B.C. His father's will had left the kingdom jointly to Ptolemy and Cleopatra, his sister, but the latter was expelled after only three years in power. Cleopatra then put together an army, and with the aid of Julius Caesar defeated her brother. Ptolemy drowned while trying to escape after his downfall.

70–72. *On Juba, next, it struck:* In 46 B.C., Caesar conquered Juba, king of Numidia (in North Africa) and ally of Pompey. During the next year he attacked the army raised by Pompey's sons in Spain.

73–75. *And what it did with its succeeding chief:* After Caesar's murder, his nephew Augustus became Emperor, the second bearer of the standard. He defeated Marc Antony at Modena in 43 B.C. and formed an alliance with him. The two men defeated Brutus and Cassius (*Inf.* XXXIV, 64–67) Caesar's assassins, at Philippi during the following year, and in 41 B.C. they conquered Lucius, Antony's brother, at Perugia.

76–78. *the tragic Cleopatra:* Not long after the death of Caesar, Cleopatra met Antony and became his mistress. Following Antony's defeat by Augustus at Actium (31 B.C.), Cleopatra fled to Alexandria. A false report of her death reached Antony, and he stabbed himself. Cleopatra committed suicide (see *Inf.* V, 63) shortly thereafter, in order to avoid being taken captive by the Roman forces under Augustus.

79–81. *the shore of the Red Sea . . . Janus' temple locked:* After Antony's death, Augustus ruled all the way to the Red Sea, and the Empire was at peace. As the gates to the temple of Janus (god of beginnings, porter of heaven, and guardian of all earthly doors and gates) were open continually during wartime, they could now be closed (for only the third time in the history of the Empire).

87 – 90. *in the third Caesar's hand:* Tiberius was the third Caesar or bearer of the standard, and during his reign Christ was crucified. This marked the zenith of the Eagle's flight as an instrument of God's will, for by the Crucifixion the sin of Adam was expiated. At the same time, the death of Christ was also a sin for which Divine Justice sought vengeance.

91. *Now marvel at what I shall add to this:* This verse, which reads in the Italian "Or qui t'ammira in ciò ch'io ti replico," has been interpreted in different ways. Sayers, who translates it "Marvel how plea meets counter-plea herein," comments on the verse:

Justinian here speaks in terms of Roman Law, according to which a defendant pleading special circumstances was said to put forward an *exceptio.* If the plaintiff countered this, his reply was called the *replicatio.* In the words of Justinian, the plea (*exceptio*) that the Jews might make was that the Crucifixion was the appointed atonement for the fall of man. The counter-plea (*replicatio*) would be that this in no way affected the guilt of the Jews in crucifying an innocent man. Thus, rightly, so Justinian infers, the eagle, in the hand of Titus, avenged "the vengeance for the ancient sin." The theological justification of this legal concept is the subject of Canto VII.

92 – 93. *it sped with Titus to avenge:* Titus, son and successor of Vespasian, was Emperor from A.D. 79 to 81. In A.D. 70, while his father was Emperor, Titus destroyed Jerusalem. Dante derives from Orosius (*Hist.* VII, iii, 8, ix, 9) the belief that Titus, as the destroyer of Jerusalem, was the avenger of the death of Christ. (See *Purg.* XXI, 82 – 84 and *Par.* VII, 19 – 51.)

94 – 96. *Then, Lombard fangs . . . victorious Charlemagne:* Dante now moves forward 700 years and refers to Charlemagne's defense of the Church against King Desiderius, the Lombard, whom he dethroned in A.D. 774. Charlemagne was not actually crowned Emperor of the Holy Roman Empire until 800. For Dante, he represented the tradition of the ancient Empire.

97 – 98. *those men that I accused . . . earlier:* This is a reference to the Guelphs and the Ghibellines alluded to earlier in verses 31 – 33.

100 – 105. *one group sets / the yellow lilies:* The Guelphs supported France, whose standard is the golden lily (fleur-de-lys), against the Eagle. The Ghibellines used the standard of the Eagle as their own sign and for their own purposes. The Eagle is the

symbol of universal authority and not the property of any particular party (see Chimenz, p. 673).

106. *Let not the New Charles:* This is Charles II (1248–1309), count of Anjou and Provence, king of Naples and leader of the Guelphs, who were supporters of the Church, as opposed to the Ghibellines, who supported the Empire. He was also the father of Charles Martel, whom the Pilgrim will meet in the next sphere of Venus in Canto VIII.

107. *those claws:* I.e., the talons of the imperial Eagle itself.

110–11. *let Charles not think:* These lines may refer to the misfortunes of Charles Martel, the son of Charles II, which are amplified in Canto VIII, 49–84.

112–14. *This little star:* The "little star" is Mercury, the smallest of the planets. With this verse Justinian begins to answer the Pilgrim's second question (*Par.* V. 127–29), explaining that here dwell those souls whose good works were motivated not only by love of God but by the desire for earthly fame as well.

115–26. *the more desire . . . produce sweet harmony among these spheres:* While alive, the souls' desire for worldly fame interfered with their ability to focus on God. In Heaven, they enjoy a lower degree of beatitude, and their capacity to participate in Divine Love is less than that of the souls who appear to the Pilgrim in the higher spheres. They are nonetheless full of heavenly bliss, knowing that their reward is in accordance with their merit, and in their own way, they contribute to the perfect harmony of Paradise, to the harmony of the spheres. Piccarda, earlier in Canto III, expressed the same idea in terms of the will of the Blest conforming to that of God.

127–42

In verse 127 Justinian refers to his sphere of Mercury as "this pearl." The previous sphere of the moon was also referred to as a "pearl." By calling the reader's attention to the similarity of the two "pearls" (in the *Paradise*, no other sphere will be referred to as a "pearl") the Poet is actually stressing a contrast: the simple soul of Piccarda introduced the soul of the great Constance, mother of kings, in her sphere; here it is the great light of Justinian which introduces the simple soul of Romeo.

127 – 28. there also radiates / the radiance: Again, in verse 128 of the original Dante uses language to imitate the idea of light in light: "luce la luce di Romeo."

128. Romeo: This is thought to be Romeo di Villeneuve (1170 – 1250), a minister of Raymond Berenger IV, the last of the counts of Provence. In the verses that follow Dante makes use of the legend recorded by Villani (VI, 90) in portraying Romeo as a humble wanderer who attached himself to Raymond's court and proved invaluable in arranging the marriages of the latter's daughters (the youngest of whom, Beatrice, was given to Charles I of Anjou), as well as in managing the funds and supplies for the court—all of which he did admirably. But a group of nobles at the court, jealous of Romeo's position and the esteem in which he was held, accused him of pilfering treasury funds and ordered an accounting. The count reluctantly agreed. When Romeo heard this, he put on his pilgrim's garb again and left the court and Provence to wander as he had before.

130 – 32. those Provençals who worked against him: In point of fact, the marriage of Beatrice to Charles of Anjou brought Provence under harsh Angevin control. In this way Romeo's enemies received punishment for their envy of him.

134. each one of them a queen: Margaret was married to Louis IX (St. Louis), Eleanor to Henry III of England, Sancha to Henry's brother, Richard of Cornwall, and Beatrice to Charles of Anjou.

135 – 42. this pilgrim-soul: These verses, especially in light of what we learn about Dante's future at the center of the Paradise, urge us to associate the tragic figure of Romeo who, unappreciated in his own land, left Provence "begging, door to door, his bread" (141) with the figure of Dante the Poet in exile. Momigliano (p. 544) points out that while the first part of this canto exalts the religious-political ideal of Dante, this last section deals with the sad consequences which such an ideal had for the Poet: exile and poverty.

CANTO VII

Having finished his discourse, Justinian begins to sing a
Latin hymn; then he and the other souls speed off into the dis-
tance like shooting sparks. Beatrice, reading the Pilgrim's mind,
sees that he has a question: how can a just vengeance be justly
avenged? She offers to explain. Since mankind sinned through
Adam, Christ's death on the Cross was just punishment insofar
as Christ's human nature is concerned; as far as His Divinity is
concerned, the punishment was sacrilegious and unjust. Beatrice
sees that her ward has another unexpressed question: why did
God choose this particular way to redeem mankind? Because it
was the most worthy way, Beatrice says, and explains why: there
were two ways in which God could accomplish man's redemp-
tion—by means of His Mercy or by means of His Justice. God
decided to employ both means, showing His Mercy by taking on
the flesh and His Justice by His suffering and death on the Cross.
Beatrice then formulates an objection the Pilgrim might have:
how can the primary elements created directly by God be cor-
ruptible? This would seem to contradict something she had said
earlier. She explains that God created only the material, but that
the form given to that material is determined by secondary
causes, and it is for this reason that they are perishable. Both the
human soul and the human body were created directly by God;
the fact that the soul is immortal necessitates the resurrection of
the body following the Last Judgment.

"Hosanna, sanctus Deus sabaoth
   superillustrans claritate tua
   felices ignes horum malacoth"   3

—singing these words, I saw him start to whirl
   to his own melody, this soul by twin
   lights fused, en-two-ed into one aureole,   6

and all the others joined him in the dance,
   and then like shooting sparks they instantly
   went disappearing into sudden space.   9

I stood there hesitant: "Speak, speak to her!"
   I told myself: "Speak to your lovely lady
   who slakes your thirst with her sweet drops of truth."   12

But the great awe that dominates my being,
   even at the mention of just *BE* or *ICE*,
   made me lower my head, like someone dozing.   15

Not long did Beatrice let me suffer
   before announcing with a glowing smile
   that would rejoice a man condemned to burn: 18

"My intuition which is never wrong
   informs me that you do not understand
   how just vengeance can justly be avenged;   21

but I can quickly free your mind from doubt.
   Now listen well, for what I have to say
   contains the doctrine of important truths.   24

Because for his own good, he would not let
   his will be curbed, the man who knew no birth,
   damning himself, damned all his progeny;   27

therefore, the human race lay sick below
   within their error for long centuries,
   until the Word of God chose to descend: 30

there, moved by His unselfish Love alone,
   He took unto Himself, in His Own Being,
   that nature which had wandered from its maker.   33

Now listen to my reasoning: once joined
   with its First Cause, this nature was (as it
   had been when first created) pure and good;   36

but by itself alone, by its own act,
   having abandoned truth and the true life,
   out of God's holy garden it was chased.   39

Then, if the Crucifixion can be judged
   as punishment of that nature assumed,
   no penalty could bite with greater justice,   42

just as none could be judged as more unjust,
   considering the Person who endured it
   with whom that other nature was combined.   45

Thus, one event produced different effects:
    God and the Jews both pleased by this one death
    for which earth shook and Heaven opened wide.   *48*

Now it should not be difficult for you
    to understand the concept of just vengeance
    being avenged in time by just decree.   *51*

But now I see your mind is all entangled
    with one thought and another, and you wait
    with eagerness for me to loose the knot.   *54*

You say: 'I clearly understand your words,
    but why God did not choose some other way
    for our redemption still remains unclear.'   *57*

The reason, brother, for that choice lies buried
    from all men's eyes until their inner sight
    has grown to ripeness in the warmth of love;   *60*

nevertheless, since men have always aimed
    their arrows at this mark they rarely strike,
    I shall explain why this choice was the best.   *63*

Divine Goodness, which from Itself rejects
    all envy, sparkles so, that It reveals
    the eternal beauties burning in Itself.   *66*

That which derives directly from His Being
    from then on is eternal, for His seal,
    once it is stamped, can never be effaced.   *69*

That which derives directly from His Being
    is wholly free, not subject to the law
    of secondary things. Created thus,   *72*

it most resembles Him, most pleases Him;
    the Sacred Flame which lights all of creation
    burns brightest in what is most like Himself.   *75*

These are the gifts with which humanity
    was privileged; and if it fails in one
    of these, it must fall from its noble state.   *78*

Sin is the only power that takes away
    man's freedom and his likeness to True Good,
    and makes him shine less brightly in Its light;   *81*

nor can he win back his lost dignity
  unless the void left by that sin be filled
  by just amends paid for illicit joy.   84

Your nature, when it sinned once and for all
  in its first root, was exiled from these honors,
  as it was dispossessed of Paradise;   87

nor could mankind recover what was lost,
  as you will see if you think carefully,
  except by crossing one of these two fords: 90

either that God, simply through clemency,
  should give remission, or that man himself,
  to pay his debt of folly, should atone.   93

Now fix your eyes on the infinity
  of the Eternal Counsel; listen well,
  as well as you are able, to my words.   96

Given his limits, man could never make
  amends: never in his humility
  could man, obedient too late, descend   99

as far as once, in disobedience,
  he tried to climb, and this is why mankind
  alone could not make his amends to God.   102

Thus, it remained for God, in His own ways
  (his ways, I mean, in one of them or both),
  to bring man back to his integrity: 105

But since the deed gratifies more the doer,
  the more it manifests the innate goodness
  of the good heart from which it springs—so, then,   108

that Everlasting Goodness which has set
  its imprint on the world was pleased to use
  all of Its means to raise you up once more.   111

Between the final night and the first day
  no act so lofty, so magnificent
  was there, or shall there be, by either way,   114

for God, Who gave Himself, gave even more
  so that mankind might raise itself again,
  than if He simply had annulled the debt;   117

and any other means would have been less
  than Justice, if God's only Son had not
  humbled Himself to take on mortal flesh.   120

But now, to satisfy all your desires
  I go back to explain a certain point
  so that you may perceive it as I do.   123

You think: 'I see that fire, I see that air,
  that water, earth, and all which they compose
  last but a little while, and then decay;   126

and yet all of these are of God's creation,
  and so if what you said before is true,
  should they not be secure against decay?   129

The angels, brother, and all this pure space
  around us, were created—all agree—
  just as they are, unchanging and entire;   132

the elements, however, that you named
  and all those things produced from them are given
  their form by powers that are themselves created.   135

Created was the matter they contain,
  created, too, was the informing power
  within the constellations circling them.   138

The soul of every animal and plant
  is drawn from a potentiated complex
  by the stars' rays and by their sacred motion,   141

but the Supreme Beneficence breathes forth
  your life directly, filling it with love
  for Him Whom it desires evermore.   144

From what I have just said you may infer
  your resurrection, if you will recall
  how human flesh first came into its being,   147

when our first parents came into the world."

NOTES

1 – 148

The Pilgrim's meeting with Justinian continues from the
sixth into the opening tercet of the seventh canto. It is interesting

to note that Beatrice's discourse takes as its starting point a rephrasing of those verses from the preceding canto that metaphorically describe the destruction of Jerusalem. While Canto VI treats the role of the Empire from a historical or rational point of view, Canto VII deals with it from the viewpoint of the mysteries of the Passion and Redemption, linking it with the doctrine of the creation of man.

Canto VII in each of the three canticles of the *Divine Comedy* appears to deal in some way with the greater workings of history. In the *Inferno* the discussion focuses on Fortune, in the *Purgatory* on the negligence of princes, and in the *Paradise* on Divine Providence. Moreover, Canto VII in each case follows a canto of a primarily political nature. For further discussion on these points as well as the binary structures in this canto, corresponding, perhaps, to the dual nature of Christ, see Galimberti.

1 – 3. *"Hosanna, sanctus Deus sabaoth:* These words are sung by Justinian and the souls with him, and are a combination of Latin and Hebrew, such as customarily occurred in liturgical hymns. The words mean, "Hosanna, holy God of hosts, who illumine with your brightness the blessed fires of these realms." The "blessed fires" are the souls of heaven. The word "malacoth" should be "mamlacoth." Dante did not know Hebrew, and is believed to have copied the words from the *Prologus Galeatus* of St. Jerome.

Sansone (p. 7) sees the second book of the *De monarchia* as the conceptual model for this and the preceding canto.

6. *lights fused, en-two-ed into one aureole:* The double light may symbolize a number of things: Justinian's dual earthly role as Emperor and Lawgiver, or the two heavenly lights of God and the soul. They may also represent the powers of natural intelligence and illuminating grace, or one light may symbolize Justinian's predestined role in the history of the Empire and the other light that of Divine Grace.

For this special verse the Poet creates the word *s'addua* which I render as "en-two-ed." In two other places in the *Paradise* Dante invents a word made from a number (see *Par.* IX, 40 and XIII, 57 where verbs using the numbers 3 and 5 respectively are constructed).

10 – 12. *"Speak, speak to her!":* A new doubt has come into the Pilgrim's mind. Notice how in verse 10 where he begins to tell

what it was that he said to himself, he starts with a doubling of the verb: "Speak, speak" (*"Dille, dille"*). As the reader will come to see (it is already visible in verse 6 with Dante's creation of the verb "en-two-ed"), the motif dictating many of the poetic effects in this canto is the number 2. It is about to appear again in verse 14. And the Pilgrim and his guide happen to be in sphere 2 of Paradise!

13 – 15. *But the great awe:* But all the reverence he has for his lady, all that "awe" which possesses his entire being at the mere mention of the first (*BE*) or the last (*ICE*) syllable of her name made him keep his head bent low and prevented him from questioning her. *BE* stands for the first letter in Beatrice's name (the letter *B* in Italian is pronounced *BE*) and *ICE* are the last three letters which, when combined, form the shortened and more endearing form of Beatrice's name: BICE. The contrast of imagery here between the Pilgrim's intense desire to ask his lady a question and his attitude of dozing seems rather strange. It could be that in the unusual combination of anxiety ("Speak, speak") and rest ("dozing") what the Poet is attempting to stress here is the conflict between the Pilgrim's great urgency to speak and quickly be satisfied with answers and his need to struggle on his own with his doubts no matter how tiring it becomes.

The tercet does, however, seem to recreate an atmosphere reminiscent of the *Vita nuova*.

20 – 21. *you do not understand:* The question which Beatrice senses is puzzling Dante (it must be remembered that Beatrice's ability to read the Pilgrim's thoughts is infallible) stems from Justinian's reference to Titus as one who avenged "the vengeance taken for the ancient sin" (*Par.* VI, 93). Dante wonders why, if the Crucifixion was a just vengeance for Adam's sin, it in turn was avenged with the destruction of Jerusalem.

26. *the man who knew no birth:* This is Adam, who was created by God directly.

28 – 30. *lay sick below:* As a result of Adam's sin, the human race lay sick in sin down on earth, separated from God and living under paganism and idolatry ("within their error"), until the second person of the holy Trinity, the Son of God ("the Word of God"), came to earth.

31 – 33. *moved by His unselfish Love . . . that nature:* "that na-

ture" refers to human nature, which was fused with Divine nature in the Incarnation. At the Fall of Adam, human nature was alienated from God, and did not regain its pure state until it was reunited with God in the person of Christ.

34 – 39. *once joined . . . it was chased:* Before the Fall Adam was endowed with a sinless human nature ("pure and good," 36) and with free will. When, of his own choice, he disobeyed God, he and Eve were banished from Eden ("the true life," 38): human nature was banished from the Earthly Paradise ("out of God's holy garden it was chased," 39).

42 – 45. *no penalty could bite with greater justice:* The Crucifixion was just in that Christ took upon Himself human nature so as to expiate Adam's sin. But because Christ is divine, and was on earth judged and made to suffer by men for the wrong reasons, His divinity was outraged. In this sense, the Crucifixion was a great injustice. See *Summa theol.* III, q. 31, a.1 and q. 46, a.12, ad 3; also *De mon.* II, 12 – 13.

47. *God and the Jews both pleased by this one death:* With this one verse, the Poet summarizes a dialectical paradox of the type favored by the scholastic mind. In the eyes of God, the Crucifixion atoned for the sin of Adam and, by extension, of all human nature. As part of the Divine plan, the death of Christ was just, and pleased God. It also pleased the Jews, but in an entirely different way. Their motives, in seeking and effecting the death of Christ, were wicked ones (see Acts 2:28), and the satisfaction they derived from the event was sinful and deserving of God's punishment. On the accountability of the Jews, see *Summa theol.* III, q. 44, a.4, 5, 6.

48. *for which earth shook and Heaven opened wide:* When Christ died on he Cross, an earthquake occurred (see Matt. 27:51), and it was also through the Passion of Christ that the Redemption occurred and the gate to the Kingdom of Heaven, closed to mankind since the time of the Fall, was opened. See *Summa theol.*, q. 49, a.5.

50 – 51. *just vengeance / being avenged in time by just decree:* Even though they actually carried out God's will in crucifying Christ, the Jews sinned, for their motives were evil. The "just decree" of Titus resulted in revenge on the Jews for their sin, through the

destruction of Jerusalem. (See *Purg.* XXI, 82–85 and *Par.* VI, 92–93.)

55. *You say:* Again Beatrice is reading the Pilgrim's mind.

56–57. *but why God did not choose some other way:* The Pilgrim's question was one that many a theologian of Dante's day was asking: why did God choose this particular way for mankind's redemption, why did He take on man's human nature and suffer death on the Cross (when He could have done it an easier way) to save man? (See *Summa theol.* qq. 46, 47.) According to Bosco and Reggio (p. 107) the solution to this problem that Dante uses here is the one given by St. Anselm in his famous treatise *Cur deus homo?*

61–62. *men have always aimed / their arrows at this mark:* It is the nature of man to attempt to grasp matters that he cannot hope to comprehend without spiritual enlightenment. In this instance the Pilgrim has failed to understand the mystery of God's justice—a question, as Beatrice points out, that has always perplexed those whose "inner sight" (59) has not "grown to ripeness in the warmth of love" (60). Because the Pilgrim has not yet attained the necessary spiritual vision to understand God's choices, his guide must explain to him why God chose to work man's redemption as He did.

64–66. *Divine Goodness . . . sparkles so:* In the same way as a fire produces sparks, God in His great Love brings forth both angels and men, thereby endowing His "eternal beauties" with form in the created world.

67–72. *That which derives directly from His Being:* The order of the universe is determined by God, the First Cause, and it reflects Divine Perfection. Angels and the human soul are also the direct creation of God. As such, they are also the image of Divine Perfection: they are eternal and above the forces of mutability, or changes brought about by secondary causes (influence of the heavenly spheres on the sublunar world).

75. *what is most like Himself:* I.e., men and angels. The love of God shines in all things, but it shines the most in what is most like himself.

76–84. *These are the gifts:* These "gifts" given to the human soul are immortality and freedom of the will, both of which bring man closer to the likeness of God. Sin deprives the soul of its gifts, and only through individual virtue and God's grace can the soul be redeemed.

86–87. *Your nature . . . .:* When mankind or human nature sinned through Adam, it lost the gifts referred to in verses 76–77 (free will and immortality), and in losing these gifts it had to give up the Earthly Paradise.

97–102. *Given his limits:* Man is incapable, by his nature, of humbling himself to the extent that Adam, in his sinful pride ("in disobedience," 100), attempted to exalt himself ("tried to climb," 101). Thus, man could only overcome Adam's legacy and gain redemption with God's help. Adam's sin of Pride was such that mankind without the help of God could not possibly atone for it.

104. *his ways, I mean, in one of them or both:* Because of this, man's inability to regain what he lost through Adam's sin, God had to intervene and effect redemption through mercy, justice, or a combination of the two. He chose to exercise both justice and mercy.

112. *Between the final night and the first day:* Between the Final Judgment and the Creation—that is to say, from the very beginning of the world to the moment of its extinction—no act of God could ever approach the excellence that He wrought with the Redemption. It is interesting to note that Beatrice inverts the order of events (*hysteron proteron*), mentioning the end (the Judgment) before the beginning. By means of this simple device, Beatrice's words convey a point of view that is both retrospective and prophetic.

114. *by either way:* either by justice or by mercy.

119–20. *if God's only Son had not / humbled Himself:* The Incarnation of Christ, then, is seen as the only act of humility which would allow human nature to descend low enough—as low as it had wished to ascend high in pride—to atone for Adam's sin (see 97–102).

122–23. *I go back to explain a certain point:* The point in question is in verses 67–72 where Beatrice mentions "That which derives directly from His Being (67) and "to the law / of secondary things" (71–72).

124 – 29. *I see that fire, I see that air, / that water:* Fire, water, air, and earth were believed to be the four elements of which all substances were composed in the sublunar world. Therefore they and their various combinations would constitute the whole of material creation. The Pilgrim wonders why, if these things come from God, they are corruptible. This fact seems to contradict a statement made earlier by Beatrice (67 – 72).

130 – 35. *The angels, brother, and all this pure space:* Here Beatrice distinguishes between the fruits of direct creation (the angels and the realm of God where the Pilgrim and his guide are situated at this moment) and the fruits of secondary causation (the elements of material creation, such as plants and animals). While the former participate in infinity, the latter are finite (see also *Par.* II, 112 – 38).

139 – 41. *The soul of every animal and plant:* The "informing power" (137) of the stars causes the spark of life to be "drawn from" the different "potentiated" or inert combinations of elements (pre-disposition in matter) that form the different plants and animals. This "soul" of created material is its life force, but it is mortal because it is not the direct creation of God.

142 – 44. *the Supreme Beneficence breathes forth / your life:* At the moment when God infuses a human being with its immortal soul, He also instills the soul with eternal love for its Maker. This love which is breathed into the human soul at creation is called natural love. (See also *Purg.* XXV, 70 – 75.)

145 – 48. *From what I have just said:* Through the resurrection of the body and through eternal life of the soul, man, as witnessed by the creation of Adam and Eve directly by God, participates in immortality.

CANTO VIII

THE CANTO OPENS with an explanation for the origin of the name of the planet Venus. Without realizing it, the Pilgrim has been ascending with his guide to the sphere of Venus, and he knows that he has arrived there only because he sees that Beatrice has grown more beautiful. Joyful lights appear to welcome the traveller. The soul who addresses the Pilgrim is Charles Martel of the renowned Anjou family, though he never mentions himself by name. What interests the Pilgrim who listens to Martel's account of the line of rulers in Naples is the doctrine of heredity implied therein. It is not clear to the Pilgrim how good seed can produce bad. Martel explains that it is not a matter of heredity or lineage but rather the workings of Nature through the influence of the stars upon each individual, influencing the formation of his own character without taking into consideration the ancestors of that particular individual. Martel concludes by telling the Pilgrim that the reason many men have gone astray is that they have not been encouraged to follow their inherent character or nature.

The world once dangerously believed the lovely
    Cyprian, whirling in third epicycle,
    rayed down her frenzied beams of love on man,   *3*

so that the ancients in their ancient error
    offered their sacrifice and votive cries
    to honor her and not just her alone: *6*

Dione too they honored, as her mother,
    and Cupid as her son who they believed
    had nestled once in Dido's loving lap.   *9*

And from that goddess who begins my canto
    they took the name and gave it to the star
    which woos the sun at both its nape and brow.   *12*

I was not conscious of ascending there,
    but that I was within the sphere, I knew,
    for now my lady was more beautiful.   *15*

Even as sparks are visible in fire,
   and as within a voice a voice is heard,
   one note sustained, while others rise and fall,   18

so I saw lights revolving in that light,
   their movements slow or swift, each, I suppose,
   according to how clearly it sees God.   21

From chilly clouds no seen or unseen winds
   ever shot down to earth with such rapidity
   as not to seem slow-motioned, cumbersome,   24

to any one who saw those holy lights
   approaching us, abandoning the dance
   begun among the lofty Seraphim;   27

and from the foremost ranks of light I heard
   "Hosanna" sung in tones so marvelous,
   my soul still yearns to hear that sound again.   30

Then one came closer and announced to us:
   "We all are ready here to do your pleasure;
   we want you to have fullest joy of us.   33

We circle in one orbit, with one rhythm,
   in one desire with those heavenly Princes
   whom once you called upon from down on earth: 36

'O you whose intellect spins Heaven's third sphere,'
   We are so full of love that, if you wish,
   we happily will stop awhile for you."   39

I raised my eyes with reverence to meet
   my lady's light, who with her eyes bestowed
   on me all her assurance and her joy;   42

then to that light who had so generously
   offered himself, I turned again: "Who are you?"
   I said, my voice vibrant with tenderness.   45

How that light glowed and grew more beautiful
   from those few words of mine as it took on
   new happiness upon its happiness!   48

Radiant, it spoke: "The time I spent on earth
   was very brief; if my life had been longer,
   much evil that will be would not have been.   51

My happiness which wraps me in its glow
  conceals me from you: I am swathed in bliss
  just like the worm that spins itself in silk.   54

You loved me greatly once, you had good cause;
  had I not died so soon, you would have seen
  more than the first leaves of my love for you.   57

The left bank, washed by waters of the Rhone
  when this has mingled with the River Sorgue,
  was waiting for me to become its lord;   60

as did the region of Ausonia's horn,
  bound by Catona, Bari, and Gaeta
  whence Tronto and the Verde turn to sea.   63

Already was reflected on my brow
  the bright crown of the land the Danube bathes
  once it has left behind the German shores.   66

And on the gulf most plagued by the Sirocco
  lying between Pachymus and Pelorus
  darkened by sulphur fumes, not by what some   69

believe to be the monster Typhoeus,
  beautiful Sicily would still have looked
  to have its kings through me from Charles and Rudolph,   72

if evil rule, which always alienates
  those subject to it, had not moved Palermo
  to cry out in its streets, 'Death, death to them!'   75

And could my brother have foreseen the facts,
  he would shun all the greedy poverty
  of Catalans before he is disgraced;   78

for clearly some provision must be made
  by him or someone else, lest on his ship,
  already weighted down, more weight be laid.   81

His stingy nature, that derived from one
  more generous, would have required men
  who cared for more than filling chests with gold."   84

"Oh Sire, I know that the deep joy your words
  have given me is clear to you, as clear
  as to myself, there where all good begins   87

and ends—so this deep joy is dearer still,
    and still more precious to me is the fact
    that you discern it as you look in God.   90

You made me happy, now make me as wise;
    your words have raised a question in my mind:
    how can sweet seed produce such sour fruit?"   93

I said. And then he said, "If I can make
    just one truth plain to you, then you will see
    what is behind your back in front of you.   96

The Good that moves and satisfies the realm
    that you now climb, endows these mighty orbs
    with all the power of His own providence;   99

and in that One Mind perfect in Itself
    there is foreseen not only every type
    of nature but the proper goal for each,   102

and thus, when this bow bends, the arrow shot
    speeds ready to a predetermined end:
    a shaft expertly aimed to strike its mark.   105

Were it not so, the heavens you climb through
    would fashion their effects in such a way
    that chaos would result, not works of art;   108

this cannot be, unless the Intellects
    that move these stars are flawed, and also flawed
    the First One Who created them with flaws.   111

Would you like me to make this truth more clear?"
    And I: "Oh no, there is no need—I see
    that Nature cannot fail in what must be."   114

And he, once more: "Tell me, would it be worse
    for man on earth were there no social order?"
    "Of course," I said, "and here I seek no proof." 117

"And can this be, unless men had on earth
    different natures, serving different ends?
    Not so, if what your master writes is true."   120

By reasoning step by step he reached this point
    and then concluded: "So, the very roots
    of man's activities must be diverse: 123

one man is born a Solon, one a Xerxes,
   one a Melchizedek, another he
   whose flight cost him the life of his own son.   *126*

For Nature in its circling stamps its seal
   on mortal wax, perfecting her fine art,
   with no concern about man's lineage.   *129*

So Esau, once conceived, differed from Jacob;
   and Romulus sprang from so base a sire,
   that men imagined him the son of Mars.   *132*

The procreated being would always walk
   the procreator's path, if it were not
   for Holy Providence that overrules.   *135*

Now, you can see what was behind your back.
   The great joy you give me urges me now
   to wrap you in this corollary-gift: *138*

Should natural disposition find itself
   not in accord with Fortune, then it must
   fail as a seed in alien soil must die.   *141*

If men on earth were to pay greater heed
   to the foundation Nature has laid down,
   and build on that, they would build better men.   *144*

But those men bent to wear the sword you twist
   into the priesthood, and you make a king
   out of a man whose calling was to preach: *147*

you find yourselves on roads not meant for you."

NOTES

1 – 2. *the lovely / Cyprian:* This is the goddess Venus, believed
to have risen from the sea off Cyprus. Venus was the daughter of
Jupiter and Dione, and the mother of Cupid. In addition to
Venus, Dione and Cupid were worshipped in pagan times as
deities with the power to inspire sensual love.

2. *third epicycle:* According to Ptolemaic astronomy, the planets
possessed three kinds of motion: that of their diurnal cycles, that

of their periodic orbits, and that of the turns of their epicycles. It was thought that each planet had a small sphere attached to it, at some point on its circumference, that "carried" the planet. This small sphere was the planet's epicycle (see Fig. 5).

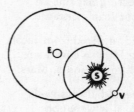

S (Sun), revolves around E (Earth)
The Sun carries with it V (Venus)
Venus revolves around the Sun in a small
circle--that is, the epicycle.

4. *the ancients in their ancient error:* The ancients (the pagans) believed the force of Venus to be irresistible, and that the planet's rays drove people mad with carnal desire.

7. *Dione:* The daughter of Oceanus and Tethys and mother of Venus by Jupiter. Venus herself is sometimes referred to as Dionaea or even Dione.

8. *Cupid:* Son of Venus. Like Dione and Venus he was worshipped as a god of love.

9. *Dido's loving lap:* Also known as Elissa, Dido was the daughter of Belus, King of Tyre, and the sister of Pygmalion. She married her uncle Sichaeus, who was later murdered by Pygmalion. Dido then fled to Africa, where, according to legend, she founded Carthage. While there, she fell in love with Aeneas, and then killed herself when Aeneas went to Italy. Virgil (*Aen.* I, 657–722) tells how Cupid, in the form of Aeneas' young son Ascanius, came to sit in Dido's lap, thereby inspiring love in her for Aeneas.

12. *which woos the sun at both its nape and brow:* This is a reference to the motion of the planet Venus with relation to the sun. Positioned between Mercury and the sun, Venus is both the morning and the evening star. Twice during her daily orbit, she

travels out of the sun's ray. At one point, she follows behind the sun ("woos . . . its nape"), and at another time, she precedes the sun ("woos . . . its . . . brow"). The physical references to "nape" and "brow" are suggestive of the carnal love that Venus was thought to inspire.

As we shall see later on, verses 1 – 12 of this canto will provide the material for the second half of the canto.

14 – 15. *but that I was within the sphere:* Beatrice grows in beauty as she and the Pilgrim rise closer to God. Her heightened loveliness at this point is an indication to Dante that they have ascended, imperceptibly, to the sphere of Venus.

16 – 18. *as sparks are visible in fire, / and as within a voice a voice:* Here Dante constructs a double simile to describe the appearance of the souls in this sphere. First, he compares them to sparks within the flame of a fire. Next, he uses a sound image from polyphonic music to evoke a similar idea. While the two voices blend together as long as they sing the same notes, the sound of each can be distinguished when one sings various notes and the other holds the same note.

19. *so I saw lights:* These "lights" are the souls who appear to the Pilgrim in the heaven of Venus, souls that gave way during their earthly lives to immoderate passion. Having possessed ardent and magnanimous natures, however, they did not become lost in carnality, but performed beneficent works and never turned from God. The nature of the souls is evident in their rapid approach toward Dante and Beatrice (22 – 24) and in the imagery of the canto in general.

22. *From chilly clouds no seen or unseen winds:* According to Aristotle (*Meteor.* III, i), lightning is wind rendered visible by ignition in the presence of cold. Here, the image is used to convey a notion of the swiftness with which the souls move toward the travellers. (See also *Purg.* V, 37 – 39.)

26 – 27. *abandoning the dance / begun among the lofty Seraphim:* Here the motion of the spheres (and the souls within them) is expressed as a dance. The circling motion of the spheres is transmitted through the universe from the Primum Mobile, the outermost of the material heavens and the sphere influenced by the Seraphim where motion begins.

The soul who speaks to the Pilgrim in these verses never identifies himself by name, but we know from what he says that he is Charles Martel (1271 – 1295), first son of Charles II of Anjou and Mary, daughter of the King of Hungary. Charles Martel married Clemence of Hapsburg in 1291 and had three children before he died of cholera at the young age of 24. Dante probably met Charles the year before he died (1294) while he was on a visit to Florence where he was warmly received. According to Villani (*Cron*. VIII, 13), when Charles Martel visited Florence, he remained there about twenty days. The fact that Dante has Charles quote the opening verse of one of his famous *canzoni* in verse 37 and that he talks in such affectionate terms to Dante (see also 55 – 57) would suggest that the two men were more than acquaintances.

35. *with those heavenly Princes:* The souls appear to the Pilgrim in the third sphere, which is governed by the order of angels known as the Principalities ("Princes").

37. *'O you whose intellect spins Heaven's third sphere':* This is the first verse of one of Dante's famous *canzoni* which is the subject of a commentary in the second book of his *Convivio*.

38 – 39. *We are so full of love:* The souls in this sphere are so happy to have the Pilgrim with them that they offer to interrupt their dance for his pleasure.

46 – 48. *How that light glowed and grew:* The growing intensity of this soul's light is all in the anticipation of making the Pilgrim happy by answering his questions.

49 – 51. *"The time I spent on earth:* Charles Martel implies here that the political situation that developed after his death, which ultimately led to the overthrow of the White Guelphs and to the eventual exile of Dante from Florence, would not have come about had he been alive to rule.

54. *just like the worm that spins itself in silk:* The image used by Charles Martel to describe himself hidden in the light of his own happiness is a sensuous and rather elegant one.

56 – 57. *had I not died so soon:* The implication in verses 49 – 51 is restated here. Had Charles Martel lived, the friendship

would have developed and Dante would have seen the fruits of Charles' love.

58 – 60. *The left bank, washed by waters of the Rhone:* The land indicated here is Provence, whose west boundary was marked by the Sorgue and Rhone rivers. Charles I acquired Provence through marriage, and passed it on to Charles II, who would in turn have passed it on to his son, Charles Martel.

61 – 63. *as did the region of Ausonia's horn:* "Ausonia" is the name the Latin poets used for Italy. These verses refer to the kingdom of Naples and Apulia to which Charles Martel was also heir. The towns of Catona, Bari, and Gaeta indicate the southern, eastern, and western boundaries of the Kingdom. The Tronto and Verde rivers separated the kingdom of Naples from the papal states.

65. *the land the Danube bathes:* This is Hungary, of which Charles Martel became King in 1290.

67 – 69. *And on the gulf most plagued:* This is the gulf of Catania in Sicily, where the prevailing wind is the stormy southeast Sirocco. Pachymus (now called Cape Passero) is the promontory at the southeast tip of Sicily, and Pelorus (now called Cape Faro) the promontory at the extreme northeast.

70. *the monster Typhoeus:* Typhoeus, or Typhon, a 100-headed giant who attempted to rule gods and men, was conquered by Jupiter and buried under Mount Aetna. According to Ovid (*Metam.* V, 346 – 56), the volcanic eruptions of this mountain were caused by Typhoeus' attempts to free himself. Dante, however, ascribes the eruptions to a surfeit of sulphur fumes. He may have derived his view from Isidore of Seville (*Etym.* XIV, 8), who maintained that the eruptions were caused when sulphur was ignited by air currents driven by waves through the mountain's caves.

72. *from Charles and Rudolph:* Charles is Charles I of Anjou, grandfather of Charles Martel. Rudolph is Rudolph of Hapsburg, father of Clemence, Charles Martel's wife.

73 – 75. *if evil rule:* Charles Martel refers here to the rebellion against French tyranny known as the Sicilian Vespers, which took place on March 30, 1282. The French were killed by the Sicil-

ians, and the crown of Sicily was passed from the house of Anjou (to which Charles Martel belonged) to the house of Aragon.

76–78. *And could my brother have forseen the facts:* Charles Martel's brother Robert collected Catalan supporters for his father while he was held hostage in Catalonia by the king of Aragon. After Robert became king of Naples and Sicily in 1309, the Catalans occupied powerful positions in his government, and in their greed they were extremely oppressive.

80–81. *lest on his ship:* The "ship" of state inherited by Robert was already burdened with administrative difficulties. These troubles could only be exacerbated by the combination of Robert's supposed avarice and greed with that of his Catalan supporters. (Modern historical opinion no longer supports the avaricious reputation of Robert of Anjou.)

82–84. *His stingy nature:* Robert's mean nature descended from a more generous one, that of his father, Charles II. It has been suggested that the reference here may actually be to Robert's grandfather, Charles of Anjou, since in the *Purgatory* (XX, 79–81) Dante has Hugh Capet describe Charles I as avaricious. The comment made here about Robert's nature leads to the Pilgrim's question in verse 93, the answer to which occupies the remainder of the canto.

85–90. *I know that the deep joy:* What Dante is saying in these two tercets is that the words of Charles Martel have given him "deep joy" and that he is even more joyful because he knows that Charles knows exactly how joyful he is, because Charles can read Dante's happiness in the mind of God ("there where all good begins / and ends," 87–88), and Dante could not possibly express the extent of his joy in words as clearly as Charles can see it. Also "precious" to Dante "is the fact" that Charles is able to know his joy because Charles is among the Blest in Heaven: that Charles is saved ("that you discern it as you look in God," 90). These verses ring with formal elegance and respect as well as with the warmth of a man addressing a superior who is also his friend.

93. *how can sweet seed produce such sour fruit?":* Dante wonders, as a result of Charles Martel's reference to his brother, how a generous nature can generate a mean or stingy one.

95–96. *Then you will see / what is behind your back:* Charles is saying that if he is able to explain a certain concept to the Pilgrim, then what has been unclear ("behind your back") will become comprehensible as soon as he explains it ("in front of you"). The Poet will return to this idea of having a person's back turned on something that is not clear to him when concluding in verse 136 his answer to the Pilgrim's question as stated in verse 93. It is not one of Dante's most poetic turns of phrase!

100 – 105. *and in that One Mind:* Charles Martel describes here the law of individuality, or differentiation, which Beatrice explained earlier (*Par.* II, 127 – 48). The natures and characters of individuals are influenced by heavenly bodies, in a way and toward an end ordained by God. God has foreseen not only what manifestations of individuality are necessary to fulfill His creation, but the proper fashions in which these manifestations should be exercised. He has created each of us to carry out particular goals.

114. *that Nature cannot fail in what must be":* The word "Nature" as used here must be understood as including both God and the things God created. The idea is an Aristotelian one (cf. *De anima* III, 14) which was widely accepted by the scholastic philosophers.

115 – 16. *would it be worse . . . were there no social order?":* This, too, is a basic Aristotelian idea. Dante in his *Convivio* (IV, iv, 1) says, "The Philosopher says that man by nature is a social animal."

120. *your master:* Aristotle, referred to by Dante in the *Inferno* (IV, 131) as "the master sage of those who know."

122 – 23. *the very roots:* These are the different dispositions or tendencies inspired by the heavens.

124 – 25. *a Solon, one a Xerxes / one a Melchizedek:* One man is born to be a lawgiver, another a general, and still another a priest. Solon was a famous Athenian legislator, and one of the Seven Sages of Greece. He brought about important changes in the constitution of Athens. Xerxes was king of Peroria from 485 – 465 B.C. He led a campaign against Greece in 480 B.C. Melchizedek is referred to in Genesis (14:18) as "king of Salem" and "the priest of the most high God."

126. *whose flight cost him the life of his own son:* This refers to

Daedalus, the mythical artificer whose son, Icarus, plunged into the sea after flying too near the sun with wax wings fashioned by his father (cf. *Inf.* XVII, 109 – 11). This is a rather elaborate way of indicating the profession of a mechanic.

129. *with no concern about man's lineage:* No genealogical line has a monopoly on fineness of character or on human attributes.

130 – 32. *So Esau . . . differed from Jacob; / and Romulus:* Having made the general statement that Nature makes its determinations of character regardless of heredity, Charles Martel provides Dante with two illustrations. Though Jacob and Esau were twins (and therefore presumably similar in every way), they were different in character, even in the womb. Because Romulus (or Quirinus) was so great a man, his peers, falsely believing in the necessity of noble lineage for a hero, refused to believe that he was of lowly birth and therefore believed his father to be Mars.

136. *Now you can see what was behind your back:* See note to verses 95 – 96.

138. *to wrap you in this corollary-gift:* The Italian for this verse is "un corollario voglio che t'ammanti," which means literally, "I would have you cloak yourself with a corollary." Charles, in a manner befitting his princely charm, elegantly tells the Pilgrim that he has one more thing to add to the conclusions he has just drawn.

139 – 48

Attributes bestowed by God cannot be brought to fruition when subjected by men to unfavorable conditions. When men compel those who would naturally bear arms to be priests, and those who would be priests to be kings, they are perverting the law of differentiation and, thus, acting counter to the will of God.

140. *Fortune:* This refers to Fate or, more precisely, to those other circumstances in which the individual who possesses certain dispositions finds himself.

141. *fail as a seed in alien soil must die:* In this image the "seed" is the individual's "natural disposition" (139) and the "alien soil" is "Fortune" (140).

CANTO IX

CHARLES MARTEL HAS made some tragic predictions about his own successors to the Pilgrim, but he, in an address to Martel's wife, Clemence, tells her that Charles forbade him to reveal them to anyone. The light of Martel has disappeared by this time and another soul appears and reveals herself to be Cunizza da Romano, sister of the infamous tyrant Ezzelino. Cunizza, after pointing out the light of another soul nearby (without naming him) and remarking on the good reputation he left behind on earth, goes on to make a prediction concerning the inhabitants of the Marches and confirms the truth of her words with her very vision of God. Cunizza returns to her heavenly dance, and the soul whom she had pointed out earlier now addresses the Pilgrim, telling him how he was influenced by the sphere of Venus. He is the light of Folquet of Marseilles, who, after repenting for his worldly loves, entered a religious order and later became Bishop of Toulouse. Folquet, reading the Pilgrim's mind and seeing that he wishes to know the identity of a certain soul nearby, tells him that it is Rahab, the Whore of Jericho, and he explains why she is with them in Venus. Folquet makes some bitter remarks about the Pilgrim's city and the Church in general and closes the canto by predicting that Divine Providence will eventually liberate the Church from its adulterous state.

Fair Clemence, once your Charles had said these words
   for my enlightenment, he then informed me
   of future plots against his progeny,   3

but said, "Say nothing, let the years go by,"
   and for this reason I can only say
   that those who do you wrong will pay with tears.   6

By now the life within that holy light
   was turned to face once more the sun that fills it,
   as to the Good sufficient for all things.   9

Ah, souls deceived, devoid of piety,
   who turn your hearts away from the True Good,
   raising your haughty heads toward empty things!   12

And then! Another of those radiant lights
    drew near to me; its eagerness to please
    was shining through the splendor of its glow.   15

The eyes of Beatrice fixed on me
    now gave me full assurance, as before,
    that my desire met with her consent.   18

"O blessèd soul," I said, "grant me at once
    fulfillment of my wish, and prove to me
    that you can be a mirror for my thoughts."   21

Whereat the light of that still unknown soul,
    out of its depths from which it sang, now answered,
    like one whose joy is giving joyously: 24

"There in that part of sinful Italy
    which lies between Rialto's shores and where
    the Piave and the Brenta rivers spring,   27

rises a hill of no great height from which,
    some years ago, there plunged a flaming torch,
    who laid waste all the countryside around.   30

Both he and I were born from the same root:
    Cunizza was my name, and I shine here
    for I was overcome by this star's light;   33

but gladly I myself forgive in me
    what caused my fate, it grieves me not at all—
    which might seem strange, indeed, to earthly minds.   36

This precious and resplendent jewel that shines
    here, closest to me, in our heaven has left
    behind great fame, fame that will live as long   39

as this centennial year shall be five-timed—
    you see how man should strive for excellence
    so that a second life survive the first!   42

And this means nothing to that crowd that lives
    between the Tagliamento and the Adige,
    nor does the scourge of war make them repent.   45

But it will come to pass that Paduan blood,
    and soon, will stain the waters of Vincenza
    because the people shunned their duty there;   48

and where Cagnano and the Sile join
    a man lords over it with lofty head
    for whom the nets already have been spread;   *51*

Feltre shall mourn her godless shepherd's crime,
    and no man yet was ever sent to Malta
    for treachery as foul as his shall be.   *54*

Immense, indeed, would have to be the vat
    to hold Ferrara's blood, and weary the man
    who would weigh ounce by ounce that bloody flood,   *57*

blood that this generous priest will sacrifice,
    to prove his party loyalty—but then,
    such gifts become that country's way of life!   *60*

Above us there are mirrors you call 'Thrones'
    through which God shines his judgments down on us—
    this justifies the harshness of our words."   *63*

Then she was silent, and it seemed her thoughts
    were drawn to something else, for she had joined
    the dancing wheel where she had been before.   *66*

That other joy which she had just described
    as something precious, now appeared to me
    like an exquisite ruby struck by sun.   *69*

Up there joy gives those souls a brighter light,
    as here it makes us smile, while down below
    souls darken to reveal their sullen minds.   *72*

"God can see all, and your sight sees in Him,"
    I said, "O holy spirit, so no thought
    of mine can hide itself from your true sight.   *75*

Your voice, then, which eternally charms Heaven,
    in harmony with those adoring flames
    that make themselves a cowl of their six wings,   *78*

why does it leave my longing unfulfilled?
    I would not wait for you to ask of me
    were I to inyou as you now inme."   *81*

"The greatest valley into which there flows,"
    with these words he began to answer me,
    "the water of that world-encircling sea   *84*

runs on so far between opposing shores
   against the sun, that finally it makes
   meridian where it first made horizon.   *87*

I dwelt upon that valley's shores between
   the Ebro and the Magra whose short course
   divides the Tuscans from the Genoese.   *90*

Almost the same sunset and dawn are shared
   by Bougie and the city I came from,
   which with its own blood warmed its harbor once.   *93*

To those who knew it Folquet was my name;
   this sphere of heaven bears my imprint now
   as from my day of birth I bore its own.   *96*

Dido, Belus' child, did not burn more,
   wronging Sichaeus and Creusa, too,
   than I burned loving till my hair turned grey;   *99*

nor she of Rhodope who was betrayed
   by her Demophoön, nor Hercules
   when he enclosed Iole in his heart.   *102*

But we do not repent, we smile instead:
   not at the sin—this does not come to mind—
   but at the Power that orders and provides.   *105*

From here we gaze upon that art which works
   with such effective love; we see the Good
   by which the world below returns above.   *108*

But now that I may fully satisfy
   all of your wishes born within this sphere,
   let me proceed. It is your wish to know   *111*

who this one is within the luminance
   you see in all its splendor next to me
   like crystal water struck by rays of light.   *114*

Know, then, that there within Rahab has peace,
   and once joined with our order, she impressed
   her seal upon it at the highest rank.   *117*

To this sphere where the shadow of your earth
   comes to an end, she was the first to rise
   among the souls redeemed in Christ's great triumph. *120*

It was most fitting that she be received
    and left in one of our spheres as a palm
    of that great victory won by those two palms,   123

for it was Rahab who made possible
    Joshua's first glory in the Holy Land—
    which seems to matter little to the Pope.   126

Your city—which was planted by the one,
    the first to turn against his Maker's power,
    and whose fierce envy brought the world such woe—   129

creates and circulates the wicked flower
    that turns the shepherds into ravening wolves
    and breaks the fold and lets the lambs run wild.   132

The Gospel and the fathers of the Church
    lie gathering dust, and Canon Law alone
    is studied, as the margins testify.   135

The Pope and Cardinals heed nothing else;
    their thoughts do not go out to Nazareth
    where Gabriel once opened wide his wings.   138

But Vatican and every sacred place
    in Rome which marked the burial-ground of saints
    who fought in Peter's army to the death,   141

shall soon be free of this adultery."

NOTES

1. *Fair Clemence, once your Charles:* In this line, Dante seems to
be addressing Clemence of Hapsburg, widow of Charles Martel.
However, such a view presents problems of chronology, since at
the assumed time of the poet's narrative (1300), Clemence had
already been dead some seven years. It has also been suggested
that the lady in question is Charles Martel's daughter, herself
called Clemence. If this be the case, Clemence would have been
a young child at the time of the narrative, a fact that makes
Dante's style of address (his reference to "your Charles") seem
highly inappropriate. Given this complication one is led to as-
sume that Dante is speaking to the first Clemence, not in fact,
but in memory, in a kind of apostrophe. For the principle studies

on this matter as well as an excellent overview of this canto see Bergin (pp. 112–42).

3. *future plots against his progeny:* Charles Robert, or Carobert (1288–1342), son of Charles Martel and Clemence of Habsburg, became King of Hungary in 1308. He was also heir to the throne of Naples, but was deposed by his uncle, Robert, in collaboration with Pope Clement V. Charles Robert retained the crown of Hungary, and Robert was crowned King of Naples in 1309.

4. *but said "Say nothing, let the years go by":* The Poet reports in his address to Clemence that Charles told him not to reveal these "future plots" to anyone. (See also *Par.* XVII, 91–92.)

6. *those who do you wrong will pay with tears:* Perhaps Dante's prediction refers to the death of Robert's brother and nephew in 1315 at the battle of Montecatini.

10–12. *Ah, souls deceived, devoid of piety:* In this sudden address to mankind the Poet aims his wrath at those who concentrate on the vain things of this world instead of devoting their thoughts to God, the "True Good." His outburst at this moment foreshadows the bitter tone of the end of the canto.

19. *"O blessèd soul":* Here Dante addresses the soul that has approached him. It is that of Cunizza da Romano (ca. 1198–1279), sister of the tyrant Ezzelino III da Romano. Cunizza had during her life four husbands and two lovers. In 1222 she married Riccardo di San Bonifazio, whom she left for the troubadour Sordello. She was then sent for safekeeping to her brother Alberico, from whom she escaped with a knight named Bonio. When Bonio was killed in battle, she married the count of Breganze. When he died, she married a gentleman of Verona, and after his death she married Salione Buzzacarini, who was Ezzelino's astrologer. After the death of her fourth husband, she went to live in Florence, where she freed the slaves of her father and brothers in 1265. According to the early commentators of the *Comedy*, during her later life Cunizza was known for her acts of compassion and mercy.

21. *you can be a mirror for my thoughts":* Since this as yet unidentified soul whom the Pilgrim is adressing can gaze upon the mind of God, it can see the Pilgrim's thought reflected in it and thus fulfill his wish all the more quickly. In verses 19–21 the Pilgrim

seems to be making his request in a way that sounds as if he were testing this soul's ability to read his thoughts in the mind of God.

22. *the light of that still unknown soul:* As yet Cunizza has not identified herself to the Pilgrim.

25–27. *"There in that part of sinful Italy:* The March of Treviso, the land of Cunizza's birth, is described here. It was bordered on the south by the Duchy of Venice (here indicated by the Rialto, its largest island) and on the north by the Alps of the Trentino, in which the River Brenta has its source, and the Alps of the Cadore, where lies the source of the River Piave.

28. *rises a hill:* The Ezzelino family castle stood on the hill of Romano, northeast of Bassano.

29. *there plunged a flaming torch:* The "flaming torch" (an allusion to the belief that his mother before giving birth to him dreamed she gave birth to a torch or firebrand) is Ezzelino III da Romano (1194–1259), brother of Cunizza. He was placed by Dante with the tyrants in the first round of circle VII of the Inferno, in the river of boiling blood (*Inf.* XII, 110). As ruler of the March of Treviso, Ezzelino was exceedingly bloodthirsty, and was rumored to have committed all manner of atrocities. By Dante's time he had become a legendary figure of evil. Most of the accounts of his deeds are based on the chronicle of Rolandino. See Kantorowicz, pp. 612–13.

33–36. *for I was overcome by this star's light:* Cunizza here admits the extent to which the influence of the planet Venus, with its power to inspire carnal desire, marked her life. Her "fate" (vs 35) was determined by her susceptibility to the influence of Venus. She is not, however, expressing remorse for her past sins. As one of the Blest, she has no regret for her transgressions as a mortal, since such bitter remembrance has been washed away by the waters of Lethe. In recalling the past, she can feel only thankfulness to God, a fact that mortal man finds very difficult to understand. This feeling of thankfulness to God will be elaborated upon later on in verses 103–108.

37. *This precious and resplendent jewel:* Here Cunizza points out another soul who is next to her and who will be the next to speak.

39–40. *fame . . . as this centennial year shall be five-timed:* Cunizza, talking about the fame of the soul next to her, says that it will endure on earth for as long as five centuries. Dante coins the word *s'incinqua* ("five-timed").

42. *a second life:* A life of fame on earth. It seems rather strange for a soul of one of the Blest in Heaven to be so concerned with the fame or reputation that another soul left on earth; but, as we soon shall see, the remark paves the way for the rest of Cunizza's speech, which, in turn, puts the statement on worldly fame into proper perspective.

43–48. *And this means nothing:* The Tagliamento and Adige rivers enclose the March of Treviso. Paduan blood shall stain Vincenza because Paduans have neglected to display allegiance to the empire. These lines seem to refer to the defeat of the Paduans outside Vincenza in 1314 by Can Grande della Scala, patron of Dante and reigning Ghibelline.

49. *and where Cagnano and the Sile join:* The Sile and Cagnano rivers join at Treviso.

50–51. *A man lords over it:* The reference is to Riccardo da Cammino, a son of the "good Gherardo" (*Purg.* XVI, 124), who took his father's place as Lord of Treviso and ruled like a tyrant. He was murdered while playing chess in 1312, probably by order of the nobility who were outraged by his arrogance ("with lofty head," 50).

52. *Feltre shall mourn her godless shepherd's crime:* This is a reference to an incident that took place in 1314, involving Alessandro Novello of Treviso, Bishop of Feltre (1298–1320). It seems that a group of Ghibellines from Ferrara, having failed in a conspiracy, took refuge in Feltre under the protection of the Bishop. Having accepted them under his protection, he then turned them over to the Ferrarese authorities, and the men were executed.

53–54. *no man yet was ever sent to Malta:* For the ancient commentators Malta was the clerical prison of Lake Bolsena; there were two other Maltas of this type, one in Viterbo, another in Padua. Bergin (p. 125) suggests that Dante had no particular location in mind but was saying simply that no criminal was ever incarcerated anywhere for a fouler crime. See also Flamini (p. 100). The idea in verses 53–54 is that none who were sent to Malta had committed a crime as treacherous as that of Alessandro Novello, the Bishop of Feltre.

56. *Ferrara's blood:* The Ghibellines who died as a result of the Bishop's treachery were from Ferrara.

58. *this generous priest:* A sarcastic reference to the Bishop of Feltre.

59. *to prove his party loyalty:* The Bishop was of the Guelph party.

60. *such gifts become that country's way of life:* The "gifts" refers to the "blood" (vs. 58) which the Bishop was so happy to donate for his party's cause (vs. 59). This verse brings to a close two of the bitterest tercets found in the Poem.

61–63. *Above us there are mirrors you call 'Thrones':* Cunizza is referring to the angels which move and direct the seventh heaven or the sphere of Saturn. What Cunizza is saying in this tercet is that in the heavens above there are angels ("mirrors") through whom they are able to see God's judgments or punishments for men on earth, so that if her words seem harsh (and she speaks with satisfaction of men's crimes) they are, in truth, good because they come from God.

67–68. *That other joy:* This is the soul to whom Cunizza referred earlier (37). This soul now comes forward to speak to the Pilgrim.

69. *an exquisite ruby:* The term used by Dante is *balasso,* or the balas ruby, taking its name from the central Asian country in which it is found. The balas ruby was thought to possess the power to repress vain and lascivious thoughts. This property seems appropriate to this soul who renounced his earthly passions and now enjoys purity of heart as one of the Blest.

70–72. *Up there joy gives those souls a brighter light:* In this tercet the Poet comments on the relationship between joy and light in Paradise ("Up there"), and on earth ("here," 71) and in Hell ("down below," 71). The Poet presents this "aside to the reader" as an interesting observation that occured to his Pilgrim when he saw the exquisite ruby light of this new soul who has just appeared to him in verses 67–69.

73. *"God can see all:* Since the souls in heaven are one with God, they share his omniscience, their vision becoming fused with His. It is therefore possible for them to penetrate Dante's thoughts.

77–78. *those adoring flames:* The flames are the Seraphim, ministers of Divine Love. In Isaiah (6:2) these angels are said to have six wings. There, however, the wings are not a "cowl": "with twain he [each angel] covered his face, and with twain did he fly." Dante may have drawn his image from St. Bonaventure, who spiritualizes the passage from Isaiah by associating each of the six wings with one of the six virtues necessary for prelates of the Church. The two wings above the head represent love of justice and piety, or fraternal compassion; the two over the body and feet are patience and an exemplary life; and the two wings used for flying represent circumspection and devotion to God.

Dante's statement that Folquet's voice is "in harmony with those adoring flames" suggests that as a Bishop of the Church, Folquet was endowed with the six virtues.

81. *were I to inyou as you now inme:* In the Italian, the line reads "s'io m'intuassi, come tu t'inmii." Dante constructed these two reflexive verbs from the personal pronouns *tu* ("you") and *mi* ("me") in order to convey the notion of interpenetration of minds. He is saying that if he were capable of knowing the question to be directed to him, as the soul is, he would answer it without delay.

In the *Divine Comedy* Dante creates thirteen verbs, all of which are used in the *Paradise*. Five of them—four of which are in this canto—are found in the sphere of Venus (see von Richthofen, p. 103).

84. *"the water of that world-encircling sea:* The Mediterranean Sea ("the greatest valley," 82), into which the Atlantic ("the world-encircling sea") flows at Gibraltar. Medieval geographers held that the Atlantic Ocean surrounded all dry land, thereby "encircling" the entire globe.

85–87. *runs on so far:* The Mediterranean runs so far east, "against the sun," that it was thought to extend 90° of longitude (it actually covers 42°). For one standing at the west end of the sea, at the zenith or meridian, the east end appears as a horizon. Conversely, one standing at the east sees the western point as a horizon. As the waters of the sea move from west to east, the eastern point which once appeared as a horizon becomes the zenith.

89 – 90. *I dwelt upon that valley's shores:* The speaker lived, while on earth, at Marseilles, which is halfway between the mouth of the Ebro River in Spain and the mouth of the Magra River in Italy.

91 – 93. *Almost the same sunset:* Marseilles and Bougie, on the coast of Africa, have longitudinal proximity. In 49 B.C., during the Civil War, Caesar conquered Marseilles in bloody victory at sea against Pompey's supporters. The verse 93, "which with its own blood warmed its harbor once," may well be an echo of Lucan's *Pharsalia* (III, 572 – 73).

94. *Folquet was my name:* The soul who speaks to Dante here is Folquet of Marseilles (born ca. 1160), a troubadour and poet. The son of a rich merchant of Genoa, Folquet devoted much of his life to pleasure, and was well known for his amorous affairs. Later, however, he became a Cistercian monk, and rose to become Abbot of Torronet in 201, and Bishop of Toulouse in 1205. He died in 1231. It is interesting to note that in his portrayal of Folquet, Dante makes no mention of his role in the persecution of heretics in the south of France, during the so-called Albigensian Crusade in 1209. For the critical edition of Folquet's poetry and facts about his life see Stronski.

97 – 98. *Dido . . . wronging Sichaeus and Creusa:* Sichaeus was the husband of Dido, to whom she made a vow of timeless constancy, but whom she wronged, after his death, by her passion for Aeneas. Creusa was Aeneas' wife, who perished after she became separated from Aeneas during the fall of Troy. In seducing Aeneas, Dido thus wronged both Sichaeus and Creusa.

100 – 102. *Rhodope . . . Demophoön, nor Hercules . . . Iole:* Rhodope is a mountain in Thrace. Phyllis, daughter of King Sithon of Thrace, was to marry Demophoön. When he did not appear on the wedding day, she hanged herself and was changed into an almond tree.

Hercules loved Iole, daughter of Eurytus, King of Thessalian Oechalia, and abducted her after killing her father. His wife, Deianira, in order to recover his love, sent Hercules a shirt bathed in the blood of the centaur Nessus, believing that blood to carry a love potion. The centaur had tricked her, however, and Hercules was poisoned. In despair and grief, she killed herself. (See Ovid, *Heroides* II, 147−48 and IX.)

With this tercet and the preceding one into which so much mythology is packed Dante, perhaps, is hinting at Folquet's fame as a poet on earth. In the rest of the canto his role as a religious figure on earth will be stressed.

103−105. *But we do not repent:* See note to 33−36 above.

107−108. *. . . the Good / by which the world below returns above:* God, as loving Creator, desires the return of every soul to its original home in Him. Through the operation of the heavenly spheres, God's influence works on the created world below. It is this loving influence (Providence) that eventually brings the souls of the elect back to God. (There is controversy as to the precise meaning of this tercet.)

115. *there within Rahab has peace:* This is Rahab, the Whore of Jericho. When Joshua sent spies to scout that city prior to battle, Rahab hid them from the king's men, and aided their escape. In doing this, she helped the people of Israel to regain the promised land, and as a result her soul rose from Limbo to heaven immediately after the Crucifixion. (See Joshua 2, 6:17; also James 2:25 and Hebrews 11:31.)

116−17. *she impressed . . . the highest rank:* Rahab, when she joined the ranks of those in the third sphere of Venus, became the brightest light among all the souls there. She was, as we learn in verses 119−20, "the first to rise / among the souls redeemed in Christ's great triumph."

118−19. *To this sphere where the shadow of your earth:* According to Ptolomy and Alfraganus, the Arabic astrologer, the shadow of the earth extended in a kind of cone shape with its point reaching no farther than the sphere of Venus. Metaphorically, these verses suggest that Venus is the last of the spheres containing souls that once were marked by an excess of earthly inclination.

120. *Christ's great triumph:* This is a reference to the Harrowing of Hell (cf. *Inf.* IV, 46−63).

122−23. *as a palm . . . victory won by those two palms:* The "palm" is the symbol of victory over Hell by means of the Crucifixion. The "two palms" are those of Christ which were willingly extended and nailed to the Cross for the redemption of mankind.

125. *Joshua's first glory in the Holy Land:* Joshua, who was the successor of Moses, had his first victory ("glory") by taking Jericho.

126. *which seems to matter little to the Pope:* Pope Boniface VIII devoted his energies to strengthening his position in Europe rather than to liberating the Holy Land from the infidel. (See also *Inf.* XXVII, 85–90.)

127–32

Florence is referred to here as a plant of the Devil, the flowers of which are florins ("the wicked flower"), the Italian currency which was stamped on one side with the lily. The city's evils are attributed to its leaders, especially its ecclesiastical ones ("the shepherds") who have become greedy ("ravening wolves") and have led those Christians ("the lambs") under their care ("the fold") astray ("run wild").

127–29. *the one . . . whose fierce envy brought the world such woe:* Lucifer, the first to fall away from God, envied the happiness of Adam and Eve and made them sin, the result of which was Original Sin and the world's grief.

134–35. *Canon Law:* The books of Canon Law (the decretals) are the papal decrees or epistles, usually composed in reply to a question of ecclesiastical law, and forming the foundation of a large part of general church law. In 1234, Pope Gregory IX issued a compilation of them, with his own additions. It was reissued, with further additions, by Popes Boniface VIII and Clement V, in 1298 and 1314, respectively. The papal decretals were promulgated as the great law of all Christendom, taking precedence over secular law. Dante's reference to the enthusiastic study of Canon Law by popes and cardinals is intended as criticism, inasmuch as the decretals were studied for the purpose of financial gain. Their margins were filled with notes and they were soiled and worn from continual use ("as the margins testify," 135).

137–38. *Nazareth / where Gabriel:* It was at Nazareth in the Holy Land that the Annunciation took place and the angel Gabriel "opened wide his wings" in homage to Mary.

The Vatican hill is located on the right bank of the Tiber. On it are located St. Peter's basilica and the Vatican palace (in Dante's time the papal residence was the Lateran palace). As the supposed place of the martyrdom of Peter, and of other early Christians, the Vatican hill is considered to be the most sacred quarter in Rome. The prophecy inherent in these closing verses may refer to the removal in 1305 of the Papal Court to Avignon or perhaps to the death of Boniface VIII or even the coming of Henry VII. I feel, however, that it is a reference, one of the many in the *Comedy*, to that unnamed savior or leader who will come at some future time to liberate Italy and restore justice.

142. *this adultery:* Perpetrated by greedy pontiffs, this is the corrupt government of the Church and the prostitution of holy things for personal gain. (See also *Inf.* XIX, 1–4.)

CANTO X

PRAISING THE CREATED order which reflects its Creator, Dante the Poet marvels at the exactitude of the structure and workings of the universe. The Pilgrim, unaware of rising there, discovers himself in the sphere of the sun, surrounded by spirits of such brilliance that their lights are distinct from the light of the sun. Dancing and singing in their joy, the spirits form a circle, making Dante and his guide their center, but they soon pause in their movement to provide an answer to Dante's evident, though unexpressed, desire to have the souls identified. Thomas Aquinas steps forward to introduce his fellow spirits, all known for their wisdom and learning. The spirits then resume their song and motion, singing and turning with such harmony that they resemble the workings of a clock which calls the faithful to prayer.

Looking upon His Son with all that love
 which each of them breathes forth eternally,
 that uncreated, ineffable first One,   3

has fashioned all that moves in mind and space
 in such sublime proportions that no one
 can see it and not feel His Presence there.   6

Look up now, Reader, with me to the spheres;
 look straight to that point of the lofty wheels
 where the one motion and the other cross,   9

and there begin to revel in the work
 of that great Artist who so loves His art,
 His gaze is fixed on it perpetually.   12

Consider how the wheel the planets ride
 branches from there obliquely; this it does
 to satisfy the earth that calls on them;   15

for if their track had not been set aslant,
 then the great powers of Heaven would be vain
 and Earth's potentialities stillborn;   18

and if its deviation from the straight
    were greater than it is, or less, disorder
    would come about in both our hemispheres.   21

Now, Reader, do not leave the table yet,
    reflect upon what you have only tasted,
    if you would dine on joy before you tire.   24

I put the food out; now you feed yourself,
    because the theme which makes of me its scribe
    demands all of my concentration now.   27

The most sublime of Nature's ministers,
    which stamps the plan of Heaven on the world
    and with its light measures the time for us,   30

now being in conjunction with that place
    I pointed out, was wheeling through the spirals
    in which we see it earlier each day;   33

and I was in the sun, no more aware
    of my ascent than one can be aware
    of how a thought will come before it comes.   36

She it is, Beatrice, guides our climb
    from good to better instantaneously—
    her action has no measurement in time.   39

How brilliant in its essence must have been
    what shone within the sun, where I had come,
    not with its color but with light on light!   42

Even if I called on genius, art, and skill,
    I could not make this live before your eyes—
    a man must trust and long to see it there.   45

If our imagination cannot rise
    to such a height, no need to be surprised.
    No eye has known light brighter than the sun's;   48

So, there within, shone God's fourth family
    whom the High Father keeps in constant bliss
    showing them how He breathes, how He begets.   51

Then Beatrice said: "And now give thanks,
    thanks to the Sun of Angels by whose grace
    you have ascended to this sun of sense."   54

No mortal heart was ever more disposed
    to do devotion and to yield itself
    to God so fully and so readily   57

than mine was at her words. So totally
    did I direct all of my love to Him,
    that Beatrice, eclipsed, had left my mind.   60

But this did not displease her, and she smiled
    so that the splendor of her laughing eyes
    broke my mind's spell. Again I was aware   63

of many things: flashes of living light
    made us a center and themselves a crown—
    their voices sweeter than their aspect bright: 66

the way Latona's daughter sometimes seems,
    girt by her halo when the pregnant air
    catches the threads of moonlight in her belt.   69

In heaven's court from where I have returned
    there are some jewels too precious and too rich
    to be brought back to Earth from out that realm,   72

and one such gem—the song those splendors sang:
    who does not grow the wings to fly up there,
    awaits these tidings from the tongueless here.   75

When singing, circling, all those blazing suns
    had wheeled around the two of us three times
    like stars that circle close to the fixed poles,   78

they stopped like ladies still in dancing mood,
    who pause in silence listening to catch
    the rhythm of the new notes of the dance.   81

Then from within its light a voice spoke: "Since
    the ray of grace by which true love is kindled
    and then grows lovingly the more it loves,   84

shines forth in you so greatly magnified
    that it allows you to ascend these stairs
    which none descends except to mount again—   87

one could no more deny your thirsty soul
    wine from his flask than could a moving stream
    refuse to keep on flowing to the sea.   90

It is your wish to know what kinds of flowers
    make up this crown which lovingly surrounds
    the lovely lady who strengthens you for Heaven.   93

I was one of the sacred flock of lambs
    led by Saint Dominic along the road
    where all may fatten if they do not stray.   96

This spirit close by, at my right, was brother
    and master to me: Albert of Cologne
    he was, and I am Thomas of Aquino.   99

If you would like to learn about the rest,
    let your eyes follow where my words shall lead
    all the way round this blessèd wreath of souls.   102

The next flame is the light of Gratian's smile,
    who served so well in the two courts of law
    that Heaven finds great joy in having him.   105

The next one who illuminates our choir
    was that same Peter who, like the poor widow,
    offered his modest treasure to the Church.   108

The fifth light, the most beautiful of all,
    breathes from a love so passionate that men
    still hunger down on earth to know his fate;   111

his flame contains that lofty mind instilled
    with wisdom so profound—if truth speak truth—
    there never arose a second with such vision.   114

Look at the burning candle next to him
    who, in the flesh, on earth saw to the depths
    of what an angel is and what it does.   117

And next, inside this tiny light, there smiles
    the great defender of the Christian Age
    whose words in Latin Augustine employed.   120

If your mind's eye has moved from light to light
    behind my words of praise, you must be eager
    to know what spirit shines in the eighth flame.   123

Wrapped in the vision of all good, rejoices
    the sainted soul who makes most manifest
    the world's deceit to one who reads him well.   126

The body that was torn from him below
   Cieldauro now possesses; to this peace
   he came from exile and from martyrdom.   129

See those next flames: they are the fervent breath
   of Isidore, of Bede, and of that Richard
   whose contemplations made him more than man.   132

This light from which your eyes return to me
   shines from a soul once given to grave thoughts,
   who mourned that death should be so slow to come: 135

this is the endless radiance of Siger,
   who lectured on the Street of Straw, exposing
   invidiously logical beliefs."   138

Then, as the tower-clock calls us to come
   at the hour when God's Bride is roused from bed
   to woo with matin song her Bridegroom's love,   141

with one part pulling thrusting in the other,
   chiming, *ting-ting*, music so sweet the soul,
   ready for love, swells with anticipation;   144

so I was witness to that glorious wheel
   moving and playing voice on voice in concord
   with sweetness, harmony unknown, save there   147

where joy becomes one with eternity.

NOTES

1 – 27

This canto, which opens with this grandiose cosmological
prelude, marks the arrival at another beginning, as it were, of
the *Paradise*. In the first three heavenly spheres we noticed that
the souls present (but only for the Pilgrim's benefit) were there
for some negative quality characteristic of that particular sphere,
for those spheres are still within reach of the Earth's shadow (see
Par. IX, 118 – 19). Those spirits who broke their sacred vow are
in the sphere of the moon, those whose love of earthly things was
excessive are in Mercury, and those whose love of the flesh was
disordered are found in Venus. But now, from the heaven of the
sun onward, we will meet only souls of positive influence. Here,
with this cosmological prelude in praise of the infinite wisdom

of the Creator, we are introduced to the sphere of the sun or the heaven of the theologians and other great thinkers. And we will discover that the souls of the Blest from this point on will appear in a more structured way: in this sphere, for example, the souls in the sun will present themselves in the shape of a circle (the symbol of perfection as well as Divinity) formed around the Pilgrim and Beatrice at the center.

8–9. *look straight to that point of the lofty wheels:* The motions of the "wheels" are (1) the daily movement of the planets around the earth (on a line parallel to the equator), and (2) the yearly movement of the sun along its ecliptic (oblique to the equator). These two wheels, which move in opposite directions, cross each other at the first point of Aries (at the vernal equinox) and at the first point of Libra (at the autumnal equinox). It is the oblique north-to-south and south-to-north movement of the sun, in a slanting spiral, that brings about the change of seasons.

13–18. *Consider how the wheel the planets ride:* The attraction of one wheel to the other is heightened by the tension resulting from the fact that there are only two points at which they intersect. Were the courses of the solar and stellar wheels parallel rather than oblique, their influence on the earth would be weakened because there would be no tension between the wheels. Thus, there would occur no change in seasons and no regeneration.

14. *branches from there obliquely:* "There" refers to the point where the ecliptic slants across the equator at Aries.

20–21. *disorder:* Seasonal change would be disrupted.

22–24. *Now, Reader, do not leave the table yet:* Aware that he has presented difficult yet tantalizing material, Dante uses the eating-at-table metaphor to suggest that those readers who stay with him will go beyond superficiality and come to understand with satisfaction what he has said. (See also *Par.* XXIV, 4–9 for a similar use of this metaphor.) The modern commentators, for the most part, take the last word of verse 22, *banco,* to mean "desk" or "place where one reads or studies." But I agree with Tommaseo who sees the word in relation to other words associated with food and eating in the following tercet (25–27).

26. *because the theme which makes of me its scribe:* The Poet refers to himself as "scribe," since it is his function to record the journey

as it took place. Thus, the emphasis is on rendition rather than invention: the journey really did take place.

28. *The most sublime of Nature's ministers:* The sun. As the symbol of intellectual power and illumination, it represents the Creator Himself. This is appropriate, inasmuch as the goal of wisdom is understanding of the Divine Essence.

29. *stamps the plan of Heaven:* See *Paradise* II, 112–48 and note.

31–33. *now being in conjunction:* The sun has reached a point at which the wheels intersect, and from there it begins a spiral-like course around the earth. Between the winter and summer solstices, the sun moves from south to north, rising a little earlier each day in the northern hemisphere.

34–36. *and I was in the sun:* The Pilgrim is in the sphere of the sun almost without realizing it. His entrance there was as rapid as a thought, which springs into the mind the instant we think of it! The speed is no less rapid than in that other favorite way of Dante's to express quick motion, in terms of the arrow hitting its mark almost before it leaves the bowstring (cf. *Par.* II, 22–24).

41–42. *what shone within the sun:* The souls of the wise were even brighter than the sun itself. They were hardly visible because they were the same color as the sun, only more intense.

45. *a man must trust and long to see it there:* It is man who makes himself fit for Heaven and who must see this spectacle for himself in order to believe it.

48. *No eye has known light brighter than the sun's:* The human eye can experience no brighter light than that of the sun. It is no wonder, then, that Dante cannot show light brighter than the sun to his reader.

49–51. *shone God's fourth family:* These souls found in the fourth sphere of the heavens are those who were endowed with great wisdom: the theologians and philosophers and other great and wise thinkers. The verses here are reminiscent of the opening of the canto where the relationship existing in the Trinity is described: the Father "breathes" forth the Spirit and "begets" the Son. Appropriately, here the Father keeps the "family" of the

Wise happy by revealing through demonstration this relationship which on earth is beyond even the imagination of the wisest.

53–54. *thanks to the Sun of Angels:* God is the "Sun of Angels" who has made it possible for Dante to rise to the sphere of the sun, God's visible counterpart, "this sun of sense." Dante in his *Convivio* (III, xii, 7) says: "No object of sense in all the universe is more worthy to be made the symbol of God than is the sun which enlightens with the light of sense, itself first. . . ."

60. *Beatrice, eclipsed, had left my mind:* This is the only place in the Poem where we can imagine Beatrice ever being "eclipsed" or forgotten. Where else but in the sphere of the sun, the symbol of God Himself, the home of the theologians whose task on earth it was to prove His existence, could Dante have forgotten his lady?

61. *But this did not displease her:* Earthly jealousy, of course, has no place in the heavenly spheres; thus, Beatrice rejoices in Dante's preoccupation with the spectacle before his eyes. It is precisely what he should be doing, and it is for this reason that she smiles with approval.

63. *broke my mind's spell. Again I was aware . . . :* This is an especially powerful line. The original reads: "mia mente unita in più cose divise." The Pilgrim's mind is divided among a number of things: he is contemplating Beatrice, God, the things around him, but at the same time his mind is united; that is to say, it is one in the sense that those things dividing the mind are, in effect, the same thing in that they all bear the same significance.

67–69. *the way Latona's daughter:* Diana or the moon. The circle of light, made up of the souls of the wise, within which Dante and Beatrice are girdled is compared here to a vaporous "halo" around the moon.

70–75

In order to hear this song, the Poet says, the Reader must make the flight himself to that realm or else dismiss the idea of ever hearing it at all, for even one who has heard it (i.e., Dante) is speechless when he tries to describe the indescribable. In other words, it would be like waiting for a man who cannot speak (who is "tongueless") to describe things.

74. *who does not grow the wings to fly up there:* Isa. 40:31 reads: "Qui sperant in Domino assument pennas sicut aquilae"

(Whoever hopes to reach God must take on the wings of the eagle). This journey to God which the poet is making, and which the allegory of the poem from the beginning has asked its reader to make, has been referred to many times in terms of "wings" and flight upward.

76–81

The circling spirits who are first referred to as "burning suns" that circle around the Poet and his lady three times are then compared to ladies engaged in dancing. The comparison is striking for its levity and its worldliness. The dancing lights, after all, are the souls of the wise and learned. Dante probably had a particular dance in mind: the ballata. In this type of dance the leader sings the first stanza while standing still. The other ladies then repeat (*ripresa* or *ritornello*) the stanza as they move in circular fashion. The leader sings the second stanza, the ladies repeat it, and the dance continues as before. It will not be until verse 99 that we are told who this "leader," who starts speaking in verse 82, is.

78. *like stars that circle close to the fixed poles:* That is to say, those "flashes of living light" (64), now called "blazing suns" (76), are slowing down their movement around the Pilgrim and Beatrice. For a similar verse, see *Purg.* VIII, 87; also *Conv.* II, 3. I disagree with Chimenz (p. 709), who believes that slowness is the primary concern of the image.

83. *true Love:* The love of God.

86–87. *it allows you to ascend these stairs:* This refers to the contemplative journey through Paradise which no one leaves except to return. The verses provide assurance that Dante, who like St. Paul has been granted special grace to make this journey, will be saved. See also *Purg.* XXXII, 100–102.

88–89. *deny your thirsty soul / wine from his flask:* The Pilgrim's "thirsty soul" wishes to know who these spirits are who have formed a circle around himself and Beatrice.

91–93. *what kinds of flowers:* The image of the jeweled crown, which begins with verse 65, now becomes that of a garland. The use of delicate feminine imagery (the dancing maidens) in this canto is in complete accordance with the allegorical aspect of Beatrice who, standing at the center of the circle, is the symbol of Theology itself and represents the light of Grace, or Revelation, which is Divine Wisdom, the subject to which these great thinkers and wise men have dedicated a life of study.

94. *I was one of the sacred flock of lambs:* The speaker here is Thomas Aquinas (?1225 – 1274) referred to in his time as the Angelic Doctor, the most famous of Catholic theologians, although he does not identify himself until verse 99. Born of a noble family (his father was the Count of Aquino), he was educated by the Benedictines; he then entered the Dominican order and studied under Albertus Magnus in Cologne. He studied six years at the University of Naples which he left at the age of sixteen. Thereafter he taught at Cologne, Paris, Rome, and Bologna, finally returning to the University of Naples where he assumed a professorship. His most famous work is the *Summa theologica,* an exposition of the teachings of the Church written in light of Aristotelian philosophy. He was also the author of the *Summa contra Gentiles,* a summary of the Christian faith for the refutation of unbelief. His major contribution to Christian theology lies in his synthesis of Christian and Aristotelian philosophy. In January of 1274 he was summoned by Pope Gregory X to attend the Council of Lyons whose purpose was to bring the Greek and Latin Churches together. On his way there he fell ill and died at the Cistercian monastery of Fossanova on March 7, 1274. He was canonized by Pope John XXII in 1323, fifty years after his death.

96. *where all may fatten if they do not stray:* The followers of St. Dominic, if they adhered to his teachings, enjoyed plentiful spiritual food. This particular reference provides the subject matter of the next canto.

98. *Albert of Cologne:* Albertus Magnus (?1193 – 1280), also from a noble family, was a fellow Dominican and teacher of Thomas Aquinas. He studied philosophy at Paris, Padua, and Bologna and was known as the Universal Doctor because of his vast learning. In 1260 he was named Bishop of Regensburg. His writings were extensive and included his *Summa theologiae,* the *Summa de Creaturis,* commentaries and paraphrases on all the works of Aristotle (he was the first to make known the complete doctrine of Aristotle), and various scientific treatises, including one on alchemy.

99. *Thomas of Aquino:* Thomas Aquinas. See note 94.

103 – 105. *The next flame is the light of Gratian's smile:* Gratian,

a Benedictine monk, was born around the end of the eleventh century at Chiusi in Tuscany and was the originator of the science of canon law. His *Decretum Gratiani* (also called the *Concordia Discordantium Canonum*), published between 1140 and 1150, is a reconciliation between the laws of secular and ecclesiastical courts. His goal in this reconciliation was to demonstrate the harmony between the two bodies of law and thereby provide a firm basis for the interpretation of canon law.

Souls of the Wise and Learned

1. St. Thomas Aquinas
2. Albertus Magnus
3. Gratian
4. Peter Lombard
5. Solomon
6. Dionysius the Areopagite
7. Orosius
8. Boethius
9. Isidore of Seville
10. Bede
11. Richard of St. Victor
12. Siger of Brabant

106–108. *The next one who illuminates our choir:* Peter Lombard, born in Novara (ca. 1100–ca. 1160), known as the "Master of the Sentences" from the title of his *Sententiarum libri quatuor,* studied at Bologna and Paris where he held a chair in theology. In 1159, shortly before his death, he was appointed Bishop of Paris. In the preface to his book of sentences he offers his work to the Church in emulation of the poor widow (Luke 21:1–4) who gave her small offering to the temple. The text of this work is essentially a collection of the sayings of the Church Fathers arranged under the headings of the Godhead, the incarnation, creation, and the sacraments. It was widely read and gained popularity as a textbook in theological schools. It was also the subject of a great many commentaries.

109–14. *The fifth light, the most beautiful of all:* Solomon, son of David and King of Israel, appears here as the only Old Testament figure, and he is honored as the "most beautiful," apparently for his superior wisdom and the fact that he is the author of the Canticle of Canticles which came to be interpreted as the mystical marriage of Christ and the Church. Besides being credited as the author of *Proverbs* and the *Book of Wisdom*, Solomon was singled out by God to receive a unique gift of wisdom. In answer to Solomon's request for an understanding heart with which to govern his people, God granted him such wisdom that neither before or after him would anyone like him exist (1 Kings 3:12). Verses 112 – 14 are a paraphrase of the biblical promise which Dante felt to be so important that Canto III of the *Paradise* (34 – 111) is an explication of it.

On earth Solomon's salvation was a matter of controversy (Augustine, for one, believed he was damned), and therefore men were eager to learn of his fate.

115 – 17. *Look at the burning candle next to him:* This is the soul of Dionysius the Areopagite, the Athenian who was converted by St. Paul (Acts 17:34). He was credited in Dante's day with having written *The Celestial Hierarchy*, a treatise explaining the angelic orders, their nature and function. Dante employs his particular system in the *Paradise* (see *Par.* XXVIII, 130 – 39 and note).

118 – 20. *And next, inside this tiny light:* This light is not named by the poet, but the majority of the commentators believe this to be Paulus Orosius, a fifth-century Spanish priest and disciple of Augustine whose *Seven Books of History against the Pagans* was intended to prove through historical evidence that, contrary to pagan belief, the world had not deteriorated since the adoption of Christianity. It was probably written as a type of historical confirmation of Augustine's *City of God.* His work was highly regarded in Dante's time.

120. *whose words in Latin Augustine employed:* Augustine made use of ("employed") Orosius' Latin treatise, *Historiarum libri*, which was written at the suggestion of the saint, as a means of historical confirmation for his own *City of God.*

This is the only mention of St. Augustine until St. Bernard points him out in his position in the Celestial Rose (*Par.* XXXII, 35). St. Augustine was considered one of the four great fathers of the Latin Church (the others being St. Ambrose, St. Jerome, and St. Gregory the Great), and it is a wonder that we do not find him here, somewhere among the souls of the wise and learned in the fourth sphere of the Sun. But see the note to *Paradise* XXXII, 34 – 36.

125 – 29. *the sainted soul who makes most manifest:* This is Boethius (born in Rome ca. 480 and died at Pavia in 524), a Roman patrician, statesman, and philosopher, and author of the celebrated *The Consolation of Philosophy*, which he wrote while in prison in Pavia. In 510 he became the consul of Theodoric the Ostrogoth, but was later imprisoned by him on false charges of treason and magic, and was finally executed. Boethius' work provided much of the knowledge of Aristotle up to the thirteenth century, and it had a tremendous influence throughout Europe during the later Middle Ages. In time his death came to be regarded as a martyrdom. In the Church he is known as St. Severinus.

128. *Cieldauro:* This refers to the Church of Saint Peter in Ciel d'Oro ('with the ceiling of gold') in Pavia where Boethius was buried.

131. *of Isidore, of Bede:* The Spaniard St. Isidore of Seville (ca. 570 – 636), one of the most influential writers of the early Middle Ages, was a distinguished ecclesiastic and the author of an important and much-used encyclopedia of scientific knowledge of the time (*Etymologiarum Libri XX* or *Origines*). He was made Archbishop of Seville in 600.

The Venerable Bede (ca. 673 – 735), an English monk known as the father of English history, was the author of the *Ecclesiastical History of the English Nation* in five volumes. He also wrote hagiography, homilies, hymns, works on grammar and chronology, and commentaries on the Old and New Testaments.

131 – 32. *that Richard / whose contemplations:* This is Richard of St. Victor, who was thought to have been born in Scotland (d. 1173). He was known as the great Contemplator after his treatise, *De Contemplatione.* He was a celebrated twelfth-century mystic, theologian, and scholastic philosopher who studied at the University of Paris and then became a canon-regular at the Augustinian monastery at St. Victor. St. Victor was known for its adherence to a system of contemplative philosophy and deep-thinking practiced in a state of profound seclusion. Richard's works, which included commentaries on the Old Testament and moral writings, were often quoted by Thomas Aquinas.

135. *who mourned that death should be so slow to come:* This soul was most eager to have his questions ("grave thoughts," 134) answered in Heaven. See note 136 – 38.

136–38. *the endless radiance of Siger:* This is the soul of Siger of Brabant (?1226–?1284), a distinguished Averroist philosopher who taught at the University of Paris, which was located in the Rue de Fouarre or "Street of Straw." His belief that the world had existed from eternity and doubt in the immortality of the soul involved him in a lengthy dispute with his colleague Thomas Aquinas, and eventually led to charges of heresy. Adversaries in life, Siger and Thomas Aquinas now stand side by side in Paradise—at the top of the clock, as it were, as will become clear in the next verse. Because of his questionable position with regard to the Church, Siger's presence in this canto has been a problem for commentators. (See Nardi and Corti.) There may be a clue in the three words of verse 138: "silogizzò invidiosi veri" (invidiously logical beliefs). Could it be that among the 219 propositions taken from Siger's teachings that were condemned as heretical were some that even Thomas Aquinas found "enviable"? (See Momigliano, p. 632.) Or has this illustrious Averroist, the prime example of radical Aristotelianism, simply been put in Paradise as incontrovertible proof of the incorrectness of his theory about the immortality of the soul?

139–48. *Then, as the tower-clock calls us to come:* The closing image of this canto provides a good example of an important aspect of Dante's style, that of the multifaceted, shifting metaphor. Here the image of the clock operates on two basic levels: first, in a strictly religious sense Dante compares the sound and motion of the souls to the working of a great clock as it chimes matins to the ears of the faithful. The use of the terms "Bride" and "Bridegroom" is entirely appropriate in this context, since by tradition they are epithets applied to the Church and Christ respectively. At the same time, mention of the Bride and Bridegroom, along with the terms used to suggest the physical workings of the clock, carries strongly erotic overtones. The pulling and thrusting movements (142), as well as the swell of anticipation (144), are obviously sensual and thereby create surprising interplay within the metaphor. In addition the matin song can be interpreted in a secular manner as the amorous tribute sung to the beloved from beneath her window (141). But perhaps the light of Solomon, the fifth and "most beautiful" light of all (109–14) has prepared us for such a sensual ending. For me this is the most spiritually erotic closing to all of the one hundred cantos of the *Divine Comedy*.

CANTO XI

DANTE'S POSITION IN the sun, among the Wise who sought
Heaven's truth, gives him the opportunity to admonish mortals
who seek earthly satisfaction, while he, in Paradise, stands effort-
lessly with Beatrice, having risen through no merit of his own to
the realms of the Blest. The souls of the Wise once again cease
their circling and singing in order that St. Thomas may respond
to the Pilgrim's puzzlement. In the previous canto Thomas had
referred to the flock of Dominic as that in which the sheep "may
fatten if they do not stray" and had pointed out the soul of
Solomon, saying, "there never arose a second with such vision."
It is the first of these two statements which is now to be explained
(the second will be dealt with in Canto XIII), but by way of
explanation, Thomas, as a courtesy to the companion order of St.
Dominic, relates first the love story of St. Francis and Lady
Poverty. Thomas then returns to the contemporary state of his
own order, the Dominicans, to condemn their degeneracy and
thereby elucidate the meaning of the statement "where all may
fatten if they do not stray."

(Insensate strivings of mortality—
   how useless are those reasonings of yours
   that make you beat your wings in downward flight!   3

Men bent on law, some on the *Aphorisms,*
   some on the priesthood, others in pursuit
   of governing by means of force or fraud,   6

some planning theft, others affairs of state,
   some tangled in the pleasures of the flesh,
   some merely given up to indolence,   9

and I, relieved of all such vanities,
   was there with Beatrice in high Heaven,
   magnificently, gloriously welcomed.)   12

When each light on the circle had returned
   to where it was before the dance began,
   they stopped as still as candles in a stand.   15

And from within the splendid radiance
　　that had already spoken came more words,
　　and as it smiled, a more effulgent light:　　　　　　　*18*

"Just as I shine reflecting His own rays,
　　so, as I gaze into the endless light,
　　I understand the reason for your thoughts.　　　　　*21*

You are perplexed and want me to explain
　　in simple terms, with clear, explicit words,
　　on your mind's level, what I meant to say　　　　　*24*

when I said earlier: 'where all may fatten,'
　　and 'never arose a second with such vision,'
　　indeed, a clear distinction must be made.　　　　　*27*

The Providence that governs all the world
　　with wisdom so profound none of His creatures
　　can ever hope to see into Its depths,　　　　　　　*30*

in order that the Bride of that sweet Groom,
　　who crying loud espoused her with His blood,
　　might go to her Beloved made more secure　　　　*33*

within herself, more faithful to her Spouse,
　　ordained two noble princes to assist her
　　on either side, each serving as a guide.　　　　　*36*

One of the two shone with seraphic love,
　　the other through his wisdom was on earth
　　a splendor of cherubic radiance.　　　　　　　　*39*

Now I shall speak of only one, for praise
　　of one, no matter which, is praise of both,
　　for both their labors served a single end.　　　　*42*

Between the Topine and the stream that flows
　　down from that hill the blest Ubaldo chose,
　　a fertile slope hangs from a lofty mountain　　　*45*

which sends Perugia gusts of cold and heat
　　through Porta Sole, and behind it Gualdo
　　grieves with Nocera for their heavy yoke.　　　　*48*

Born on this slope where steepness breaks the most,
　　a sun rose to the world as radiantly
　　as this sun here does sometimes from the Ganges;　　*51*

thus, when this town is named let none call it
  Ascesi, for the word would not suffice—
  much more precise a word is *Orient*.   54

Only a few years after he had risen
  did his invigorating powers begin
  to penetrate the earth with a new strength: 57

while still a youth he braved his father's wrath,
  because he loved a lady to whom all
  would bar their door as if to death itself.   60

Before the bishop's court *et coram patre*
  he took this lady as his lawful wife;
  from day to day he loved her more and more.   63

Bereft of her first spouse, despised, ignored
  she waited eleven hundred years and more,
  living without a lover till he came,   66

alone, though it was known that she was found
  with Amyclas secure against the voice
  which had the power to terrify the world;   69

alone, though known was her fierce constancy
  that time she climbed the cross to be
  with Christ, while Mary stayed below alone.   72

Enough of such allusions. In plain words
  take Francis, now, and Poverty to be
  the lovers in the story I have told.   75

Their sweet accord, their faces spread with bliss,
  the love, the mystery, their tender looks
  gave rise in others' hearts to holy thoughts;   78

The venerable Bernard was the first
  to cast aside his shoes and run, and running
  toward such great peace, it seemed to him he lagged.   81

O unsuspected wealth! O fruitful good!
  Giles throws his shoes off, then Sylvester too—
  they love the bride so much, they seek the groom.   84

And then this father, this good lord, set out
  with his dear lady and that family
  that now was girded with the humble cord.   87

It mattered not that he was born the son
   of Bernardone, nor did he feel shame
   when people mocked him for his shabbiness;   90

but he announced, the way a king might do,
   his hard intent to Innocent who gave
   the seal establishing his holy Order.   93

The souls who followed him in poverty
   grew more and more, and then this archimandrite—
   whose wonder-working life were better sung   96

by Heaven's highest angels—saw his work
   crowned once again, now by Honorius
   through inspiration of the Holy Spirit.   99

Then in the haughty presence of the Sultan,
   urged by a burning thirst for martyrdom,
   he preached Christ and his blessèd followers,   102

but, finding no one ripe for harvest there,
   and loath to waste his labors, he returned
   to reap a crop in the Italian fields;   105

then on bare rock between Arno and Tiber
   he took upon himself Christ's holy wounds,
   and for two years he wore this final seal.   108

When it pleased Him who had ordained that soul
   for such great good to call him to Himself,
   rewarding him on high for lowliness,   111

he, to his brothers, as to rightful heirs,
   commended his most deeply cherished lady,
   commanding them to love her faithfully;   114

and in the lap of poverty he chose
   to die, wanting no other bier—from there
   that pristine soul returned to its own realm.   117

Think now what kind of man were fit to be
   his fellow helmsman on Saint Peter's boat,
   keeping it straight on course in the high sea—   120

and such a steersman was our Patriarch;
   and those who follow his command will see
   the richness of the cargo in their hold.   123

But his own flock is growing greedy now
    for richer food, and in their hungry search
    they stray to alien pastures carelessly;   *126*

the farther off his sheep go wandering
    from him in all directions, the less milk
    they bring back when they come back to the fold.   *129*

True, there are some who, fearing loss, will keep
    close to their shepherd, but so few are these
    it would not take much cloth to make their cowls.   *132*

Now, if my speech has not been too obscure,
    and if you have been listening carefully,
    and if you will recall my former words,   *135*

your wish will have been satisfied in part,
    for you will have seen how the tree is chipped
    and why I made the qualifying statement: *138*

'where all may fatten if they do not stray.' "

NOTES

1 – 12

    The canto begins with an unusual address to Everyman, reproaching him for his foolishness in seeking material gain. The combination of professions and pursuits is an odd one, for it censures the pious as well as the simply licentious. The first three tercets, which are very much tied to earthly concerns, provide a striking contrast to the fourth tercet, which magically returns us to Dante with Beatrice in the heavens. Looking at the canto as a whole, the tone of the first three tercets, along with that of St. Thomas' admonition (124 – 40), serves as a frame to the rest of the canto in which the love story of St. Francis and Lady Poverty is recounted.

    3. *downward flight:* Frequently throughout the *Paradise* the imagery of flight and wings is used as a metaphor for transcendence. Downward flight symbolizes man's perverted desire to pursue material rather than spiritual ends.

    4. *on law:* the study of civil and canonical law.

on the Aphorisms: Attributed to Hippocrates, the *Aphorisms* served as a medical textbook.

5. *on the priesthood:* Those who pursue their priestly duties out of greed for money or in search of worldly fame. (See *Conv.* III, xi, 10.)

6. *by means of force or fraud:* Those who govern by means of violence or fraud. The word Dante used for "fraud" in the Italian is *sofismi,* something which all of the sinners in the lower Inferno practiced to a greater or lesser degree.

12. *magnificently, gloriously welcomed:* The verse that ends the twelve-line prelude to this canto reads in Italian: "cotanto gloriosamente accolto," another most impressive three-word verse. The reader is forced, in order to read this verse correctly and maintain the rigors of the endecasyllabic line, to divide the word *gloriosamente* into six syllables; that is to say, he is made to linger over this adverb placed precisely at the center of the line (as the Poet himself is at this moment at the center of a circle). The effect achieved is one of glorious freedom in joyous harness expressed with a sigh of relief.

15. *as still as candles in a stand:* What began in the preceding canto as a crown of lights surrounding Dante and Beatrice (65) was soon after transformed into a circle of dancing ladies (79) and then a garland (92) and finally the workings of a great tower-clock (139). Here, the image of the circle of souls becomes static once again as it changes to the motionless form of candles in a circular candle stand or chandelier. The verse stresses the idea of total immobility as well as brilliant light pouring upward. Perhaps the reader is also invited to think in terms of twelve votive candles, each fixed in its own holder in a circular rack, burning straight and bright in a church.

16. *the splendid radiance:* St. Thomas once again comes forth to answer Dante's questions. He ascertains the Pilgrim's doubts before he is able to express them, for he sees them directly through the mind of God.

18. *a more effulgent light:* The light of this soul becomes brighter with love because it is about to resolve the Pilgrim's doubts. In the *Paradise* such generosity always results in more light.

22–26. *You are perplexed:* St. Thomas now poses the questions that have sprung up in the Pilgrim's mind. He was puzzled by Thomas' reference in Canto X to the path where there is good fattening if the lambs do not stray (96) as well as the saint's statement that Solomon was never equalled in wisdom (114). The first question is answered in this canto, the second in Canto XIII.

27. *indeed, a clear distinction must be made:* There are two possible interpretations for this verse: (1) the speaker is saying that each of the two points made in verses 25 and 26 needs separate clarification, or (2) he could be alluding to the second statement only ("never arose a second with such vision," 114) where a distinction is made later on (*Par.* XIII, 103 – 109) between Solomon's vision as a man and as a king. The latter interpretation, I feel, is too sophisticated for the Pilgrim to grasp at this point.

28 – 36. *The Providence that governs all the world:* St. Thomas introduces the two most important mendicant orders of the Middle Ages and their leaders in this preface to his story of Francis of Assisi. Providence, which governs all, ordained two princes, Francis and Dominic, to help sustain the Church, the Bride of Christ, on either side (Francis with love, Dominic with wisdom) in order to keep her faithful to the Bridegroom who had "married" her by means of His Crucifixion.

37 – 42. *One of the two shone with seraphic love:* Francis is characterized by his "seraphic love," the Seraphim being the highest order of angels and symbolic of the greatest love for God. Dominic, known for his learning, is associated with the Cherubim, the second order of angels and those acknowledged as the wisest. The complementary nature of the qualities each represents, coupled with the fact that both men worked for the dissemination and practice of the faith ("a single end," 42), makes praise of one man a praise of both. Here, St. Thomas, a Dominican, courteously retells the life of St. Francis; in the next canto (XII), Bonaventure, a Franciscan, returns the compliment paid to his founder by offering a narration of Dominic's life.

43 – 48. *Between the Topine:* The geographical description is that of Assisi, which lies between the Topino and Chiascio rivers. Ubaldo, before becoming bishop of Gubbio, had lived as a hermit on a hill from which the Chiascio rises. The "lofty mountain" is Mount Subasio, which reflects the rays of the sun on Perugia (to

the west) in the summer, and sends out icy winds to the same town during the winter. Porta Sole is the gate of Perugia facing in the direction of Assisi. Gualdo and Nocera, towns located to the east of the mountain, were oppressed by Perugia.

49–54. *Born on this slope:* St. Francis, himself a "sun," rose on the world in the manner of the real sun (the Ganges River marking the easternmost point of the habitable world), the sun they are all standing in at this moment. "Ascesi" was in Dante's time the name of the town of Assisi, and it also meant "I have risen." While "Ascesi" suggests this second meaning, Dante points out that the word "Orient" carries a more immediate meaning of the sun rising and therefore is more symbolically appropriate as a name for the town from which this great saint arose.

St. Francis was born Giovanni Francesco Bernardone, son of a wool merchant, in 1181 or 1182, at Assisi. As a young man he pursued a life of pleasure but changed his ways after a series of hardships (including two illnesses) befell him. He resolved to renounce the worldly life and devote himself to poverty, which he called his bride. Several years later, inspired by Christ's injunction to the Apostles (Matt. 10:9–10), Francis gave up shoes (following the example of the Apostles), girdle, and staff and began wearing a simple brown tunic girt with a hemp cord. This became a distinguishing mark of his order, the rules of which were drawn up in 1290. In 1219 he went to Egypt in an unsuccessful attempt to convert the Sultan. Four years later his order received solemn confirmation by papal bull from Honorius III. In 1224 he received the stigmata on his hands, feet, and side, the same five wounds inflicted on Christ at the Crucifixion. After two years of suffering, he died on October 4, 1226, near Assisi. He was canonized by Gregory IX in 1228.

58–60. *while still a youth he braved his father's wrath:* Francis was in love with Lady Poverty, whom he embraced against his father's wishes and whom most men fear as much as they do death itself.

61–63. *et coram patre:* This is the Latin expression meaning "in the presence of his father." In his father's presence and before the bishop of Assisi, in the spring of 1207, Francis gave up his inheritance and took his vow of poverty.

64. *Bereft of her first spouse:* Poverty's first husband was Christ.

67–69. *She found / with Amyclas:* This story, which is taken from Lucan's *Pharsalia* (V, 515–31) tells how Amyclas, a poor fisherman, because he possessed absolutely no worldly goods (thus representing poverty) remained tranquil, unafraid, and unimpressed when Caesar, who had been waging war in his area, appeared at the door of his shack to ask to be ferried across the Adriatic.

71–72. *she climbed the cross to be / with Christ:* Because Christ was crucified naked, Poverty is said to have remained loyal to him even to his death. The idea of Poverty as the spouse of Christ and St. Francis could have come to Dante from a number of Franciscan sources, but see in particular the *Arbor vitae crucifixae* of Ubertino da Casale.

I have accepted the reading of *salse* ("climbed") in verse 71 instead of Petrocchi's more authoritative reading of *pianse* ("wept") for aesthetic reasons. See also Auerbach and Chimenz (p. 721).

74. *take Francis, now, and Poverty to be:* Not until this point in the eulogy of St. Francis does St. Thomas reveal the names of the main characters of his narrative. See note 49–54 for details of St. Francis' life.

76–78. *Their sweet accord:* Referring to the harmony between St. Francis and Lady Poverty.

79–81. *the venerable Bernard:* Bernardo da Quintavalle, a wealthy merchant of Assisi, was the first follower of St. Francis. His casting aside his shoes and running suggest his eagerness to follow Francis' example of poverty. Dante's Italian for this tercet reads:

> tanto che 'l venerabile Bernardo
> si scalzò prima, e dietro a tanta pace
> corse, e correndo li parve esser tardo.

The use of enjambement between verses 80 and 81 as well as the repetition of the verb "run" ("corse e correndo") almost back to back—separated only by the conjunction "and"—underscore Bernard's zest for poverty.

83. *Giles . . . Sylvester:* Giles was the third disciple of St. Francis. He preached in the Holy Land and in Tunisia and died in 1262.

Sylvester was another early follower of St. Francis. He was said to have been very greedy for money until he met St. Francis and had a miraculous dream. He died in 1240. For more details, see Singleton (p. 202).

84. *they love the bride so much, they seek the groom:* The "bride" is Poverty, the "groom" Francis.

85–87. *And then this father:* Francis, accompanied by Lady Poverty and his followers, set forth to Rome; they were girded with rope as a sign of their poverty.

88–90. *It mattered not:* Francis was not ashamed of the fact that his father, Pietro Bernardone, was only a common merchant; in fact the saint would often have his disciples call him *filius Petri Bernardonis* in order to remind himself of his humble origins. See Bonaventure, *The Legend of St Francis* (VI, I).

92. *his hard intent:* This is an allusion to the difficult and rigid rules followed by the Franciscans. Even Pope Innocent III, who would eventually sanction the order, found them extremely rigid. Innocent III was raised to the papacy in 1198 and died in 1216; he verbally sanctioned the order of St. Francis in 1209 or 1210.

95. *archimandrite:* This is a Greek Church term meaning "head of the fold," or one who supervises convents. Dante found the word in Uguccione da Pisa's *Magnae Derivationes.*

97–98. *saw his work / crowned once again:* Pope Honorius III now officially ("once again") approved the Franciscan Order in 1223.

100–105. *Then in the haughty presence of the Sultan:* In 1219 St. Francis accompanied the Fifth Crusade to Egypt where he entered the Sultan's camp to preach. He was treated kindly there but was unsuccessful in making conversions.

106–108. *then on bare rock:* In 1224, while fasting on Mount Alvernia between the upper Arno and the source of the Tiber, Francis received from Christ through a seraph the stigmata, the marks of Christ's five wounds. He bore them until his death at Porziuncola below Perugia in 1226.

115–17. *and in the lap of poverty:* Francis requested that after his death his body lie naked on the bare ground.

118. *Think now what kind of man:* St. Dominic is Francis' "fellow helmsman." Having finished his encomium on St. Francis, St. Thomas turns to his own order, and thus returns to the Pilgrim's first doubt: what he meant when he said, in Canto X, 94 – 96, that the lambs of the Dominican flock fattened if they did not stray.

119. *Saint Peter's boat:* The Church.

121. *our Patriarch:* St. Dominic, the founder of St. Thomas' order, whose life is described in the next canto.

126. *they stray to alien pastures carelessly:* The Dominican Order, having become greedy for worldly honors and favors, has deviated from the principles governing the order.

128 – 29. *the less milk / they bring back:* Since they have gained no spiritual nourishment outside the flock, they have nothing to offer their followers.

137. *the tree is chipped:* Refers to the corruption ("chipped") of the Dominican Order ("the tree").

CANTO XII

ST. THOMAS HAVING completed his discourse, the ring of
souls now resumes its circling and is joined by another circle
which forms around it. The two move with such harmony that
the outer seems an echo of the inner one, and their beauty is such
that they resemble concentric rainbows or a double garland of
roses. The double rings cease their singing and motion, and
Bonaventure, a spirit from that new circle and himself a Francis-
can, steps forward to return the compliment made to his leader
by St. Thomas. In relating the story of Dominic, Bonaventure
follows the pattern set up in Thomas' story of St. Francis, so that,
just as the two rings of souls are twin garlands, the stories of the
mendicant leaders are nearly line-by-line parallels. After finish-
ing the story of Dominic, Bonaventure comments, as did
Thomas, on the present state of his own order: the Franciscans
have been divided by those who would misread his rule. Then,
turning from these concerns, Bonaventure introduces himself and
the other spirits in this outer circle to Dante.

The very moment that the blessèd flame
    had come to speak its final word, the holy
    millstone began revolving once again;   3

before it could complete its first full round
    a second circle was enclosing it:
    motion with motion, matching song with song—   6

song that in those sweet instruments surpassed
    the best our Sirens or our Muses sing,
    as source of light outshines what it reflects.   9

As two concentric arcs of equal hue,
    are seen as they bend through the misty clouds
    when Juno tells her handmaid to appear—   12

the outer from the inner one an echo,
    like to the longing voice of her whom love
    consumed as morning sun consumes the dew—   15

and reassure the people here below
　　that by the covenant God made with Noah,
　　they have no need to fear another Flood—　　　　18

even so those sempiternal roses wreathed
　　twin garlands round us as the outer one
　　was lovingly responding to the inner.　　　　21

When dancing and sublime festivity
　　and all the singing, all the gleaming flames
　　(a loving jubilee of light with light),　　　　24

with one accord, at the same instant, ceased
　　(as our two eyes responding to our will,
　　together have to open and to close),　　　　27

then, from the heart of one of those new lights
　　there came a voice that drew me to itself
　　(I was the needle pointing to the star);　　　　30

it spoke: "The love that makes me beautiful
　　moves me to speak about that other guide,
　　the cause of such high praise concerning mine.　　　　33

We should not mention one without the other,
　　since both did battle for a single cause,
　　so let their fame shine gloriously as one.　　　　36

The troops of Christ, rearmed at such great cost,
　　with tardy pace were following their standard,
　　fearful and few, divided in their ranks,　　　　39

when the Emperor who reigns eternally,
　　of His own grace (for they were not deserving)
　　provided for his soldiers in their peril—　　　　42

and, as you have been told, He sent His bride
　　two champions who through their words and deeds
　　helped reunite the scattered company.　　　　45

Within that region where the sweet west wind
　　comes blowing, opening up the fresh new leaves
　　with which all Europe is about to bloom,　　　　48

not far from where the waves break on the shore
　　behind which, when its longest course is done,
　　the sun, at times, will hide from every man,　　　　51

lies Calaroga, fortune-favored town,
 protected by the mighty shield that bears
 two lions: one as subject, one as sovereign.   54

There the staunch lover of the Christian faith
 was born into the world: God's holy athlete,
 kind to his own and ruthless to his foes.   57

His mind, the instant God created it,
 possessed extraordinary power: within
 his mother's womb he made her prophesy.   60

The day that he was wed to Christian Faith
 at the baptismal font, when each of them
 promised the other mutual salvation,   63

the lady who had answered for him there
 saw in a dream the marvellous rich fruit
 that he and all his heirs were to produce,   66

and that he might be known for what he was,
 a spirit sent from Heaven named the child
 with His possessive, Whose alone he was: 69

Dominic he was named. I see in him
 the husbandman, the one chosen by Christ
 to help Him in the garden of His Church.   72

Close servant and true messenger of Christ,
 he made it manifest that his first love
 was love for the first counsel given by Christ.   75

Often his nurse would find him out of bed,
 awake and silent, lying on the ground,
 as if to say, "For this end was I sent."   78

O father Felix, felicitously named!
 O mother called Giovanna, 'grace of God!'
 And these names truly mean what they express.   81

Not like those men who toil for worldly gain,
 studying Thaddeus and the Ostian,
 but for the love of the eternal bread,   84

he soon became a mighty theologian,
 a diligent inspector of the vineyard,
 where the vine withers if the keeper fails.   87

And from the See which once was so benign
  to its deserving poor (but now corrupt,
  not in itself but in its occupant)   90

no right to pay out two or three for six,
  nor first choice of some fat and vacant post,
  nor *decimas quae sunt pauperum Dei,*   93

did he request, but just the right to fight
  the sinful world for that true seed whence sprang
  the four and twenty plants surrounding you.   96

Then, armed with doctrine and a zealous will
  with apostolic sanction, he burst forth
  —a mighty torrent gushing from on high;   99

sending its crushing force against the barren
  thickets of heresy, and where they were
  toughest, it struck with greatest violence.   102

And from him many other streams branched off
  to give their waters to the Catholic fields
  so that its saplings might have greener life.   105

If such was one wheel of the chariot
  that Holy Church used to defend herself
  and conquer on the field of civil strife,   108

you cannot fail to see how excellent
  the other must have been, about whom Thomas,
  before I came, spoke with such courtesy.   111

But now the track made by the topmost part
  of that great wheel's circumference is gone,
  and there is only mold where once was crust.   114

His family, which once walked straight ahead
  in his own footprints, now are so turned round
  they walk along by putting toe to heel.   117

Soon comes the harvest time and we shall see
  how bad the tillage was: the tares will mourn
  that access to the storehouse is denied.   120

I will admit that if you search our book
  page after page you might find one that reads:
  'I still am now what I have always been,'   123

but such cannot be said of those who come
   from Acquasparta or Casal and read
   our rule too loosely or too narrowly.   126

I am the living soul of Bonaventure
   from Bagnoregio; temporal concerns
   always came last when I was in command.   129

Illuminato and Augustine are here,
   they were the first of God's barefooted poor
   who wore the cord to show they were His friends.   132

Hugh of St. Victor is among them too,
   with Peter Mangiador, and Peter of Spain
   who in twelve books illumines men below,   135

Nathan the prophet, and the Patriarch
   Chrysostom, Anselm, and Donatus who
   devoted all his thought to the first art.   138

Rabanus, too, is here, and at my side
   shines the Calabrian Abbot Joachim
   who had received the gift of prophecy.   141

The glowing courtesy of Brother Thomas,
   his modesty of words, have prompted me
   to praise this paladin as I have done   144

and moved this fellowship to join with me."

NOTES

1—21

The opening image of this canto is that of two circles of
light, one reflecting the other and both moving in perfect har-
mony. The circle of the twelve spirits named in Canto X has been
joined by another circle, which surrounds the first to act as its
echo or reflection. Theologically, the arrangement of the circles
is also significant. The inner one, which is the source of the outer
one, is made up largely of Dominicans, characterized principally
by their wisdom. The outer circle, composed at least partially of
Franciscans, known for their love, acts as the reflection. Accord-
ing to the theology of St. Thomas, understanding precedes the
act of love, thus the learned are appropriately the "source" of

those who love. The idea of reflection and the harmony of these two circles is repeated in the work of the two great leaders, Francis and Dominic, and in Dante's method of presenting their stories. The careful reader will discover a meticulous parallelism in the narratives of the two men.

1. *the blessèd flame:* The spirit of St. Thomas who had been speaking up to this point.

2–3. *the holy / millstone:* The circle of spirits. The image suggests horizontal gyration.

6. *motion with motion, matching song with song:* The verse in the Italian, "e moto a moto, e canto a canto colse," imitates in its double duality the circle within the circle.

7–9. *song that in those sweet instruments surpassed:* The song of the souls surpasses the best of earth's music ("our Sirens") or poetry ("our Muses"), just as the source of a light outshines its reflection.

12. *Juno tells her handmaid:* Juno's handmaiden is Iris, goddess of the rainbow and messenger of the gods. (See *Metam.* I, 271 and *Aen.* IV, 694; V, 606; IX, 2, 5.)

14–15. *the longing voice of her whom love / consumed:* The wood nymph Echo had helped to expedite Jupiter's amorous adventures, and thus incurred the wrath of Juno, who deprived her of the power of speech except to repeat the last syllables of others' words. Because Narcissus failed to return her love, Echo faded away until only her voice remained. (See *Metam.* III, 356–401.)

17–18. *the covenant God made with Noah:* The appearance of the rainbow was a promise to Noah that God would never again destroy the earth by water (Gen. 9:8–17).

22–33

At this point, simultaneously and with one will, the circling spirits cease their singing and dancing. The focus shifts to the movement of the Pilgrim as he turns in the direction of one spirit, whose voice he hears. This pause sets the stage for the introduction of St. Bonaventure, who offers an account of the life of St. Dominic. This image, like the one comprising verses 10–21, is rather long and filled with asides or parentheses. It emphasizes the parallelism as well as the circularity of the two concentric circles.

29. *a voice that drew me to itself:* The voice is that of St. Bonaventure (Giovanni di Fidanza), born 1221 at Bagnoregio near Orvieto, a Franciscan monk who became general of the Franciscan Order in 1255 or 1256. As a child he was miraculously cured of a serious disease by St. Francis. There is a story that when St. Francis heard that the young boy had been cured, he exclaimed "buona ventura!" The boy's mother on hearing this changed her son's name to Bonaventure. Among his many works is a biography of St. Francis, *The Legend of St. Francis,* which provided Dante with one of his sources for the story in Canto XI. He died in 1274 and was canonized in 1482 by Sixtus IV. The title of "Doctor Seraphicus" was later bestowed on him by Sixtus V.

30. *I was the needle pointing to the star:* Dante and Beatrice stand in the center of the circles. On hearing a voice from one of the spirits, Dante turns toward it in the same way the compass needle is attracted to the North Star.

32. *that other guide:* The other leader is St. Dominic.

33. *the cause of such high praise concerning mine:* St. Thomas for love of his own leader, St. Dominic, has been praising St. Francis who is Bonaventure's leader.

34–45

Note the similarities between this preface to Dominic's story and the preface of St. Francis' (XI, 28–42). The tercet 34–36, for instance, corresponds to verses 40–42 of the preceding canto while verses 37–45 correspond to 28–36 of Canto XI. While the imagery associated with St. Francis was mostly of a pastoral nature with overtones of courtly chivalry—his image might be summed up in the word "archimandrite" (XI, 99)—the figure of St. Dominic will be couched in military terms: he is "God's holy athlete" (56); in fact, the tercet 55–57 seems to contain all of the imagery that will be associated with St. Dominic in this canto.

37. *The troops of Christ, rearmed:* Christ's troops, or humanity, were "rearmed" with the blood of Christ, through His sacrifice on the Cross.

43. *as you have been told:* As St. Thomas had said in verses 31 – 36 of the preceding canto.

46. *that region:* Spain, near the Bay of Biscay, which is the area nearest the source of the west wind, or Zephyr.

47 – 48. *fresh new leaves:* It will be spring soon in Europe.

51. *the sun, at times, will hide from every man:* At the summer solstice, the sun sets in the Atlantic across from the west coast of Spain. The word "every man" refers to the inhabitants of the northern hemisphere; the southern hemisphere, in Dante's cosmography, contained only water and the Mountain of Purgatory.

52 – 54. *Calaroga, fortune-favored town:* The village blessed by Fortune (because Dominic was born there) is Caleruega in Old Castile which was ruled by kings whose arms consisted of quartered castles and lions, one lion below a castle and one above, thus "one as subject, one as sovereign."

55. *the staunch lover:* Dominic, born between 1170 and 1175, supposedly into the noble family of Guzmán, studied theology, beginning at the age of fourteen, at the University of Palencia. He later participated in diplomatic missions, in the Albigensian Crusade, during which period he preached and even bore arms against the heretics, and finally founded his order of Preaching Friars at Toulouse in 1215. It was officially recognized by Honorius III the following year. In 1219 he moved the center of the order to Bologna, where he died in August 1221. He was canonized in 1234 by Gregory IX.

56. *God's holy athlete:* In the sense of defender of the Faith. See note 34 – 45.

58 – 60. *His mind, the instant God created it:* Even within the womb, Dominic's mind had such strength that he caused his mother to dream that she would give birth to a black and white dog with a flaming torch in its mouth. The Dominicans were called the "dogs of the Lord" from the Latin *Domini canes;* the flaming torch is representative of the order's zeal, and black and white are its colors.

61 – 63. *The day that he was wed . . . mutual salvation:* Just as Francis (XI, 61 – 63) wed Poverty, Dominic married Faith (note the correspondence in the lines). The faith acquired through

baptism freed Dominic from Original Sin and he, in turn, defended the Faith from heresy.

64–66. *the lady who had answered for him there:* Dominic's godmother, who answered for him at his baptismal ceremony, is said to have dreamed of him with a star on his forehead, indicative of his great intellect and his role as guide for all mankind (as the North Star is the guide for every navigator). This particular fact is recorded by Vincent di Beauvais (XXIX, 94) in his *Speculum Historiale,* a widely read work in the Middle Ages (see Casini-Barbi).

67–68. *that he might be known for what he was:* So that he would be called by the name of what he really was, the inspiration for that name came directly from Heaven. See note 79–81.

69. *with His possessive:* The name Dominic means "the Lord's" in Latin, (Dominicus, possessive adjective from Dominus).

75. *first counsel given by Christ:* the first of the Beatitudes: "Blessed are the poor in spirit" (Matt. 5:3); that is, love of poverty. Notice that in verses 71, 73, 75 the word "Christ" is in rhyme with itself. This happens three more times in the *Paradise:* Cantos XIV, 104–108; XIX, 104–108; XXXII, 83–87 (see respective notes to these cantos).

76–78. *Often his nurse would find him out of bed:* Dominic, even as a child, denied himself the comforts of a bed in order to lie on the floor in imitation of the humility of Christ whose words: "For this is why I have come" (Mark 1:38) are echoed in verse 78.

79–81. *O father Felix . . . and these names truly mean what they express:* Names were believed to derive from the quality of the things named. Medieval philosophy adhered to this aspect of platonic doctrine. Dante in the *Vita nuova* (XIII, 4) says, "nomina sunt consequentia rerum" (names are the consequences of the things they name). Dominic's father, Felix de Guzmán, was seen to be happy in his son's greatness (79), while the name Giovanna, that of Dominic's mother, comes from the Hebrew and signifies "abounding in the grace of Jehovah" (80). See also verse 67 and note.

83. *Thaddeus and the Ostian:* This is probably Thaddeus of Alderotto (ca. 1235–95), a well-known physician and the presumed founder of the school of medicine at the University of

Bologna, who wrote commentaries on the works of Galen and Hippocrates.

Enrico da Susa, "the Ostian" (from the village of Ostia about twenty miles southwest of Rome), was a theologian who taught canon law in Paris and Bologna and was famous for his commentary on the decretals or papal decrees on ecclesiastical law. He was cardinal bishop of Ostia from 1261 until his death in 1271.

84. *the eternal bread:* True knowledge or "the bread of angels," as opposed to learning for material gain (see also *Purg.* XI, 13, and *Par.* II, 11).

88–90. *And from the See which once was so benign:* Dante here distinguishes between the office of pope and the particular occupant of that office. The papacy itself has always been good to the poor; at present it has been corrupted by the reigning pope, Boniface VIII.

91–93. *no right to pay out:* Dominic, unlike some other ecclesiastics, did not petition the Pope for a dispensation to pay out only one-third or one-half of what was supposed to be given to the poor (and keeping the rest, 91); nor for the first vacant post or benefice (92); nor for "the tithes that are for God's poor" (*"decimas quae sunt pauperum Dei"*).

94–96. *but just the right to fight:* Dominic asked to fight the "sinful world" (heretics, especially the Albigensians, against whom the Dominicans preached) for the sake of the faith, from which have sprung the twenty-four spirits in the double garland surrounding Dante.

98. *with apostolic sanction:* Dominic's order was officially sanctioned in 1216 by Pope Honorius III.

101–102. *where they were / toughest:* In Provence the Albigensians had their strongest foothold.

103. *many other streams:* Here, Dominic becomes the source of many other streams, which may refer to Dominic's individual followers or to the establishment of particular groups within the Dominican Order.

106. *If such was one wheel of the chariot:* The chariot is the Church of which St. Dominic is one wheel and St. Francis the other. (See *Purg.* XXIX, 107.) The word for "chariot" in the

Italian is *biga,* an ancient two-wheeled war-cart usually drawn by two horses.

110. *the other:* St. Francis.

112–13. *But now the track:* The path St. Francis made is no longer followed; his order, like Dominic's, has degenerated.

114. *there is only mold where once was crust:* From the metaphor of the wheel (112–13), Dante makes an abrupt shift to one of wine-making. A good wine will leave a crust in the barrel; bad wine leaves mold.

115–17. *His family, which once walked straight ahead:* The metaphor now shifts from the track left by the wheel of St. Francis to the mark of his order's footprints. In the description of the degeneracy of the Franciscans, it is stated that they are walking in the wrong direction, back instead of ahead, thereby placing their toes into the heels of the footprints left by their predecessors. Not only does this image evoke a notion of regression, but it also suggests total lack of accord between past and present members of the order.

118–20. *Soon comes the harvest time:* The reference is to Matt. 13:24–30, in which the tares are bundled together to be burned and the wheat is gathered into the barn. The verses may refer to the failure of the corrupt Franciscans to enter heaven, but they may also be a reference to the condemnation of the "Spirituals" (a faction within the Franciscan order, opposed by the so-called Conventionals) by Pope John XXII in 1318.

121–23. *if you search our book:* The metaphor now shifts to that of the book that is the Franciscan Order in which, after searching through many pages, it might be possible to find one page that reads, "I still am now what I have always been" (123); that is, there still might be a few Franciscan brothers who adhere to the rules of the Order as set down by their founder. The implication, however, is that there are very few indeed.

125. *Acquasparta or Casal:* Acquasparta (a town in Umbria) refers to Matthew of Acquasparta who was appointed general of the Franciscan order in 1287. As general he introduced relaxations in the Franciscan rule which paved the way for abuses.
Casal (a town in Northern Italy thirty miles east of Turin) specifically refers to Ubertino of Casal, leader of the Franciscan

"Spirituals," who opposed the relaxations and preferred a more literal adherence to the rule.

127. *I am the living soul of Bonaventure:* See above, verse 29, and the note for details concerning the speaker.

128–29. *temporal concerns / always came last:* Contemplation was the primary concern of the saint. Bonaventure was the author of a well-known treatise on the journey of the mind to God, the *Itinerarium mentis in Deum* which, as Singleton says, "might even stand as an appropriate title of the *Paradiso* and of Dante's journey to Paradise" (p. 219).

130. *Illuminato and Augustine:* Bonaventure begins his introduction of the spirits in the outer circle (Fig. 7) with these two early followers of St. Francis. Both men joined the saint in 1210. Illuminato, from a noble family of Rieti, went with Francis on his mission to the Orient, which was referred to in the preceding canto (XI, 100ff.). He died ca. 1280, late enough to have witnessed the corruption already present in his Order.

Augustine, like St. Francis, was from Assisi. He became head of the Franciscan Order in Campania (1216) and was said to have died on the same day and at the same hour as his leader, St. Francis.

133. *Hugh of St. Victor:* A famous theologian and mystic of the early twelfth century, born in Flanders around 1097 (or in Saxony as some believe), Hugh of St. Victor wrote numerous works characterized by great learning. They were much admired and much quoted by Thomas Aquinas. Two of his students, Richard of St. Victor and Peter Lombard, stand in the inner circle of souls. He was also the good friend of St. Bernard of Clairvaux.

134. *Peter Mangiador, and Peter of Spain:* Peter Mangiador, also known as Petrus Comestor, born in Troyes, France, became Dean of the Cathedral there in 1147, and later assumed the position of Chancellor of the University of Paris. His best-known work, the *Historia scholastica*, is a compilation of the historical books of the Bible accompanied by a commentary.

Peter of Spain, born in Lisbon (ca. 1226), became Archbishop of Braga and in 1276 became Pope John XXI. His reign lasted only eight months; he was killed when a ceiling collapsed in one of the rooms in his palace at Viterbo. His *Summulae logicales*, a manual of logic, was divided into twelve parts and expanded the traditional logic of the Scholastics.

136. *Nathan the Prophet:* Nathan was the Hebrew prophet who rebuked King David for having caused the death of Uriah the Hittite in order to marry Bathsheba (2 Sam. 12:1 – 15).

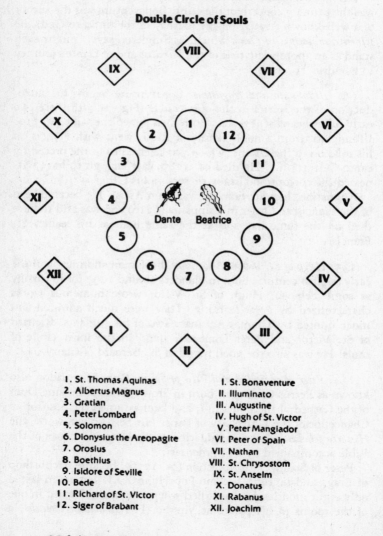

Double Circle of Souls

1. St. Thomas Aquinas
2. Albertus Magnus
3. Gratian
4. Peter Lombard
5. Solomon
6. Dionysius the Areopagite
7. Orosius
8. Boethius
9. Isidore of Seville
10. Bede
11. Richard of St. Victor
12. Siger of Brabant

I. St. Bonaventure
II. Illuminato
III. Augustine
IV. Hugh of St. Victor
V. Peter Mangiador
VI. Peter of Spain
VII. Nathan
VIII. St. Chrysostom
IX. St. Anselm
X. Donatus
XI. Rabanus
XII. Joachim

137–38. *Chrysostom. Anselm. and Donatus:* St. John Chrysostom, fourth-century Patriarch of Constantinople, was noted for his preaching.

Anselm, eleventh-century Archbishop of Canterbury, was author of *Cur Deus Homo,* a treatise on the Atonement which attempts to prove the necessity of the Incarnation. Beatrice summarizes his arguments in Canto VII.

Donatus, a fourth-century Roman rhetorician, was author of commentaries on Virgil and Terence but was best known for his widely used Latin grammar *Ars grammatica.* Grammar is "the first art" (138) of the seven liberal arts of the trivium and quadrivium.

139. *Rabanus:* Archbishop of Mainz from 847 until his death in 856, Rabanus Maurus Magnentius (born ca. 776) was considered one of the most learned men of his time. He wrote commentaries on much of the Bible and numerous theological works.

140. *Calabrian Abbot Joachim:* Joachim, preacher and prophet, born 1145 in Calabria, originated the doctrine that the dispensation of the Father (Old Testament) and of the Son (New Testament) would be followed by the dispensation of the Holy Spirit, a period of perfection and peace. Though himself a Cistercian, Joachim was very influential among the Franciscan "Spirituals" who adopted his teachings. He died ca. 1202.

As the last of the circle to be introduced, Joachim stands in the same relation to Bonaventure as does Siger de Brabant to Thomas Aquinas in the inner ring. Joachim stands to the left of Bonaventure and is acknowledged as prophet, whereas on earth Bonaventure had attacked the Joachimite Franciscans. In the same way, St. Thomas had opposed the teachings of Siger de Brabant.

144. *this paladin:* St. Dominic, God's athlete and warrior.

CANTO XIII

DANTE, IN ATTEMPTING to convey the grandeur of the two encircling wreaths of illustrious souls, opens the canto with a grandiose image of the heavenly contellations. Once the singing ceases, St. Thomas begins to speak again, explaining to the Pilgrim what he meant when he said earlier in regard to Solomon: "there never arose a second with such vision" (*Par.* X, 114). After demonstrating that the greatest amount of wisdom was that which God gave Adam and Christ when he created them (they were direct products of the Creator and therefore perfect), St. Thomas explains that what he meant when he used the phrase in relation to Solomon was that God had given Solomon the greatest amount of wisdom that He ever gave to a king, not a man. So, then, it was in the context of kingly prudence or perfection that Solomon had no equal. St. Thomas uses this occasion to warn the Pilgrim about drawing rash conclusions and making quick judgments, and he mentions a number of ancient philosophers and heretics as examples of those who fell into error precisely because they did not examine all the circumstances and make clear distinctions. He concludes by saying that one must be especially prudent when it comes to second-guessing the Almighty: just because we see one man steal and another make offerings does not necessarily mean that the thief will be damned and the do-gooder saved by God.

Imagine, you who wish to visualize
    what I saw next (and while I speak hold hard
    as rock in your mind's eye this image),　　　　　　3

the fifteen brightest stars in all of heaven,
    the ones whose light is of such magnitude
    that it can penetrate the thickest mist;　　　　　　6

imagine next the turnings of the Wain
    through night and day and all contained within
    the spacious vault of heaven's hemisphere;　　　　9

imagine, too, the bell-mouth of that Horn
    whose tip is marked by that bright star which serves
    as axis for the Primum Mobile—　　　　　　12

all joined into a double constellation
    (like that one which the daughter of Minos
    left in the sky when stricken by Death's chill),   *15*

one's rays within the other shining forth,
    and both of them revolving, synchronized
    at different speeds but moving light with light—   *18*

and you will have some shadowy idea
    of the true nature of that constellation
    and of the double dance encircling me,   *21*

for these things far exceed our cognizance,
    as far as movement of the swiftest sphere
    outspeeds the current of Chiana's flow.   *24*

No Bacchic hymn or Paean did they sing,
    but of three Persons in one God they sang
    and in One Person human and Divine.   *27*

When song and circling reached the final note,
    those holy lights then turned to wait on us,
    rejoicing as they moved from task to task.   *30*

The hush of that concordant group of souls
    was broken by that light from which had poured
    the wondrous story of God's pauper-saint;   *33*

and he said: "Now that one sheaf has been threshed
    and all its grain is garnered, God's sweet love
    invites me now to thresh the other one.   *36*

Into that breast, you think, from which was drawn
    the rib that was to form the lovely face
    whose palate was to cost mankind so dear,   *39*

and into That One Who pierced by the lance
    gave satisfaction for future and past,
    such that it outweighed all of mankind's guilt,   *42*

as much of wisdom's radiance as is given
    to human nature was infused by Him
    whose power created their humanity;   *45*

and so, you must have been surprised to hear
    what I said earlier of our fifth light:
    that he possessed a wisdom without equal.   *48*

Open your eyes to what I now reveal,
  and you will see your thoughts and my words join
  as one truth at the center of the round.   51

All that which dies and all that cannot die
  reflect the radiance of that Idea
  which God the Father through His love begets: 54

that Living Light, which from its radiant Source
  streams forth Its light but never parts from It
  nor from the Love which tri-unites with them,   57

of Its own grace sends down its rays, as if
  reflected, through the nine subsistencies,
  remaining sempiternally Itself.   60

Then it descends to the last potencies,
  from act to act, becoming so diminished,
  it brings forth only brief contingencies;   63

and by this term I mean things generated,
  things which the moving heavens produce from seed
  or not from seed. The wax of things like these   66

is more or less receptive, and the power
  that shapes it, more or less effective—stamped
  with the idea, it shines accordingly.   69

So trees of the same species may produce
  dissimilar fruit, some better and some worse;
  so men are born with diverse natural gifts.   72

And if the wax were perfectly disposed,
  and if the heavens were at their highest power,
  the brilliance of the seal would shine forth full;   75

but Nature never can transmit this light
  in its full force—much like the artisan
  who knows his craft but has a trembling hand.   78

But if the Fervent Love moves the Clear Vision
  of the First Power and makes of that its seal,
  the thing it stamps is perfect in all ways.   81

And this is how the dust of earth was once
  made fit to form the perfect living being
  and how the Virgin came to be with child.   84

And so you see how right you are to think
    that human nature never has been since,
    nor ever will be such, as in those two.   87

Now, if I were to end my discourse here,
    you would be quick to ask: 'Then, how can you
    say that the other was without an equal?'   90

To clearly understand what seems unclear,
    consider who he was and his request
    that time God said to him, 'Ask what you will.'   93

My words were meant to bring back to your mind
    the fact he was a king, and asked his Lord
    for wisdom to suffice a worthy king;   96

he did not ask to know so that he might
    count angels here, or know whether *necesse*
    with a conditioned premise yields *necesse;*   99

nor *si est dare primum motum esse,*
    nor if without right angles, triangles
    in semicircles can be made to fit.   102

So, when I talked of unmatched wisdom then,
    royal prudence was the wisdom upon which
    I had my arrow of intention drawn.   105

If you recall the word I used, 'arose,'
    it should be clear that only kings were meant,
    of which there are full many, but few good.   108

And if my words are taken in this sense,
    they will not contradict what you believe
    of our first father and of our High Bliss.   111

Let this be leaden weight upon your feet
    to make you move slow as a weary man
    both to the 'yes' or 'no' you do not see,   114

for he ranks low, indeed, among the fools,
    who rushes to affirm or to deny,
    no matter which, without distinguishing.   117

Opinions formed in haste will oftentimes
    lead in a wrong direction, and man's pride
    then intervenes to bind his intellect.   120

Worse than useless it is to leave the shore
   to fish for truth unless you have the skill;
   you will return worse off than when you left.   123

Of this Parmenides offers clear proof
   and Bryson and Melissus and the rest
   who went their way but knew not where to go;   126

so did Sabellius and Arius
   and all those fools who were to Holy Scripture
   swordblades distorting images of truth.   129

Nor should one be too quick to trust his judgment;
   be not like him who walks his field and counts
   the ears of corn before the time is ripe,   132

for I have seen brier all winter long
   showing its tough and prickly stem, and then
   eventually produce a lovely rose,   135

and I have seen a ship sail straight and swift
   over the sea through all its course, and then,
   about to enter in the harbor, sink.   138

No Mr. or Miss Know-It-All should think,
   when they see one man steal and one give alms
   that they are seeing them through God's own eyes,   141

for one may yet rise up, the other fall."

NOTES

1 – 24

In the opening verses of this canto, the tone becomes increasingly emphatic as the poet exhorts his reader to imagine what is essentially (for mortal man) an unimaginable scene. Anaphoric use of the word "imagine" (in verses 1, 7, 10) underscores the poet's awareness of the difficulty of his task in portraying the ineffable.

4. *the fifteen brightest stars:* According to Ptolemaic astronomy, there were fifteen stars of the first magnitude in the sky.

7. *the Wain:* The Great Bear (Ursa Major, or Big Dipper) consists of seven conspicuous stars and can always be seen in the northern hemisphere.

10. *bell-mouth of that Horn:* The Horn was another name for the Little Bear (Ursa Minor, or Little Dipper); "bell-mouth" refers to the two stars at the opposite end from the Pole (North) Star.

11. *that bright star:* The Pole Star was located at one end of the Horn and also served as the axis upon which the Primum Mobile supposedly turned.

13-24

Imagining the brightest stars in the heavens forming two circles conveys inadequately the splendors of the twenty-four souls encircling Dante and Beatrice. The heavenly experience exceeds the human grasp to the same degree that the speed of the Primum Mobile (the swiftest motion in the universe) surpasses that of the Chiana river, whose waters in some places were nearly stagnant.

13-15. *a double constellation / like that one:* When the daughter of Minos, Ariadne, died ("stricken by Death's chill"), the wreath she wore at her wedding to Bacchus was transformed into a constellation called Ariadne's crown, or the Corona Borealis. (See *Metam.* VIII, 174-82; also *Inf.* V, 4.) The reader is supposed to imagine a double circle of lights as bright as the twenty-four stars mentioned earlier.

24. *Chiana's flow:* The Chiana is a river in Tuscany that was nearly stagnant in Dante's day.

25-27. *No Bacchic hymn:* Just as devotees of the gods Bacchus and Apollo used to sing their praises, these heavenly spirits sing of the nature of God in the Trinity and of the dual nature of Christ.

30. *from task to task:* The spirits rejoice as they turn from their task of song and dance to that of attending Dante in order to answer his questions.

32. *that light:* St. Thomas, who told the story about St. Francis, "God's pauper-saint" (33), in Canto XI.

34-36. *"Now that one sheaf has been threshed:* St. Thomas, remarking that one of Dante's questions has been answered ("where all may fatten if they do not stray"), now addresses himself to the other: the question of the fifth light (Solomon), whose wisdom was unequalled (see Canto X, 109-114).

Adam and Christ were granted the fullest wisdom ever given to human kind, and therefore it is understandable that Dante, knowing this, would be confused by the statement that Solomon (the fifth light) had unparalled wisdom.

37. *that breast:* Adam.

39. *the lovely face:* Eve.

40. *That One:* Christ.

49–51. *Open your eyes:* Just as the center of a circle is one specific point and no other, truth also is specific. Thomas' words will coincide with Dante's understanding to represent one truth.

52–87

The following discourse on the universe resembles that one pronounced by Beatrice in Canto II concerning the moon spots, except that St. Thomas' purpose here is to explain how imperfection can exist in a universe created and sustained by a perfect being.

All creation—both immortal and mortal—reflects the Light of the Idea (the Son of the Trinity, or the Word). This Living Light streams forth from its Source (the Father or First Cause) throughout creation though itself remaining unseparated from its Source and from the Love (Holy Spirit) which binds the Trinity. The Divine Light becomes reflected through the nine orders of angels which in turn convey it through the varying degrees of creation.

Through continual reflection, the light becomes diminished, and creation becomes indirect as, via the power of the moving spheres, it infuses the elements on earth: the organic, or plants and animals (produced "from seed," 65), and the inorganic, or minerals (produced "not from seed," 66). The basic material, "wax" (see *Par.* VIII, 127–29), of these creations receives the Divine Light according to each one's varying capacity; this phenomenon explains the vast diversity within Creation.

If primal matter were perfectly receptive to Divine Light and if the light were undiminished when it reached the basic material, perfection would exist in all creation. This, however, is not the case, because Nature (second cause), the process of causation or distribution of light, is incapable of passing the light throughout creation without the light's attenuation. Therefore, Nature resembles the artist who conceives his idea but cannot execute it perfectly ("the artisan . . . who knows his craft but has a trembling hand," 77–78).

Perfection, however, did occur in two cases in the material universe: in the creation of Adam and the conception of the human nature of Christ. These perfections occurred as a result of direct creation—from the Love (the Spirit) which moved the Vision (Son) of the Power (the Father) directly to infuse matter with its likeness. Thus, Dante was correct in believing that Adam and Christ were created having perfect wisdom.

59. *through the nine subsistencies:* These are the nine orders of angels that reflect the "Living Light" (55) of God within Whom rests the plan of the universe.

60. *remaining sempiternally Itself:* This impressive three-word verse reflecting the Trinity Itself reads as follows in the Italian: "eternalmente rimanendosi una."

61–62. *the last potencies, / from act to act:* The "Living Light" (55) of God finally reaches the sublunar world, having been transmitted from sphere to sphere.

63–66. *only brief contingencies:* The result of this filtering down of God's light is the creation of things that do not have a lasting existence.

72. *so men are born with diverse natural gifts:* See *Par.* VIII, 124–32.

75. *the seal:* God's Divine Plan.

76. *Nature:* Here the word means the entire operation of the heavens.

79–81. *But if the Fervent Love moves the Clear Vision:* Up until this point Thomas Aquinas has been talking about how the Creator works through Nature (52–60); here he describes direct creation. While this tercet is not clear in the original, the general sense is not difficult to grasp. The emphasis here is on the perfect coordination of the three Persons of the Trinity: "Fervent Love" (the Holy Spirit), "Clear Vision" (the Son), and the "First Power" (the Father). See last paragraph of note 52–87.

88 – 90. *if I were to end my discourse here:* St. Thomas anticipates an objection the Pilgrim might have.

93. *'Ask what thou wilt':* When the Lord asked Solomon what he desired, Solomon replied, "Give therefore to Thy servant an understanding heart, to judge Thy people and discern between good and evil" (1 Kings 3:5 – 13).

97 – 102. *he did not ask to know:* Solomon did not ask for theological or scientific knowledge, such as: (1) how many angels there are (as discussed by Plato, Aristotle, and by Dante himself in the *Convivio,* II, iv and v); (2) whether, in logic, an absolute premise (*necesse*), existing with a contingent one, can yield an absolute conclusion (a problem also discussed by Plato and Aristotle); (3) whether there exists a first mover, i.e., a motion without a cause (*"si est dare primum motum esse"*); and (4) whether geometry exists similarly throughout the universe. These are all highly speculative questions, having little to do with practical wisdom.

103 – 105. *when I talked of unmatched wisdom then:* When, in Canto X, 112 – 14, St. Thomas concluded his argument, he was not talking about wisdom in the sense of doctrine but wisdom as "prudence"—that is, royal prudence in connection with government. And this is all he meant.

106. *'arose':* Apparently, Thomas' word "arose" is meant to suggest that kings "rise" to power or that they "rise" above ordinary men. Adam and Christ were not kings, nor could they rise above men, being already created "above" ordinary men (see *Par.* X, 114).

111. *our High Bliss:* Christ.

123. *you will return worse off than when you left:* You will be worse off because you will return with the false and dangerous belief of having found it. You would be better off to have remained ignorant.

124. *Parmenides:* A Greek philosopher born at Elea in Italy (ca. 513 B.C.), Parmenides was the founder of the Eleatic school of philosophy in which he was succeeded by Zeno.

125. *Bryson . . . Melissus:* Bryson, a Greek philosopher, is mentioned by Aristotle as having attempted to square the circle by using dishonest nongeometrical methods. Melissus, a philosopher of Samos, was a follower of Parmenides.

127. *Sabellius . . . Arius:* Sabellius, a third-century heretic, rejected the doctrine of the Trinity, holding instead that the individual terms Father, Son, and Holy Spirit were simply alternate names for the One God. Arius, responsible for the Arian heresy, believed the Father and Son were not of "one substance." The Son was the first created being, inferior to the Father, and the Holy Spirit was created by the power of the Son. The followers of the Arian heresy brought about major controversies within the Church.

128–29. *all those fools:* Instead of properly reflecting the truths from Scripture, these men distorted truth in the same way that the blade of a sword will reflect a distorted image because it is somewhat curved. The image is a forceful one, since the word "swordblades" (129) carries overtones of heretical violence.

130–42

The diverse images of the corn field, the brier, the ship, and the thief all serve to emphasize the idea that mortal man is easily deceived by the appearance of things and, worse, that in his presumption man takes what he sees to be true, never questioning his own judgment. Man must realize that the only true and perfect vision is that possessed by the Divine Being.

139–41. *No Mr. or Miss Know-It-All should think:* In the Italian, verse 139 reads "Non creda donna Berta o ser Martino." Berta and Martino were very common feminine and masculine names at that time. Dante adds *donna* (Lady or Miss) to Berta and *ser* (Sir or Mister) to Martino, giving the verse a certain flavor of sarcastic pretentiousness. In the background to this warning lies the controversy on earth over the question of Solomon's salvation. Men should not presume to judge as God judges (see note to *Par.* X, 111).

CANTO XIV

CONCENTRIC RINGS OPEN this canto as well, this time with
an image of water rippling in a round container, as Beatrice
speaks from the center of the rings of lights. The Pilgrim has
another question for these lights, and Beatrice expresses it for
him: will the brilliant light of these souls remain with them after
the resurrection of the body and, if so, how will their reacquired
sight resist such splendor? The souls dance and sing with delight
at being able to answer the Pilgrim's question. Then from the
inner circle Solomon reassures the Pilgrim that the light sur-
rounding them will last eternally and always in proportion to the
vision they have of God. And since they will be more perfect
once they have their bodies back, their vision will be strong
enough to support their great brilliance. Suddenly a third ring of
bright lights begins to surround the other two concentric rings,
but their intensity is too much for the eyes of the Pilgrim. Then,
looking into Beatrice's eyes, he finds himself rising, without
realizing it, to the next sphere. Because of the red glow of this
planet he knows that he is on Mars. Two enormous bands of light
form, upon which for a brief moment flashes the image of Christ,
and within the transparent arms of this cross specks of souls, like
dust in shafts of light, move in all directions as a hymn is sung
in praise of Christ. Never before, he says, has the Pilgrim been
so overwhelmed by something as beautiful as this, and then he
apologizes for making this remark since, he admits, he has yet to
gaze into his lady's eyes since arriving here!

The water in a round container moves
　　center to rim rippling or rim to center,
　　when struck first from within, then from without:　　　3

this image suddenly occurred to me
　　the moment that the glorious, living light
　　of Thomas had concluded its remarks　　　6

because of the resemblance that was born
　　between his flow of words and Beatrice's,
　　she being moved to speak once he had spoken:　　　9

"This man, though he cannot express his need,
and has not even thought the thought as yet,
must dig the roots of yet another truth.   *12*

Explain to him about the radiance
with which your substance blooms. Will it remain
eternally, just as it shines forth now?   *15*

And if it does remain, explain to him
how, once your sight has been restored, you can
endure the brilliance of each other's form."   *18*

As partners in a dance whirl in their reel,
caught in a sudden surge of joy, will often
quicken their steps and raise their voices high,   *21*

so at her eager and devout request
the holy circles showed new happiness
through their miraculous music and their dance.   *24*

Those who regret that we die here on earth
to live above, have never known the freshening
downpour of God's eternal grace up here.   *27*

That One and Two and Three which never ends
and ever reigns in Three and Two and One,
uncircumscribed and circumscribing all,   *30*

three separate times was sung by all those spirits,
and unbelievably melodious
it sounded—Heaven's consummate reward.   *33*

Then, from the brightest of the lights I heard
come from the inner round a modest tone
as was the angel's voice that Mary heard: *36*

"Long as the joyous feast of Paradise
shall last," it said, "so long our burning love
shall clothe us in this radiance you see.   *39*

Our brilliance is in ratio to our love,
our ardor to our vision, and our vision
to the degree of grace vouchsafed to us.   *2*

When our flesh, sanctified and glorious
shall clothe our souls once more, our person then
will be more pleasing since it is complete;   *45*

wherefore, the light, generously bestowed
   on us by the Supreme Good, is increased—
   the light of glory that shows Him to us.   48

It follows, then, that vision must increase,
   as must the ardor kindled by the vision,
   as must the radiance the ardor gives.   51

But as a coal burns white in its own fire
   whose inner glow outshines its outer flame
   so that its form is clearly visible,   54

so this effulgence that contains us now
   will be surpassed in brilliance by the flesh
   that for so long has lain beneath the ground;   57

nor will such light be difficult to bear,
   the organs of our bodies will be strengthened
   and ready for whatever gives us joy."   60

So quick and eager to cry out "Amen!"
   were both those choirs that it was very clear
   how much they yearned to have their bodies back—   63

not for themselves as much as for their mothers,
   their fathers, and for all those they held dear
   before they turned into eternal flame.   66

And suddenly! around us was a light
   growing as bright as all the light it circled,
   like an horizon brightening with the dawn.   69

Just as at twilight all across the heavens
   new things appear—the faint appearances
   of what we see or what we seem to see,   72

so I began to see, it seemed, new shapes
   of spirits forming there, making a ring
   around the other two circumferences.   75

Oh sparks of truth that are the Holy Spirit!
   How quick, how bright the brilliance of that light
   grew for my eyes, now overwhelmed by glory!   78

But Beatrice showed herself to me
   smiling so radiantly, it must be left
   among those sights the mind cannot retrace.   81

It gave me strength to raise my eyes again,
　　and looking up I saw myself translated,
　　alone with her to more exalted bliss.　　　　　　*84*

I was aware of having risen higher
　　because I saw the star's candescent smile
　　glow redder than it ever had before.　　　　　　*87*

Then in the language common to all men,
　　with all my heart, I made an offering
　　unto the Lord befitting His fresh grace.　　　　　*90*

Nor had the sacrifice within my breast
　　ceased burning when I knew my prayer of thanks
　　had been accepted, and propitiously,　　　　　　*93*

for with such mighty sheen, such ruby glow,
　　within twin rays, such splendor came to me,
　　I cried: "O Helios, who adorns them so!"　　　　*96*

Just as the Milky Way adorned with stars,
　　some large, some small, gleams white between the Poles,
　　baffling the wisest of astrologers,　　　　　　　*99*

so, constellated in the depths of Mars,
　　these rays of light crossed in the holy sign
　　which quadrants make when joining in a circle;　*102*

but here my memory defeats my art:
　　I see that cross as it flames forth with Christ,
　　yet cannot find the words that will describe it.　*105*

But who takes up his cross and follows Christ
　　will pardon me for what I leave unsaid
　　beholding Heaven's whiteness glow with Christ.　*108*

From top to base, across from arm to arm
　　bright lights were moving, sparkling brilliantly
　　as they would meet and pass each other's glow.　*111*

So, here on earth, along a shaft of light
　　that sometimes streaks the shade that men devise
　　by means of arts and crafts for their protection,　*114*

our eyes see particles of matter move
　　straight or aslant, some swift, some floating slow—
　　an ever-changing scene of shapes and patterns.　*117*

And as the viol and harp, their many strings
    tuned into harmony, will ring out sweetly
    even for the one who does not catch the tune,   120

so from the spread of lights along the cross
    there gathered in the air a melody
    that held me in a trance, though I could not   123

tell what the hymn was—only that it sang
    of highest praise: I heard "Arise" and "Conquer"
    as one who hears but does not understand.   126

This music raised my soul to heights of love:
    until that moment nothing had existed
    that ever bound my soul in such sweet chains—   129

but this, perhaps, may seem too rash a statement,
    forgetting, as it were, those lovely eyes,
    the source of bliss in which my gaze finds rest,   132

but since those vivid crowning beauties grow
    in strength the higher they ascend, and since
    I had not turned to look at them as yet,   135

one must excuse me for what I accuse
    myself of to excuse myself, and see
    the truth: that sacred joy is not excluded,   138

since it grows in perfection as we rise.

NOTES

1 – 3. *The water in a round container moves:* Bearing in mind that
Dante and Beatrice stand in the center of the two circles of souls,
we see here the movement of water in a round container compared
to the direction and flow of the sound waves of the voices of
Thomas Aquinas (from rim to center) and Beatrice (center to
rim). For a similar analogy see Boethius' *De musica,* I, 14.

10 – 18

Beatrice addresses the souls, requesting that someone reply
to the as-yet unformed question in Dante's mind: "Will the light
which surrounds these souls be there forever, even after the res-
urrection of the body, and, since the body will be one day reu-
nited to the soul, how will the eyes of each physical body be able

to endure the splendor of the other's appearance?" The first part of the question was frequently debated in Dante's day. Dante was in accord with Aquinas (see *Summa theol.* III, Suppl., q.85, a. 1 – 3).

12. *must dig the roots of yet another truth:* Actually, it is a matter of getting to the bottom of two truths that Dante has in mind (see note 10 – 18).

19 – 24. *As partners in a dance:* The physical and spiritual attitudes of the souls are once again conveyed by a dance image. (See *Par.* X, 79 – 81; also *Par.* XII, 22.)

25 – 27. *Those who regret that we die here on earth:* It must be remembered that Dante the narrator is speaking in these verses (he began in verse 19 and will go on uninterrupted until the end of verse 36) from his vantage point "here on earth" about the place where his Pilgrim is "up here" (27).

28 – 31. *That One and Two and Three:* God, the dual nature of Christ, three Persons in one Trinity. This tercet offers another fine example of Dante's use of language to imitate action. These verses in the original Italian read:

Quell' uno e due e tre che sempre vive,
  e regna sempre in tre e 'n due e 'n uno,
    non circunscritto, e tutto circunscrive,

tre volte era cantato da ciascuno . . .

34. *the brightest of the lights:* This is the light of Solomon (see *Par.* X, 109 – 14), author of the Canticle of Canticles, which celebrates the union of the human and the divine as well as the resurrection of the body.

35. *a modest tone:* The stress is on the humility with which King Solomon will speak, aware that he is in the presence of great theologians.

36. *the angel's voice:* That of the angel Gabriel (see Luke 1:28).

40 – 42. *Our brilliance is in ratio:* The souls shine in proportion to the strength of their love, which in turn depends upon the power of their understanding. Knowledge exists according to the amount of grace bestowed upon each—a factor wholly dependent upon God. According to Christian doctrine, vision comes first, then love, and finally radiance. (See also *Par.* XXVIII, 106 – 11.)

45. *will be more pleasing since it is complete:* Man is "more pleasing" (to himself and to God) when, after the Last Judgment, his body is reunited with his soul, for then he is complete and as perfect as when God created him. The idea of completeness as "more perfect" derives from Aristotle and was adapted to Christian theology by St. Thomas. (See also *Inf.* VI, 103–108.)

49–51. *It follows, then, that vision must increase:* Here, the actual sequence (vision, love, radiance) is clearly expressed (cf. above, note 40–42). And because of this increase of grace, it follows that the vision of God increases too.

52–57. *But as a coal burns white in its own fire:* The glowing coal, then, is like the resplendent body once it is resurrected; the flame surrounding the coal is like the brilliance of the souls in Heaven, burning with love. The greater light will be the one inside (the body) the brilliance surrounding it (the soul).

63–66. *how much they yearned to have their bodies back:* One aspect of the doctrine of bodily resurrection, as discussed by medieval theologians, was that the soul, once reunited with the flesh, became more personal and individual. In this state of completeness, the soul appreciates in eternity the strength of its old earthly, human ties. This does not, obviously, indicate a yearning on the part of the soul to return to mortal life; it suggests, rather, the joyful anticipation of the day when the souls and their loved ones (mothers and fathers and children) will, all together, enjoy the perfection bestowed after the Last Judgment.

73–76. *new shapes . . . the Holy Spirit:* A third circle consisting of a multitude of lights, representing, perhaps, the remaining blessed souls in this sphere (or minor theologians?) forms itself around those two concentric rings already present. The number and identity of the spirits in this circle, as well as its significance, are much disputed by the critics. Dante's exclamation (76) does suggest, however, some association of this ring with the Holy Spirit. Perhaps this association is meant simply to complete, on a symbolic level, the theme of the Trinity, which began in Canto X at Dante's emergence into the heaven of the sun. Dronke (p. 11) views this third circle as representing a new age, connecting it with Joachim's idea of a third or a future *status mundi* of the Holy Spirit.

83–87. *translated . . . redder than it ever had before:* Dante and

Beatrice are now in the fifth sphere, that of Mars. Then as now known for its red appearance (see *Conv.* II xiii, 21), Mars is the sphere of the warriors who fought in defense of the Faith. Dante says that Mars appears even redder now than it was before because of the arrival therein of Beatrice.

88–90. *Then in the language common to all men:* This is the unspoken language of the heart, expressing devotion and gratitude through silent prayer and thanksgiving. It is "the language common to all men" because, since it exists only in the minds and hearts of men, no verbal or specific language is necessary.

95. *within twin rays:* This is a reference to the two bands of light which intersect to form the enormous cross of light referred to in verses 101–102 in which the souls of the warrior saints will appear.

96. *Helios:* God. The word combines the connotations of the Greek *helios* (Sun) and the Hebrew *Ely* (God). The sun is a common symbol for God in Christian thought (see *Conv.* III, xii, 7).

97–102. *Just as the Milky Way:* The precise composition of the Milky Way was a disputed subject. Dante correctly assumed it to be composed of stars. See *Convivio* (II, xiv, 5–8) for his discussion of the various theories on the subject, which he found in Albertus Magnus (*De meteoris* I. ii. 2–5). Here he compares the clustering of those white stars to the red spirits of Mars which gather now to form a Greek cross—two diameters of one circle intersecting at right angles.

104–108. *Christ . . . Christ . . . Christ:* Dante, out of respect for the name of Christ, never rhymes it with any other word except itself. Three times in the *Paradise* (XIV, 104–108; XIX, 104–108; XXXII, 83–87) Dante makes the word Christ rhyme with itself, and at exactly the same point or verse in each of the three cantos.

Verses 106–108 may be understood in two ways: (1) the true Christian will forgive the Poet for what he leaves unsaid, because while he was watching Christ flash forth upon that cross he was so bewildered by the spectacle, he could not express himself, or (2) that whoever follows Christ on earth and reaches Heaven to see this spectacle will certainly forgive him (Dante the Poet) for not describing it, because he will see for himself that it is beyond description. Verse 106 is a paraphrase of Matthew 10:38.

109−11. *From top to base, across from arm to arm:* The spirits move along the arms of the cross sparkling with greater light as they meet or pass each other.

112−17

The spirits move within the form of the cross in the same way that specks of dust are seen to float in a shaft of light streaking down through some opening in a shaded area. They change their appearance as they move in all different directions. It is interesting to note that the poet employs a rather common-place image to give his reader a picture of such glorious warriors of the Faith. While the mention of the cross recalls, albeit vaguely, medieval iconography, in this passage there is no strong visual image of Christ.

113−14. *the shade that men devise:* That is, the many and ingenious means men have invented to protect themselves from the light of the sun, such as blinds, curtains, etc.

118−26

This is the first substantial musical image in the *Paradise.* It is probably placed here as a reminder to the reader of the affinity that this planet has with music, as Dante confirms in his *Convivio.* In this sphere, the heaven of Mars, the symbol of Christ will dominate. And the words "Arise" and "Conquer" of the hymn the Pilgrim hears may apply to Christ as well as to the Old Crusader (whom we are about to meet in the next canto) who died for it, and also to the mission of Dante the Poet. For more details see Bergin (pp. 143−66).

118. *And as the viol and harp:* The musical instrument that Dante calls a viol—*giga*—is difficult to define; however, it was probably similar to the lyre. From the verses that follow we can be certain that it consisted of more than one string (see *E.D.,* pp. 159−60). The harp (*arpa*) was probably much like the instrument of today.

124−26. *only that it sang:* The song Dante hears is suggestive of Christ's victory over sin and death. It is a triumphal hymn, even though the precise nature of the song is unclear. See also *Par.* XVIII, note 49−51, and Momigliano (pp. 673−74), who discusses these verses in connection with the next three cantos.

130–32. *this, perhaps, may seem too rash a statement:* Dante suggests he may be overhasty in claiming that the song he hears gives him greater pleasure than anything he has previously experienced, because he has not yet had the pleasure of gazing into the eyes of his lady since reaching this new sphere of Mars.

133. *those vivid crowning beauties:* Beatrice's eyes, which increase in brilliance as she and the Pilgrim rise from one heaven to the next. They are referred to in the original as *i vivi suggelli*, literally living seals. Many commentators see these words not as a reference to Beatrice's eyes but rather to the spheres through which the Pilgrim and his guide have risen thus far. See Sayers (p. 185).

136–39. *one must excuse me . . . as we rise:* these verses in the original read:

escusar puommi di quel ch'io m'accuso
   per escusarmi, e vedermi dir vero,
   ché 'l piacer santo non è qui dischiuso,

perché si fa, montando, più sincero.

With a rather complicated verbal play with *p* and *o* sounds and the coupling and doubling of these sounds, the Pilgrim accuses himself of becoming so taken with the song of those spirits that he has forgotten about Beatrice's eyes. But he accuses himself in order to excuse, or explain, that this is not true. He has not forgotten her; the fact is, he has not yet looked upon her in this sphere. Therefore the pleasure of seeing her eyes is not to be taken as of less account than the delight derived from the song. Indeed, that particular pleasure grows greater as her eyes glow brighter as she and the Pilgrim rise from sphere to sphere.

The playing off of one sound or word against another in these verses that close the canto seems to recall the opening of this canto, and the sound waves of concentric circles of water, which the poet compares to his own mind as it perceives the similarities between what St. Thomas and Beatrice have to say. We must also keep in mind verses 28–31 of this canto in which numbers are played off each other (see note 28–31), for this is part of the same pattern.

CANTO XV

As THE SOULS of the cross conclude their hymn, the Pilgrim perceives what he imagines to be a star falling from the right arm of the cross down to its base without leaving the arms of the cross. Then this light glowing like fire behind alabaster addresses him in Latin. At first the Pilgrim has difficulty comprehending the soul's words, but gradually the language descends to his level of understanding. The light says that he understands why the Pilgrim does not ask him who he is or why he appears so joyful to him, because he rightly believes that souls in Paradise know the thoughts of mortals through the mirror of God's love, but he asks the Pilgrim to be bold and speak just the same, since his answer is already decreed. With the approval of Beatrice he asks the light its name. The soul replies that he is Dante's great-great-grandfather Cacciaguida and that Dante's great-grandfather is on the first terrace of the mountain of Purgatory. He exhorts Dante to pray for his great-grandfather and then begins a description of the Florence of his day, his birth, his marriage to a woman of the Alighieri line, and his death during the crusade led by Conrad.

The magnanimity in which true love
    always resolves itself (as does that other,
    self-seeking love into iniquity)   3

silenced the notes of that sweet-sounding harp
    and hushed the music of those holy strings
    tuned tight or loose by Heaven's hand itself.   6

How could such beings be deaf to righteous prayers,
    those beings who to encourage my desire
    to beg of them fell silent, all of them?   9

And right it is that he forever mourn
    who out of love for what does not endure
    loses that other love eternally.   12

As now and then through calm and cloudless skies
    a sudden streak of fire cuts the dark,
    catching the eye that watches listlessly,   15

as if a star were changing places there
   (except that from the place where it flared up
   no star is missing, and the blaze dies down),   18

so, from the right arm of the cross a star
   belonging to that brilliant constellation
   sped to the center, then, down to the foot,   21

and as it coursed along the radial lines,
   this gem contained within its setting seemed
   like fire behind an alabaster screen.   24

With like affection did Anchises' shade
   rush forth, if we may trust our greatest Muse,
   when in Elysium he beheld his son.   27

"O sanguis meus, o superinfusa
   gratïa Deï, sicut tibi, cui
   bis unquam celi ianüa reclusa?"   30

So spoke that brilliance, and I stared at him.
   Then I turned round to see my lady's face;
   I stood amazed between the two of them,   33

for such a smile was glowing in her eyes,
   it seemed that with my own I touched the depths
   of my beatitude, my paradise.   36

And then this light of joy to eye and ear
   began to add to his first words such things
   I could not grasp, his speech was so profound.   39

It did not hide its thought deliberately;
   there was no other choice: its argument
   soared far beyond the target of man's mind.   42

Then once the bow of his affection had
   released its love, allowing what he said
   to hit the mark of human intellect,   45

the first words that I comprehended were:
   "Blessèd be Thou, Three Persons in One Being,
   Who showest such great favor to my seed!"   48

Then he went on: "A long-felt, welcome thirst
   born from perusal of that mighty book
   whose black and white will never altered be,   51

you have assuaged, my son, within this flame
  from which I speak to you, thanks be to her
  who gave you wings to make this lofty flight.   54

Since you believe your thought flows forth to me
  from Primal thought, as five and six from one,
  if understood, ray forth from unity,   57

therefore, you do not ask me who I am
  or why I show more joy in seeing you
  than any other in this joyful throng.   60

What you believe is right. We in this life,
  greatest or least alike, gaze in that Mirror
  where thoughts are thought before they are expressed.   63

Yet, that the Sacred Love in which I gaze
  eternally on God, and which creates
  sweet thirstiness in me, be best fulfilled,   66

let your own voice, confident, bold, and joyous,
  express your will, express your heart's desire—
  my answer has already been decreed."   69

I turned to Beatrice who had heard
  my words before I spoke, and with her smile
  she gave strength to the wings of my desire.   72

Then I began: "Love and intelligence
  achieved their equipoise in each of you
  once you saw plain the First Equality,   75

because the sun that warmed and lighted you
  with heat and light is poised so perfectly
  that all comparisons fall short of it.   78

But utterance and feeling among mortals
  for reasons which are evident to you,
  have different feathers making up their wings.   81

I, too, as man feel this disparity
  deeply, so only with my heart can I
  give thanks for your paternal welcome here.   84

I beg of you, rich topaz, living gem
  within the setting of this precious jewel,
  to satisfy my wish to know your name."   87

"Branch of my tree, the mere expectancy
   of whose arrival here gave me delight,
   I was your root"—this was his preface, then   *90*

he said: "He after whom your family
   was named, whose soul a hundred years and more
   still circles the first terrace of the Mount,   *93*

father of your grandfather, was my son.
   And meet it were that you offer your prayers
   to shorten the long sentence of his weight.   *96*

Florence, enclosed within her ancient walls
   from which she still hears terce and nones ring out,
   once lived in peace, a pure and temperate town: *99*

no necklace or tiara did she wear,
   no lavish gowns or fancy belts that were
   more striking than the woman they adorned.   *102*

In those days fathers had no cause to fear
   a daughter's birth: the marriageable age
   was not too low, the dowry not too high.   *105*

Houses too large to live in were not built,
   and Sardanapalus had not yet come
   to show to what use bedrooms can be put.   *108*

Not yet had your Uccellatoi surpassed
   Rome's Montemalo, which in its ascent
   being surpassed, will be so in its fall.   *111*

Bellincion Berti I have seen walk by
   belted in leather and bone, and his good wife
   come from her mirror with unpainted face;   *114*

de' Nerli I have seen, del Vecchio too,
   content to wear plain leather, and their wives
   to handle flax and spindle all day long.   *117*

O happy wives! Each one of them was sure
   of her last resting place—none of them yet
   lay lonely in her bed because of France.   *120*

One watching tenderly above the cradle,
   soothing her infant in that idiom
   which all new parents love to use at first;   *123*

another, working at her spinning-wheel
  surrounded by her children, would tell tales
  about the Trojans, Rome, and Fiesole.   126

A Lapo Salterello, a Cianghella
  would have amazed them then as much as now
  a Cincinnatus or Cornelia would.   129

To this serene, this lovely state of being
  within this comity of citizens,
  joined in good faith, this dwelling-place so sweet,   132

Mary, besought by pains of birth, gave me;
  and then within your ancient Baptistry
  a Christian I became, and Cacciaguida.   135

Eliseo and Moronto were my brothers;
  my wife came from the valley of the Po
  and brought with her the surname that you bear.   138

And then I served Conrad the Emperor
  who later dubbed me knight among his host,
  so pleased was he by all my gallant deeds.   141

Along with him I fought against the evil
  of that false faith whose followers usurp—
  only because your Shepherds sin—your rights.   144

There the vile Saracen delivered me
  from the entanglements of your vain world,
  the love of which corrupts so many souls—   147

from martyrdom I came to this, my peace."

NOTES

1 – 3. *The magnanimity in which true love:* This solemn opening,
while it sets the tone that will dominate the entire canto, also
establishes one of its main structural features: the juxtaposition
of opposites, in particular that of the Florence of old as opposed
to the Florence of Dante's day—the main theme of this and much
of the following two cantos. The reader would do well to keep in
mind that with Cantos XV, XVI, and XVII we are at the center
of the *Paradise*'s thirty-three cantos, and the "center" for Dante is
always a position of importance and one reserved for significant

matters. Also worth noting is the fact that the Pilgrim and his guide have arrived at the central heaven: the sphere of Mars is the fifth of the moving heavens. As we shall soon see, it is here in these central cantos of the *Paradise* that the Poet is told of his great mission, and it is here that the Pilgrim and Poet become one.

4 – 6. *that sweet-sounding harp:* The cross of souls is compared to a harp, the individual spirits being the strings of the instrument which God's hand plays. This is a continuation of the harp and viol image, the only substantial musical one so far in the *Paradise*, introduced toward the close of the preceding canto (see *Par.* XIV, 118 – 26).

7 – 12. *How could such beings:* These two tercets reflect the theme of the opening tercet in which true love and self-serving love are juxtaposed. Verses 7 – 9 suggest the "magnanimity" of the spirits who stop their music and singing in order to please Dante. Following this example of true love, Dante depicts one who is a self-lover (10 – 12), who neglects true love for the impermanent, material good. It is right that this lover should suffer the punishment of mourning forever, for his love resolves itself in iniquity.

16. *a star were changing places there:* A meteor or "falling star." In Dante's time, meteors were thought to be the result of dry vapors that rose high enough above the earth to catch fire before falling back down.

19 – 21. *from the right arm of the cross:* Like a meteor blaze, one of the spirits shoots across the right arm of the cross and down to the foot of it where Dante stands.

22. *radial lines:* The two radial lines are those that divide a circle into quadrants, which means that the cross is a Greek cross, the four arms of which are of equal length.

24. *like fire behind an alabaster screen:* A flame behind an alabaster screen would appear as an intense light amidst diffused light. This spirit, then, shines more brilliantly than the light surrounding it.

25 – 27. *With like affection did Anchises' shade:* Anchises, the father of Aeneas, joyously greeted his son when Aeneas visited the Elysian Fields. (See *Aen.* VI, 684 – 88.) The comparison pre-

pares us for the familial relationship that exists between Dante and the soul who has approached him. The reference to "our greatest Muse" is to Virgil, who is the inspiration for other poets. And once again the association between Dante and Aeneas is reinforced, and especially in light of what is said (in Latin) in the following tercet.

28–30. *"O sanguis meus . . . ianüa reclusa?":* "O blood of mine, O grace of God. To whom, as to thee, was heaven's gate ever twice opened?" Once again, as in Canto X, 87, there is an assurance of Dante's future salvation. The soul's use of Latin lends an air of solemnity to his greeting; the words "sanguis meus" are also those used by Anchises in the *Aeneid* (VI, 835): "Proice tela manu, sanguis meus" (cast from thy hand the sword, thou blood of mine). And this is the first and only time in the *Comedy* that a character will greet the Pilgrim in Latin. Martinelli associates the speaker of this tercet with Christ and in terms of a Christian oracle. In any case, there is no doubt that Dante the Poet is about to introduce to his Pilgrim a character of major importance.

32. *Then I turned round to see my lady's face:* Up to this point in the heaven of Mars Dante has not looked at Beatrice.

50–53. *that mighty book / whose black and white will never altered be:* In the book of the future that can never be changed this spirit had learned of Dante's journey and grew eager to see him. Now, upon Dante's arrival, the spirit's waiting has been rewarded.

The speaker's language here is very dignified and rather archaic; hence my translation of verse 51, for example: "whose black and white will never altered be."

54. *who gave you wings:* As his guide, Beatrice in her role of Revelation gives Dante the ability to ascend. (See also *Par.* XXV, 49–50.)

55–57. *Since you believe your thought:* Dante's thoughts, as all things, are reflected in God; in the same way, numbers have their source in unity.

61–69. *What you believe is right:* Dante is correct in believing that the soul knows his thought, for all gaze at God and in seeing God they see and know everything; therefore there is no necessity to speak, though there is pleasure in hearing the voice. This soul already knows what Dante will say and, in fact, he has his answer ready (69); nevertheless he insists on hearing the sound of Dante's voice.

70–72. *who had heard / my words before I spoke:* Beatrice already knows that the Pilgrim is going to ask her for her permission to speak, and with her smile she grants it.

73–78. *"Love and intelligence:* Once the soul sees God, its intelligence or will becomes equal to its love or desire and therefore whatever is willed is obtained. God, in whom all qualities are equally balanced, bestows this light (intellect) and heat (desire) in equal measures to make this perfection possible. It would seem, as Momigliano (p. 679) implies, that the Pilgrim here is attempting to match the elevated style and tone of his ancestor who has just addressed him.

79–84

Verse 79 in the Italian reads: "Ma voglia e argomento ne' mortali." *Voglia* I take to mean "feeling" and *argomento* the capacity to argue or discuss, thus "utterance." These words vaguely correspond to the words "Love and intelligence" of verse 73. The general sense of the passage is that while the Blest have no imbalance in their faculties ("Love and intelligence"), mortals, who also have the faculties that allow them to feel and to react, may have the desire to do something but not the ability to carry it through—in Dante's case, he has the desire to express his feelings to the person who has addressed him, but cannot find the proper words.

80. *for reasons which are evident to you:* Since the Blest see everything in God, these reasons are clear to them.

81. *have different feathers making up their wings:* That is to say, the capacity to express oneself has fewer feathers in its wings than does the actual feeling—the feeling is stronger than the ability to express it.

85. *rich topaz:* a yellow gem that turns red (the color of love) when exposed to high heat.

86. *the setting:* The metaphor is a continuation of that in verse 23 and refers to the cross of spirits.

90. *I was your root":* This is Dante's great-great-grandfather. All that is definitely known of him comes from Dante's account

in these cantos. It is not until verse 135 that he identifies himself as Cacciaguida.

91—92. *"He after whom your family / was named:* Alighiero, Dante's great-grandfather, was the first member of the family to bear that name (as his Christian name).

93. *the first terrace of the Mount:* The circle of Pride on the Mountain of Purgatory. The reason for this placement is unknown; however, the sin of Pride does seem to run in Dante's family. Earlier (*Purg.* XIII, 136—38) he made it quite clear that he, too, was guilty of this sin.

96. *to shorten the long sentence of his weight:* His "sentence" refers to the punishment in Purgatory of carrying a large stone on his back.

98. *terce and nones:* Near the old walls of the city stood the abbey of Badia whose bells, even in Dante's day, rang the canonical hours. Terce is the third hour (9 A.M.) and nones is the ninth (3 P.M.).

100—105. *no necklace or tiara did she wear:* The city of Florence once fostered a way of life without ostentation or luxury; hers was the beauty of simplicity, like that of an unadorned lady. In addition, the marriage age for young women was not unduly low, nor were fathers burdened with excessive dowries.

107—108. *Sardanapalus:* The last king of Assyria, who was famous for his wantonness and effeminacy.

109—11. *Not yet had your Uccellatoi surpassed:* Approaching Florence from Bologna, the traveller first views the city from Mount Uccellatoio; one approaching Rome from the north first sees that city from Montemalo. At the time of which Cacciaguida speaks, Florence had not yet surpassed the pride and splendor of Rome; later she would outdo Rome both in her magnificence and her decline.

112. *Bellincion Berti:* A distinguished Florentine citizen and member of the honorable Ravignani family, he lived in the late twelfth century and was father of the "good Gualdrada" (see *Inf.* XVI, 37).

115. *de' Nerli . . . del Vecchio:* The Nerli were a noble Florentine

family which received knighthood from the Marquis Hugh of Brandenburg, "the great Baron" (*Par.* XVI, 128).

The del Vecchio family, or "Vecchietti," were another ancient Florentine family. Being Guelphs, the family was expelled from Florence in 1248, and in 1260 they went into exile after the Ghibelline victory at the Battle of Montaperti (see Villani, v–viii).

118–20. *O happy wives:* In the past, Florentine women did not live in fear of exile, or of being deserted by husbands trading in France.

122–23. *that idiom:* Baby talk.

126. *about the Trojans, Rome, and Fiesole:* These were stories of the founding of Rome by the Trojans and of the establishment of Fiesole and then Florence by the Romans.

127–29. *A Lapo Salterello, a Cianghella . . . a Cincinnatus or Cornelia:* Cianghella, a contemporary of Dante, was a Florentine woman of questionable reputation and loose and profligate life style. Lapo Salterello, a prominent Florentine citizen belonging to the Bianchi faction, was a corrupt lawyer and judge. He adhered to the same party as Dante and in fact served in the office of prior of Florence during the two-month period preceding Dante's priorate. In the banishment decree that included Dante's name, his was listed as well.

In the period of the Roman republic Cincinnatus was called from the plough to be dictator, during which time he conquered the Aequians (458 B.C.). Following this victory, he returned to his farm (see *Par.* VI, 46). Cornelia, daughter of the elder Scipio Africanus, was mother of Tiberius and Gaius Gracchi, Roman tribunes who died attempting to preserve the republic. Dante placed her in Limbo among other noble souls of antiquity (*Inf.* IV, 128).

What the tercet is saying is that the corrupt Lapo Salterello and the dissolute Cianghella would have astonished the pious Florentines of old in the same way that a noble Cincinnatus or Cornelia would surprise the corrupt Florentines of the present.

130–32. *To this serene . . . so sweet:* In this tercet which contains a good dose of adjectives conveying an atmosphere of tranquility, faithfulness, goodness, Cacciaguida (who will reveal his identity in the next tercet (135) summarizes his description of Florence in his day.

133. *Mary, besought by pains of birth:* Women in labor called upon the Virgin Mary for the safe delivery of the child.

136. *Eliseo and Moronto:* Nothing at all is known about Cacciaguida's brothers.

137. *my wife came from the valley of the Po:* Four cities have been nominated for the privilege of being the birthplace of Dante's great-great-grandmother: Bologna, Verona, Parma, and Ferrara. Dante's thirteenth-century commentators seem to favor the city of Ferrara because of the documented existence there of an Aldighieri family.

138. *and brought with her the surname that you bear:* Cacciaguida married Alighiera degli Alighieri, and they named their son Alighiero (the first), and the descendants of this son took his Christian name for their surname.

139. *Conrad the Emperor:* Conrad III (1093–1152) was the son of Frederick, the Duke of Swabia. Having become the Duke of Franconia, he fought Lothair II, Duke of Saxony. As a result, with the support of Lothair's adversaries he was crowned King of Saxony in 1128 in Milan and was recognized as emperor thereafter. He, along with Louis VII of France, undertook the Second Crusade.

142–44. *I fought against the evil:* The Mohammedans, in their occupation of the Holy Land, usurp the rights of Christians to that land. "Your Shepherds sin" refers to the fact that the popes were indifferent to the recapture of the area.

145. *There the vile Saracen delivered me:* "There" refers to the Holy Land, where Cacciaguida was killed during the Second Crusade.

148. *from martyrdom I came to this, my peace":* Those who died on crusade were considered martyrs whose souls ascended directly to Heaven.

The canto closes most appropriately with the word "peace," the word that best describes the Florence of Cacciaguida's day which Dante, through his illustrious ancestor, yearns to see again.

CANTO XVI

THE PILGRIM TELLS the reader that he can no longer wonder at those on earth who glory in their family lineage, since he himself in Paradise, where wills are perfect, gloried in it too. When Cacciaguida finishes speaking, Dante addresses him with the formal "you" (*voi* in Italian), at which Beatrice smiles. At Dante's request, Cacciaguida gives an account of the family history and goes on to describe his Florence, in contrast to the corrupt Florence of Dante's time, discoursing on the changing fortunes of the city and her old families and lamenting the loss of the peace and glory of the earlier period.

Ah, trivial thing, our pride in noble blood!
　　That you can make men glory in you here
　　on earth where our affections are weak-willed,　　　　3

will never again amaze me, for up there
　　where appetite is always in the right,
　　in Heaven itself, I gloried in my blood!　　　　　　6

Nobility, a mantle quick to shrink!
　　Unless we add to it from day to day,
　　time with its shears will trim off more and more.　　9

I spoke again addressing him as "*voi*"
　　(a form the Romans were the first to use,
　　though now her children make less use of it),　　　12

and Beatrice, not too far from us,
　　smiling, reminded me of her who coughed
　　to caution Guinevere at her first sign　　　　　　15

of weakness. I began: "You are my sire.
　　You give me confidence to speak. You raise
　　my heart so high that I am more than I.　　　　　18

My soul is overflowing with the joy
　　that pours from many streams, and it rejoices
　　that it endures and does not burst inside.　　　　21

Tell me, then, cherished source from which I spring,
about your own forefathers, who they were;
what years made history when you were young?   24

Tell me about the sheepfold of St. John,
how large it was and who among the folk
were worthiest to hold the highest seats?"   27

As glowing coals in a quick breath of air
burst into flame, just so I saw that light
grow brighter when it heard my loving words,   30

and as his beauty grew before my eyes,
so, in a voice sweeter and more refined
(so different from our modern Florentine),   33

his light said: "From the day 'Ave' was said
to that on which my mother, now a saint,
heavy with child, gave birth to me, her son,   36

to its own Lion this fiery star returned
five hundred fifty times and thirty more
to be rekindled underneath his paw.   39

The house where I and all of mine were born
stands at the place the last ward is first reached
by all those running in your annual games.   42

About my forefathers, let this suffice,
for what their names were and from where they came
is better left unsaid than boasted of.   45

All those who lived at that time fit for arms
between Mars and the Baptist were no more
than just one fifth of those who live there now;   48

The population then, polluted now
by Campi, and Certaldo and Fighine,
was pure down to the humblest artisan.   51

Oh how much better it would be if they
were still your neighbors and your boundaries
Galluzzo and Trespiano as they were,   54

than have such folk within and bear the stench
of Aguglione's churl and him from Signa,
already with a sharp eye out for swindling!   57

If that group of the world's most despicable
    had not played a stepmother's role to Caesar,
    but been a loving mother to her son,   60

a certain nouveau-Florentine who trucks
    and trades would now be back in Semifonte
    where once his own grandfather begged his bread,   63

and Montemurlo would still have its Counts,
    the parish of Acone have its Cerchi,
    and Valdigreve still its Buondelmonti.   66

A mingled strain of men has always been
    the source of city decadence, as when
    men stuff their stomachs sick with food on food;   69

a bull gone blind is more likely to fall
    than a blind lamb; often a single sword
    will cut more efficaciously than five.   72

If you consider Luni and Urbisaglia,
    how they have perished, how Sinigaglia
    and Chiusi too now follow them to ruin,   75

you should not find it hard to understand
    or strange to hear that families dwindle out
    when even cities pass away in time.   78

All of your works must die, as you must too,
    but they conceal this fact since they endure
    a longer time, and your life is so short.   81

And as the turning of the lunar sphere
    covers and then uncovers ceaselessly
    the shore, so Fortune does with Florence now;   84

and so, you should not be surprised to hear
    me talk about the noble Florentines
    whose fame has disappeared, concealed by time.   87

I knew the Ughi and the Catellini,
    Greci, Filippi, Alberichi, Ormanni,
    illustrious citizens even in decline;   90

I also knew, as great as they were old,
    the families dell'Arca and Sannella,
    the Soldanieri, Ardinghi, and Bostichi.   93

Close to the gate now laden with the weight
    of unbelievable iniquity,
    a cargo that will soon submerge the ship,   96

once lived the Ravignani from whom came
    Guido the Count and all of those who took
    as theirs the noble Bellincione name.   99

The della Pressa were already versed
    in governing as one should, and Galigaio
    already had his hilt and pommel gilded.   102

Already great the pale of vair, the Galli,
    Sacchetti, Giuochi, Fifanti, and Barucci
    and those who blush now for the stave affair.   105

The stock from which sprang the Calfucci branch
    already had grown great, the Arrigucci,
    the Sizii occupied high seats of offices.   108

How great I saw them once who now are ruined
    by their own pride! And how those balls of gold
    shone bright as Florence flowered in great deeds!   111

Such were the fathers of those who today
    prolong some vacant office in the Church
    and grow fat sitting in consistory.   114

That insolent, presumptuous clan that plays
    the dragon to all those who flee, the lamb
    to anyone who shows his teeth—or purse—   117

was on the rise, though still of such low class
    that Ubertin Donato was not pleased
    when his father-in-law made him their kin.   120

By then, the Caponsacchi had come down
    from Fiesole to the marketplace; the Giudi
    and Infangati were good citizens.   123

Here is a fact incredible but true:
    one entered the small circle by a gate
    named for the della Pera family.   126

All those who bear the handsome quarterings
    of the great Baron Hugh whose name and worth
    are celebrated on Saint Thomas' Day,   129

received from him knighthood and privilege,
  though he who decks that coat of arms with fringe
  today has taken up the people's cause.   132

The Gualterrotti and the Importuni
  existed then; their Borgo would have been
  a quieter place had they been spared new neighbors.   135

The House that was the source of all your tears,
  whose just resentment was the death of you
  and put an end to all your joy of life,   138

was highly honored as were all its clan.
  O Buondelmonte, wrong you were to flee
  the nuptials at the promptings of another!   141

Many who now are sad would have been pleased
  if God had let the Ema drown you when
  you started for our city the first time.   144

How fitting for Florence to sacrifice
  a victim to the mutilated stone
  that guards her bridge to mark the end of peace!   147

With these and other men who ruled like them
  I saw a Florence prospering in peace
  with no cause, then, to grieve as she has now.   150

With families like these in charge I saw
  the glory and the justice of her people:
  never the lily on the staff reversed,   153

nor through dissension changed from white to red."

NOTES

1 – 9. *Ah, trivial thing, our pride in noble blood:* Dante's unashamedly contradictory introduction to this canto juxtaposes his detached, indeed scornful, view of "nobility of blood" as being both pathetic and transitory, with his personal pride in his own lineage. The canto itself, while recalling the temporary nature of fine family lines, does so with prideful nostalgia as Cacciaguida mourns the Florentine past, which he remembers as one dominated by proud and noble families which have since gone to ruin.

10 – 12. *addressing him as* "voi": The *voi* form (second person plural "you") indicates the honor with which Dante regards his ancestor. According to tradition, this form (*vos* in Latin) was first used to address important individuals during Julius Caesar's time. Besides Cacciaguida, the only other individuals addressed this way in the *Commedia* are Farinata and Cavalcante (*Inf.* X, 51 and 63), Brunetto Latini (*Inf.* XV, 80), Corrado Malaspina (*Purg.* VIII, 122), Pope Adrian V (*Purg.* XIX, 131), Guido Guinizelli (*Purg.* XXVI, 112), and Beatrice (until the end of the poem, when he shifts to the familiar *tu* form). Dante will also shift back to *tu* in addressing his noble ancestor in the next canto, and the reader will have no problem seeing why he does so.

13 – 15. *Beatrice . . . smiling, reminded me of her who coughed:* In the *Lancelot du Lac,* the book that played such an important role in the life and tragic death of Francesca da Rimini (see *Inf.* V, 127 – 38), the Dame de Malehaut, witnessing the first clandestine meeting of Guinevere and Lancelot, coughed when she heard their confessions of love as a warning to them that she was aware of their secret. Beatrice's smile, suggesting her knowledge of Dante's pride in his ancestry, makes him aware of his own weakness, perhaps. (Is her smile one of encouragement, disapproval, or warning? For the various opinions on this account see Aglianò, who points out that it cannot be taken as a rebuke because Dante has gone through the process of purgation, and cannot err in Paradise, and that Dante's misjudgments and misunderstandings of the workings of Paradise are often received by the Blest and Beatrice with smiles.)

It seems to me that the use of this image from Arthurian romance in which the Poet suggests the relationship Beatrice = Dame de Malehaut (the lady in waiting), Cacciaguida = Lancelot (the warrior-knight), and Dante = Guinevere—coming, as it does, immediately after his aside to the reader on the nobility of blood—is most appropriate. The fact that the reputation of Lancelot and Guinevere is threatened by their wrongdoing underscores what the Poet has just said (7 – 9): that nobility of blood can be modified by time or actions. Notice that the emphasis is on Guinevere. The other two are not named, only evoked. It is Guinevere and Dante who are at fault: the former revealed her illicit love for Lancelot with a kiss; the latter reveals his pride in his ancestry with the use of the formal *voi*.

16 – 18. *I began: "You are my sire:* The Pilgrim's tone is one of

affection and reverence; he addresses his forebear three times in this tercet with the formal *voi*.

19–20. *the joy / that pours from many streams:* That is, there are many reasons why the Pilgrim is so happy.

25. *the sheepfold of St. John:* The Florentines. St. John the Baptist is the patron saint of Florence.

32–33. *in a voice sweeter and more refined:* Cacciaguida, whose first words to Dante were in solemn Latin (*Par.* XV, 28–30), is now speaking the genteel vernacular of his own day, which the Poet wishes to distinguish from the Florentine spoken at the time of the Poem. Again, the stress is on the refinement and greatness of Cacciaguida's Florence as compared to the uncouth and corrupt city of Dante's time.

34–39. *the day 'Ave' was said:* From the time of the Annunciation (Luke 1:28) to the time of Cacciaguida's birth, the planet Mars had revolved 580 times, returning to its position in the constellation Leo. One revolution of Mars was estimated to take 687 days; by multiplying 580 by 687 and dividing by 365, we can calculate that Cacciaguida's birth year was 1091.

39. *to be rekindled underneath his paw:* Besides their astronomical relationship, Mars and Leo may also be related as symbols of courage.

40–42. *The house where I and all of mine were born:* The horse race, the *palio*, was run every year on St. John's Day—June 24—along the Corso, and at the beginning of the "last ward" or district (that of Porto San Piero) stood the house of the ancient Elisei family, from whom Cacciaguida probably was descended.

44–45. *from where they came / is better left unsaid:* To boast would be to display overweening pride, an impossibility in the heavenly spheres. Cacciaguida is content to let the family record speak for itself. (In addition, Dante probably knew no more about the family than what is actually disclosed in this passage.)

47–48. *between Mars and the Baptist:* These landmarks, the statue of Mars (on the north side of the Ponte Vecchio) and the Baptistry of St. John, mark the southern and northern boundaries, respectively, of the old city. Those able to bear arms ("fit for

arms," 46) during Cacciaguida's time (about 6,000) were equal
to one-fifth of the total Florentine population in 1300.

50. *by Campi, and Certaldo, and Fighine:* Small towns near
Florence whose inhabitants, according to Cacciaguida, polluted
the purity of Florentine blood by moving to the city.

54. *Galluzzo and Trespiano:* Galluzzo is an ancient Tuscan vil-
lage two miles south of Florence on the road to Siena. Trespiano
lies three miles to the north of Florence on the Bologna road.

56. *Aguglione's churl and him from Signa:* Baldo d'Aguglione, a
prominent Guelph political leader, became prior of Florence in
1298. Banished from Florence for fraud in 1299, Aguglione
returned in 1302 after which he became a very influential figure.
In 1311, when he was prior of the city for the second time, in
his *riforma,* he rescinded a number of exile sentences against
Guelphs, though some of the orders were expressly excepted,
among these being that of Dante Alighieri.
  "Him from Signa" is probably a reference to Fazio de' Moru-
baldini da Signa (a town ten miles west of Florence). He was
prior of Florence several times and was sent in 1310 as ambassa-
dor to Pope Clement V to aid in organizing opposition to Em-
peror Henry VII's coming into Italy.

58. *the world's most despicable:* The pope and cardinals of the
Church in particular.

59. *a stepmother's role to Caesar:* Stepmother implies a hostile
relationship. "Caesar" refers to the Emperor of the Holy Roman
Empire.

61–63. *a certain nouveau-Florentine:* The specific allusion is
unknown; nevertheless, "nouveau-Florentine" apparently refers to
an upstart of less-than-noble parentage from Semifonte, a fortress
(destroyed by the Florentines in 1202) southwest of Florence.

64. *Montemurlo would still have its Counts:* The Conti Guidi,
unable to defend the castle of Montemurlo against the Pistoians,
were forced to sell it to Florence. This allusion emphasizes the
aggressive policy Florence came to adopt.

65. *the parish of Acone have its Cerchi:* According to Cacciaguida,
among the many results of the feud between the Church and the
Empire was the immigration of the Cerchi family from the small

town of Acone to Florence where a feud with the noble Donati family resulted in much civil disturbance. Originally of low birth, the Cerchi rose to wealth and political prominence in Florence.

66. *Valdigreve still its Buondelmonti:* When their castle in the valley of the Greve was destroyed to permit Florence to expand its borders, the Buondelmonti family moved in 1135 to that city. The Buondelmonti became leaders of the Guelph party in Florence.

67–69. *A mingled strain of men:* A mixed population, "polluted" (see 49) by outsiders, is compared to undigested (and therefore unassimilated) food in a stomach. It was believed at that time that food added to undigested food in the stomach caused sickness.

70–72. *a bull gone blind:* Size of a city is no guarantee of quality of life or wise government; often a smaller city is more effective than a larger one.

73. *Luni . . . Urbisaglia:* An ancient Etruscan city, on the border between Etruria and Liguria, Luni decayed during the Roman period and was eventually destroyed. The date of its final destruction is unknown. "Urbisaglia," the ancient Urbs Salvia, in the region of the Marches, had once been an important town, but by Dante's time it had fallen to ruin.

74. *Sinigaglia:* Now Senigallia, the ancient city of Sena Gallica, this city on the Adriatic was ruined in the thirteenth century during the wars between the Guelphs and Ghibellines and more especially by the devastation wrought by Guido da Montefeltro (see *Inf.* XXVII).

75. *Chiusi:* The ancient Clusium, located halfway between Florence and Rome, had once been one of the twelve great Etruscan cities. Its downfall may have been caused by its unfavorable geographical situation in the malarious area of the Val di Chiana.

79–81. *All of your works must die:* A city may appear to be eternal to a human being because the span of his lifetime is comparatively short, but even a city must come to an end.

82–84. *as the turning of the lunar sphere:* Just as the revolving of the moon causes the tides of the ocean to be in a state of flux, so Fortune's wheel causes constant change in the condition of Florence.

88–93. *I knew the Ughi . . . and Bostichi:* The families mentioned in these verses were noble Florentine families which were extinct by Dante's time. (See Villani IV, 9–13.)

94–96. *Close to the gate now laden with the weight:* The Cerchi (see n. 65), responsible for much civil strife, in 1280 had bought the houses of the Conti Guidi (inherited from the Ravignani) near the old gate at the Porta San Piero. The "ship" (96) is the city of Florence. This tercet has been variously interpreted (see Bosco and Reggio, pp. 268–69).

97–99. *the Ravignani from whom came:* The Ravignani were another noble family extinct in Dante's day. Bellincione Berti (see *Par.* XV, 112), in Cacciaguida's time, was the head of the family and the father of Gualdrada, the wife of Guido Guerra IV. The Conte Guido here is probably their grandson (see *Inf.* XVI, 38).

100. *the della Pressa:* A prominent Ghibelline family who were among those driven out of Florence in 1258.

101. *Galigaio:* Galigaio de' Galigai was a member of an ancient Florentine family. Like the della Pressa, the Galigai were exiled with other Ghibellines in 1258.

102. *his hilt and pommel gilded:* A sign of nobility.

103–104. *the pale of vair, the Galli . . . Barucci:* A representation of a strip of ermine ("vair") longitudinally bisected the escutcheon of the Pigli family arms. The Galli were a family of Ghibellines whose houses in Florence, like those of the Galigai, were destroyed (by provision of the *ordinamenti di giustizia*) in 1293. The Sacchetti were Guelphs and among those who fled Florence after the Ghibelline victory at Montaperti. The Giuochi, the Fifanti, and the Barucci were Ghibelline families; the Barucci were extinct by Dante's time.

105. *those who blush now for the stave affair:* The verse refers to the Chiaramontesi family, one of whom was responsible for fraud in the salt trade. Durante de' Chiaramontesi, as head of the Salt Import Department in Florence, had reduced the size of a bushel-measure by one stave, appropriating the balance (see *Purg.* XII, 105 and note).

106 – 108. *Calfucci branch . . . the Sizii:* An ancient Guelph family extinct in Dante's time, the Calfucci were ancestors of the Donati.

The Arrigucci and the Sizii held public offices during Cacciaguida's time and as Guelphs were among those who fled Florence in 1260 after the Ghibelline victory at Montaperti.

109 – 10. *How great I saw them once:* The Uberti, a Ghibelline family of Germanic origin, had come to Florence in the tenth century. Farinata, a famous member of the family, is among the heretics in Hell (see *Inf.* X). The Uberti family was responsible for the Ghibelline victory at Montaperti in 1260 which resulted in the Guelph exile from Florence.

110 – 11. *those balls of gold:* The Lamberti, whose arms bore golden balls on a field of blue, were of Germanic origin. The infamous Mosca (*Inf.* XXVIII, 106), a member of their family, was responsible for the incitement of the Amidei to murder Buondelmonte. This family quarrel was credited with beginning the Guelph-Ghibelline feud.

112 – 14. *Such were the fathers:* The Visdomini and the Tosinghi families administered episcopal revenues of the Florentine bishopric whenever the See was vacant. Cacciaguida accuses the descendants of these once-honorable families of prolonging vacancies of the See in order to enjoy the revenues.

115 – 20. *That insolent, presumptuous clan:* The Adimari family were Guelphs and as such were expelled from Florence in 1248. They were among those who sought refuge in Lucca following the Ghibelline victory in 1260. A member of the Cavicciuli branch took possession of Dante's property when he was exiled and continued to oppose Dante's recall. Ubertino Donati, whose family was probably in a feud with the Adimari long before their split into opposing Guelph factions, was displeased when his wife's sister was bestowed in marriage to one of the Adimari.

121. *The Caponsacchi:* Originally from Fiesole, this family was among the first Ghibelline families in Florence. After 1280, on their return from exile, they joined the Bianchi faction of the Guelphs, and were exiled with that group in 1302.

122 – 23. *The Guidi / and Infangati:* Two ancient Ghibelline families.

124. *Here is a fact incredible but true:* When Cacciaguida says this, he is not referring to the smallness of the city at the time when this was one of its gates, but rather to the fact that the della Pera family, in Dante's time of little renown, had once been so important and were of such antiquity that a gate of the old city was named after them. It was said to have been called Porta Peruzzi. (See the *E.D.* under "Pera.")

127 – 32. *the handsome quarterings / of the great Baron:* The Marquis Hugh of Brandenburg, vicar of Emperor Otto III, conferred knighthood upon six Florentine families (the Giandonati, the Pulci, the Nerli, the Gangalandi, the Alepri, and the della Bella) who adopted variations of his coat of arms as their own.

Giano della Bella, whose family had decked "that coat of arms with fringe," introduced strict reforms against the nobles in 1293; he was banished in 1295.

133 – 35. *The Gualterrotti and the Importuni:* Ancient Guelph families who lived in the Borgo Santi Apostoli quarter. The "new neighbors," the Buondelmonti, came to live in the Borgo when their castle in Montebuono was destroyed in 1135.

136 – 37. *The House that was the source of all your tears, / whose just resentment:* The Amidei family. Buondelmonte de' Buondelmonti, betrothed to a daughter of the Amidei, forsook her on their wedding day at the instigation of Gualdrada Donati, whose daughter he later married. This was a serious insult, and members of the indignant Amidei family murdered Buondelmonte, thereby beginning the feud that caused civil unrest in Florence for many years.

139. *as were all its clan:* The Ucellini and Gherandini.

142 – 44. *Many who now are sad would have been pleased:* Cacciaguida laments all the tragedy brought to his city as a result of the arrival of the Buondelmonti family. The Ema river lies between Florence and the castle of Montebuono, the former home of this family.

145 – 47. *How fitting for Florence to sacrifice:* The "mutilated stone" is the statue of Mars (first patron of Florence) which stood at the Ponte Vecchio, marking the southern limit of the city. Buondelmonte, "the victim," was murdered at the foot of the statue on Easter morning. Cacciaguida remarks on the appropri-

ateness of this "sacrifice" to the god of war which served to ignite civil discord.

153–54. *never the lily on the staff reversed:* During the wars between the Guelphs and Ghibellines, it was the custom of the victor to drag the opposing standard in the dust, thus the lily was "reversed" on its staff. After the expulsion of the Ghibellines in 1251, the Guelphs reversed the Florentine standard from a white lily in a red field to a red lily in a white field (cf. *Cron.* VI, 43).

CANTO XVII

WHEN CACCIAGUIDA finishes speaking, Beatrice encourages Dante to ask his ancestor what he wishes to know concerning the grave future that souls during his journey have predicted for him. Cacciaguida clarifies the prophecies by revealing to Dante that he will be exiled from Florence and that his place of refuge will be first with the great Lombard whose coat of arms is the ladder and the eagle and then with the younger one whose greatness is not yet known. Cacciaguida adds that Dante should not envy his neighbors, because his life will continue long after their perfidies are punished. Having heard the prophecy, Dante is troubled on the one hand by the bitterness of his fate and on the other by the fact that he may be too timid to reveal what he has seen and heard during his journey. His illustrious ancestor, however, urges him to tell the whole truth and assures him that while his *Comedy* and the criticism it levels against great and important men may at first seem harsh, it is bound to nourish mankind, and this honor should be a consolation. The fact that Dante has been introduced only to famous souls as examples of conduct in Hell, Purgatory, and Paradise will give his work an enduring fame, because it is through the example of illustrious men that mankind can best learn.

Like him who came to Clymene to learn
   the truth of those things said against him, he
   who still makes fathers chary of their sons,   *3*

was I, and just so was I felt to be
   by Beatrice and that holy light
   who for my sake had moved from where he was.   *6*

Wherefore my lady said: "Release the flame
   of your consuming wish; let it come forth
   marked clearly with the stamp of your desire,   *9*

not that your words would add to what we know,
   but that you better learn to speak your thirst
   in order that your cup be filled for you."   *12*

"O my own cherished root, so highly raised
    that, as men see no triangle contains
    among its angles two that are obtuse,   15

you see, gazing upon the final Point
    where time is timeless, those contingent things
    before they ever come into true being.   18

While I was still in Virgil's company,
    climbing the mountain where the souls are healed,
    descending through the kingdom of the dead,   21

ominous words about my future life
    were said to me—the truth is that I feel
    my soul foursquare against the blows of chance;   24

and so, it is my keenest wish to know
    whatever fortune has in store for me:
    fate's arrow, when expected, travels slow."   27

These were the words I spoke to that same light
    who spoke to me before, and so my wish,
    as Beatrice wished, was now confessed.   30

Not with dark oracles that once ensnared
    the foolish folk before the Lamb of God,
    Who takes away all sins, was crucified,   33

but in plain words, with clarity of thought,
    did that paternal love respond to me,
    both hidden and revealed by his own smile: 36

"Contingency, which in no way extends
    beyond the pages of your world of matter,
    is all depicted in the eternal sight;   39

but this no more confers necessity
    than does the movement of a boat downstream
    depend upon the eyes that mirror it.   42

As organ music sweetly strikes the ear,
    so from this Vision there comes to my eyes
    the shape of things the future holds for you.   45

As Hippolytus was forced to flee from Athens
    by his devious and merciless stepmother,
    just so you too shall have to leave your Florence. 48

So it is willed, so it is being planned,
    and shall be done soon by the one who plots
    it there where daily Christ is up for sale.   51

The public will, as always, blame the party
    that has been wronged; vengeance that Truth demands,
    although, shall yet bear witness to the truth.   54

You shall be forced to leave behind those things
    you love most dearly, and this is the first
    arrow the bow of your exile will shoot.   57

And you will know how salty is the taste
    of others' bread, how hard the road that takes
    you down and up the stairs of others' homes.   60

But what will weigh you down the most will be
    the despicable, senseless company
    whom you shall have to bear in that sad vale;   63

and all ungrateful, all completely mad
    and vicious, they shall turn on you, but soon
    their cheeks, not yours, will have to blush from shame.   66

Proof of their bestiality will show
    through their own deeds! It will be to your honor
    to have become a party of your own.   69

Your first abode, your first refuge, will be
    the courtesy of the great Lombard lord
    who bears the sacred bird upon the ladder,   72

and he will hold you in such high regard
    that in your give and take relationship
    the one will give before the other asks.   75

With him you shall see one who at his birth
    was stamped so hard with this star's seal that all
    of his achievements will win great renown.   78

The world has not yet taken note of him;
    he is still very young, for Heaven's wheels
    have circled round him now for just nine years.   81

But even before the Gascon tricks proud Henry,
    this one will show some of his mettle's sparks
    by scorning wealth and making light of toil.   84

Knowledge of his munificence will yet
　　be spread abroad: even his enemies
　　will not be able to deny his worth.　　　　　　　　*87*

Look you to him, expect from him good things.
　　Through him the fate of many men shall change,
　　rich men and beggars changing their estate.　　　*90*

Now write this in your mind but do not tell
　　the world"—and he said things concerning him
　　incredible even to those who see　　　　　　　　*93*

them all come true. Then he said: "Son, you have
　　my gloss of what was told you. Now you see
　　the snares that hide behind a few years' time!　　*96*

No envy toward your neighbors should you bear,
　　for you will have a future that endures
　　far longer than their crime and punishment."　　*99*

When, by his silence, that blest soul revealed
　　that he had ceased weaving the woof across
　　the warp that I had set in readiness,　　　　　　*102*

I said, as one who is in doubt and longs
　　to have the guidance of a soul who sees
　　the truth and knows of virtue and has love:　　*105*

"Father, well do I see how time attacks,
　　spurring toward me to deal me such a blow
　　as falls the hardest on the least prepared;　　*108*

so, it is good that foresight lend me arms;
　　thus, should the place most dear to me be lost,
　　my verse, at least, shall not lose me all others.　*111*

Down through the world of endless bitterness
　　and on the mountain from whose lovely crown
　　I was raised upward by my lady's eyes,　　　　*114*

then through the heavens, rising from light to light—
　　I learned things that, were they to be retold,
　　would leave a bitter taste in many mouths;　　*117*

yet, if I am a timid friend to truth,
　　I fear my name may not live on with those
　　who will look back at these as the old days."　*120*

The light that was resplendent in the treasure
  I had found there began to flash more light,
  just like a golden mirror in the sun,   *123*

and then replied: "The conscience that is dark
  with shame for his own deeds or for another's,
  may well, indeed, feel harshness in your words;   *126*

nevertheless, do not resort to lies,
  let what you write reveal all you have seen,
  and let those men who itch scratch where it hurts.   *129*

Though when your words are taken in at first
  they may taste bitter, but once well-digested
  they will become a vital nutriment.   *132*

Your cry of words will do as does the wind
  striking the hardest at the highest peaks,
  and this will be for honor no small grounds;   *135*

and so you have been shown, here in these spheres,
  down on the Mount and in the pain-filled valley
  only those souls whose names are known to fame,   *138*

because the listener's mind will never trust
  or have faith in the kind of illustration
  based on the unfamiliar and obscure—   *141*

or demonstration that is not outstanding."

NOTES

1. *Like him who came to Clymene to learn:* On hearing that he was not Apollo's son as he had always believed, Phaëthon went to his mother Clymene for the truth. She swore that, indeed, he was Apollo's son and urged him to ask for himself. Phaëthon did so, and at that interview he persuaded his father to let him drive the chariot of the Sun, an action that proved fatal to him (see *Metam.* I, 750–61).

3. *who still makes fathers chary of their sons:* The tragic consequence of Phaëthon's request continues to make fathers wary of granting their sons' requests (cf. note to *Inf.* XVII, 106–108). This verse, which carries with it the fatal overtones of Phaëthon's tragic ending, overshadows the entire canto.

4. *was I:* Dante in his journey through Hell and Purgatory has heard ominous words concerning his future. He now wishes to know the truth of these rumors and looks to his great-great-grandfather for the answer just as Phaëthon went to his mother, Clymene, to learn the truth. Actually, from what we were told in the *Inferno*, it was Beatrice who would clarify what he had heard (see *Inf.* X, 130–32 and XV, 89–90). Dante, for poetic reasons, felt that here, in the central cantos of the Paradise featuring his great-great-grandfather, was the best place to clarify the predictions running through the poem.

10. *not that your words would add to what we know:* Beatrice and the souls of all the Blest can gain no additional knowledge from anything the Pilgrim says, for they have already read all there is to know in the mind of God (see *Par.* XV, 61–69). The Pilgrim is encouraged to speak up so as to get used to expressing his questions or wishes; after all, he will not be in Paradise forever. He will have to return to earth and communicate with living men again.

13–18. *"O my own cherished root, so highly raised:* Just as earthly minds can grasp elementary and unchangeable concepts (such as the geometrical principle cited here), the heavenly spirits can see contingencies and causalities. The souls, in gazing at God, are able to see all past, present, and future time.

At the end of verse 13 Dante coins a verb, this time by combining a preposition (*in*) with the adverb *suso: insusi.* He used the same type of construction in *Paradise* X, 148.

19–21. *While I was still in Virgil's company:* During his journey through Hell and Purgatory the Pilgrim heard things said against him ("ominous words," 22) by Farinata (*Inf.* X, 79–81); Brunetto Latini (*Inf.* XV, 61–72); Vanni Fucci (*Inf.* XXIV, 142–51); Corrado Malaspina (*Purg.* VIII, 133–39); and Oderisi da Gubbio (*Purg.* XI, 139–41).

24. *foursquare:* The word Dante uses in the Italian is *tetragono,* which is a "cube," the symbol of stability. The Poet, then, is planted "squarely" on all sides against the blows of fortune.

27. *fate's arrow, when expected, travels slow:* This popular saying implies that the arrow will not hit its mark with such force, because the person it is aimed at would have time to defend himself somehow.

31 – 36. *Not with dark oracles:* Not with such ambiguous and enigmatic prophesying as the oracles used in order to fool the ancient peoples, but with clear and unequivocal speech, Cacciaguida tells Dante's future.

36. *both hidden and revealed by his own smile:* Cacciaguida's joy increases his brilliance, thus he is enclosed in his own brilliance, yet he reveals his great joy.

37 – 42. *"Contingency, which in no way extends:* Contingent things (i.e., things derived from secondary causes) do not exist beyond the material world, as contingency has no place in eternity. The fact that these things can be seen within God does not mean that His foreknowledge necessitates events any more than the eyes, seeing a boat move downstream, determine the course of the vessel. The comparison used here does not work all that well, however, for while a boat may be seen floating downstream by the human eye and the eye have no control of the boat's course, the mind of God has control over everything.

46 – 48. *Hippolytus:* When Phaedra, Hippolytus' stepmother, fell in love with him, Hippolytus rejected her advances and was forced to flee Athens when she subsequently accused him of attempting to dishonor her (see *Metam.* XV, 497 – 505). What is stressed here is the innocence of the person exiled.

49 – 51. *So it is willed:* In these words of Cacciaguida, Dante seems to express his belief that Pope Boniface VIII was already planning the exile of Dante and his fellow Bianchi party members from Florence when he turned the city over to the Neri faction. By the time Dante and other ambassadors arrived in Rome to protest papal actions, Boniface had already sent to Florence his representative, Charles of Valois, whose appointment the Bianchi opposed. Shortly thereafter, in 1302, before he could return to Florence from Rome, Dante, along with other compatriots, was exiled from Florence. He was never to return there. Cacciaguida is not saying that Boniface VIII actually planned Dante's exile ("so it is being planned," 49), but rather that he was planning the events that would eventually lead to the Poet's exile.

53 – 54. *vengeance that Truth demands:* God's punishment (that is bound to come) will be the proof that Dante and his party were unjustly accused. The punishment or Divine retribution probably

refers to all the bad that came to Florence in a general sense as well as to the disgraceful death of Boniface VIII.

59–60. *others' bread . . . others' homes:* Dante will know the sadness of depending on others for food and lodging. Notice in verse 60 how the normal word order for "going up and down stairs" is reversed: ". . . down and up the stairs of others' homes." This reversal heightens the pathos of the situation. The person who is exiled and must beg his food and lodgings starts off by being rejected: we see him descending the stairs in someone's house before he is forced to ascend stairs in another's. Mattalia also points this out and cites *Convivio* I, 3. This tercet and the preceding one are considered to be two of the most poignant tercets in all of the *Divine Comedy.*

62–69. *the despicable, senseless company:* The Bianchi, or White Guelphs, who were exiled with Dante. After the exile in 1302, they made several attempts to march on Florence. Dante did not participate in the last attempt in 1304, and about this time he broke from the party. Specific reasons for this severance are unknown. See, however, the *Ottimo Commento* which provides some possible explanation.

70–72. *the great Lombard:* The reference is believed to be to a member of the Scaliger family, Bartolommeo della Scala of Verona, whose arms consisted of the Imperial eagle perched upon a golden ladder. Dante took refuge with him in Verona immediately after separating from the other exiled members of his party.

75. *the one will give before the other asks:* Unlike many benefactors who wait for requests before granting favors, "the great Lombard lord" will give before he is asked.

76–78. *With him you shall see one:* The young man is Can Grande della Scala, younger brother of Bartolommeo, who was born in 1291. In 1308 he and his other brother Alboino were associated in the lordship of Verona, and they jointly received the title of Imperial Vicar from Henry VII. In 1311, on his brother's death, he became sole Lord of Verona which he remained until his death in 1329. Dante dedicated the *Paradise* to Can Grande in a letter to him (*Epist.* XIII), in which the title and subject of the poem are discussed.

Can Grande is said to have been "stamped so hard with this star's seal" (77) in the sense that, born under the influence of

Mars, his great achievements would be in the field of the martial arts, which was the case (cf. Villani, IX – X).

80 – 81. *Heaven's wheels I have circled . . . just nine years:* Can Grande, born in March of 1291, would have been just nine years old in 1300, the fictional date of the *Comedy.*

82. *But even before the Gascon tricks proud Henry:* Before 1312, Pope Clement V, the Gascon, had supported Emperor Henry VII and invited him to Italy; however, Clement apparently changed his mind, withdrew support, and even fostered opposition to Henry.

83 – 84. *this one will show some of his mettle's sparks:* Even before 1312 Can Grande will show signs of his generosity "by scorning wealth" and his energetic character by "making light of toil." Because of the words "scorning wealth" in verse 84 many commentators would connect this verse to verse 103 of Canto I of the *Inferno:* "He will not feed on either land or money," and they identify the mysterious "greyhound" who will eventually come to save Italy as Can Grande. (See my note to *Inf.* I, 101 – 11.)

90. *rich men and beggars changing their estate:* Cf. Luke 1:52 – 53. "He hath put down the mighty from their seats and exalted them of low degree. He hath filled the hungry with good things; and the rich he hath sent empty away."

91 – 94. *Write this in your mind but do not tell I the world":* Dante the Poet cannot tell the world (only the Pilgrim knows) because these things which Can Grande did still have to be done. We must remember that the time of the Poem is 1300, and Can Grande is only nine years of age. What comes through in these four verses is all the heartfelt hope and faith the Poet placed in the young boy, this savior.

95. *my gloss:* Cacciaguida's clarification of the many predictions Dante heard during his journey through the Inferno and Purgatory (cf. note 19 – 21 for specific predictions).

95 – 96. *Now you see I the snares that hide behind a few years' time:* In fact, not even two years after the fictional date of the poem, which is 1300, will pass before the bans of Dante's exile are posted (January 27 and March 10 of 1302).

97 – 99. *No envy toward your neighbors:* Literally speaking,

Dante lived longer than either his adversary Pope Boniface VIII or his neighbor, Corso Donati (see *Purg.* XXIV, 82–87), so this is a reference to a neighbor in the strict sense. In a figurative sense, these verses suggest that Dante's fame will last beyond that of his enemies.

101–102. *he had ceased weaving the woof across / the warp:* Cacciaguida after answering ("weaving the woof") the Pilgrim's questions or doubts ("the warp") falls silent. He has woven the pattern of Dante's future into the cloth of his doubts. This weaving image recalls the tenderness with which the Old Crusader spoke of the Old Florence early in Canto XV (97ff.). Dante uses the same metaphor earlier in the *Paradise* (see Canto III, 95–96) in connection with Piccarda's vow.

104–105. *who sees / the truth and knows of virtue and has love:* In these three qualities Dante gives us a portrait of his ancestor in miniature.

110. *the place most dear to me:* Florence.

111. *all others:* I.e., other places of refuge in his exile.

112. *the world of endless bitterness:* Hell.

113. *on the mountain:* Purgatory. The summit is beautiful because the Earthly Paradise is located there, and Dante was able to reach it by virtue of the power of Beatrice's eyes.

116–17. *I learned things:* These are the unpleasant and often scandalous things the Pilgrim heard said (and said himself) about many of the souls he encountered during his journey through the three realms of Hell, Purgatory, and Paradise. And if he were to repeat some of these things, he may lessen his chances of receiving hospitality from them in his exile.

118–20. *yet, if I am a timid friend to truth:* Dante is compelled to relate the truth of what he has experienced out of duty to posterity, and out of concern for his reputation.

121–23. *The light . . . the treasure / I had found there:* That is to say, Cacciaguida himself, whom he had found in the heaven of Mars, now glows brighter because he is joyful at having the opportunity to satisfy Dante by answering his question.

129. *and let those men who itch scratch where it hurts:* If any man

should react unfavorably to what the Poet has said about him in his poem, it would be more an indication of guilt on the part of that man than bad taste on the part of the Poet. This statement is in the same spirit as "If the shoe fits, wear it!" Notice how Cacciaguida has in a sense run the gamut of language: from Latin and words the poet could not understand when Cacciaguida addressed him for the first time in Canto XV to the use of vulgar proverb here.

130–32. *your words . . . will become a vital nutriment:* Cacciaguida here is referring to the entire *Comedy*, which will provide mankind with spiritual nourishment once those who have been offended have licked their wounds and the contents of the great Poem have been digested.

134. *the highest peaks:* Powerful and eminent men such as popes and politicians will hear his words.

135. *and this will be for honor no small grounds:* Striking at "the highest peaks" takes much courage.

136–42. *and so you have been shown:* Only by using well-known persons as examples can the *Comedy* be efficacious; Dante can convince no one by citing unknown examples or proof drawn from obscure facts. Obvious examples and clear demonstrations will be more persuasive to the Poet's audience. But it is not true that all of the characters inhabiting Dante's three realms are of great stature. His theory seems to hold more true for the world of the *Paradise* than for that of the *Inferno*.

CANTO XVIII

While Dante and Cacciaguida are rapt in thought, Beatrice calls to the Pilgrim to look into her eyes that are filled with Divine Love, the love that releases him from all other desires. Beatrice breaks his rapture by telling him to turn and listen once more to his ancestor, because Paradise is not only in her eyes. Then Cacciaguida introduces Dante to a number of famous soldier-souls who appear in the cross flashing like lightning at the mention of their names. Dante turns to Beatrice and is again lost in her gaze when suddenly he realizes that he has been transported from the rosy glow of the fifth sphere of Mars to the silvery sixth sphere of Jupiter. In this sphere the shining souls group together to form, one at a time, the letters of the first verse of the Book of Wisdom: DILIGITE IUSTITIAM QUI IUDICATIS TERRAM, appearing as gold against silver. Having formed the final letter M, the souls stop. More lights descend singing on the summit of the M and then suddenly shoot up to form the neck and head of an eagle. The souls of the M now move to fill out the rest of the design of the eagle. Moved by this vision of Justice Dante, in a bitter apostrophe against the Pope, accuses him of having forgotten the example of his predecessors Peter and Paul who died for the Church he is now in the process of ruining.

That holy mirror was rejoicing now
    in his own thoughts, and I was left to taste
    and temper mine, the bitter with the sweet.   3

Then she who was my guide to God said: "Stop,
    think other thoughts. Think that I dwell with Him
    Who lifts the weight of every wrong man suffers."   6

Those loving words made me turn round to face
    my Solace. What love within her holy eyes
    I saw just then—too much to be retold;   9

not only do I fear my words may fail,
    but to such heights my mind cannot return
    unless Another guides it from above.   12

I can recall just this about that moment:
  as I was gazing at her there, I know
  my heart was freed of every other longing,   15

for the Eternal Joy was shining straight
  into my Beatrice's face, and back
  came its reflection filling me with joy;   18

then, with a smile whose radiance dazzled me,
  she said: "Now turn around and listen well,
  not in my eyes alone is Paradise."   21

As here on earth the eyes sometimes reveal
  their deepest wish, if it is wished with force
  enough to captivate all of the soul,   24

so, in the flaring of the sacred fire
  to which I turned, I recognized his wish:
  I saw that he had something more to say.   27

He spoke: "Upon the fifth tier of the tree
  whose life comes from its crown and which bears fruit
  in every season, never shedding leaves,   30

blest spirits dwell whose fame below on earth,
  before they came to Heaven, was so widespread
  that any poet would be enriched by them.   33

Now look up and observe the cross's arms,
  each soul that I shall name there you will see
  flash quick as lightning flashes through a cloud."   36

I saw, as he pronounced the name of Joshua,
  a streak of light flashing across the cross—
  no sooner was it said than it was done.   39

And at the name of the great Maccabees
  I saw another whirling light flash through—
  the cord that spun that top was its own joy!   42

Then came the names Roland and Charlemagne,
  and eagerly I followed these two lights,
  as hunters watch their falcons on the wing.   45

William of Orange, then, and Renouard
  and the Duke Godfrey drew my sight with them
  along the cross; then came Robert Guiscard.   48

The light who spoke to me now moved away
  to mix with other lights and let me hear
  the artist that he was in Heaven's choir.   51

I turned to Beatrice at my right
  to learn from her by word or by a sign
  what she thought I should do, and I beheld   54

new brilliance in her eyes, such purity,
  such ecstasy, her countenance was now
  more beautiful than it had ever been.   57

And as a man feeling from day to day
  more joy in doing good, becomes aware
  thereby that virtue grows in him, just so,   60

seeing that miracle grow lovelier,
  I noticed that my circling with the heavens
  had taken on a greater arc of space.   63

And such a transformation as is seen
  upon a fair-skinned lady's face when shame
  recedes, and blushes vanish instantly,   66

I saw when I turned round: before my eyes
  there was the pure white of the temperate star,
  the sixth, that had received me in its glow;   69

I saw within that Jovial torch the light
  of all the sparkling love rejoicing there
  and forming words of speech before my eyes.   72

As birds just risen from the water's edge,
  as if in celebration for their food,
  flock now in circles, now in drawn-out lines,   75

so there, within those lights the blessèd beings
  were circling as they sang, turning themselves
  first to a *D*, then *I*, then into *L*.   78

They first flew, singing, to their music's rhythm,
  then having made a letter of themselves,
  they held their form and stopped their song a while.   81

O sacred Muse of Pegasus who gives
  glory to men of genius and long life,
  as they, through you, give it to realms and towns—   84

let your light shine on me that I may show
   these letter-shapes of souls fixed in my mind;
   let your power show through these few lines of mine!   87

They showed themselves to me in five times seven
   vowels and consonants, and I was able
   to understand the written words they formed.   90

The first words of the message, verb and noun:
   DILIGITE IUSTITIAM; then came
   QUI IUDICATIS TERRAM after them.   93

And in the final letter, in the M
   of the fifth word they stayed aligned—and Jove's
   silver became the background of their gold.   96

I saw more lights descend, and they alighted
   upon the M, and from its peak they sang,
   I think, about the Good that summons them.   99

Just as one sees innumerable sparks
   go flying up when smoldering logs are poked
   (which once encouraged fools to prophesy),   102

so, there I seemed to see more than a thousand
   lights rising up, mounting to different heights,
   as chosen by the Sun that kindles them;   105

and once each spark had found its place of rest,
   I saw the crest and neck of a great eagle
   now patterned in the fire of those sparks.   108

(The One who paints there has no one to guide
   his hand. He guides Himself. It is from Him
   that skill in birds to build their nests is born.)   111

The other blessèd ones who seemed at first
   content to lilify themselves into the M
   with a slight shift completed the design.   114

O lovely star, how many and what jewels
   shone there declaring that justice on earth
   comes from that Heaven which you yourself begem.   117

Therefore, I pray the Mind—for there begins
   your movement and your power—to examine
   the place whence comes the smoke that dims your rays,   120

so that its wrath descend upon, once more,
    all those who buy and sell within the temple
    whose walls were built with miracles and martyrs.   *123*

O Heaven's army to whom my mind returns,
    pray for those souls on earth who are misled
    by bad example and have gone astray.   *126*

It used to be that wars were waged with swords,
    but now one fights withholding here and there
    the bread our Father's love denies to none.   *129*

And you who write only to nullify,
    remember that Peter and Paul, who died
    to save the vineyard you despoil, still live.   *132*

But you will answer: "I, who have my heart
    so set on him who chose to live alone
    and for a martyr's crown was danced away,   *135*

know nothing of your Fisherman or Paul."

NOTES

1. *That holy mirror:* Cacciaguida, whose soul reflects the light of God, as do the souls of all the Blest.

2–3. *I was left to taste . . . the bitter with the sweet:* Dante's thoughts focus on the predictions, good and bad, which he has heard concerning his future. One must admit that he has heard more bitter news than sweet. The "sweet" must refer to the coming greatness of Can Grande.

5–6. *I dwell with Him:* Beatrice will pray for Dante in his time of suffering to come.

8. *my Solace:* Cf. Virgil's role in *Purg.* III, 22; IX, 43, where he is addressed with the same words, *mio conforto.*

16–18. *Eternal Joy was shining:* God's joy shines into the Pilgrim indirectly through the face of Beatrice. Not until the final canto of the poem will the Pilgrim be able to look directly at God.

20. *"Now turn around:* I.e., back toward Cacciaguida.

21. *not in my eyes alone is Paradise":* the Divine Light of Paradise

is reflected in all that Dante experiences around him, not just in Beatrice's eyes. The word "Paradise" is used in the same sense earlier (cf. *Par.* XV, 36).

25–27. *in the flaring of the sacred fire:* By now we should be accustomed to the fact that the souls of the Blest express their emotions by giving off greater light. In this case, Cacciaguida, by shining more brightly, expresses his desire to say more to his great-great-grandson.

28–30. *"Upon the fifth tier of the tree:* The heavens are conceived of as a tree whose crown is the outermost limit of the universe where God dwells. This being the case, the "tree" derives its nourishment not from its roots but from its crown. The sphere of Mars is the fifth of ten tiers. (Cf. Ezek. 47:12 for reference to the tree that never sheds its leaves.)

34. *observe the cross's arms:* The reader will remember that these spirits of those warriors who fought for the Faith had formed a cross earlier in Canto XIV, 100ff.

36. *quick as lightning flashes through a cloud:* Against the deep red background of the planet Mars the souls, as they speed by, resemble flashes of lightning (which was believed at that time to come from the explosion of fire in a cloud).

37. *Joshua:* The successor of Moses and conqueror of Canaan. (See *Par.* IX, 124–25.)

40. *Maccabees:* Judas Maccabaeus, the great warrior, succeeded in resisting the attempts of the kings of Syria to destroy the Jewish religion. After restoring and purifying the Temple of Jerusalem (ca. 164 B.C.), he was defeated and slain by the Syrians at Elasa a few years later.

42. *the cord that spun that top was its own joy:* This lovely metaphor of a child's top made to spin by its own cord of joy probably originates from a similar one in the *Aeneid* (VII, 378ff.).

43. *Roland and Charlemagne:* Charlemagne (742–814), king of the Franks and Emperor of the Holy Roman Empire, and Roland, his nephew and greatest warrior, are presented here for their efforts against the Saracens. (See also *Inf.* XXXI, 16–18.)

46. *William of Orange, then, and Renouard:* William, Count of Orange, is the hero of a group of Old French epics, the *Aliscans*

being the best known. He fought the Saracens in southern France. Renouard, a giant of Saracen birth, though later baptized a Christian, was the companion and brother-in-law of William.

47. *Duke Godfrey:* Godfrey of Bouillon, leader of the First Crusade (1096), became the first Christian king of Jerusalem.

48. *Robert Guiscard:* In the latter half of the eleventh century the Norman Robert Guiscard took southern Italy and Sicily from the Saracens. He died in Salerno in 1085 (see *Inf.* XXVIII, 14).

49 – 51. *The light who spoke to me now moved away:* Cacciaguida returns now to his place among the other spirits and demonstrates his artistry in song. Just as the Cacciaguida episode may be said to have opened with the notes of the hymn the Pilgrim heard— "Arise" and "Conquer" (*Par.* XIV, 125)—so here in verse 51 it comes to its magnificent close with the old warrior returning to the glowing choir of the cross and to the singing of the same hymn, probably the same notes or words that brought him on stage in Canto XV.

Cacciaguida has filled three full cantos (XV, XVI, XVII) and parts of two others (XIV and XVIII). Dante dedicates 550 verses to his illustrious ancestor, which is the most given to any other character (with the exception of Virgil and Beatrice) in the *Comedy.* For more on these important cantos see Bergin.

61 – 63. *seeing that miracle grow lovelier:* Seeing Beatrice become more beautiful, Dante becomes aware that he has risen to the next sphere. Because each successive sphere encloses those below it, as Dante moves up he also moves outward, thus his circling encompasses a larger space.

64 – 66. *such a transformation:* Dante compares his movement from Mars with its red color to Jupiter with its whiteness to the passing away of a blush on a fair-skinned lady's face. The emphasis this time is more on change of color than on speed.

68 – 69. *the pure white of the temperate star, / the sixth:* In the *Convivio* (II, xiii, 25) Dante quotes Ptolemy as characterizing Mars as hot, Saturn as cold, Jupiter between them as temperate.

70. *that Jovial torch:* I.e., belonging to Jupiter; also suggesting a joyful disposition, which those born under its influence were said to possess.

72. *forming words of speech before my eyes:* The souls now position themselves to spell out a message. This is reminiscent of the "visible speech" on the Terrace of the Proud in *Purgatory* (X, 95).

75. *flock now in circles, now in drawn-out lines:* In this verse describing birds that, having fed well along the water's edge, have just taken to flight in order to express their contentment, the letters the souls will form before our eyes in verse 78 are already taking shape. The birds Dante probably had in mind were cranes, which were said to form different shapes while in flight (see Lucan, *Phars.* V, 711–16).

79–81. *They first flew, singing, to their music's rhythm:* Dante takes pains in this tercet to describe exactly how this skywriting was done before his eyes: a flock of lights would first fly up, keeping time to the music they themselves were chanting, and form an individual letter of the alphabet. The group would then hold the formation and stop singing—a kind of punctuation— long enough for the Pilgrim to record the letter in his memory.

82. *O sacred Muse of Pegasus:* Pegasus, the winged horse, was associated with the Muses. Here, Dante invokes one of the Muses, though which particular one is unclear. He may be appealing to Poetry in general.

91–93. *The first words of the message, verb and noun:* The message, "Love justice, you who judge the earth," comes from the first verse of the Book of Wisdom of Solomon in the Apocrypha. The souls in Jupiter are those of the just, and justice is the product of this sphere.

94. *in the final letter, in the "M":* The souls who were forming the last letter of the word TERRAM hold their position in the *M*, which must not have been the angular Roman-style capital *M* with its twin peaks that is often found in stone inscriptions and illuminated manuscripts of the twelfth through fifteenth centuries but rather another popular style, the uncial-derived *M*, having one peak only, according to what Dante says in verse 98: "and from its peak they sang." (See Anderson, pp. 61–63 and 98–100.)

95–96. *Jove's / silver became the background of their gold:* The planet Jupiter is of a silvery whiteness which forms a background for the golden letters which the souls form. This mass of silver inlaid with an *M* of gold is a fitting background for the presentation of the sign for Monarchy. (Steiner, however, discusses the possibility that the *M* at this point signifies the World [*Mondo*]; see pp. 876–77.) Dante in his *De monarchia* (I, xi, 2) says: "The highest justice is attained only under a Monarch; therefore, in order to have perfect order in the world, there must be a Monarchy or Empire."

97–99. *I saw more lights descend:* As they settle on the top ("its peak," 98) of the *M,* the souls change its configuration (see Fig. 8). The *M* of Monarchy is now changing into an heraldic lily, but the reader is not aware of this particular change until verses 112–14.

By saying "I think" in verse 99 the Pilgrim is implying that he could not hear or understand all the words sung by those sparks of souls (and this is not the first time) who have just descended on the neck of the *M*.

102. *which once encouraged fools to prophesy:* It was believed in some parts of Italy that it was possible to read omens and portents in the sparks sent up from a burning log. See Dante's early commentators, such as Benvenuto, for details.

104. *mounting to different heights:* All these lights on the neck of the *M* now begin to ascend to different heights: a new shape is being formed, and the design shifts "to the crest and neck of a great eagle" (107).

112–14. *The other blessèd ones:* This is the final stage in the formation of the eagle. Atop the center vertical line of the uncial-derived *M* the spirits form the neck and head of an heraldic eagle. Then the other spirits which have curved the flanking lines of the verticle center forming a temporary fleur-de-lys shift slightly to complete the wings and body of the eagle.

The *M* from which the eagle took its shape stands for Monarchy, and the eagle itself is the symbol of the Empire. It has been suggested that the lily, which was first formed, then abandoned, represents the French monarchy which had, under Charlemagne, restored the empire, though it was soon lost by them to the Germans (see Chimenz, p. 792).

Verse 113 reads in the original "pareva prima d' ingigliarsi a l' emme." Dante, as he will do from time to time, coins a verb for this miraculous occasion: *ingigliarsi,* which I have rendered as "lilify themselves." All of the commentators are not in agreement on the formation of a lily in verse 113 (see Porena, pp. 178–79; also the *E.D.* under *ingigliarsi*).

To summarize the transformation of the *M* into the Eagle we must think in terms of four stages:

1) The *M* is isolated (94–96).
2) Other lights descend upon the peak of the *M* (98–99) —they are the souls referred to in verses 112–13 of stage 4.
3) Lights rise to different levels forming head and neck of an eagle.
4) The other souls (some from stage 2) of verses 112–14 (those who seemed "content to lilify themselves into the *M*") re-arrange themselves to form the body and wings of the eagle.

The fact that the Poet does not mention the heraldic lily in stage 2, but instead only refers to it belatedly in a single word in verse 113 ("lilify"), as a passing stage in the formation of the eagle, is indicative of what Dante thought of the French monarchy, whose heraldic device was the lily or Fleur-de-lys.

115. *O lovely star:* Jupiter.

116–17. *justice on earth / comes from that Heaven:* Justice on earth is governed by this sphere of which the planet is the gem.

120. *the smoke that dims your rays:* The avarice of the popes is the smoke which blocks imperial authority and prevents the clear administration of justice on earth (see n. 121–23).

121–23. *so that its wrath descend upon, once more:* That God's wrath may descend again, as it had before, upon all those in the Church who practice simony. The verses are reminiscent of when Christ drove the money-changers from the Temple of Jerusalem (cf. Matt. 21:12–13).

124. *O Heaven's army to whom my mind returns:* This apostrophe to the Blest in this sphere of Justice is uttered by Dante not at the fictitious time of the poem but rather while he is back on earth (at his writing desk?), remembering.

126. *by bad example and have gone astray:* Dante once again in the *Comedy* charges the papacy with setting a bad example. (See also *Purg.* XVI, 100–11; *Par.* IX, 127–32.)

127–29. *It used to be that wars were waged with swords:* Wars are

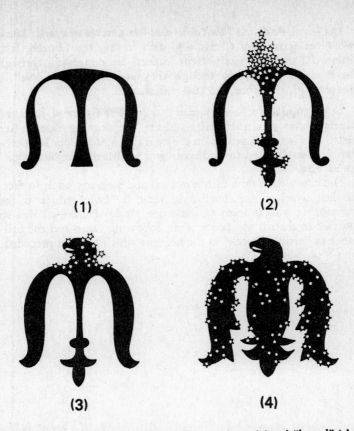

(1)
(2)
(3)
(4)

now waged by denying the sacraments, the spiritual "bread" (the holy sacrament of the Body of Christ) through the issuance of interdicts and excommunications. Parodi suggests that this could be an allusion to Pope John XXII's excommunication of Can Grande della Scala in 1317, and from this arises the possibility that these verses, and perhaps even the Cacciaguida cantos (XV, XVI, XVII), which are at the center of the *Comedy*, might have been written while Dante was at the court of Can Grande in Verona.

130–132. *And you who write only to nullify:* Pope John XXII was supposed to have issued and rescinded many orders of excommunication. The cancellation of excommunications was a source of revenue for the papacy.

131 – 32. Peter and Paul, who died / to save the vineyard: These two great apostles of Christ who died to save the Church ("the vineyard") that you (its present leaders) are destroying through the practice of simony, though they are dead, "still live" in Heaven and, therefore, can still punish you.

133 – 36. I, who have my heart / so set: The figure of John the Baptist, who was martyred to please the dancing Salome (see Matt. 14:1 – 12), appeared on the gold florin. The Pope's concentration is so directed toward acquiring wealth that he has forgotten all else.

The canto ends on a rather cynical and sarcastic note; in fact, the last word of the concluding verse is *"Polo,"* which is the common or vulgar form of the name Paolo (Paul)—all this in contrast to the magnificence of the following canto and the brilliance of "visible speech" in the heavens which has just preceded.

CANTO XIX

THE EAGLE NOW appears to the Pilgrim with open wings
and as if composed of countless sparkling rubies. The lights of
the souls who form the beak of the eagle move, and a voice that
speaks for all of those composing the sacred emblem informs the
Pilgrim that it is exalted in this sphere as the symbol for Divine
Justice, and that, although its memory is preserved on earth, its
example is not followed. He then asks the eagle to elucidate the
meaning of Divine Justice and to help him to resolve a doubt he
has had for some time: what justice is there in damning a good
soul who, through no fault of his own, has not heard of Christ
and has not been baptized? Before he has the chance to express
this doubt the eagle goes into a long discourse on the unfathom-
able nature of God and the inability of His creatures to under-
stand His infinite wisdom. The eagle, showing displeasure,
circles above Dante as its souls sing an incomprehensible song
which the eagle likens to the mystery of Eternal Judgment which
cannot be understood by mortals. Finally, the eagle condemns all
those rulers of the times who governed without justice.

And there before my eyes with wings spread wide
    that splendid image shone, shaped by the souls
    rejoicing in their interwoven joy.   3

They were set there like splendid rubies lit
    each of them by a gleaming ray of sun
    which was reflected straight into my eyes.   6

And what I have to tell you here and now
    no tongue has told or ink has written down,
    nor any fantasy imagined it,   9

for I could hear the beak and see it move;
    I heard its voice use words like *I* and *Mine*
    when in conception it was *We* and *Ours*.   12

"Because of my justice and piety,"
    it said, "I have been raised up to this glory,
    the highest our desires can conceive,   15

and I have left on earth a memory
   which even wicked men are wont to praise,
   though they refuse to follow in my course."   18

Just as from many burning coals will come
   one glow of heat, so from that image came
   a single sound composed of many loves.   21

And I exclaimed: "O everlasting flowers
   of the eternal bliss who concentrate
   all of your many fragrances in one,   24

breathe forth your words now, breaking at long last
   the fasting that has kept me hungering
   for food that I could never find on earth.   27

I know that though God's justice is beheld
   within some other mirror in these spheres,
   your kingdom apprehends its light unveiled.   30

You know my eagerness to hear you speak,
   you also know the nature of the question
   whose answer I have hungered for so long."   33

Then as the falcon, now freed from its hood,
   stretches its neck and starts to beat its wings,
   and preens itself—to show its eagerness—   36

so moved the ensign made of woven voices
   in exaltation of God's grace with song
   known only to the souls who dwell in bliss.   39

Then it said: "He Who with His compass drew
   the limits of the world and out of chaos
   brought order to things hidden and revealed,   42

could not impress his quality so much
   upon the universe but that His Word
   should not remain in infinite excess.   45

The proof of this is in that first proud one,
   the highest of all creatures, who plunged down
   unripe because he would not wait for light;   48

hence, clearly, every lesser nature is
   too small a vessel to contain that Good
   which knows no bounds, whose measure is Itself.   51

Therefore, our vision which can only be
  one of the rays that come from that prime Mind
  which penetrates every created thing,   54

cannot of its own nature be so weak
  as not to see that its own Principle
  is far beyond what our eyes can perceive.   57

And so the vision granted to your world
  can no more fathom Justice Everlasting
  than eyes can see down to the ocean floor: 60

while you can see the bottom near the shore,
  you cannot out at sea; but nonetheless
  it is still there, concealed by depths too deep.   63

There is no light except from that clear sky
  forever cloudless—darkness is the rest,
  the shadow or the poison of the flesh.   66

Now you can see what hiding place it was
  concealed from you the truth of living Justice
  concerning which you were so plagued with doubts;   69

for you would say: 'Consider that man born
  along the Indus where you will not find
  a soul who speaks or reads or writes of Christ,   72

and all of his desires, all his acts
  are good, as far as human reason sees;
  not ever having sinned in deed or word,   75

he dies unbaptized, dies without the faith.
  What is this justice that condemns his soul?
  What is his guilt if he does not believe?'   78

Now who are you to sit in judgment's seat
  and pass on things a thousand miles away,
  when you can hardly see beyond your nose?   81

The man who would argue fine points with me,
  if holy Scripture were not there to guide us,
  surely would have serious grounds for doubt.   84

O earthbound creatures! O thick-headed men!
  The Primal Will, which of Itself is good,
  never moves from Itself, the Good Supreme.   87

Only that which accords with it is just.
  It is not drawn to any finite good,
  but sending forth its rays creates that good."   90

Just as the stork once it has fed its young
  will fly around the nest, and as the chick
  she fed will raise its head to look at her,   93

so did that sacred image circle me,
  those many wills joined there to move its wings,
  and so did I lift up my head to it.   96

Circling, it sang, then spoke: "Even as my notes
  are too high for your mind to comprehend,
  so is Eternal Judgment for mankind."   99

Those blazing fires of the Holy Spirit
  stopped still, and then still in that ensign shape
  which had brought Rome the reverence of the world,   102

it raised its voice again: "And to this realm
  none ever rose who had not faith in Christ,
  before or after he was crucified.   105

But then there are all those who cry, 'Christ, Christ!'
  and at the Judgment Day will be less close
  to Him than will be those who know not Christ.   108

Such Christians shall the Ethiop condemn
  the Day those two assemblies separate,
  one rich, the other poor forevermore.   111

What will the Persians say, then, to your kings
  when they shall see God's open Book and read
  what has been written of their infamies?   114

There they will read, where Albert's deeds are found,
  that act already trembling on the pen,
  which shall lay waste to all the realm of Prague.   117

There they will read about the Seine's distress
  provoked by that debaser of the coin
  whose death will wear the hide of a wild boar;   120

there they will read about the thirsting pride
  by which the Scot and Englishman are maddened,
  neither content to stay within his bounds.   123

The book will show the lecherous, soft life
   of him of Spain, and the Bohemian
   who knew no valor nor had wish to know;   *126*

the book will mark an *I* for all the good
   the Cripple of Jerusalem has done,
   and *M* for all of his perversities;   *129*

the book will show the cowardice and greed
   of him who guards the island of the fire
   on which Anchises ended his long life,   *132*

and just to show how little he was worth,
   he will be written up in bits of words
   which will say much in very little space;   *135*

and clear to all will be the filthy deeds
   of his brother and uncle, who cuckold
   a splendid lineage, a double crown;   *138*

and Norway's king and Portugal's shall be
   recorded there, and Rascia's, who debased
   the coin of Venice and disgraced himself.   *141*

Oh happy Hungary, if she escapes
   further abuse! Happy Navarre if she
   but make a rampart of her mountain-chain!   *144*

In proof of this let everyone pay heed
   to Nicosia's and Famagosta's lot
   whose own beast makes them wail and shriek as he   *147*

keeps pace with all the others in this pack."

NOTES

2. that splendid image: The eagle formed by the spirits.

11 – 12. I heard its voice use words like I and Mine: The eagle,
representing Justice, is composed of a multitude of souls, but it
speaks with one voice and as one being. This conformity of the
wills of the individual souls suggests the single nature of Justice
which conforms to the will of God.

13 – 15. justice and piety": God's two ways of operating (see
Par. VII, 103) should guide the Empire and its rulers, whose

authority is received from God. The souls who appear in this sphere enjoy the degree of bliss to which they are entitled, by dint of their activities on earth as good and just rulers. Thus, they can aspire to no higher glory than that which they now have.

16. *I have left on earth a memory:* I.e., the memory of good deeds.

19—21. *Just as from many burning coals:* The image contained in this tercet and the next emphasizes, once again, the notion of unity.

22. *everlasting flowers:* By calling these sparks of light eternal blooms the Poet is preparing us for the final picture of the entire Paradise as the Celestial Rose (see *Par.* XXXIII, 9).

26. *the fasting that has kept me hungering:* The souls read in Dante's mind the question that has long perplexed him: are men who live in ignorance of Christ, without baptism or faith, damned or not?

28—30. *some other mirror:* The sacred mirror of God's justice. The angelic order of Thrones, which guides the sphere of Saturn, is the order which reflects Divine judgments. While the souls in other spheres see the reflection of God's judgment in the Thrones, the souls in the heaven of Jupiter (sphere of justice) seem to receive this light directly.

Sayers (p. 229) says: "If elsewhere in Heaven Divine Justice is mirrored, it is beheld by the souls of the Just more clearly than by any other."

34. *as the falcon, now freed from its hood:* Hunting with falcons was a popular sport among the nobility of the middle Ages. The falcon remained hooded until, once in the area of the hunt, its hood was removed.

37—39. *so moved the ensign made of woven voices:* By calling the eagle an "ensign" (*segno*) the reader is invited to think in terms of the banner of the Roman Empire. Here the eagle sings a hymn in praise of God before answering the Pilgrim's question.

40—45. *"He Who with His compass drew:* The eagle's discussion of Divine Judgment begins with an affirmation of the might and superiority of God over his creation. Since God is infinite, His power surpasses all things, and it is impossible for Him to create anything greater than Himself. Cf. Proverbs 8:27–29.

46–51. *The proof of this is in that first proud one:* The enormous superiority of God over his creatures is illustrated in the example of Lucifer who, though being the most beautiful angel and the closest of all creatures to God, fell because he refused to wait for Divine Grace which would have perfected or "ripened" him. If God's greatest creature failed to attain perfection, how much less likely it is that lesser beings can contain the goodness of God. (Cf. *Inf.* XXXIV, 34–36.)

52–57. *Therefore, our vision:* Human intellect, though only a fraction of that knowledge which God possesses, nevertheless is sufficient to realize that it cannot comprehend the mind of God.

58–60. *And so the vision granted to your world:* The eagle now addresses the Pilgrim's question.

64–66. *There is no light . . . darkness is the rest:* There is no truth ("light") except that which is found in God ("that clear sky"); all else is error, either ignorance ("shadow") or vice ("poison").

67. *you can see what hiding place:* I.e., the mystery of God's justice and judgment.

70–76. *'Consider that man born / along the Indus:* The eagle poses a particular example of the problem that had perplexed the Pilgrim: how is it just to condemn a nonbeliever if he had no opportunity to believe, yet was an upright man in every other respect? The problem recalls the situation of the virtuous pagans in Limbo (see *Inf.* IV, 33–42). The Indus River in India is used to suggest that area of the world isolated from Christianity. India was believed to mark the eastern limit of the inhabited world.

79–81. *Now who are you to sit in judgment's seat:* The answer to Dante's question is not an answer at all but a rebuke for the presumption of even attempting to second-guess God's justice. Verse 81 in the Italian reads "con la veduta corta d'una spanna," which means "with the short sight of a hand's span."

82–84. *The man who would argue fine points with me:* The eagle concedes that without the Scriptures to guide men, the ways of Divine Justice would be matter for dispute. Dante writes in the

De monarchia (II, vii, 4–5): "There are also certain judgments of God to which human reason, albeit unable to attain of its proper strength, is nevertheless raised by dint of faith in what is said to us in the sacred writings; as for instance this: that no one, however perfect in the moral and intellectual virtues, both as to disposition and practice, may be saved without faith, if he has never heard aught of Christ. For human reason of itself cannot see that this is just, but helped by faith it may" (Wicksteed).

85. *O earthbound creatures! O thick-headed men:* Here, in an unusual Address to the Reader, the eagle addresses all mankind. Boethius uses a similar address (cf. *Consol. philos.* III, iii).

88. *Only that which accords with it is just:* Since God is supremely just, what He does cannot be construed as anything but just. Likewise, whatever is seen to be in accordance with the will of God must be just. The only question to be asked, therefore, is whether an earthly judgment is in conformity with the Divine Will.

91. *Just as the stork:* This tender image of the stork that has just fed its young, describing the movement of the souls around the Pilgrim, is a surprising one, as it contrasts with the magnificence of the enormous (one feels) figure of the eagle.

100–105. *Those blazing fires of the Holy Spirit / stopped still:* The souls cease their circling, and, maintaining the shape of the imperial eagle ("ensign shape," see note 37), speak once more.

104–108

Dante for the third time in the *Comedy* uses the word "Christ" three times in rhyme position with itself here in verses 104, 106, and 108.

106. *there are all those who cry, 'Christ:* The eagle at this point suggests that those who say they are Christians are in fact less like Christ than those who never knew him (cf. Matt. 7:21–23: "Not every one that saith unto Me, Lord, Lord, shall enter into the Kingdom of heaven," etc.). There follows a condemnation of contemporary monarchs who are engaged in political or moral misdeeds.

109–11. *Such Christians:* The Ethiop (i.e., heathens in general) will condemn these "Christians" on Judgment Day, when the saved ("rich") and the damned ("poor") shall be separated ("the day those two assemblies separate," 110). Cf. Matt. 25:31 – 46; also 8:11 – 12.

112. *Persians:* Like "Ethiop" in verse 107, the word here stands for heathens in general.

113. *God's open Book:* The Book of God's judgment. (See note to *Par.* XV, 51.

115 – 41

In this series of nine tercets condemning the Christian rulers of Dante's time the device of anaphora is used: in the Italian text the first three tercets begin with the adverb *Li* (there), the next three tercets with the verb *Vedrassi* (The book will show) and the third three with the conjunction *E* (And). So then, in Italian the first group begins with *l*, the second with *v* (which is the same as *u*), and the final group with *e*, spelling out the word *lue*, which means "pestilence." This is not the first time Dante makes use of the anaphoric device (see *Purg.* XII, 25 – 63).

115 – 17. *they will read, where Albert's deeds are found:* Albert of Austria, though never crowned, was elected Emperor in 1298. Becoming jealous of the power of Wenceslaus IV of Bohemia, Albert in 1304 invaded that country and laid waste to it, "which shall lay waste to all the realm of Prague," (117)—the reason for the use of the future tense, of course, is that the event has not taken place by the time of the fictional date of the poem.

118. *the Seine's distress:* The grief which the French people were made to suffer. The Seine River stands for all of France.

119 – 20. *provoked by that debaser of the coin:* To pay for the wars against Flanders, Philip the Fair inflated French currency, resulting in economic ruin for many. In 1314 he was killed by a fall from his horse when a wild boar charged between the horse's legs: "whose death will wear the hide of a wild boar" (120). The prediction of his death is couched in vague terms precisely to give it the mysterious air of something that is seen happening sometime in the future.

121 – 23. *about the thirsting pride:* In the early fourteenth century Edward I and Edward II were at war with Scotland under Wallace and Bruce. The "thirsting pride" is their desire for do-

minion. There is some confusion as to Dante's referent with the word "Englishman" in verse 122.

125. *him of Spain, and the Bohemian:* Ferdinand IV, King of Castile and Leon (1295 – 1312) is "him of Spain." The king of Bohemia is Wenceslaus IV (1270 – 1305). (See *Purg.* VII, 101.)

127 – 29. *The book will mark an I for all the good:* "The Cripple" is Charles II of Naples, titular king of Jerusalem. Charles is characterized here as having one (*I*) virtue as opposed to one thousand (*M*) vices. His one good quality was said to have been his liberality.

131. *him who guards the island of the fire:* Frederick II of Sicily had at one time supported the Imperial cause, but on the death of Emperor Henry VII, he abandoned it. Sicily is "the island of the fire."

132. *Anchises:* The father of Aeneas, Anchises died in Sicily after the arrival of the Trojans (see *Aen.* III, 707 – 15).

133 – 35. *to show how little he was worth:* As a mark of Frederick's baseness and insignificance, in the book of judgment he will be allotted a small place, but shorthand will be needed to fill that space with his many deeds.

137. *his brother and uncle:* Frederick's brother was James II of Aragon. His uncle was James, King of the Balearic Islands.

138. *a double crown:* The kingdoms of Aragon and Mallorca.

139. *Norway's king and Portugal's:* Norway's king was Haakon V (1299 – 1319) who engaged in wars with Denmark. Diniz (or Dionysius), the king of Portugal (1279 – 1325), is thought to have been one of the better rulers of the time. The reason for his inclusion here is unclear.

140. *Rascia's:* The King of Rascia. The capital of Serbia, Rascia was commonly used to refer to that country. Stephen Urosh II, (1275 – 1321), Rascia's king, counterfeited the Venetian coinage by issuing coins of debased metal in imitation of the Venetian *grosso*.

142 – 43. *O happy Hungary, if she escapes:* The throne of Hungary which had belonged to Charles Martel (see *Par.* VIII, 64 – 66) was usurped by Andrew III.

143 – 44. *Happy Navarre if she / but make a rampart:* The king-dom of Navarre, if she could use the Western Pyrenees Mountains to protect her from French annexation, might remain happy as she is. Navarre came under French rule in 1304.

145 – 48. *In proof of this:* Navarre (and any who are at peace) should take the examples of Nicosia and Famagosta as represen-tative of the evils that may befall them. These towns of Cyprus were suffering under the corruption of the rule of Henry II of Lusignan, a Frenchman, He is "the beast" who keeps up with the evil deeds of other monarchs who are "the others in this pack" mentioned above.

CANTO XX

When the individual souls composing the eagle have
finished singing, the eagle tells the Pilgrim to watch its eye
closely as it points out six famous souls who were champions of
justice on earth. First the eagle introduces King David, who is
the pupil of the eye, after which come the five lights that form
the eyebrow of the great bird: the Emperor Trajan, who is the
soul closest to the eagle's beak, then Hezekiah followed by the Em-
peror Constantine, then King William II of Naples and Sicily, and
last the Trojan Ripheus. The Pilgrim is puzzled by the presence of
the two pagans, Trajan and Ripheus, and he asks why they are here.
The eagle explains that they were Christians when they died through
the power of Divine Grace and that the workings of predestination
are even beyond the understanding of the souls in Paradise. As the
eagle speaks the two lights of Trajan and Ripheus flash in accompani-
ment.

When he who floods the whole world with his light
   has sunk so far beneath our hemisphere
   that day on every side has disappeared,   *3*

the sky which he, the sun, alone had lit
   before, now suddenly is lit again
   by many lights, reflections of the one;   *6*

I was reminded of this heavenly change
   the moment that the emblem of the world
   and of its lords was silent in its beak,   *9*

for all those living lights were now ablaze
   with brighter light as they began their songs,
   whose fleeting sweetness fades from memory.   *12*

O sweetest love which wraps you in its smiles,
   how ardent was your music from those flutes
   played with the breath of holy thoughts alone!   *15*

And when those precious, light-reflecting jewels
   with which I saw the sixth planet begemmed
   imposed silence upon their angel tones,   *18*

I seemed to hear the murmur of a stream
    as its clear waters flow from rock to rock
    revealing the abundance of its source.   *21*

And as at the lute's neck the sound of notes
    take form, as does the breath that fills a flute
    escape as music through an opening,   *24*

just so without a moment of delay,
    the murmur of the eagle seemed to climb
    up through its neck, as through a hollow space,   *27*

where it became a voice, and from the beak
    emerged the words which I had longed to hear
    and which are now inscribed upon my heart.   *30*

"That part of me which in a mortal eagle
    sees and endures the sun," it said to me,
    "I want you now to fix your gaze upon.   *33*

Of all the fire-souls which give me form
    the ones that give the eye within my head
    its brilliant lustre are the worthiest.   *36*

He at the center as the pupil's spark
    wrote songs inspired by the Holy Spirit
    and once conveyed the ark from town to town,   *39*

and now he knows the value of his psalms
    so far as his own gifts contributed,
    for his bliss is commensurate to it.   *42*

Of those five souls that form my eyebrow's arch
    the one who shines the closest to my beak
    consoled the widow who had lost her son,   *45*

and now he knows from living this sweet life,
    and having lived its opposite, how dear
    it costs a man to fail to follow Christ.   *48*

He who comes next on the same curving line
    along the upper arch of which I speak
    delayed his death by his true penitence,   *51*

and now he knows that God's eternal laws
    are not changed when a worthy prayer from earth
    delays today's events until tomorrow.   *54*

The next light went to Greece bearing the laws
    and me to let the Shepherd take his place—
    his good intentions bore the worst of fruits;   57

and now he knows that all the evil sprung
    from his good action does not harm his soul,
    though, thereby, all the world has been destroyed.   60

And at the down sweep of the arch you see
    that William, mourned for by the land which now
    deplores the fact that Charles and Frederick live;   63

and now he knows how much is loved in Heaven
    a righteous king, and splendidly he makes
    this clear to all through his effulgence here.   66

Who in your erring world would have believed
    that Ripheus of Troy was here, the fifth
    in this half-circle made of holy lights?   69

And now he knows much more about God's grace
    than anyone on earth and sees more deeply,
    though even *his* eye cannot probe God's depths."   72

Then like the lark that soars in spacious skies,
    singing at first, then silent, satisfied,
    rapt by the last sweet notes of its own song,   75

so seemed the emblem satisfied with that
    reflection of God's pleasure, by Whose will
    all things become that which they truly are.   78

Though my perplexity must have shown through,
    as color shows clear through a piece of glass,
    I could no longer bear to hide my doubt—   81

it burst forth from my lips: "How can this be?"—
    such was the pressure of its weight—at which
    I saw a festival of flashing lights.   84

And then, its eye more radiant than ever,
    the blessèd emblem answered me at once
    rather than keep me wondering in suspense: 87

"I see that you believe these things are true
    because I say them, but you see not how;
    thus, though they are believed, their truth is hid.   90

You do as one who apprehends a thing
    by name, but cannot see its quiddity
    unless someone explains it for his sake.   93

Regnum celorum suffers violence
    gladly from fervent love, from vibrant hope
    —only these powers can defeat God's will: 96

not in the way one man conquers another,
    for That will wills its own defeat, and so
    defeated it defeats through its own mercy.   99

The first soul of the eyebrow and the fifth
    cause you to wonder as you see this realm
    of the angelic host adorned with them.   102

They did not leave their bodies, as you think,
    as pagans, but as Christians with firm faith
    in feet that suffered and in feet that would.   105

One came from Hell (where there is no return
    to righteous will) back to his flesh and bones,
    and this was the reward for living hope;   108

the living hope that fortified the prayer
    made unto God that he be brought to life
    so that his will might be set free to choose.   111

This glorious soul, having regained the flesh
    in which it dwelt but a short space of time,
    believed in Him Who had the power to save;   114

and his belief kindled in him such fire
    of the true love that at his second death
    he was allowed to join our festival.   117

The other soul, by means of grace that wells
    up from a spring so deep that no man's eye
    has ever plumbed the bottom of its source,   120

devoted all his love to righteousness,
    and God, with grace on grace, opened his eyes
    to our redemption and he saw the light,   123

and he believed in this; from that time on
    he could not bear the stench of pagan creed,
    and warned all its perverse practitioners.   126

He was baptized more than a thousand years
    before baptism was—and those three ladies
    you saw at the right wheel were his baptism.   *129*

Predestination! Oh, how deeply hid
    your roots are from the vision of all those
    who cannot see the Primal Cause entire!   *132*

You men who live on earth, be slow to judge,
    for even we who see God face to face
    still do not know the list of His elect,   *135*

but we find this defect of ours a joy,
    since in this good perfected is our good;
    for whatsoever God wills we will too."   *138*

Thus, with these words did the supernal sign
    administer to me sweet medicine
    to remedy the shortness of my sight.   *141*

And as a good lute-player will accord
    his quivering strings to a good singer's voice
    making his song all the more beautiful,   *144*

so, as the eagle spoke, I can recall
    seeing the holy lights of those two souls
    (as if two blinking eyes were synchronized)   *147*

quiver in perfect timing with the words.

NOTES

1 – 3. *he who floods the whole world with his light:* The sun that
sets.

4 – 6. *the sky:* In Dante's time it was generally thought that
the stars took their light from that of the sun.

7 – 12. *I was reminded of this heavenly change:* Just as the one
light of the sun is fragmented into many lights when reflected
by the stars, so the voice of the eagle, which was heard as from
one being, now is broken into the voices of the individual souls
who sing in chorus.

12. *whose fleeting sweetness fades from memory:* The beauty of the

souls' light and song is impossible to recount, since it is impossible to recapture in the mind.

13. *O sweetest love which wraps you in its smiles:* The love which the souls have for God is expressed, as is the case with all the souls in Paradise, through the joy of their light.

17. *the sixth planet:* The sphere of Jupiter. As the reader will soon see for himself, when the eye of the great eagle is described, the number six is stressed.

19–30

These tercets build sound imagery upon that of light in the preceding tercets, and do so in a shifting yet progressive manner. The murmur of a flowing stream becomes the gentle music of a lute, and then of a flute. Finally, the murmur is recognized as a voice. Each phase of the progression is deeply effective.

30. *and which are now inscribed upon my heart:* The names of some of the spirits occupying this heaven which the Pilgrim is longing to hear are now "inscribed" in his memory ("heart").

31–32. *"That part of me which in a mortal eagle / sees and endures the sun":* The eagle directs the Pilgrim to look at his eye, of which there is only one, since the heraldic emblem of Empire was always pictured in profile. (See also *Par.* I, note to 47–48.)

37–72

Again, as in the preceding canto (cf. *Par.* XIX, 115–41), Dante makes use of the device of anaphora, though here it is less complicated: two tercets are allotted to each of the six great souls composing the eye and brow of the eagle, and the second of each pair of tercets (twelve in all) will begin with the words "and now he knows" *(ora conosce).* The anaphora works as a heavenly echo sounding loud and clear that underscores with austere dignity the great distance and difference between then and now, the then of life and God's justice on earth and the now of it in Paradise (see also *Purg.* XII, 25–63 for a different use of anaphora).

Concerning this portion of the canto Grandgent (p. 803) says: "In the description of this company we find a sort of formal symmetry that reminds us of the architectural structure of lines 25–63 in *Purgatorio,* where are pictured the carvings on the floor of the terrace of Pride: in our canto lines 37–72 fall into six sections of six verses each, and the second tercet of every section begins with Ora conosce.' Thus the number six is made conspicuous in the sixth heaven."

37–39. *He at the center:* King David, whose psalms were inspired by the Holy Spirit, had the ark of the covenant moved to Jerusalem (2 Kings 6:2–17; cf. also *Purg.* X, 55–64). He forms the pupil of the eagle's eye. See Figure 9.

40–42. *and now he knows the value:* Now, in heaven, David knows just what proportion of the creative effort of the psalms may be attributed to his individual creativity and what proportion is due to Divine inspiration. As each soul in turn is distinguished, the eagle informs Dante of the knowledge gained by each since arriving in Paradise. The difference in man's limited ability to understand the Divine plan is thus underscored in each soul's example.

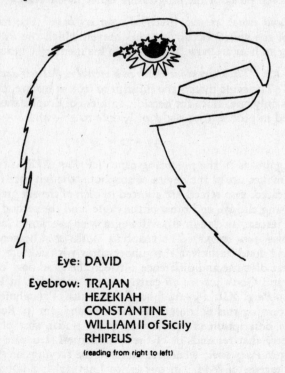

Eye: DAVID

Eyebrow: TRAJAN
HEZEKIAH
CONSTANTINE
WILLIAM II of Sicily
RHIPEUS

(reading from right to left)

44–48. *The one who shines the closest to my beak:* The Roman Emperor Trajan (who lived in Christian times but was a pagan at his death) was said to have granted a widow's request for compensation for the death of her son (*Purg.* X, 73–93). Further, a legend existed that Pope Gregory so prayed for Trajan's redemption that the Emperor was brought to life from his place in Limbo (the "opposite" [47] of Heaven), and Gregory baptized him to salvation.

49–54. *He who comes next on the same curving line:* Hezekiah, King of Judah, when told of his impending death, prayed that God remember his faithful service, and he was rewarded with fifteen more years of life (see 2 Kings 20:1–6).

55–60. *The next light went to Greece:* The Emperor Constantine, who occupies the highest point on the arch of the eagle's eyebrow, moved the capital of the Roman Empire to Byzantium, thereby leaving Rome to the Popes. This act, in itself, was not bad—only its consequences proved harmful. (Cf. Thomas Aquinas: ". . . if the consequences [of an action] follow by accident and seldom, then they do not increase the goodness or malice of the action . . . ," *Summa theol.* I–II, q. 20, a.5, resp.)

61–62. *you see / that William:* This is William II, "the Good," King of Naples and Sicily (1166–1189), a just ruler whose death was mourned by his people. He was known for his generosity toward religious institutions and toward his people, as his father, William I, "the Bad" (who ruled from 1154 to 1166) was the opposite.

63. *Charles and Frederick:* The kings of Naples and Sicily (see *Par.* XIX, 127–35, where they are reproached).

68. *Ripheus of Troy:* One of several Trojan heroes who fell during the sack of Troy and whom Virgil points out as "foremost in justice and zealous for the right" (*Aen.* II, 426–27). The presence of this relatively obscure pagan in Paradise is a further proof of the incomprehensible nature of Divine Justice.

It is interesting to note that of the six souls composing the eye of the eagle two are Jews, two are pagans, and two are Christians (see Porena, p. 199).

73–75. *Then like the lark that soars in spacious skies:* The lark was a lyrical figure in Provençal poetry and in the work of early

Italian poets. A number of commentators suggest that Dante may have had in mind the opening four lines of a poem by Bernart de Ventadorn:

> Can vei la lauzeta mover
> de joi sas alas contra 'l rai,
> que s'oblid' e's laissa chazer
> per la dussor c'al cor li vai . . .

> (When I see the lark joyously moving
> its wings against the rays of light,
> then, caught up in ecstasy, falling
> from sweetness rushing to its heart . . .)

But I see no reason to think that Dante had this or any other particular poem in mind when he composed this tercet. Sometimes Dante the Poet did get up from his desk, leave his library, walk out into the open air and look up into the sky. He may even have seen a lark on that particular day! The lark here should be seen in the same relationship to the eagle as was the stork in the preceding canto (cf. XIX, 91–96): the lyrical side of the great eagle of Justice.

76–78. *satisfied with that / reflection of God's pleasure:* God's "pleasure" is justice, represented by the presence in this heaven of two souls thought to be pagans. Love of justice conforms to God's will, and brings a soul to its true self.

80. *as color shows clear through a piece of glass:* Dante's feelings of confusion are as poorly concealed as a painted surface would be if covered by glass.

82. *"How can this be?":* Dante, once again attempting to understand God's justice, wants to know how Trajan, a pagan who lived after the birth of Christ, and Ripheus, a pagan before Christ, could have attained salvation.

84. *I saw a festival of flashing lights:* The souls grow brighter in anticipation of answering Dante's question.

91–93. *You do as one who apprehends a thing:* Dante, though knowing the truth of the salvation of Ripheus and Trajan, does not understand how this can be. The "quiddity" is the essence of something.

94. Regnum celorum *suffers violence:* The kingdom of heaven

(the term comes from Scriptures [Matt. 11:12]: "Regnum caelorum vim patitur" [The kingdom of heaven has been enduring violent assault]) willingly endures the assault of love or of hope. Either of these has the power to "defeat God's will" (96) which allows itself to be defeated ("for That will wills its own defeat," 98).

100. *The first soul of the eyebrow and the fifth:* Trajan and Ripheus.

103 – 105. *They did not leave their bodies:* Trajan and Ripheus were not pagans at their deaths: Trajan believed in the crucified Christ ("feet that suffered"), Ripheus in Christ to come ("in feet that would").

106 – 108. *One came from Hell:* Trajan, whose soul had been in Limbo. "Righteous will" (107) was not enough to lift the soul of Trajan out of Limbo: he needed God's sanctifying grace for his salvation, a grace which is granted only to the living.

109. *the living hope:* The desire of Gregory whose prayers brought Trajan to life and to be baptized to salvation. Concerning the salvation of Trajan and Gregory's prayers for him Thomas Aquinas says (*Summa theol.* III, Suppl., q. 71, a.5):

> Concerning the incident of Trajan it may be supposed with probability that he was recalled to life at the prayers of blessed Gregory, and thus obtained the grace whereby he received the pardon of his sins and in consequences was freed from punishment.

112 – 14. *This glorious soul, having regained the flesh:* Trajan was brought back to life so that he might know Christ and thereby gain salvation.

118. *the other soul:* Ripheus.

122 – 23. *God, with grace on grace, opened his eyes:* God bestowed special grace on Ripheus enabling him by means of implicit faith, comparable to that which God had given those who were harrowed from Hell, to believe in Christ before His coming. For this point of doctrine concerning the two kinds of grace: operating and cooperating grace ("grace on grace") see Thomas Aquinas (*Summa theol.* I – II, q. III, a.2, resp.) quoted by Singleton (pp. 342 – 43).

128. *those three ladies:* The theological virtues of Faith, Hope,

and Charity which Dante saw at the right wheel of the chariot of the Church in the Earthly Paradise at the top of the Mountain of Purgatory (*Purg.* XXIX, 121–29). And so, with these three ladies as proxies, Ripheus fulfills the requirement for salvation, which is baptism.

130–32. *Predestination:* Having accounted for the presence of Trajan and Ripheus in Paradise, the eagle reiterates man's inability to know the Divine plan. This "predestination" is in the restricted sense of salvation as is made clear in the following verses (133–35); it is, according to Thomas Aquinas, God's predestination *ab aeterno* which is then verified through the intervention of divine grace (*Summa theol.* III, q. 24, a.1).

136–38. *but we find this defect of ours a joy:* Here for the first time the eagle shifts from the first person singular (*I*) to speak from the point of view of the many (*we*) representing God's justice. In this tercet we are reminded of what Piccarda said earlier (*Par.* III, 52–54, 70–87) about the "good" or happiness of the souls in Paradise existing totally in the love of or conformity to the will of God.

142–48. *And as a good lute-player will accord:* The ending of the canto recalls its opening (10–30), in which the building voice of the eagle is compared to, among other things, the sound of the lute. The interplay of sound and light is also present in both these parts of the canto. What are stressed here in the canto's final image (one which the modern-day reader might find a bit gaudy) are the ideas of "concordance" and "symmetry," the first being certainly one of the major aesthetic themes of the *Paradise* and the second, without a doubt, an idea that is essential to the structure of the whole of the *Divine Comedy* as well as to its parts.

CANTO XXI

BEATRICE AND THE Pilgrim have now reached the sphere of
Saturn, and Beatrice tells him that she cannot smile here; her
beauty is now so great that if it were to shine forth in her smile,
the Pilgrim's mortal eyes could not withstand it. Countless lights
descend and circle about a golden ladder rising up beyond his
sight. A soul approaches; the Pilgrim asks why it has come to
him and why there is no music in this sphere. The soul explains:
there is no music here for the same reason that Beatrice does not
smile; and he has simply come to welcome him as a gesture of
love. In an attempt to understand the nature of predestination
the Pilgrim insists on asking why it was he and not another who
was chosen to welcome him. The soul whirls about, and then it
says that not even the highest order of angels could answer that
question, and that the Pilgrim should warn mankind, once he
has returned to earth, not to presume to know more than the
Blest themselves can understand. Humbled, the Pilgrim only
asks who the soul was on earth. He identifies himself as Peter
Damian, and, after describing his simple life as a contemplative,
with bitter sarcasm he criticizes the self-indulgence of the pres-
ent-day leaders of the Church. At his final words the other lights
descend and group around him, raising such a strange and thun-
derous shout that the Pilgrim is completely overwhelmed.

By now I had my eyes fixed once again
    upon my lady's face, and with my eyes,
    my mind, which was oblivious of all else.   3

She was not smiling, but, "Were I to smile,"
    she said to me, "what Semele became
    you would become, burned to a heap of ashes: 6

my beauty, as you have already seen,
    becomes more radiant with every step
    of the eternal palace that we climb,   9

and if it were not tempered, such effulgence
    would strike your sight the way a bolt of lightning
    shatters the leafy branches of a tree.   12

We have ascended to the Seventh Light
   which underneath the Lion's blazing breast
   sheds down its radiance mingled with his might.   *15*

Now back your eyes with an attentive mind;
   make of them perfect mirrors for the shape
   that in this mirror shall appear to you."   *18*

If one could understand with what delight
   my eyes were feeding on that blessèd face
   when I, at her command, turned them away,   *21*

then he would know how much joy it gave me
   to be obedient to my heavenly guide,
   were he to weigh one joy against the other.   *24*

Within the crystal which still bears the name,
   as it goes round the world, of that dear king
   under whose rule all evil was extinct,   *27*

I saw—color of gold as it reflects
   the sun—a ladder gleaming in the sky,
   stretching beyond the reaches of my sight.   *30*

And I saw coming down the golden rungs
   so many splendors that I thought the heavens
   were pouring out the light of every star.   *33*

As crows, obedient to instinctive ways,
   will flock together at the break of day
   to warm their frigid feathers in the sky,   *36*

some flying far away not to return,
   some coming back to where they started from,
   some staying where they were, wheeling about,   *39*

just such a rush of movement happened here,
   with all that sparkling having flocked as one,
   and then alighted on a chosen rung.   *42*

A splendor from the sparkling nearest us
   became so bright that I said to myself,
   "I see the love for me with which you glow,   *45*

but she, who teaches me the how and when
   to speak and not to speak, keeps still, so I,
   against my will, do well not asking now."   *48*

Then she who saw my silence in the sight
of Him whose vision can behold all things
said to me: "Satisfy your deep desire."   51

"I know I am not worthy in myself
to have an answer from you," I began,
"but for the sake of her who gives me leave   54

to speak, O blessèd life, hidden within
your happiness, I pray you, let me know,
what is it made you come so close to me,   57

and tell me why Heaven's sweet symphony
is silent here in this sphere while below
in all the rest its pious strains resound."   60

"Your hearing is but mortal like your sight,"
he said. "There is no singing here just as
there is no smile on Beatrice's face.   63

Only to welcome you with words and light
with which my soul is mantled do I come
this far down on the sacred ladder's steps;   66

nor was it greater love that prompted me:
as much and even more love burns above—
you see it in the flaming lights up there.   69

But that deep charity which urges us
to serve the wisdom governing the world
assigns each soul his task, as you can see."   72

"O holy lamp," I said, "I clearly see
how in this court a love entirely free
gladly obeys Eternal Providence;   75

what I find hard to understand is this:
why you alone among your fellow souls
have been predestined for this special task."   78

I had not finished speaking when the light
just like a millstone at full speed began
to spin around its inner luminance;   81

and then the love that was inside it said:
"A ray of God's light focuses on me
and penetrates the light enwombing me,   84

whose force once joined to that of my own sight
   lifts me above myself until I see
   the Primal Source from which such might is milked.   87

From this derives the joy with which I burn;
   the clearness of my flame will ever match
   my clarity of spiritual vision.   90

Yet even heaven's most illumined soul,
   that Seraph who sees God with keenest eye,
   could not explain what you have asked to know.   93

The truth you seek to fathom lies so deep
   in the abyss of the eternal law,
   it is cut off from every creature's sight.   96

And tell the mortal world when you return
   what I told you, so that no man presume
   to try to reach a goal as high as this.   99

The mind that shines here smolders down on earth;
   how, then, can it accomplish down below
   what it cannot even once it reaches heaven?"   102

I put aside that question which his words
   had so proscribed me from and only dared,
   with humble voice, to ask him who he was.   105

"Between two shores of Italy, not far
   from your own birthplace, rise great crags so high
   that thunder sounds from far below their peaks;   108

they form a humpback ridge called Catria
   below which stands a holy hermitage
   once dedicated to God's praise alone."   111

Thus he began his third address to me,
   and then went on to say: "There I became
   so steadfast in God's service that I lived   114

on nothing but plain foods in olive oil,
   suffering gladly heat and cold all year,
   content in only thoughts contemplative.   117

That cloister once produced for all these heavens
   harvests of souls, but now it is so barren,
   and soon its decadence must be exposed.   120

There I was known as Peter Damian—
   Peter the Sinner in Our Lady's house
   that lies along the Adriatic shore.   123

Little of mortal life remained to me
   when I was called and forced to wear the Hat
   which seems to pass only from bad to worse.   126

Lean and barefooted Cephas came, and came
   the mighty vessel of the Holy Spirit,
   both taking food wherever it was offered.   129

Your modern pastors need all kinds of help:
   one here, one there, to lead, to prop and hold
   up their behinds—they are so full of food;   132

their flowing cloaks cover the horse they ride:
   two beasts beneath one hide appear to move!
   O Heaven's Patience, what you must endure!"   135

As he spoke these last words, I saw more flames
   descending, whirling rung to rung, and they
   grew lovelier with every whirl they made.   138

Around this light they came to rest, and then,
   in one voice all those lights let out a cry
   the sound of which no one on earth has heard—   141

nor could I hear their words for all the thunder.

NOTES

1 – 15

Beatrice, here, seems to have taken on a new attitude. We
have never seen her quite like this before. She is both regal and
threatening as she prepares the Pilgrim for this new realm, where
singing and dancing will be absent. No mention is made of
entering into the sphere of Saturn, the heaven of the contempla-
tives. Beatrice simply announces with another "burning" image
(13 – 15), matched by the violence of verses 11 – 12, that they
are there in the "Seventh Light" (13). Just as the monastery, the
home of the contemplative, is that place between the life of our
world and the life in Heaven, so the sphere of Saturn is the

transition point between the six lower spheres and those above in the hierarchy of Heaven.

1 – 3. *I had my eyes fixed:* It is as though the Pilgrim were in deep contemplation, and well he might be considering the sphere he has reached.

5. *What Semele became:* At the instigation of Jupiter's jealous wife, Juno, Semele asked to see Jupiter, her lover, in his full splendor. The God's radiance was so great that Semele was burned to ashes (*Metam.* III, 253 – 315).

8 – 9. *with every step / of the eternal palace:* The steps leading to the palace can be thought of as the spheres that lead to the highest heaven of the Empyrean.

13 – 15. *the Seventh Light:* Saturn in the Spring of 1300, the fictional date of the *Comedy,* was in conjunction with the constellation of Leo. Del Lungo suggests that the astronomical reference serves to underscore the austere silence of Saturn and the burning soul of the contemplatives.

18. *this mirror:* The planet Saturn.

19 – 24. *If one could understand:* These two tercets are somewhat cold and complex. The idea the Poet is trying to convey, however, is simple: the Pilgrim's pleasure in contemplating the beautiful face of Beatrice is weighed against the pleasure of his obeying her command to turn his gaze elsewhere. If one could conceive of the joy he received from gazing at her, then one would understand how it gave him even greater joy to obey her commands, since he gave up the first joy (of looking at Beatrice) for the second joy (of obeying her).

26 – 27. *that dear king / under whose rule all evil was extinct:* Saturn, the father of Jupiter, was said to have ruled during a Golden Age of peace and harmony. Notice that the ladder described in the following tercet (28 – 30) is of gold.

29. *a ladder gleaming in the sky:* The ladder, a symbol of contemplation, appropriately appears in this planet of the contemplatives. Compare Dante's vision of the ladder with its golden lights to that of Jacob's heavenly ladder of angels (see Gen. 28:12). The ladder, unlike the eagle or the cross in the preceding cantos, is not formed out of the souls of the Blest; it is an

independent symbol of truth upon which the souls of the contemplatives move in no fixed order.

31. *the golden rungs:* The steps of the ladder "represent either the virtues by which contemplative souls mount upward, or the truths that are mastered one by one in consideration in the ascent to universal truth" (see Gardner, pp. 153–54).

34–42. *As crows:* The spirits are compared to crows that flock together and then break into varieties of motion. The particular movements may suggest the varieties of the contemplative calling—those who come to the contemplative life but find their work to be in the world; those who return to their monastic houses after brief excursions into the world; and those who remain secluded in their retreats. (See Sinclair, p. 311.) But, although it may be manifested differently, the contemplatives are unified in their aim. Note the energy of the metaphor: contemplatives are not static beings; they are active in their desire for God. The color of the crow suggests the garb of the monks or contemplatives on earth.

In these three tercets we see the two contrasting tones (warmth and coldness) established earlier in the canto now working together: the "frigid feathers" (36) of the crow-like souls that are "sparkling" (41) as they move.

45. *"I see the love for me with which you glow:* Many editors and translators end the Pilgrim's thought to himself with the last word of this verse. I choose to end it with verse 48, as does Petrocchi, who mentions the sequence of present tenses in verses 45–48 in support of this choice.

46. *but she:* Beatrice.

49–51. *Then she who saw my silence:* Beatrice again reads the Pilgrim's thoughts and tells him to express them. All human thought is reflected in the mind of God where the Elect are privileged to see it.

61–63. *"Your hearing is but mortal:* The spirit answers Dante's second question first, concerning the silence of this sphere: like the smile of Beatrice, which would be too strong for Dante's mortal eyes to bear, the song these spirits might sing is not sung because Dante is not yet spiritually strong enough to bear its sweetness.

The spirit, as yet unidentified, answers the Pilgrim's first question (the second having been answered in 61 – 63) as to why he in particular was chosen to speak to the Pilgrim. It was no greater love which prompted this spirit; the assignment was merely the soul's particular task. Clearly the Pilgrim's second question, which is quickly answered in one tercet, is of less importance that the first question, which seems to involve the mystery of predestination once again; however, this time it is of a different sort.

68 – 69. *as much and even more love burns above:* As we know by now, the measure of a soul's love in this realm is revealed by the brightness with which it shines, and, according to the speaker on the ladder, there are souls above him shining as brightly and even brighter than he.

70. *that deep charity:* God's love.

74 – 75. *a love entirely free / gladly obeys:* With this statement the Pilgrim seems to be clarifying the words of the soul who has just spoken to him. He wishes to show him that he understood the meaning of the words "to serve" in verse 71: serving the Divine Will is something the souls of the Elect do instinctively and freely out of their love for God.

76 – 78. *what I find hard to understand:* Dante once again returns to the perplexing problem of predestination, as he desires to understand why this soul was singled out to be given special grace, whereas others were not. (See also *Par.* XIX, 52 – 66, 79 – 90; XX, 130 – 38.)

79 – 81. *I had not finished speaking when the light:* As we have seen many times before in other heavens of the Paradise, souls become brighter in their eagerness to answer the Pilgrim's questions. This soul expresses his joy in a sudden spinning movement. (See also *Par.* XVIII, 41 – 42.)

82 – 102

The spirit does not in fact answer Dante's question involving predestination. He states that his individual power to love is in proportion to his ability to know God, the "clarity" of spiritual vision, bestowed by grace. The spirit acknowledges that this is no satisfactory explanation, but no one in heaven or on earth can penetrate the mysteries of God's will—even the Seraphim, the highest order of angels and closest in understanding to God. He warns of the foolishness of men who try to discover God's justice for, on earth, even the brightest mind sees but darkly. How can mortals begin to learn what even angels cannot discover?

84. *the light enwombing me:* Dante, as he sometimes does in this canticle, invents a word for the concept of "enclosed"; in this case it is *m'inventro,* which I interpret as "enwombing me."

87. *is milked:* The words in the Italian are *è munta,* literally meaning "is milked."

88. *From this:* By beholding the "Primal Source."

99. *a goal as high as this:* Mankind should not attempt to fathom the workings of Providence.

106. *two shores of Italy:* The Adriatic and Tyrrhenian seas.

109. *a humpback ridge called Catria:* Monte Catria in the Apennines is on the border of Umbria and the Marches.

110. *a holy hermitage:* The monastery of Santa Croce di Fonte Avellana.

112. *Thus he began his third address to me:* The first time this spirit addressed the Pilgrim was in verses 61−72 and the second in 83−102.

113. *"There I became:* In the "holy hermitage" (see above, n. 110).

115. *plain foods in olive oil:* Lenten fare, or foods that are not prepared with animal fat.

120. *and soon its decadence must be exposed:* The meaning of this verse is not clear. Is Dante alluding to a particular event that will make the degeneracy of that monastery clear to all the people or, as Casini and Barbi suggest, to the financial condition of the monastery which by 1321 was so bad that the papacy had to intervene. Or does it simply mean, as Momigliano seems to suggest, that since the monastery has so few monks now, eventually it will have to suffer the consequences. My translation tries to allow for all three interpretations.

121−23. *Peter Damian:* Known also as "Peter Sinner in Our

Lady's house," that is, in the monastery of Santa Maria in Porto near Ravenna, Peter Damian (ca. 1007 – 1072) rose from humble parentage to be an abbot, then a cardinal of the Church. As abbot of the Benedictine monastery at Fonte Avellana, he served a number of Popes and was a zealous reformer of church discipline. Much against his will, he was made cardinal of Ostia in 1057.

There has been much discussion of these three verses. See Singleton (pp. 354 – 55), Chimenz (pp. 818 – 19), and Palmieri (pp. 62 – 83). The basic problem with this tercet is one of identification of the speaker: is Peter Damian presenting himself to the Pilgrim with two different names (are the two Peters the same person?) by which he was known in two different places, or is Peter Damian one person and Peter Sinner a certain Pietro degli Onesti who died 1119 and was buried in the church of Santa Maria in Porto along the Adriatic and upon whose tombstone are inscribed the words *Petrus Peccans?*

But why would Dante want to introduce the name of another Peter in order to avoid a confusion which has nothing to do with the text? What Peter Damian is saying, perhaps, is that while he lived in the monastery of Fonte Avellana he was known as Peter Damian and when he moved to the monastery of Santa Maria in Porto in Ravenna he was known as Peter Sinner. What I feel he is not saying is: "I am the Peter Damian who lived in one place, not to be confused with Peter Sinner who lived in another." While it is true that the church and convent of Santa Maria in Porto were founded and inhabited not by Peter Damian but by Pietro degli Onesti, it is also true that Peter Damian was known to have signed many a letter with the words *Petrus Peccator monacus,* and Dante having seen the words *Petrus Peccator* on Pietro degli Onesti's tombstone in Ravenna may well have thought that Peter Damian was buried there.

131 – 32. *to lead, to prop and hold / up their behinds:* Every important official of the Church had a large retinue of lackeys. Those needed "to lead" were probably the *portantini,* who carried his chair; those needed "to prop" were the *bracciere,* who supported him while he was on his horse. Those employed to "hold up their behinds" is either a reference to those lackeys who held up the long train of the prelate's rich and elegant gown to keep it from dragging on the ground (*caudatari*) or to those who assisted him onto his horse (*staffieri*). In light of the fact that Dante makes fun of the size of these prelates in verse 132 ("they are so

full of food"), I prefer to think of these lackeys as *staffieri*, struggling to get some fat cardinal's opulent rear end onto the horse! My translation, however, allows for both interpretations.

134. *two beasts beneath one hide appear to move:* The cloaks of the modern prelates are so long and rich that they cover both the prelate in question and his horse, making the two appear as one beast beneath its covering or "hide."

136–42. *As he spoke these last words . . . all the thunder:* The other spirits now join in the whirling motion begun by Peter Damian in verses 79–81. In addition, the quiet of the sphere is now broken by a tremendous, thundering roar, which carries the reader on to the next canto where in verses 13–15 the reason for this explosion—certainly the loudest noise made in the *Comedy*—is explained. What started out to be a rather conventional canto with a few interesting touches, such as the absence of Beatrice's smile and the general silence of the sphere (reflecting the contemplative life), ends up in a very original fashion.

CANTO XXII

THE PILGRIM, STUNNED by the deafening shout at the close
of the last canto, turns for comfort to Beatrice. Like a mother
consoling her child, she tells him to remember that he is in
Heaven where everything is done for the good; had he understood
the words that he heard shouted, he would know the just venge-
ance that is to befall the corrupt clergy in his own lifetime. The
bright light of another soul, St. Benedict, now approaches and
speaks. After the saint gives a brief account of his life, the Pil-
grim asks the saint if it would be possible to see him without his
veil of light. St. Benedict explains that this will be possible only
in the highest of heavens where there is perfection and all desires
are satisfied. St. Benedict hoped that his order would climb the
ladder that reaches this highest heaven, but men no longer climb
and the monastic orders have relaxed their original spiritual dis-
cipline. Having said this the saint, together with his compan-
ions, rises in the form of a whirlwind up the ladder, and the
Pilgrim and his guide swiftly follow them up into the next
heaven: the sphere of the fixed stars. There they enter the con-
stellation of Gemini, the sign under which the Poet was born. In
order to put the world in its proper perspective Beatrice suggests
that the Pilgrim look back down through the seven celestial
spheres. He sees the earth and smiles at its puny insignificance.
Then turning to Beatrice, he fixes his eyes on her great beauty.

Shocked, in amazement, like a little boy
    who always runs back to the one in whom
    he trusts the most, so I turned to my guide;   3

and she, just like a mother quick to help
    her pale and breathless son by giving him
    her voice whose calmness always reassures,   6

said, "Don't you know that you are up in Heaven,
    and don't you know that all is holy here
    and every act here springs from righteous zeal?   9

Imagine had they sung or had I smiled,
    what would have happened to you then, if now
    you are so shaken by a single cry?   12

If you had heard the prayer within their shout
    you now would know the vengeance yet to come,
    though you will witness it before you die.   15

The sword of Here on High cuts not in haste
    nor is it slow—except as it appears
    to those who wait for it in hope or fear.   18

But now turn your attention to the rest;
    if you allow my words to guide your eyes,
    many illustrious spirits you will see."   21

As she directed me I turned my eyes
    and saw hundreds of little globes of fire
    growing in beauty through each other's light.   24

I stood there like the anxious man restrained,
    forced to hold back the thrust of his desire,
    longing to ask while fearing to offend;   27

and then the largest and the brightest one
    among those pearls came forward to fulfill
    my silent longing to know who he was.   30

Then from inside it I heard words: "If you
    could see, as I do, with what love we burn,
    you would have shared your silent thought with us.   33

But rather than to cause you some delay
    in reaching your high goal, I shall reply
    directly to the question you hold back.   36

The summit of that mountain on whose slope
    Cassino lies was once inhabited
    by people with perverse and false beliefs;   39

I was the first to carry up to them
    the name of Him Who brought down to the earth
    that truth which gives mankind the strength to rise;   42

such grace shone down on me that I reclaimed
    all the surrounding towns, converting them
    from pagan worship that seduced the world.   45

These other flames were all contemplatives,
    men who were kindled by the warmth that breeds
    the flowers and the fruits of holiness.   48

Here is Macarius and Romuald,
   here are my brothers who kept to the cloisters,
   and, never roaming, kept a steadfast heart."   51

And I to him: "The love you have shown me
   in speaking this way and the good intentions
   I truly see glowing in all your fire   54

allow my confidence to open wide:
   it grows, unfolding petals like a rose
   warmed by the sun, till now it is full blown: 57

therefore, I pray you father, please tell me,
   assure me: do I have sufficient grace
   to see the unveiled image of your face?"   60

Whereon he said: "Brother, your high desire
   shall be fulfilled in the last sphere, for there
   not only mine but every wish comes true;   63

for there, and only there, is every wish
   become a perfect, ripe, entire one,
   there where each part is always where it was: 66

that sphere is in no space, it has no pole,
   and since our ladder reaches to that height,
   its full extent is stolen from your sight.   69

It was the patriarch Jacob who saw
   our ladder stretch to touch the final height,
   the time he dreamed of it so thronged with angels.   72

But now no man will lift a foot from earth
   and try to climb it, and my Rule is worth
   the wasted parchment it is written on.   75

The walls that used to be our abbey cells
   are dens for beasts now, and the cowls monks wear
   are just so many sacks of rotting meal.   78

The greed of usury, however gross,
   offends God less than does that holy fruit
   which drives the hungry hearts of monks insane;   81

for what the Church has in its keeping should
   be for the poor who ask it in God's name,
   not for the families of monks—or worse.   84

The flesh of mortals is so weak: on earth
   a good beginning does not last as long
   as the oak's springing to the acorn's birth.   *87*

Peter built his without silver or gold,
   and I constructed mine with prayer and fast
   while Francis, his convent, with humbleness;   *90*

if you examine each one's origins,
   then look again at what became of it,
   you see the white has withered into dark.   *93*

Yet Jordan's waters at the will of God
   flowed backward and the Sea fled—miracles
   far greater than if God now helped His Church."   *96*

These were his words to me; then he drew back
   into his company whose flames closed in,
   and like a whirlwind, they were swept on high.   *99*

With a mere gesture my sweet lady sped
   me up behind them, up the ladder's rungs,
   my nature conquered by her greater power.   *102*

Down here on earth where men go up or down
   by natural means, there never was a speed
   to match the motion of my wings up here.   *105*

Reader, as I hope ever to return
   here to this holy triumph for whose sake,
   I weep my sins and beat my breast—no quicker   *108*

could you have pulled your finger from a flame
   and thrust it in, than I caught sight and was
   already in the sign that follows Taurus.   *111*

O glorious constellation! O mighty stars
   pregnant with holy power which is the source
   of all of whatever genius may be mine,   *114*

in company with you there rose and set
   He who is father of all mortal life
   when I drew my first breath of Tuscan air;   *117*

and then, when that grace was bestowed on me
   to enter the great sphere that makes you turn,
   to your own zone of stars I was assigned!   *120*

To you devoutly my soul breathes its prayer
    to grant it strength enough for what is now
    the hardest phase to reach the journey's end.   123

"You are so close to final blessedness,"
    said Beatrice, "that you now must keep
    your eyes unclouded and your vision keen;   126

and so, before insiding further here,
    look down and see how vast a universe
    I have already put beneath your feet,   129

so that your heart, knowing the utmost joy,
    may greet that host of the Triumphant
    who come in joy through this ethereal round.   132

My vision travelled back through all the spheres,
    through seven heavens, and then I saw our globe;
    it made me smile, it looked so paltry there.   135

I hold that mind as best that holds our world
    for least, and I consider truly wise
    the man who turns his thoughts to other things.   138

I saw Latona's daughter glowing full
    without those shadows which had led me once
    to think that she was rare and dense in parts.   141

On your son's face, Hyperion, my eyes
    could gaze, and I saw, circling close to him,
    how Maia and Dione's children move;   144

From there I saw the tempering of Jove
    between his son and sire—and it was clear
    how they could change position in their course.   147

All seven at one time were visible:
    I saw how vast they were, how swift they spun,
    and all the distances between the spheres;   150

as for the puny threshing-ground that drives
    us mad—I, turning with the timeless Twins,
    saw all of it, from hilltops to its shores.   153

Then, to the eyes of beauty my eyes turned.

Beatrice's role as the Pilgrim's guide takes on a maternal aspect in response to his reaction to the noise he has just heard. Dante's inability to comprehend what is happening around him is indicative, in a general sense, of his lack of understanding of the contemplative life. It is now up to Beatrice to reassure him and up to the souls in this sphere to instruct him. The mother-child relationship present in these opening verses will recur at the opening of the next canto, where it plays an important part in setting the tone for the action that follows (see note 1–12 of *Par.* XXIII).

9. *every act here springs from righteous zeal:* The contemplative life is not a passive one; its adherents are not detached from what transpires around them. The souls in this sphere react with indignation ("righteous zeal") to the wrongs committed on earth in the name of the Church. Righteous zeal or indignation, St. Thomas tell us, springs from intense love.

13–15. *If you had heard the prayer within their shout:* The "cry" heard by Dante at the end of the preceding canto was a prayer for retribution against corrupt prelates and monks. The "vengeance yet to come" is unspecified: Beatrice may be referring to the attack on Boniface VIII at Anagni, or to the debasement of the Roman Curia by the relocation of the papal court at Avignon. It could also be a reference to the fulfillment of the prophecy made in the *Purgatory* (XXXIII, 43–44: the "five hundred, ten, and five").

16–18. *The sword of Here on High:* This is God's judgment, which is never premature or tardy except to those who either fear it or desire it.

23–24. *little globes of fire / growing in beauty through each other's light:* The spirits shine individually and collectively, as they respond to one another's joy and love.

25–27. *like the anxious man restrained:* The Pilgrim, having been overwhelmed by the great cry he heard from the souls in this sphere, still feels bewildered and unsure. He also displays humility, as befits his status as a mortal visitor. Some critics (Sayers, Carroll) have suggested that his fear of presumption is tied to the Rule of St. Benedict, which holds: "The 9th degree of humility is that a monk restrain his tongue from speaking and, keeping silence, do not speak until he is spoken to." Thus, is it a kind of instinct that causes Dante to respect the Rule? Or is it just his awe?

28. *the largest and the brightest one:* This is the spirit of St. Benedict, founder of monasticism in the Western Church. Born in 480 of a noble Umbrian family, he was educated in Rome. As a young man he isolated himself in a cave near Abruzzi for three years, and afterwards was elected abbot of a monastery at nearby Vicovaro. His rule was such a severe one that the monks under his direction attempted to poison him. In 528 he moved to Monte Cassino, where he founded his own monastery. He died there in 543. The light of this saint does not declare himself until verse 40, and he does so without mentioning his name.

St. Benedict's precepts were set down in his *Regula monachorum.* Originally intended as a set of rules to govern the lives of ambulatory monks, the work became the rule of conduct for all Western monks. Within the Benedictine order, manual labor and instruction of the young are emphasized.

31–33. *I heard words: "If you:* St. Benedict assures Dante that he need not have hesitated to speak (however, his questions are ascertained without his having to articulate them!).

35. *your high goal:* That is, the end of the journey and the vision of God.

37–39. *that mountain on whose slope / Cassino lies:* This is Monte Cassino, which overlooks the Liri Valley, approximately halfway between Naples and Rome. The town of Cassino is located at the mountain's base. When St. Benedict arrived there, pagan worship existed; a temple to Apollo and a grove sacred to Venus were destroyed on his orders. It was upon the ruins of the Temple of Apollo that St. Benedict built his famous monastery.

46. *These other flames were all contemplatives:* This is the first explicit reference to the souls of the contemplatives in the sphere of Saturn.

47–48. *the warmth that breeds / the flowers and the fruits of holiness:* The fire of Divine Love provides the warmth that in turn produces pious ideas (flowers) and good works (fruits).

49. *Macarius and Romuald:* Several saints are known by the name Macarius, the two most famous being St. Macarius the Elder (301 – 391), also called the Egyptian, and St. Macarius the Younger of Alexandria (d. 404). Both were disciples of St. Anthony. St. Macarius the Elder spent 60 years in the Libyan desert, engaged in manual labor and prayer. St. Macarius the Younger directed the activities of 5,000 monks, and is known as the founder of Eastern monasticism. As such, he can be viewed as the counterpart of St. Benedict, and is probably the saint to which Dante refers in this sphere.

Born ca. 950 in Ravenna of the Onesti family, Romuald founded the Order of Camaldoli, or reformed Benedictines. He entered the Benedictine order around 970 and lived as a hermit. He later established hermitages, including the monastery of Camaldoli in the Casentino near Florence. His order (which was sanctioned by Pope Alexander II in 1072) prescribed a life of pure contemplation. Under his direction, the monastic habit was changed from the Benedictine black to white. Romuald died ca. 1027.

52 – 57. *"The love you have shown me:* This powerful image of the unfolding rose in these verses is a reiteration as well as development of the image in verses 47 – 48. Here, Dante relates his own experience to that of the contemplatives: divine love (the sun's warmth) provides knowledge and understanding (the blooming rose), which then lead to appropriate conduct (fruit). See also verses 64 – 66.

60. *to see the unveiled image of your face?":* It is not clear why Dante desires to see the human features of this soul in particular. There is no evidence that the Poet held Benedict in more reverence than he did any of the other saints. Certainly there are other souls of the Blest whom Dante would have preferred to see in the flesh. On a symbolic level, the "unveiling" could represent the bestowal of understanding upon Dante through special grace, but it is too early in the journey for this; he will, however, attain this kind of vision at the end of his journey (see *Par.* XXX, 43 – 45). Viewed another way, these verses could suggest that Dante is asking to see the soul in its true essence, behind its radiance— this is one of the questions central to contemplative life.

61 – 65. *in the last sphere:* Dante's wish for vision (or understanding) will be granted in the Empyrean where he will see all

of the Blest in their human form. Vision is the reward of all those who climb the ladder of contemplation to the top. It is in the Empyrean that every "desire" (61) becomes "perfect, ripe, entire" (64) in the presence of God. Dante uses these three adjectives, all of them meaning basically the same thing, as a reflection of the Trinity in whose presence all desire is perfected.

66–67. *there where each part is always where it was:* The Empyrean is eternal and unchanging; it does not revolve like the lower spheres. It exists "in no space," that is, only in the mind of God.

70–72. *Jacob:* "He dreamed that a ladder was set upon the ground with its top reaching to heaven; angels of God were ascending and descending on it" (Gen. 28:12).

73–96

St. Benedict now undertakes to denounce the monastic orders and the Church for the corruption that has overtaken them. His condemnation is expressed in very strong terms, as he decries the fact that the ladder, representing the journey of contemplation, has been seriously neglected.

74–75. *my Rule is worth / the wasted parchment:* This is a reference to St. Benedict's *Regula monachorum,* which is no longer followed, and therefore worth very little. In other words, his Rule or Order is not worth the paper it is written on.

79–80. *The greed of usury . . . offends God less:* Usury, the lending of money with an interest charge, is not as offensive to God as the greed of monks for Church money ("holy fruit" [80], intended to assist the needy).

84. *not for the families of monks—or worse:* Not only do the greedy monks use Church money for themselves and their families, but they also use it for their concubines and illegitimate children.

85–87. *a good beginning does not last as long:* Using the fruit image again, St. Benedict states that, like the acorn, human nature must have the proper conditions in which to flourish, otherwise it becomes corrupt in a very short time; that is, in the world a good beginning does not last as long as it takes the oak to sprout and produce its fruit or acorn. Beatrice expresses a similar idea in an even more complicated fashion later on in the

Paradise (XXVII, 136–38). Benedict is of course referring here to the members of his Order who start out with good intentions which are soon corrupted.

93. *you see the white has withered into dark:* The wilting of a flower usually brings on a change in its color as it falls into decay. Likewise, the holy orders on earth have withered and decayed. This verse points back to verse 87.

94–96. *Yet Jordan's waters:* The Jordan was turned back and the Red Sea was parted, both as a result of Divine intervention. These miracles far exceed the intervention now required to cure the Church of its ills; therefore, it could very well happen!

99. *like a whirlwind:* The souls move away in a swirling, spinning motion, continuing the theme of movement in the previous canto. This motion also recalls the spinning top image in Canto XXI, 81.

101–102. *With a mere gesture:* Dante and Beatrice now rise up the ladder to the eighth sphere, that of the fixed stars. Verse 102, "my nature conquered by her greater power" is another indication that the journey to Paradise was taken in the flesh (see also *Par.* I, 73–75).

106. *Reader, as I hope ever to return:* This is the sixteenth and last time that Dante addresses himself to the reader. For the other three Addresses to the Reader in the *Paradise,* see V, 109; X, 7 and 22. There are five such Addresses in the *Inferno* (VIII, 94; XVI, 128; XX, 19; XXV, 46; XXXIV, 22) and seven in the *Purgatory* (VIII, 19; IX, 70; X, 106; XVII, 1; XXIX, 98; XXXI, 124; XXXIII, 136). See also the articles on the subject by Spitzer and Auerbach.

108–11. *—no quicker / could you have pulled your finger:* The speed image in these verses, like that of the bow and arrow in Canto II, 23–24, is an example of the rhetorical figure *hysteron proteron,* or "last first." Here, the action of recoiling from the heat of a flame is evoked before that of touching it. Dante insists here in his final Address to the Reader in the poem not only on the veracity of the journey, but that he was actually taken up and into the constellation under which he was born: "the sign that follows Taurus" is, of course, Gemini.

Dante the Pilgrim now addresses his own constellation as if it were his Muse, invoking its aid. Because he was born under the sign of Gemini, he is subject to its influence; in fact, in *Purg.* II, 73 – 81 he is careful to establish this influence of the heavenly bodies. Belief in the power of the stars to affect human character was an ancient one. It predated Christian belief but was eventually reconciled with the new religion when it was decided that the planets derived their power from God. (See Seznec.)

113 – 14. *the source / of all of whatever genius may be mine:* Dante attributes all the talent he possesses to the constellation of Gemini. Those born under the sign of "the Twins" were supposedly inclined to intellectual endeavors and the arts. We remember what Brunetto Latini tells the Pilgrim-Poet in *Inf.* XV, 55 – 56: "Follow your constellation / and you cannot fail to reach your port of glory."

115 – 16. *with you there rose and set / He who:* The sun was rising and setting in Gemini (May 21 – June 21) when Dante was born in 1265. We do not know the precise day of Dante's birth, however.

121 – 23. *To you devoutly my soul breathes its prayer:* It is no longer sufficient for the Poet to appeal, in an Invocation, to the Muses for their assistance as he did earlier in the *Paradise* as well as in the *Inferno* and *Purgatory;* he feels now that he must call on the very source of his talent or genius itself in the form of his own constellation. This devout appeal shows how strong and sincere was the Poet's belief in the influence of the heavenly bodies. Dante is about to enter the most important phase of his journey to God, and Beatrice makes this clear in the following tercet when she says, "You are so close to final blessedness. . . ."

127. *and so, before insiding further here:* The Poet invents a verb for the occasion. The verse in the original reads: "e però, prima che tu più t'inlei." He takes the pronoun *lei* and coins a verb from it: *inlei.* He has done this before (see *Par.* IX, 81).

130 – 32. *so that your heart:* In fact, what Beatrice announces here takes place in the following canto, where the Pilgrim witnesses the Triumph of Christ.

133 – 35. *My vision travelled back through all the spheres:* Dante,

now in the position of a soul elevated by contemplation, looks back down through the spheres he has traversed. The idea of the soul's return to its native star is a platonic one, and has already been established in Canto IV, 52–57. Other parallels are found in Cicero (*De re publica*, VI, in Scipio's dream): ". . . indeed the earth seemed to me so small that I was scornful of our empire, which covers only a single point, as it were, upon its surface." And in Boethius (*Consol. philos.* II, vii, 1–6):

> He that to honour only seeks to mount
> And that his chiefest end doth count,
> Let him behold the largeness of the skies
> and on the strait earth cast his eyes;
> He will despise the glory of his name,
> which cannot fill so small a frame.

See Singleton, who quotes Grandgent (pp. 366–68) for the above parallels and details concerning them.

136–38. *I hold that mind as best that holds our world / for least:* The man who holds the things of this world in high regard does not have his mind set on the right object. This idea is also found in Scipio's dream from the *De re publica* (VI, 20). See note 133–35 above.

139–41. *Latona's daughter:* This is the moon, or Diana, sired by Jupiter. For an explanation of the reference to the spots on the moon, see Canto II, 49ff. and note. The moon's other side, the side not facing the earth, was thought to be without markings.

142–43. *your son's face, Hyperion:* Hyperion, one of the Titans, was father of Helios, the Sun-god in earliest Greek mythology (called Sol by the Romans). For the first time in the poem the Pilgrim can bear to look into the sun. This is certainly an indication of his growth in vision and understanding.

144. *Maia and Dione's children:* Maia, the daughter of Atlas, produced Mercury by Jupiter. Dione's child was Venus. It is interesting to note that all of these references are to the parents of gods for whom heavenly bodies were named. A certain tenderness comes through in Dante's treatment of the spheres here as does the majesty of God's universe. All this regal affection is dropped when the Poet turns in disdain in the final tercet of the canto (151–53) to look at our earth. We can see the beginnings of the tender parent-offspring relationship at the outset of the

canto. This affection the Poet then transfers to the spheres, and in the following canto it is heightened to the point of dictating the entire mood of Canto XXIII.

145 – 47. *the tempering of Jove / between his son and sire:* Jove's son was Mars and his sire Saturn. Jove (Jupiter) is referred to as "tempering" because of its location in the planetary system: it is between the heat of Mars and the cold of Saturn. The movements of these planets as they drew near each other were observed and understood in Dante's time. From the Pilgrim's current vantage point in the Poem he is able to observe how these planets do change position, that is, in respect to the heaven of the fixed stars where he has just come to stand.

151 – 53. *the puny threshing-ground that drives / us mad:* The Pilgrim, looking down at the inhabited portions of the earth, comments on the insignificance of this "threshing-ground," our earth, where man is driven mad by his desire to possess as much as he can of the produce it yields. The same metaphor is used in Canto XXVII, 85 – 87.

154. *Then, to the eyes of beauty my eyes turned:* The Pilgrim's eyes are now averted from the visible, physical universe, and return to Beatrice's eyes, which represent the spiritual universe. As the canto ends the tone is serene and calm. All the fears and bewilderment of the canto's opening are gone; the Pilgrim is no longer "Shocked, in amazement, like a little boy" (1).

CANTO XXIII

Now in the sphere of the fixed stars Beatrice is anxiously
waiting for something to appear. Before long the sky begins to
lighten and Beatrice announces the arrival of the Church Trium-
phant. Looking up, the Pilgrim sees the light of Christ shining
on the whole assembly, and he is so transfixed and transported by
the sight of Him that he can no longer remember what he did at
that point. The Pilgrim can now look upon the smiling face of
Beatrice, and when he does, he is forced to admit that her beauty
defies description. Beatrice tells him to look again at the Triumph
of Christ. By this time Christ has ascended, but His splendid
light shines down on everyone from above as the Pilgrim fixes
his eyes on the brightest of the remaining lights, the Virgin Mary,
who is crowned by a torch borne by an angel who circles the
Virgin summoning her to follow her Son to the highest sphere.
They ascend while all the souls of the Church, their arms
stretched towards the heavens, begin to sing with unforgettable
beauty the hymn *Regina celi*.

As a bird quiet among the leaves she loves
   sits on the nest of her belovèd young
   all through the night that hides things from our sight,   *3*

anxious to look upon her longed-for ones,
   eager to go in search of food for them
   (her heavy labors she performs with joy),   *6*

foretelling daybreak from an open bough,
   she waits there for the sun with glowing love,
   her gaze fixed on the birth of a new day—   *9*

just so my lady waited, vigilant,
   intense, as she looked at that part of Heaven
   beneath which the sun's movement seems so slow;   *12*

then I, who saw her poised in longing there,
   became like one who wishes he had more
   and lets his hope feed on anticipation.   *15*

But time between the *when* was quick to pass—
  I mean the *when* of waiting and beholding
  the heavens growing bright and brighter still.   *18*

And Beatrice said: "Behold the hosts
  of Christ in triumph, and see all the fruit
  harvested from the turning of these spheres."   *21*

I saw her face aflame with so much light,
  her eyes so bright with holy happiness,
  that I shall have to leave it undescribed.   *24*

As in the clearness of a fullmooned sky
  Trivia smiles among eternal nymphs
  who paint the depths of Heaven everywhere,   *27*

I saw, above a myriad of lights,
  one Sun that lit them all, even as our sun
  illuminates the stars of his domain;   *30*

and through its living light there poured the glow
  of its translucent substance, bright, so bright
  that my poor eyes could not endure the sight.   *33*

O Beatrice, loving guide, sweet one!
  She answered: "That which overcomes you now
  is strength against which nothing has defense.   *36*

Within it dwell the wisdom and the power
  that opened between Heaven and earth the road
  mankind for ages longed for ardently."   *39*

As fire when it expands within a cloud
  must soon explode because it has no space,
  and, though against its nature, crash to earth,   *42*

so my mind there amid so rich a feast
  began to swell until it broke its bounds,
  and what became of it, it does not know.   *45*

"Open your eyes, look straight into my face!
  Such things have you been witness to that now
  you have the power to endure my smile."   *48*

As one just shaken from a dreamy sleep
  who having dreamed has now forgotten all
  and strives in vain to bring it back to mind,   *51*

so I was hearing her self-offering,
an invitation that can never be
erased within the book of my past life.   54

If at this moment all the tongues of verse,
which Polyhymnia and her sisters nourished
with their sweet milk, sang to assist my art,   57

their singing would not come to one one-thousandth
part of the truth about her sacred smile
nor how it set her holy face aglow;   60

so I find that my consecrated poem
describing Paradise will have to make
a leap, like one who finds his road is blocked.   63

Now bear in mind the weight of my poem's theme,
think of the mortal shoulders it rests on,
and do not blame me if I stagger here: 66

this stretch of sea my vessel's prow now dares
to cut is no place for a little boat
nor for a captain who would spare himself.   69

"Why are you so enamored of my face
that you do not turn to the lovely garden
flowering in the radiance of Christ?   72

There is the Rose in which the Word of God
took on the flesh, and there the lilies are
whose fragrance led mankind down the good path."   75

Thus Beatrice. And I, eager to serve
her every wish, surrendered once again
my frail eyes to the battle of the light.   78

Sometimes on cloudy days my eyes have seen
a ray of pure sunlight come streaming through
the broken clouds and light a field of flowers,   81

just so I saw there hosts of countless splendors
struck from above by ardent rays of love,
but could not see the source of such a blaze.   84

O Mighty Force that seals them with such light,
You raised yourself on high so that my eyes,
powerless in your presence, might perceive.   87

The sound of that sweet flower's name, the one
I pray to night and day, drew all my soul
into the vision of that flame of flames;   90

and when both of my eyes revealed to me
how rich and glorious was that living star
that reigns in Heaven, as it had reigned on Earth,   93

down from Heaven's height there came a flaming torch
shaped in a ring, as if it were a crown,
that spun around the glory of her light.   96

The sweetest sounding notes enrapturing
a man's soul here below would sound just like
a clap of thunder crashing from a cloud   99

compared to the melodious tones that poured
from the sweet lyre crowning the lovely sapphire
whose grace ensapphires the heaven's brightest sphere: 102

"I am angelic love encompassing
the joy supreme who breathed from out the womb
which was the place where our Desire dwelt,   105

and I shall circle you, Heavenly Lady
while you follow your Son, to highest heaven
and with your presence make it more divine."   108

With this the circling melody was sealed,
and all the other lights within that sphere
sang out the Blessèd Virgin Mary's name.   111

The regal mantle folding itself round
the turning spheres, and nearest to the breath
and ways of God it burns and quickens most,   114

was curving round us with its inner shore
at such a distance that from where I stood
as yet there was no sign that it was there;   117

and so my mortal eyes did not have strength
enough to see the crowned flame as it rose,
higher and higher, following her son.   120

And as an infant after it has suckled
will raise its arms up searching for its mother,
expressing all the love with which it glows,   123

so I saw all those radiances stretch
    their flame on high, thus making clear to me
    how deep their love, how much they cherished Mary.   *126*

There they remained suspended in my sight
    singing "*Regina celi*" in tones so sweet,
    the joy of it will never leave my mind.   *129*

O what abundant grace is stored up here
    inside those richest coffers who below
    in our world sowed the land with their good seed!   *132*

Herein they truly live and they enjoy
    the wealth their tears had won for them while they
    in Babylonian exile scorned all gold.   *135*

And here, victorious, beneath the Son
    of God and Mary and amid the good
    souls of the Old and the New Covennant   *138*

triumphs the one who holds the keys to glory.

NOTES

1 – 12

This image of the mother bird protecting her nestlings
through the night and watching the sky from an open branch,
eager for day to break so that she may care for them in a more
active way (by seeking food for them), is a mixture of tenderness,
intensity, and suspense. Beatrice is the mother bird, full of con-
cern for her nestling the Pilgrim as she fixes her gaze on the
coming of the light of day that will allow her to seek food—
spiritual sustenance—for her young one. This "maternal" simile
can be fully appreciated only if we look ahead in the canto and
discover what is about to happen: Christ, the rising sun, is about
to appear, and so is the Blessed Virgin Mary. The maternal theme
was foreshadowed by the opening verses of the preceding canto
(see *Par.* XXII, 1 – 12 and note), and reappears later on in this
canto in a more vivid way (121 – 23) in connection with the
Virgin Mary. The triumph of Mary, as we will see, receives more
attention in this canto than does the triumph of Christ, and the
imagery would seem to support this observation.

11 – 12. *as she looked:* Beatrice is looking toward the meridian,

the highest point in the heavens, where the sun at noon appears to be moving the slowest.

13–15. *I, who saw her poised in longing there:* The attitudes of Beatrice and the Pilgrim in this tercet suggest that something extraordinary is about to take place. The element of suspense is strong.

16–18. *But time between the* when *was quick to pass:* In this tercet of transition from anticipation to actuality the reader is told that the Pilgrim did not have to wait long to see the spectacle. The "heavens growing bright and brighter still" (18) is suggestive of dawn and relates back to the opening of the canto with its mother bird image.

19–21. *"Behold the hosts / of Christ in triumph:* When Dante says that Christ appeared accompanied by "all the fruit / harvested from the turning of these spheres," he is, I feel, not referring to all of heaven's Blest, including those the Pilgrim has already seen in the heavens below, but rather to those who have not appeared to him up to this point. They are of the highest category, including, as we shall soon see, the Apostles, Adam, the Virgin Mary, and Christ the Man Himself. They are the souls of those who were directly influenced by the fixed stars of this Heaven, influenced without mediation of the heavens below this one; in other words, these souls were not subject to the filtering-down process talked about earlier in the *Paradise* (II, 64–72). This is how Porena interprets the tercet (pp. 227–29).

25–27. *As in the clearness . . . Trivia:* This is the second very tender and lyrical, "feminine" image in this canto (see 1–12). Trivia is another name for Diana, the goddess of the moon. It was a name used by Virgil and other Latin poets to refer to the "goddess at the three ways" from the fact that her temple was often placed at a spot where three roads converged. (See *Aen.* VI, 13, 35; VII, 516, 774.) The "eternal nymphs" in this image stand in relation to Diana as the stars do to the moon.

28–30. *I saw . . . one Sun that lit them all:* Christ is the Sun that gives light to the many stars. The idea of multiplicity is important in this sphere, for the stars here in this heaven receive their power directly from above, from the Light of God, and they dispense it to the spheres below (see again *Par.* II, 64–72).

31 – 32. *through its living light there poured the glow:* Here the figure of Christ, the source of light in this sun, appears before the Pilgrim's eyes for the second time in the poem: he had caught a glimpse of him earlier in the Heaven of Mars. The figure of Christ that flashed on the enormous cross in that heaven remained visible to the Pilgrim for a shorter period of time there than it does here. The higher he climbs, the more he learns, the stronger is his vision.

The light that appears here is referred to as the "translucent substance." The word "substance" ("essence") is a medieval scholastic term referring to something that has its own, separate existence as opposed to "accident" ("quality") that exists within a "substance."

34. *O Beatrice, loving guide, sweet one!:* The Poet breaks the flow of his narrative with this outburst of joy, of thanks to his guide, Beatrice, as he remembers (while in the process of writing the *Comedy*) that it was she (then, in the poem's time) that had led him to this marvelous vision. The exclamation is in complete accord with the opening mood of the canto (see 1 – 12).

37. *Within it dwell the wisdom and the power:* "Christ is the power of God and the wisdom of God" (1 Cor. 1:24). This is a definition of the "substance" or essence referred to above in verses 31 – 32.

38. *that opened between Heaven and earth the road:* After the fall of Adam up until the Advent of Christ, the road to Heaven was closed to mankind. The souls of the faithful went to Limbo to wait patiently for His coming, until that day when the road would be opened again.

40 – 42. *As fire when it expands:* According to the science of the time lightning occurs when compressed air trapped in a cloud expands and eventually escapes by exploding. The resulting noise is thunder, and the ignition, if it occurs, is the lightning. Fire, by its nature, rises, but in the case of lightning, the fire "against its nature" (42) falls downward to the earth.

43 – 45. *so my mind there:* Dante compares his own state of mind, bursting with ideas ("amid so rich a feast") to the phenomenon of lightning. However, unlike lightning, once his mind has "broken its bounds," he cannot know where it will go ("and what became of it"). In other words, there are no bounds to what the

mind can know once it understands Divine Love. The Pilgrim is aware that he has exceeded his previously limited ability to know, but it is still beyond him to understand exactly where all this will lead him. It is the mystical act of the mind transcending itself.

48. *you have the power to endure my smile":* Beatrice confirms the fact that he has surpassed his old limitations because of what he has experienced in the various spheres of Paradise. He is gaining knowledge that mortal man is not normally granted. Having seen the Triumph of Christ, he can now bear to look upon Beatrice's smile. Beatrice has not smiled since she and the Pilgrim entered the heaven of Saturn.

49–53. *As one just shaken from a dreamy sleep:* Dante compares himself to someone who has just awakened from a dream and is unable to remember what he dreamed no matter how hard he tries. He has just witnessed the Triumph of Christ, which overwhelmed him to the point of going out of his mind, as it were (see 43–45). It is at this moment that Beatrice says to him, "Open your eyes, look straight into my face" (46). The same topos will reappear at the end of the *Paradise* (XXXIII, 58–60) when the Pilgrim has his final vision of God.

54. *the book of my past life:* The "book of memory" is a popular theme with Dante. See Chapter I of the *Vita nuova*, for example.

55. *all the tongues of verse:* All the poets.

56. *Polyhymnia and her sisters:* The Muse of songs to the gods, together with all the other Muses.

61–63. *So I find that my consecrated poem:* Beatrice's smile will have to remain undescribed because it is beyond the Pilgrim's power of expression. It is of such sublime quality that the Poet, after choosing a rather lofty way of saying that the smile was indescribable (the Muses and their milk, 55–57) descends to a very low level of description: his "consecrated poem" becomes like the ordinary man "who finds his road is blocked" and has to "leap" over the obstacle in the road (Beatrice's smile). The ineffability theme continues through the next tercet (64–66) always at the same relatively low level: "do not blame me if I stagger here" (66).

67–69. *this stretch of sea my vessel's prow now dares:* See the opening verses of the *Purgatory* as well as the opening of *Paradise* II.

70–72. *"Why are you so enamored of my face:* There is a similar situation earlier in the *Paradise* (XVIII, 20–21) where the Pilgrim's eyes seem to be looking in the wrong place.

73–75. *There is the Rose:* The flower imagery begun in the preceding canto becomes more specific here. Christ, Who is like the Sun, shines over a beautiful garden of many flowers. "The Rose" is the Virgin Mary and "the lilies" are the Apostles whose "fragrance" (their words and deeds) led mankind along the path of the True Faith.

78. *my frail eyes to the battle of the light:* One element, the "frail eyes," underscores (once again) the Pilgrim's weakness as a mortal, while the "battle" reminds the reader of the effort he is required to make in order to experience Paradise as he should.

79–84. *Sometimes on cloudy days my eyes have seen:* What appears as a simple picture drawn from Nature (79–81) turns into a painting (or fresco) of the Ascension of Christ: the Sun behind the clouds breaking through to shine His love down on the flowering souls of the Blest. We do not, however, see the actual ascension of Christ, for He has already ascended by the time the image opens in verse 79. The Pilgrim sees only the light pouring down from the risen Christ.

85–87. *O Mighty Force:* This is the second of the canto's lyrical outbursts. It is born of the appreciation for the vision granted the Pilgrim as well as of the amazement at the spectacle itself. It is of the same type occupying verse 34 of this canto (see also n. 34).

88–90. *the sound of that sweet flower's name:* Now the Pilgrim with great affection and tenderness, the elements dictating the general mood of the entire canto, turns his attention to the Rose, the Virgin Mary, whose name was mentioned by Beatrice in verse 73 and whose light, now that Christ has ascended, shines the brightest.

92. *that living star:* Mary in the liturgy of the Church is referred to as the "Morning Star" as well as the "Star of the Sea."

94–96. *a flaming torch:* This is probably the loving flame of the Angel Gabriel. His shaping of a ring in the form of a crown around "the glory of her light" is symbolic of the Annunciation. The Angel Gabriel will appear again in Canto XXXII of the *Paradise* in verses 91 – 96, in the same position of the verses as in this canto. There are some commentators who believe that this is not the Angel Gabriel, because they would have him appear only once (*Par.* XXXII, 94 – 96), but rather an unnamed angel of the Seraphim order representing angelic love in general (see Sayers, pp. 263 – 64, in support of Porena).

101. *from the sweet lyre crowning the lovely sapphire:* The angel who sings as he circles the Virgin Mary is compared to a musical instrument producing the "sweetest sounding notes" mentioned in verse 97. The Virgin Mary is now referred to as "the lovely sapphire," a precious stone whose blue color has always been associated with her.

102. *whose grace ensapphires the heaven's brightest sphere:* Dante, playing with the word "sapphire," makes a verb out of it: "ensapphires" (*s' inzaffira*), and in so doing he turns the Empyrean, "heaven's brightest sphere," the home of God and all the Blest, into a rich jewel set with a brilliant sapphire.

105. *our Desire:* Christ.

103 – 105. *"I am angelic love encompassing:* This is the beginning of the melody sung by the "flaming torch" first mentioned in verse 94, identified as the Angel Gabriel (see n. 94 – 96). Here he identifies himself in general terms as "angelic love," inviting the reader to think in terms of all the angels' love for Mary who is also described in a more vast way as "the joy supreme who breathed from out the womb"; then her "womb" becomes, in the final verse of this tercet, "the place where our Desire dwelt."

109. *With this the circling melody was sealed:* The song sung by the angel circling (notice how the Poet has the melody circling in this verse) the Virgin seals itself by ceasing.

112 – 17. *The regal mantle folding itself round:* The mantle or cloak encompassing all of the other eight heavens is the ninth sphere or Primum Mobile. This sphere is the one closest to God and "burns" the more with desire to be joined to His love. It is also the fastest-spinning of the nine spheres. The "inner shore" (115) refers to the curving inner surface of the ninth sphere. As

yet, the Primum Mobile is too far from the Pilgrim for him to see it (117).

121–26. *And as an infant after it has suckled:* With this mother-child image, recalling the opening verses of the canto, Dante begins to seal the circular movement of the canto itself with the great tenderness with which it opened. While in the opening verses the mother-child relationship involved Beatrice and the Pilgrim, in these two tercets the relationship is between Mary and the souls of the Blest. The Virgin has risen up beyond the sphere of the fixed stars, and the flaming souls of the Blest stretch their light on high, as a baby who has just fed at its mother's breast stretches its little arms up lovingly toward her.

127. *There they remained suspended in my sight:* With this verse Dante fixes in his reader's mind this second of the two ascension scenes present in this canto (see Christ's Ascension, especially verses 79–84). The reader feels somehow that he has seen these two magnificent scenes somewhere on a church wall in Florence.

128. *"Regina celi":* This church hymn in praise of the Virgin Mary, the "Queen of Heaven," is sung at Easter. For the text of the antiphon see Guéranger, p. 39.

130–39

The canto closes with what I take to be the third break in the narrative of the canto. The first one occupies one verse (34), the second an entire tercet (85–87), and this final one three tercets and the closing verse (130–39). It, like the preceding two, is full of joy and glorious admiration as the Poet comments on the richness of this sphere he has been privileged to see. This closing tercet plus one serves a double function: while they fix the entire action of the canto into just three verses (136–38), they also introduce, without naming him, the central character of the following canto.

130–32. *O what abundant grace:* The souls here, referred to as "those richest coffers," are now filled with the grace they deserve as a result of the good they performed on earth.

135. *in Babylonian exile:* This reference from the Old Testament came to signify the earthly life. These souls following the precept of Jesus, gave up all worldly wealth in order to have spiritual wealth. (See Matt. 19:21: "Jesus said to him 'If thou

wilt be perfect, go, sell what thou hast and give to the poor, and
thou shalt have treasure in heaven.' ")

138. *souls of the Old and the New Covenant:* The Prophets and
Apostles (the saints before and after Christ).

139. *the one who holds the keys:* "And I will give thee the keys
of the kingdom of heaven" (Matt. 16:19). It is St. Peter who
holds the keys to Heaven, and it is he who will decide, as we
shall soon see, whether or not the Pilgrim will be allowed in
Paradise proper. For this reason, Dante chooses to refer to him
not by name at this point, but rather as "the one who holds the
keys." In the Celestial Rose of Canto XXXII St. Peter sits to the
right of the Virgin Mary. Mention of him here suggests the idea
of entry, transition, and promise that the end of the journey is
not far off.

CANTO XXIV

BEATRICE SOLEMNLY REQUESTS that the Pilgrim be allowed to partake in some way of the Divine Knowledge of the souls in this sphere. From the brightest group of spinning lights the brightest light of St. Peter comes forth in answer to Beatrice's request and circles her three times. Beatrice asks St. Peter to test her ward on his faith, not that there is any question about it but rather so that he may have the opportunity to glorify it here in this heaven. St. Peter first asks the Pilgrim to define Faith, then he asks him if he possesses it, and finally he inquires about the source of his faith and how he knows that the source is valid. As a sign of their approval of his answers, all the souls there sing out *"Te Deum laudamus."* Then the great saint asks the Pilgrim to confess to him what he personally believes and to tell how it was made known to him. Because the Pilgrim has answered so well, St. Peter joyfully blesses him, and singing, he circles him three times.

"O fellowship of those chosen to feast
   at the great supper of the Lamb of God
   Who feeds you, satisfying all your needs,   *3*

if by the grace of God this man foretaste
   of what falls from the table of the Blest
   before the hour death prescribes for him,   *6*

consider his immeasurable thirst;
   bedew him with a few drops, for you drink
   forever from the Source of this man's thoughts."   *9*

Thus Beatrice. Then those blissful souls
   started to spin in circles on fixed poles,
   each looking like a comet flaming bright.   *12*

As wheels in clocks are synchronized to move,
   one slowly, looked at closely, almost still—
   the other seems to fly compared to it,   *15*

just so those whirling wheels by different-
  ly dancing, through their movement, fast or slow,
  revealed to me the measure of their bliss.   18

From one that spun the richest light I saw
  emerge a flame so radiant with joy,
  no greater brightness danced within the sphere;   21

three times it circled Beatrice's soul
  accompanied by music so divine
  my memory cannot recapture it,   24

and so, my pen skips over such detail—
  not fantasy nor words are good enough
  to paint the subtle folds of Heaven's light.   27

"O holy sister mine, the burning love
  that glows within your earnest prayer to us
  releases me to you from my bright sphere."   30

That sacred fire, once it stopped circling her,
  breathed forth his words directly to my lady,
  saying precisely what I said above.   33

And she: "Eternal light of the great man
  to whom Our Lord brought down and did bequeath
  the keys to this, our paradise of joy,   36

now test this man on questions grave or light,
  as pleases you, pertaining to that faith
  by means of which you once walked on the sea.   39

If love and hope and faith he truly has,
  you will know, for your eyes are fixed upon
  the place where everything that is is seen.   42

But since this realm was won by citizens
  of the true faith, fitting it is for him
  to glorify it by discussing it."   45

Just as a bachelor arms his mind with thought
  in silence till his master sets the question
  to be discussed but not decided on,   48

so did I arm myself with arguments
  while she was speaking, that I be prepared
  for such a questioner and such a creed.   51

"Speak up, good Christian, and declare yourself!
  Faith, what is Faith?" At which I raised my eyes
  to look upon the light that breathed these words;   54

and then I turned to look at Beatrice
  whose glance was urging me to let pour forth
  the waters welling up within my soul.   57

"May the same Grace that grants me to profess
  my faith before the great centurion,"
  I said, "grant that my thoughts be well expressed."   60

And I went on: "As the veracious pen,
  father, of your dear brother, who with you
  set Rome upon the path of true faith, wrote: 63

Faith is the substance of those hoped-for things
  and argument for things we have not seen.
  And this I take to be its quiddity."   66

Next I heard: "You are right but only if
  you understand why Faith is classified
  as *substance* first and then as *argument*."   69

I answered: "The deep mysteries of Heaven
  that generously reveal themselves to me
  are so concealed from man's eyes down on earth   72

that they exist there only in belief;
  on such a base is high hope built—it is
  substant by its own nature, one could say.   75

And since from this belief we must construct
  logical proofs for what cannot be seen,
  by nature, this partakes of *argument*."   78

Then I heard: "If, on earth, all that is learned
  by mortal minds is so well understood,
  there would be no place for the sophist's wit."   81

That burning love breathed forth these words, and then
  he added: "Now that you have thoroughly
  examined both this coin's alloy and weight,   84

tell me, do you have such coin in your purse?"
  I answered: "Yes I do, so bright and round,
  I have no doubt as to its quality."   87

Then from the depths of that light's radiance
poured the words: "This inestimable gem
upon which every other virtue sets,   90

where did you get it?" I: "The bountiful
rain of the Holy Spirit showering
the parchments, Old and New, is to my mind   93

unquestionable certainty of Faith,
so accurate that any other proof
compared to it would sound most unconvincing."   96

I heard: "These premises, the Old and New,
which you believe to be conclusive proof,
how do you know they are God's holy word?"   99

And I: "The proof that what I read is true
is in the works that followed: Nature's hand
could never heat or forge that kind of iron."   102

Then the reply: "Tell me, how do you know
that these works ever were? You use as proof,
and nothing more, what still needs to be proved."   105

"If the world turned to Christ without the help
of miracles," I said, "then that would be
a miracle far greater than them all,   108

for you, hungry and poor, entered the field
to sow the good plant of the faith that once
grew as a vine and now is but a thorn."   111

I said this, and the high and holy choir
let ring *Te Deum laudamus* through the spheres
in strains of music heard only in Heaven.   114

That Baron who had led me branch by branch,
examining my faith, to where we now
were getting closer to the topmost leaves,   117

spoke out again: "The Grace that lovingly
speaks with your mind, parting your lips, till now
has let them speak the way they should, and I   120

approve of what I heard come from your mouth.
But now you must declare your creed to me,
and then tell me the source of your belief."   123

"O holy father, spirit who now sees
    that faith confirmed that led him to the tomb,
    though younger feet than his arrived there first," 126

I answered him, "you want me to reveal
    the form of my unhesitating faith,
    and you have asked the reason for its being. 129

I tell you: I believe in one, sole God
    eternal Who, unmoved, moves all the heavens
    that spin in His love and in His desire; 132

and for such faith as mine I have the proofs
    not only of physics and metaphysics,
    but of that truth which rains down from this realm 135

through Moses, through the Prophets, through the Psalms,
    and through the Gospel and through you who wrote
    once kindled by the Holy Spirit's tongue; 138

and I believe in three eternal Beings,
    an Essence that is One as well as Three
    where *is* and *are* describe it equally. 141

Concerning this profound and holy state
    of which I speak, the teachings of the Gospel,
    in many places, has made up my mind. 144

This is the source, this is the very spark
    which then ignites into a living flame
    and like a star in Heaven lights my mind." 147

Then, as a lord delighted with the message
    delivered by his page embraces him,
    rejoicing in the happy news he bears, 150

thus, singing benedictions over me,
    the apostolic light that bid me speak,
    when I was silent, circled me three times, 153

so much delight my words had given him.

NOTES

1 – 2. "*O fellowship of those chosen to feast:* Beatrice's opening
words (1 – 9) have clear biblical overtones. The word for "fellow-

ship" in the Italian is *sodalizio,* a word, according to Dante's early commentators, associated with the Apostles. Cf. Rev. 19:9: "Blessed are they which are called unto the marriage supper of the Lamb."

3. *Who feeds you:* Cf. John 6:35. God provides spiritual nourishment to those who know Him; desire for His sustenance is never-ending, even when it has been satisfied by God.

4. *if by the grace of God this man:* Dante has been given special dispensation to enjoy knowledge of God before the time of his death.

5. *of what falls from the table of the Blest:* Food imagery abounds in the *Paradise.* See, for example, Cantos III, 91; IV, 1 – 3; V, 38 – 39; X, 22 – 24; X, 96; XIX, 25 – 33.

7 – 9. *his immeasurable thirst:* Dante's thirst is his desire for truth. The souls of the Blest feed eternally on the truth from God Who is the "Source." "Dew" is the symbol of grace bestowed by Heaven.

10 – 18

We are meant to visualize these souls spinning "in circles on fixed poles," whirling all together but in separate groups, some large, some small, and at varying speeds. This becomes evident when these spinning spirits that leave a trail of light behind them "like a comet" (12) are compared to the wheels in the mechanism of a clock (13 – 15). The clock image also underlines the idea of individual parts working together in harmony. Movement and light in the *Paradise* are always in proportion to the amount of bliss or love each soul enjoys in the sight of God.

16 – 18. *those whirling wheels by different / ly:* The Italian for this tercet reads:

così quelle carole, differente-
    mente danzando, de la sua ricchezza
    mi facieno stimar, veloci e lente.

Dante splits the adverb *differentemente* at the end of verse 16, thus underscoring the idea of dance (a *carole* is a circular dance), as well as the fact that this particular dance can be either fast or slow. The words imitate the action.

22. *three times it circled Beatrice's soul:* This light, which emerges

from the brightest of the dancing circles and which is also the most radiant within that separate spinning group, will do the same to the Pilgrim at the end of this canto (see 153).

24. *memory cannot recapture it:* Memory is that faculty which is capable of holding images.

26. *not fantasy nor words are good enough:* Fantasy is the faculty that receives the images (the imagination) and is considered to be stronger than the faculty of memory.

27. *to paint the subtle folds of Heaven's light:* Memory, imagination, and words are not enough to describe ("to paint") the depths of holiness in the song the Pilgrim heard. The "folds of Heaven's light" is an allusion to the art of painting: the deep, subtle shades of color in the folds or drapery of the garments of the subject being painted were considered very difficult to reproduce. Dante's colors, or in this case his words, are too bright for the folds.

34. *the great man:* St. Peter.

35–36. *Our Lord brought down . . . the keys:* Cf. Matt. 16:19.

37–42

The Pilgrim's entrance examination to Heaven will cover three topics: Faith, Hope, and Charity, the three theological virtues. St. Peter will examine him on Faith in this canto, St. James on Hope in Canto XXV, and St. John on Charity or Love in Canto XXVI. By means of these three virtues man ascends to God, and they can be acquired only by means of grace operating through revelation—human knowledge and understanding are not enough to reach God.

39. *you once walked on the sea:* Cf. Matt. 14:28–29: "But Peter answered Him and said, 'Lord, if it is Thou, bid me come to Thee over the water.' And he said 'Come.' Then Peter got out of the boat and walked on the water to come to Jesus."

40. *If love and hope and faith he truly has:* Dante here reverses the usual order of the three theological virtues; he will, however, be examined on each one in the normal order.

42. *the place:* God.

43–45. *since this realm was won by citizens:* It is fitting that the

Pilgrim, in order to glorify faith, discuss faith at this point, for the realm of Paradise consists of all those citizens who practiced the True Faith.

46-51

Here the reader gets a glimpse of medieval university life: an examination (the *disputatio*) taken by the "bachelor" or student at the close of a course would eventually lead to the candidate's doctorate degree (in this case in theology). Though Dante's commentators are not all in complete agreement as to the exact procedures, the examination progressed more or less along the following lines: the master or doctor proposed the question or questions to the candidate (the "bachelor," 46) who, in turn, was expected to propose "arguments" (49) both pro and con, but without drawing any definite conclusions (48) concerning the topic under discussion—this was a privilege granted the examiner only. For a discussion of the various interpretations of the "bachelor simile" see Palmieri.

49-51. *so did I arm myself:* While Beatrice is speaking (34-45) the Pilgrim, who has sensed that an examination is forthcoming, starts thinking of different answers for the questions about to be proposed to him in order to be "prepared" (50) for St. Peter ("such a questioner," 51) and for such a declaration of faith ("such a creed," 51).

52-57. *Speak up, good Christian:* St. Peter is very direct and precise. The Pilgrim turns to Beatrice for reassurance and inspiration to undertake discussion of the question. In fact, whenever the Pilgrim is about to answer a question in the *Paradise*, he always seems to turn to his guide, Beatrice, for approval.

59. *the great centurion":* Dante employs a Roman military term to describe St. Peter: he is the "high commander" of the Church.

62. *your dear brother:* St. Paul.

64-66. *Faith is the substance of those hoped-for things:* The definition of Faith given by the Pilgrim is the one according to St. Paul: "Now faith is the substance of things to be hoped for, the evidence of things that are not seen" (Heb. 11:1). St. Thomas, commenting on this statement, says "Accordingly, we may say that faith is a habit of the mind whereby eternal life is begun in us, making the intellect assent to what is non-apparent." (*Summa theol.* II – II, q. 4, a.1, resp.) Faith, then, is the basic principle upon which is based our hope for eternal life beyond. The words "substance" (64) and "argument" (65) will be defined by the Pilgrim at St. Peter's request (67 – 69) in verses 70 – 75 and 76 – 78.

67 – 69. *"You are right but only if:* St. Peter wants the Pilgrim to tell him why St. Paul refers to faith first "as *substance*" and then "as *argument*."

70 – 75. *"The deep mysteries of Heaven:* In these two tercets the Pilgrim attempts to define "substance." When mortal man aspires to the heavenly life ("hoped-for things," 64), his "high hope" (74), which is the hope for eternal beatitude, is a matter of faith or belief, and so it is the "substance" on which "hoped-for things" are based; "it is *substant*" (75) or material in itself.

76 – 78. *we must construct / logical proofs:* Here "argument" is defined. Man ordinarily bases his arguments on proven fact or evidence. In questions of religion ("things we have not seen," 65) arguments are based on belief, and so faith in religious questions takes the place of evidence in worldly matters. The hope which is faith or belief must exist before it can be applied as argument to questions of religion.

79 – 81. *"If, on earth, all that is learned:* If mortal man possessed the understanding that the Pilgrim here displays, faulty reasoning ("the sophist's wit") would cease to exist.

83 – 84. *you have . . . examined this coin's alloy and weight:* The alloy and the weight are the two measures of a coin's worth.

86 – 87. *"Yes I do, so bright and round:* The Pilgrim has defined Faith and is certain of its orthodoxy. The "coin" is not false. The words "bright and round" refer first to the coin's composition (its alloy is "bright") and then to its weight ("round"), because gold coins could be shaved around the edges.

89. *"This inestimable gem:* Faith.

90. *upon which every other virtue sets:* Hope and Charity are based on Faith as are all the other virtues. The Scriptures attest to this fact.

92. *rain of the Holy Spirit:* The inspiration of the Holy Spirit.

93. *the parchments, Old and New:* The Old and New Testaments gave the Pilgrim his faith.

94–96. *unquestionable certainty of Faith:* The Old and New Testaments are taken as God's word, and therefore they are an indisputable support of faith.

97. *"These premises:* The Old and New Testaments are the premises from which the Pilgrim deduces his conclusion.

100–102. *"The proof that what I read is true:* The proof that the Bible is God's word is in the miracles related therein. These are not the work of Nature or natural occurrences, for Nature has neither the means (to heat the iron) nor the ability (to forge that kind of iron). There is a similar metaphor in which Nature is compared to the blacksmith in *Par.* II, 127–29.

103–105. *how do you know:* St. Peter now asks the Pilgrim what evidence he has that the miracles actually took place. The Pilgrim has offered the Bible itself as proof of the miracles it recounts, and in so doing he would be arguing in circles by using as proof the very thing that still has to be proved.

106–108. *"If the world turned to Christ:* The Pilgrim replies that the fact that all the world turned to the Christian faith without the need of miracles, that is to say, without the need to prove the miracles recounted in the Bible, is in itself the greatest miracle of all.

110–11. *the faith that once / grew as a vine:* The corrupt clergy have allowed the vineyard of the Lord to be overtaken by the thorny bramble of degeneracy.

112–14. *the high and holy choir / let ring* "Te Deum laudamus": The singing by the spirits of the hymn *Te Deum* ("We praise Thee, O God"), written by St. Ambrose at the conversion of St. Augustine, acknowledges Dante as a true believer. The same hymn of rejoicing was sung when Dante passed through the gate of Purgatory (IX, 139–42).

115. *That Baron who had led me branch by branch:* St. Peter is referred to as a Baron, a title applied also to Christ and to the other great saints. (Cf. *Par.* XXV, 16 and 40–42.) Now the Pilgrim's examination on Faith is referred to metaphorically as a tree, the symbol of life, vitality, and solidity. The Pilgrim has

moved from question to question ("branch by branch") and is now reaching the end of his examination ("the topmost leaves").

118−20. *"The Grace that lovingly / speaks with your mind:* The quality of the Pilgrim's answers is ascribed to the special grace that he has been accorded and not to his own power to reason and speak.

125−26. *that faith confirmed that led him to the tomb:* St. Peter can now see in God the things he accepted on faith during his earthly life. His faith was so fervent that even though John got to the sepulchre ahead of him, Peter was compelled to be the first to go inside. (See John 20:3−8.)

130−47

Dante's credo is based on accepted Aristotelian doctrine as well as purely Christian elements. The reference to heavens in the plural sense (all the spheres) and the notion of the unmoved mover who causes the heavens to revolve out of desire to be joined to him are from Aristotle. The idea of love of God for His creation is strictly Christian.

133−34. *the proofs . . . of physics and metaphysics:* Support of his credo is drawn not only from Scripture but also from physics and metaphysics (see *Summa theol.*, I, ii, a.4, where five physical and metaphysical proofs for the existence of God are offered: "the impossibility of explaining the world without the assumption of a first motor, of a first efficient cause, of a first necessity, of a first goodness, of a first governing intelligence." Singleton, who quotes Grandgent, points this out on p. 395).

135. *that truth which rains down from this realm:* Cf. Luke 24:44: "These are the words which I spoke to you while I was yet with you, that all things must be fulfilled that are written in the Law of Moses and the Prophets and the Psalms concerning me."

137−38. *through the Gospel and . . . by the Holy Spirit's tongue:* By the Gospel is meant the New Testament; "you who wrote" indicates the Apostles. See Acts 2:1−4 where Pentecost is described, that time when the Holy Spirit came down upon the Apostles in the form of tongues of fire. The writings implied here are the Acts, Epistles, and Revelation.

139−44. *I believe in three eternal Beings:* The Trinity, which may be viewed as both singular and plural (hence, the use of *"is* and *are,"* 141), is strictly based on revelation and can be proven only by the Scriptures.

145–47. *This is the source:* This refers to the Pilgrim's entire *credo.* Thus, the existence of God as One and as Three, which is a principle provided by revelation in the Scriptures, is the source of all articles of faith. According to some commentators (see Chimenz, p. 849), the phrase "This is the source" refers only to the Gospels mentioned in the preceding tercet (143), and the conclusion is that with this the Pilgrim would have answered St. Peter's second question posed in verse 123: "tell me the source of your belief."

148–53. *as a lord delighted with the message:* The Pilgrim has passed the first of his three examinations and has pleased St. Peter greatly with his answers, as is made evident by the three circles Peter makes around the Pilgrim as he did earlier with Beatrice in verses 22–24. The simile of the page who delivers good news to his lord is in keeping with the courtly imagery found earlier in the canto ("That Baron," 115) and that will continue into the following canto. Some commentators find the simile inappropriate (see Porena, p. 239).

CANTO XXV

THE CANTO OPENS with an expression of the Poet's hope to be able to return by means of his poetic endeavors to Florence, and there at the site of his baptism into the faith receive the poet's crown. Then Beatrice points out St. James, who has just approached and greeted St. Peter. Beatrice initiates the second examination by asking St. James to make Hope heard in this sphere. Encouragingly, the saint tells the Pilgrim to look up and have confidence, and then poses the following questions: What is Hope? What is its source? What does it promise? When he answers the questions correctly, all the souls from above sing, *"Sperent in te."* Then a third light, whom Beatrice identifies as St. John, joins Peter and James in their dance. Intent on seeing with his own eyes if the legend concerning St. John's body being taken to Heaven with his soul was true, the Pilgrim stares fixedly at the glowing saint, who perceives the Pilgrim's curiosity and replies that his body has turned to dust on earth and that until the Day of Judgment only Christ and the Virgin Mary possess both body and soul. As the Pilgrim listens and looks at the light of St. John he loses his sight and is troubled that he can no longer see his guide, Beatrice.

If ever it happen that this sacred poem
   to which both Heaven and Earth have set their hand,
   and made me lean from laboring so long,   3

wins over those cruel hearts that exile me
   from my sweet fold where I grew up a lamb,
   foe to the wolves that war upon it now,   6

with a changed voice and with another fleece,
   I shall return, a poet, and at my own
   baptismal font assume the laurel wreath,   9

for it was there I entered in the faith
   that counts God's souls for Him, the faith for which
   Peter just turned himself into my crown.   12

And then a light began to move toward us
out of the sphere which had produced that rare
first fruit of Christ's own vicarage on earth;   15

whereat, my lady, radiant with joy,
said to me: "Look, look there ! You see the Baron
who draws souls to Galicia down on earth."   18

As when a dove alights beside its mate,
and it begins to coo and circle round
the other in expression of its love,   21

even so did I behold one glorious
and great lord greet the other as the two
sang praises for the feast that Heaven serves.   24

Then, once the joyful greetings were exchanged
they stopped and stood in silence *coram me*—
their brilliance was too powerful for sight.   27

And then my Beatrice, smiling, said:
"Illustrious life, the one chosen to write
of the largesse of our celestial Court,   30

make hope resound throughout this heaven's height:
you can, you were its symbol all those times
Jesus bestowed more light upon His three."   33

"Lift up your head and reassure yourself,
for all that rises from the mortal world
must ripen here in our own radiance."   36

These words of strength came from the second flame,
whereby, up to those hills I raised my eyes,
which had been lowered by excessive brilliance,   39

"Since of His grace our Emperor has willed
that you before your death come face to face
with His own Counts in His most secret hall,   42

that, having seen the truth of our Court here,
you, in yourself and others, may give strength
to Hope which makes men love the good on earth,   45

now tell me what is Hope, how much of it
thrives in your mind, and where your Hope comes from."
So spoke the second light a second time.   48

And that devout one who on my high flight
   had guided every feather of my wings
   anticipated my reply, and said: 51

"There is no son of the Church Militant
   with greater hope than his, as you can read
   in Him whose radiance lights all our host;   54

and this is why he is allowed to come
   from Egypt to behold Jerusalem
   before his fighting days on earth are done.   57

The two remaining questions you have asked
   not for your sake, but that he may report
   to men on earth how much you cherish Hope—   60

I leave to him: they are not difficult
   nor is self-praise involved. So let him speak,
   and may he answer with the grace of God."   63

As pupil answering his teacher would,
   ready and willing to display his worth,
   so well-versed in his subject, I said, "Hope   66

is sure expectancy of future bliss
   to be inherited—the holy fruit
   of God's own grace and man's precedent worth.   69

From many stars this light comes to my mind,
   but he who first instilled it in my heart
   was highest singer of the Highest Lord.   72

'Let them have hope in Thee who know Thy name,'
   so sings his sacred song. And who does not
   know of That Name if he has faith like mine?   75

And in your own epistle you instilled
   me with his dew, till now I overflow
   and pour again your shower upon others."   78

While I was saying this, within that living
   bosom of luminescence flashed a flame,
   repeating quick and bright as lightning strikes. 81

It breathed: "The love that always burns in me
   for Hope, that followed me even to the palm
   and the departure from the battlefield,   84

moves tne to speak again to you who loves
    this virtue: give me joy by telling me
    what promise does your Hope make to your soul."   *87*

And I: "The Old and the New Testaments
    define the goal—which points me to the promise—
    of those souls that Our Lord has made His friends.   *90*

Isaiah testifies that every man
    in his homeland shall wear a double raiment,
    and his homeland is this sweet life of bliss.   *93*

There is also your brother, where he writes
    about the white robes—he makes manifest
    this revelation more explicitly."   *96*

And, on the sound of my last word I heard
    ring out *"Sperent in te"* above my head,
    and all the dancing spheres gave their response.   *99*

Then, one among those lights became so bright
    that if the Crab possessed just one such star,
    winter would have one month of one long day.   *102*

As a young girl rises and in her joy
    rushes to dance in honor of the bride
    without a thought of showing off herself,   *105*

so did I see that brilliant splendor rush
    to reach the two circles that whirled in dance
    whose rhythm was in tune with their great love.   *108*

It joined them in their dance and in their song;
    and all the while my lady, like a bride,
    stood gazing at them, motionless and quiet.   *111*

"This is the one who lay upon the breast
    of our own Pelican; he is the one
    who from the Cross assumed the great bequest."   *114*

These were the words my lady said to me,
    but no more after than before she spoke
    did she once take her eyes away from them.   *117*

As one who squints and strains his eyes to see
    a little of the sun in its eclipse,
    and who through looking can no longer look,   *120*

so did I stare at that last blaze of light
 until I heard the words: "Why blind yourself
 by looking for what has no place up here?"   123

My body is in earth as earth, and there
 it lies with others till our number is
 the predetermined total set by God.   126

Two Lights and no more, were allowed to rise
 straight to our cloister clad in double robes—
 explain this to your world when you go back."   129

His voice had stopped the flaming circle's dance,
 and with it stopped the mingling of sweet sound
 breathed by that triune breath in harmony,   132

as oars, driven through water at a pace,
 stop all together when a whistle blows,
 to signal danger or prevent fatigue.   135

Ah, the strange feeling running through my mind
 when I turned then to look at Beatrice
 only to find I could not see, and she   138

so close to me, and we in Paradise!

NOTES

1 – 12

Dante never stopped hoping that he would be called back
to Florence from exile. The opening verses of this canto poig-
nantly express this hope in terms of the fame the poem that he is
writing now may bring him. What better place than here, in this
canto in which St. James will test him on Hope, for Dante to
sound the note of his own personal hope?

3. *laboring so long:* Dante is thought to have written the Com-
edy over a period of ten years, between 1310 and 1320.

4. *those cruel hearts:* These are the members of the Florentine
party of the "Blacks," who were responsible for exiling Dante
from his native city in 1302. The poet never returned to
Florence.

7 – 9. *with a changed voice and with another fleece:* Dante hopes

that when he returns to Florence after completing his poem he will do so in triumph, as a more mature individual, and in an entirely different role, that is, as a serious, celebrated poet. The phrase "with a changed voice," more than a simple reference to maturity, probably means "with a different kind of poetry": he will return not as a mere writer of love poems but as author of the sublime poem that is the *Divine Comedy.* The baptismal font referred to in verse 9 is that in the Florence Baptistry where Dante was baptized.

14 — 15. *the sphere which had produced that rare / first fruit:* The circle of the blessed souls that had already sent forth Peter, the first pope.

17 — 18. *the Baron:* This is St. James the Apostle (the same term is applied to St. Peter in Canto XXIV, 115). James was the son of the fisherman Zebedee and Salome, and the brother of John the Apostle and Evangelist. Just before Passover in the year 44, Herod Agrippa I had him put to death (see Acts 12:2). He had preached in Spain and later returned to Jerusalem. After his death his body was miraculously transferred to Santiago de Campostela, capital of Galicia, an ancient kingdom in northwestern Spain. During the Middle Ages his tomb at Santiago de Campostela was a much-visited site by pilgrims, second only to Jerusalem in popularity.

19 — 21. *As when a dove:* The use of the dove image here places emphasis on the affective qualities of mutual tenderness, fidelity, and love. The same figure appears in the introductory verses to Francesca and Paolo in *Inf.* V, 82, serving there, however, an entirely different purpose. The tenderness, fidelity, and love are as deceiving there as they are pure here.

23. *the two:* St. Peter and St. James.

24. *the feast that Heaven serves:* Cf. above, Canto XXIV, 1 — 6 and note.

26. *coram me:* Latin, meaning "in front of me." Cf. *Par.* XI, 62.

28 — 33. *the one chosen to write / of the largesse:* The Epistle of St. James speaks of Divine magnanimity. Sayers (p. 278) claims that Dante confused St. James the Great (of the Campostela shrine)

with St. James the Less (brother of Jesus and supposed author of the Epistle).

33. *His three:* Peter, James, and John were the three disciples privileged to witness Christ's character on three different occasions: the Transfiguration (Matt. 17:1–8), the Garden of Gethsemane (Matt. 26; 36–38), and the raising of the daughter of Jairus (Luke 8:50–56).

34–36. *"Lift up your head:* Cf. 27 where the Pilgrim had lowered his head, unable to look upon the brilliance of Peter and James. He is now encouraged to raise his eyes and enjoy greater vision as he looks upon the saints.

38. *those hills:* Cf. Psalms 120:1 ("I lift up my eyes"). We are invited to think of the Apostles Peter and James as hills of bright light—perhaps reflections of that greater light the Pilgrim first saw shining in all its glory around another "hill" at the beginning of his journey in Canto I of the *Inferno* (16–18).

42. *His own Counts in His most secret hall:* The "Counts" are the saints (cf. feudal terminology in 17 and 40); the "most secret hall" is the Empyrean. It is God's will that Dante witness all of this before his death. The same courtly imagery that made its first appearance in Canto II of the *Inferno* is present here. The poem in its imagery would seem to be coming full circle.

44–45. *you . . . may give strength:* It is Dante's sacred duty to recount what he has seen on his journey, and thus render hope to men on earth that they may achieve salvation in Heaven. Hope springs from faith, and love from hope.

46–47. *now tell me what is Hope:* The three questions to be answered by the Pilgrim are now stated: first, the definition of Hope, second, the degree to which he possesses hope, and third, the source of his hope. Beatrice intercedes to answer the second question (52–57), since it would be inappropriate for the Pilgrim to do so at this moment—it would imply a display of vainglory. Cf. also St. Peter's questions on Faith in Canto XXIV, 53; 85; 91.

49–51. *every feather of my wings:* The image of wings and flight is a frequent one in the poem, one usually connected with Beatrice and love. We first see the image, appropriately enough, in

Inf. II, 76 – 78. For another important reference to "wings" see *Purg.* XXIV, 58 – 60 and note 57.

52 – 57

The Church Militant (all living Christians) and the Church Triumphant ("all our host," 54) are terms from Christian doctrine. Continuing the courtly imagery, the emphasis here is on action, struggle ("fighting days," 57), and mission. Dante hoped for the regeneration of the Church, for the rise of a true political leader, as well as for his own return to his beloved city of Florence. His is the Christian hope which springs from his faith in God. Accordingly, his mission upon his return to earth will be to impart the knowledge of divine ways that he has acquired as a mortal who has been witness to the joys of Paradise.

53 – 54. *as you can read:* St. James is able to read the truth of what Beatrice says in the brilliant mind of God.

56. *from Egypt to behold Jerusalem:* Egypt represents life on earth (see Ps. 113:1), and it makes allusion to the slavery of the Jews in Egypt (see *Purg.* II, 46), while Jerusalem stands for the City of God (see Heb. 12:22).

58 – 59. *The two remaining questions you have asked:* The remaining questions are "What is Hope?" and "What is its source?"

60. *how much you cherish Hope:* Hope is a quality treasured in Heaven, but it is not needed there.

62. *nor is self-praise involved:* See above, note to 51. The degree to which the Pilgrim possesses hope cannot be stated by him, for it would be presumptuous on his part to do so here. It is for this reason that Beatrice answers this question for him.

64. *As pupil answering his teacher:* Cf. the preceding canto (XXIV, 46 – 48) where a similar comparison is made.

66 – 69. *I said "Hope / is . . . and man's precedent worth:* The Pilgrim now defines Hope. His definition comes from that found in Peter Lombard (see *Par.* X, 106 – 108), *Liber sententiarum,* III, XXVI, 1: "hope is a certain expectation of future beatitude proceeding from God's grace and antecedent merits." The motivation of hope springs from God's grace alone; "precedent worth," or merit, is necessary for the assurance of salvation. See also *Summa theol.* II, 2, q. xvii, a.1.

70. *From many stars this light comes:* The Pilgrim's spiritual illumination comes down to him from many wise minds through their writings. Cf. Daniel 12:3.

71–72. *he who first instilled:* David, the Psalmist.

73. *'Let them have hope in Thee who know Thy name':* Quoted from Ps. 9:10 ("Sperent in te . . ."). The overall mood and tone of the Psalms is one of hope.

76. *in your own epistle:* The General Epistle of St. James, in which trust (Hope) in God's promise is brought up a number of times.

76–78. *you instilled:* Beginning in verse 71 is the imagery of dew and rain in connection with the teachings of David and St. James. The notion of spiritual overflow and pouring forth of the faith to others (as Jesus did) is a recurrent one in both Old and New Testaments.

81. *quick and bright as lightning strikes:* See Mark 3:17: James and John, sons of Zebedee, were surnamed by Jesus "Boanerges, that is, Sons of Thunder." The light of James flashes in joyous applause to the Pilgrim's response.

82–84. *The love . . . for Hope . . . to the palm . . . the battlefield:* St. James was put to death in the year 44 by Herod Agrippa (see Acts 12:2). The "palm" refers to the victory of the martyr; the "battlefield" represents life itself. The courtly-war imagery is still present.

87. *what promise does your Hope make to your soul:* In the preceding canto (XXIV, 121–22), St. Peter asked the Prilgrim to define the content of his faith. Here, he is asked to state the content of his hope, or what he expects in the life to come.

88–90. *the promise:* In the Scriptures there appears the promise that some (the Elect) will know God.

91–93. *a double raiment:* This is the union of body and soul in Heaven. See Isa. 61:7, "Therefore shall they receive double in their land. Everlasting joy shall be with them." See also Isa. 61:10, "He hath clothed one with the garments of salvation."

94–96. *There is also your brother:* A reference to St. John the Evangelist and to Rev. 7:9: "I beheld a great multitude, which no man could number, of all nations and kindreds and people and tongues, standing before the throne and before the Lamb, *clothed in white robes*, and palms in their hands" (italics mine). The white robes belong to the elect. After the Resurrection the purified body is white like the spirit (see *Par.* XXX, 129). Thus, the content of Dante's hope is immortality of the soul and resurrection of the body to the same state.

98. *"Sperent in te":* The whole choir of the Blest now join in the hymn of hope. (See above, 73 and note.)

100 – 102. *one among those lights became so bright:* This new light is that of St. John which would appear to be as bright as the sun itself. If the constellation Cancer possessed a star of such magnitude, the result would be one month of continuous light from December 21st to January 21st when Cancer dominates the night sky. For a similar, rather strange (as well as scientifically impossible) astronomical image see *Par.* XIII, 1 – 12.

103 – 108

The image of the dance has already been re-evoked in verse 99 (cf. also *Par.* XXIV, 16). Here combined with the image of the young girl, it suggests innocence, ingenuousness, unselfishness, nonaffectation, and purity. The other two whirling circles are Peter and James; all three together represent the three Christian virtues. The great clock of the church doctors in *Par.* X, 79 – 81 was also compared to dancing maidens. See also *Purg.* XXIX, 121 – 29 where the three theological virtues are seen dancing in the presence of Beatrice.

112 – 13. *the one who lay upon the breast / of our own Pelican:* See John 13:23, "Now one of his disciples whom Jesus loved was reclining at Jesus' bosom." The pelican was believed to revive its dying young by allowing them to feed on its own blood; so Christ by shedding his own blood raised man from his spiritual death.

114. *the great bequest:* John was entrusted with the care of Mary when Christ died on the Cross. See John 19:26 – 27.

119 – 20. *eclipse:* In Dante's lifetime seven eclipses were witnessed in Italy. It was known that they could cause damage to the eyes when looked upon directly.

Dante tries to look through the brilliant light of John to see if the soul of the Saint is there in body too. According to a medieval belief, John was taken to Heaven in the flesh. Since the Pilgrim is, after all, travelling through Heaven in the flesh, he would naturally find the possibility of interest. John refutes the legend and charges Dante to enlighten those on earth who put credence in it.

125–26. *it lies with others till our number:* Until the number of those chosen by God as His elect is completed the Resurrection of the Flesh will not take place.

127–29. *Two Lights and no more:* Only Christ and the Virgin Mary were allowed to rise to Heaven in the body.

130–35. *His voice had stopped the flaming circle's dance:* When John had begun speaking, all dancing and whirling had ceased, as had the harmonious song of the three Apostles ("that triune breath," 132).

133–35. *as oars . . . to signal danger or prevent fatigue:* All movement stops with this strong, realistic touch of the oarsmen stopping short at the sound of their leader's whistle. This dramatic pause for silence makes the closing four verses of this canto, in which the Pilgrim comments on his blindness, all the more effective.

136–39. *the strange feeling . . . and we in Paradise!:* The Pilgrim is now blind. He is as blind as he might be after looking upon an eclipse. The strangeness of this condition strikes the Pilgrim as he remembers where he is: he is in Heaven, guided by Beatrice, and yet he seems to have fallen into imperfection. His feeling of embarrassment runs through the last four verses of this canto.

CANTO XXVI

ST. JOHN BEGINS the third and final examination on Love
by asking the Pilgrim what the final goal of his love is, assuring
him in the meantime that Beatrice has the power to restore his
sight. The Pilgrim answers that the beginning and end of his
love is God. Having satisfactorily answered this question, the
Pilgrim is required to tell precisely how and why he is drawn to
right love. When he answers correctly, the whole assembly to-
gether with Beatrice sings "Holy, Holy, Holy" and the Pilgrim
regains his sight. He is surprised to see that another light has
joined the three there beside him. It is Adam, who immediately
discerns the Pilgrim's questions in the mind of God and tells the
Pilgrim so. He has four questions for Adam: how long ago was
he created, how much time did he spend in the Earthly Paradise,
what did he do to provoke God's wrath, and what language did
he speak.

While I stood there confounded by my blindness,
    from out the effulgent flame that took my sight,
    there came a breath of voice that made me heed   3

its words: "Until you have regained the sense
    of sight which your eyes have consumed in me,
    let discourse be a means of recompense.   6

Begin then, tell what is it that your soul
    is set upon—and you may rest assured
    your sight is only dazzled not destroyed: 9

the lady who guides you through the Divine
    spheres has that power in a single glance
    that rested in the hand of Ananias."   12

I said: "At her own pleasure, soon or late,
    let her restore my eyes that were the gates
    she entered with the fire that burns me still.   15

The Good, that full contentment of this Court,
    is Alpha and Omega of all texts
    Love reads to me in soft or louder tones."   18

The same voice that had just now calmed the fear
    I felt in sudden blind bewilderment
    once more encouraged me to speak. It said: 21

"But certainly, you need a finer sieve
    to sift this matter through: you must explain
    who made you aim your bow at such a mark?"   24

I said: "Through philosophic arguments
    and through authority which comes from here
    such love as this has stamped me with its seal;   27

for good perceived as good enkindles love,
    and makes that love more bright the more that we
    can comprehend the good which it contains.   30

So, toward that Essence where such goodness rests
    that any goodness found outside of It
    is only a reflection of its ray,   33

the mind of man, in love, is bound to move
    more than toward any other, once it sees
    the truth on which this loving proof is based.   36

Such truth is made plain to my mind by him
    who demonstrates to me the primal love
    of each and every endless entity.   39

Plain it was made by the True Author's voice
    when He said, speaking of Himself, to Moses:
    "I shall show you all of my goodness now."   42

Made plain it also is from the first words
    of your great Gospel which cries out to men,
    loudest of all, the mysteries of Heaven."   45

And then I heard: "As human reason proves
    and revelation which concurs with it,
    of all your loves the highest looks to God.   48

But tell me, are there other ties you feel
    that draw you to Him? Let your words explain
    the many teeth with which your love can bite."   51

The sacred purpose in the questioning
    of Christ's own eagle here was clear to me—
    I knew which way my answer had to go.   54

I spoke again: "All of those teeth with strength
    to move the heart of any man to God
    have bitten my heart into loving Him.   57

The being of the world and my own being,
    the death He died so that my soul might live,
    the hope of all the faithful, and mine too,   60

joined with the living truth mentioned before,
    from that deep sea of false love rescued me
    and set me on the right shore of true Love.   63

I love each leaf with which enleaved is all
    the garden of the Eternal Gardener
    in measure of the light he sheds on each."   66

The instant I stopped speaking all of Heaven
    filled with sweet singing, as my lady joined
    the others chanting: "Holy! Holy! Holy!"   69

As sleep is broken by a flash of light,
    the visual spirit rushing to the gleam
    which penetrates the eyes from lid to lid,   72

and the roused sleeper shrinks from what he sees,
    confounded by his sudden wakening,
    until his judgment comes to aid his sight,   75

so Beatrice drove out every speck
    clouding my vision with her splendid eyes
    whose radiance spread a thousand miles and more;   78

so I could see much better than before,
    and then, surprised with my new sight, I asked
    about a fourth light that was with us now.   81

My lady said: "Within that blaze of rays,
    in loving contemplation of his maker,
    is the first soul the First Power first made."   84

As tops of trees will bow to sweeping gusts
    of wind, only to straighten up again
    by force of their own natural resilience,   87

so I, amazed, was bent the while she spoke;
    but then I found my confidence restored,
    and burning with the wish to speak again,   90

I spoke these words: "O one and only fruit
   who was created ripe, first, oldest sire,
   father and father-in-law of every bride,   *93*

I beg of you devoutly, I implore
   you, speak to me. You see right through my wish;
   to hear you speak the sooner, I speak less."   *96*

Sometimes an animal will tremble in its skin
   and thus reveal its feelings from within
   as he moves his own cover from inside;   *99*

so, that first soul of souls revealed to me,
   stirring transparently in his own glow,
   how joyously it moved to bring me joy.   *102*

And then it breathed: "Without your telling me,
   I know your wish much better than you know
   whatever seems most evident to you;   *105*

I see it in that Mirror of the Truth,
   Itself perfect reflector of all things,
   yet no thing can reflect It perfectly.   *108*

You wish to know how long ago it was
   God placed me in the Earthly Paradise
   where she prepared you for this long ascent,   *111*

and how long did my eyes delight in it;
   and the true reason for the wrath of God;
   the language which I spoke and formed myself.   *114*

Know now, my son, the tasting of the tree
   was not itself the cause of such long exile,
   but only the transgression of God's bounds.   *117*

Four thousand three hundred and two full suns
   I longed for this assembly from that place
   your lady summoned Virgil to your aid;   *120*

I saw the sun return to run the course
   of all its stars nine hundred thirty times
   while I was living as a man on earth.   *123*

The language that I spoke was long extinct
   before that unaccomplishable task
   entered the minds of Nimrod's followers;   *126*

no product of the human mind can last
   eternally for, as all things in Nature,
   man's inclination varies with the stars.   *129*

That man should speak is only natural,
   but how he speaks, in this way or in that,
   Nature allows you to do as you please.   *132*

Till I descended to the pains of Hell,
   I was He called on earth That Highest Good
   Who swathes me in this brilliance of His bliss;   *135*

and then He was called *El:* for naturally
   man's habits, like the leaves upon the branch,
   change as they fall and others take their place.   *138*

Atop that mountain highest from the sea
   my time of innocence until disgrace
   was from my first day's hour until the hour,   *141*

as sun shifts quadrant, following the sixth."

NOTES

1–81

In the preceding canto the Pilgrim attempted to look
through the brilliance of St. John's light in order to see his body,
which, according to medieval legend, had been raised intact to
Heaven. This effort resulted in blindness for the Pilgrim, a fact
that suggests that his ignorance and superstition have deprived
him of his vision and understanding of Divine Truth. The Pil-
grim's condition is only temporary, however; St. John reassures
him that his eyesight will be restored after he has been examined
on the subject of Love or *caritas,* the last of the three theological
virtues. The traditional link between love and blindness ("love is
blind") is also evoked here—Cupid's blindness, for example.
During the examination no definition of love will be given,
unlike what was done earlier with the other theological virtues of
Faith and Hope. The Pilgrim will be questioned only as to the
"why" and the "what" of love. At the end of the examination the
Pilgrim will be allowed to enter the realm of blessedness above.
Dante in his *Convivio* (III, xiv, 14) had said:

whence our excellent faith has its origin, from which there comes the
hope of that for which we long and which we foresee, and from this

is born the activity of charity; by which three virtues we rise to philosophize in that celestial Athens.

For a different interpretation of Dante's blindness, see Gaffney (p. 110), who proposes that it is a further stage of the Pilgrim's spiritual progress which is at this point made to turn from exterior reflections to interior impressions of Divine Love.

10–12. *the lady who guides you:* Just as St. Paul's sight was restored to him by Christ's disciple Ananias on the Damascus road (see Acts 10:17), so will the Pilgrim recover his vision through the power of Beatrice's eyes.

14–15. *my eyes that were the gates:* Dante fell in love with Beatrice the first time he saw her (see *Vita nuova,* II). The idea of beauty working on the heart of the beholder by passing through the eyes was a common image in the lyric poetry of and before Dante's time (the entire process is described in a rather banal sonnet "L'amor e il cor gentil sono una cosa" (Love and the gracious heart are a single thing) in Chapter XX of the *Vita nuova.* Virgil also elaborates on the phenomenon in *Purg.* XVIII, 19–33.

16. *The Good, that full contentment of this Court:* That is, God, or the Highest Good.

17–18. *is Alpha and Omega of all texts:* Cf. Rev. 1:8: "I am Alpha and Omega, the beginning and the ending, saith the Lord, which is and which was and which is to come, the Almighty." Alpha is the first letter in the Greek alphabet, Omega the last. What Dante is saying, then, is that in God rest the beginning and end of all his love.

This tercet, however, is open to more than one interpretation. I take it to mean that God (the "Good" of verse 16) is the beginning and end of all that Holy Scripture teaches me ("reads" of verse 18 in the sense of "teaches," as in *Par.* X, 137) both literally and figuratively ("in soft or louder tones," 18). The Poet might also be saying, as Porena mentions (p. 252), that God is reflected in all the things he loves, reflected to a greater degree in some and to a lesser degree in others.

19. *the same voice:* The voice of St. John.

22. *you need a finer sieve:* Just as the sieve strains and separates the bran from the flour, so must the Pilgrim choose his words

more carefully: he must be more refined in his statements, more precise in his explanation of how he came to love God.

24. *who made you aim your bow:* Dante makes frequent use of this image in the *Comedy* (cf. *Purg.* XXX and XXXI, where Dante's aim was not so good!).

25–26. *"Through philosophic arguments / and through authority:* Through reason (see below, 37–39) and revelation (the Holy Scriptures) Dante has come to accept God as the supreme object of his love.

27. *such love as this has stamped me with its seal:* This is another frequent image in the poem. The imprint in wax is used with reference to love in *Purg.* XVII, 38–39. Cf. also *Par.* X, 29.

28–36. *for good perceived as good enkindles love:* The philosophical arguments (see 25), taken principally from Aristotle, hold that good inspires love to the extent that it (the good) is understood. The greater the comprehension of good, the greater the love which is enkindled within us. All goodness rests within God; hence, He must be the prime object of love, and once Divine Goodness is perceived, man must love Him. Thus, it is understanding (a function of the intellect) that precedes love (a function of the will).

37–39. *Such truth is made plain to my mind by him:* The reference is to Aristotle, who argues that all things are moved by an unmoved Mover; it is out of longing (love) for this Mover that the heavens (including the Angels and the Blest: "every immortal entity") revolve.

40–42. *Plain it was made by the True Author's voice:* In Exod. 33:17–19 God says to Moses: "I will make all my goodness pass before thee."

44. *Your great Gospel:* The Gospel of St. John, which opens with the proclamation of the Incarnation ("In the beginning was the word"), and thus the great mystery of God's nature. See John 1:1–18.

46–48. *"As human reason proves:* In summary, the philosophical arguments of reason (as formulated by Aristotle and other pagan thinkers), along with the authority of theology (revelation as brought forth in the Scriptures), give proof that the highest form of love is for God.

51. *the many teeth with which your love can bite":* Dante is asked to describe the secondary loves he has experienced and that lead him to place his highest love in God. The image of teeth that bite is an oddly graphic one; it is not the sort of tender figure that one might expect in connection with love. As in verses 55–57 below, the image suggests vehemence and tenacity. But this is not the first time Dante makes use of this image in connection with love or the lack of it (see *Purg.* XIII, 39 as well as XVIII, 132). According to Bosco and Reggio (p. 432), the image has its source in the language of the mystics.

53. *Christ's own eagle:* In medieval art the eagle symbolized St. John, indicating his deeper insight into the Divine mysteries. See also Revelation 4:7 where the four beasts are identified with the four Evangelists.

55–57. *"All of those teeth . . . .:* See above, verses 49–51 and note 51.

58–63. *The being of the world:* Several things have brought the Pilgrim to recognize the true and rightful object of his love: the existence of the world, his own existence, the Redemption and Dante's appreciation of its meaning both for himself and for all men, and the hope he holds as a result of his faith—all of these have made him see that love of God must be the highest form of devotion. Dante, when he says "that deep sea of false love" is probably alluding, among other things, to the wrong way in which he loved his lady Beatrice in the *Vita nuova.*

64–66. *I love each leaf:* Now that he recognizes God as the prime object of his love, Dante can appreciate the love he feels for all of God's creation. This type of love is in direct proportion to the grace bestowed by God upon the elements of His creation. Only God is loved for Himself.

67–69. *The instant I stopped speaking:* The Pilgrim's examination is now ended, and the joyful reaction of the souls of the Blest, including Beatrice, indicates that he has answered well. The chant of "Holy! Holy! Holy!" (three times over—a nice touch) is that sung by the Seraphim around the throne of God (see Isa. 6:2 – 3); it is also heard in the Apocalypse of St. John, sung by the four beasts (see Rev. 4:8).

70 – 72. *As sleep is broken by a flash of light:* The Pilgrim's sight is now restored to him. The process is compared to the experience of a sleeping man who perceives a bright light through the lids and membranes covering his eyes. The "visual spirit" (71) which apprehends the light is the power of the sensory organ (in this case, the eyes), according to the principles of medieval physiology. Cf. *Conv.* III, ix, 7 – 10; and II, ix, 5.

The Pilgrim's examination on the three theological virtues comes to an end at midpoint in this canto. The image of the light coming through the lids and membranes of the sleeping man's eyes, bringing him to his senses, serves as an introduction to a fourth light, that of Adam (also, incidentally, seen through a kind of membrane), to whom the second half of this canto is dedicated.

76 – 78. *so Beatrice drove out every speck:* It is the power of Beatrice's gaze that reawakens Dante's sight which, progressively through the poem, gets stronger and stronger.

84. *the first soul the First Power first made":* The Pilgrim's first sight after his examination by St. John on love is that of the soul of Adam, the fourth light, joining the lights of St. Peter, St. James, and St. John.

85 – 96

It must be kept in mind that the Pilgrim as he moves through the heavens is moving through a hierarchy. He is now in the eighth sphere, which may be thought of as the summit of the "human" hierarchy, since the two remaining spheres are the angelic and the Empyrean. Adam appears here, then, as the father of the human race and the only being created mature and perfect. The Pilgrim, amazed by his newly restored sight, bows down to Adam, perhaps in homage to his ancestor, the first father.

94 – 96. *I beg of you devoutly, I implore:* Perhaps we are meant to recall verses 64 – 69 of *Inf.* XXVI, where the Pilgrim shows similar enthusiasm to speak to another great shade, that of Ulysses. In fact, echoes of Ulysses' "mad flight" which ended in failure will be heard in the next canto, which is one of summation and

looking back in time as we approach the realm of timelessness and the end of a successful journey.

97 – 102. *Sometimes an animal will tremble in its skin:* The soul of Adam reveals its inner joy to Dante by moving within its own effulgence. These two tercets in Italian read:

Tal volta un animal coverto broglia
   sì che l'affetto convien che si paia
   per lo seguir che face a lui la 'nvoglia.

e similmente l'anima primaia
   mi facea trasparer per la coverta
   quant' ella a compiacermi venia gaia.

Many critics have tried their hand at identifying the "animal coverto" of verse 97: a caparisoned horse (see Torraca and Griffin), a hooded falcon, a cat in a sack, etc.? Dante may not have had a specific animal in mind, but if he did, it was most likely a silkworm in its cocoon or what I call in my translation "its skin." The verb *broglia* was translated by Benvenuto da Imola to mean "vibrat, vel tremit" (shakes or trembles). This meaning would go along well with the vibrations of a cocoon as the caterpillar spins, or to the movement of the animal itself moving back and forth inside the cocoon, which would be, at least in its early stages, a thin, transparent sack (see Sayers, pp. 354-55, and Vernon). See also *Par.* VIII, 52-54; V, 124-26. The *broglia* (97) and *'nvoglia* (99) seem to carry the meaning of the "intricacy" involved in the spinning of the silkworm's cocoon. See the *Enciclopedia Dantesca* under "brogliare" and also Sapegno.

106 – 108. *that Mirror of the Truth:* Adam perceives Dante's questions in the mind of God which reflects all things, and yet which is Itself reflected by no one thing. Cf. *Par.* XIX, 49 – 51.

109 – 42

Adam reads the questions the Pilgrim has in his mind; he poses them himself and then answers them. Dante wishes to know (1) how long ago Adam was created, (2) how long Adam remained in the Garden of Eden, (3) the true nature of Adam's sin, and (4) what language the first man spoke. Adam responds to the questions in order of their importance: (3), (1), (4), (2). The third question is, of course, the most important for all mankind since it deals with original sin.

111. *she:* Adam is referring to Beatrice.

115–17. *the tasting of the tree / was not itself the cause:* Adam and Eve would have had in due course the knowledge of good and evil that they so hastily pursued by eating the forbidden fruit. Adam's sin, then, was not one of gluttony, but rather one of disobedience of God's warning, caused by pride (see *Summa theol.* II–II, q. 163, a.1). Lucifer committed a similar sin of haste (see *Par.* XIX, 46–48). Was not Ulysses (*Inf.* XXVI) also guilty of a similar sin (though he was a pagan), that is, the transgression of the bounds set by his God?

118–19. *Four thousand three hundred and two full suns:* Adam spent 4,302 solar years in Limbo, the place whence Virgil came to the Pilgrim's aid, before Christ rescued him. It is interesting to note that Adam knows all about Beatrice's summoning of Virgil to come to the aid of her friend Dante.

It would seem that Adam does not waste words. He answers the Pilgrim's questions quickly and precisely and in no elaborate or embellished terms. He uses only one simile, and a very simple one at that (see 137 and note). Adam is, as it were, merely presenting the facts.

121–23. *I saw the sun return . . . nine hundred thirty times:* Adam lived 930 years on earth before he died (see Gen. 5:5). Added to the number of years he spent in Limbo (4,302), this gives a total of 5,232 years between the creation of Adam and the Crucifixion. The overall chronology is as follows:

Creation of Adam: 5198 B.C.
Adam's death and descent to Limbo: 4268 B.C.
Christ's descent into Hell: A.D. 34.

124–29. *The language that I spoke:* Here Dante states that Adam's language was born of reason, it was "a product of the human mind" (127). In *De vulgari eloquentia* (I, vi, 5–7), an earlier work, he held the theory that language was a Divine creation, unsusceptible to change. There, Dante had stated that Adam spoke Hebrew and that all his descendants spoke the same language until the building of the Tower of Babel by Nimrod's people. After this, language was confused (see Gen. 11:4–9), and from that time on only the sons of Heber spoke the language of Adam, which was the language of grace. Here Dante, through the mouth of Adam, corrects his earlier theory.

127–29. *no product of the human mind can last / eternally:* The turning of the heavenly spheres affects the operation of Nature and all things beneath the sphere of the moon, including the human mind, which is a variable thing.

134. *I was He called:* Cf. Ps. 68:4: "Sing unto God, sing praises to his name: extol Him that rideth upon the heavens by his name JAH, and rejoice before Him." "JAH" is the pronunciation of the letter "I," which begins the sacred name of Jehovah. The name was so profoundly revered by the Jews that it was spoken only on certain highly solemn occasions. "Hallelujah" contains the abbreviation as its last syllable. "I" also suggests the number 1, the symbol of unity, and it may have been invented by Dante for this purpose. See the *Magnae derivationes* of Uguccione da Pisa in which "I" is interpreted as the first letter in the word "invisibilis."

136. *and then he was called* El: Along with Jehovah, the name Elohim was used throughout the Hebrew scriptures to refer to God. According to St. Isidore (*Etym.* VII, i, 3) *El* was the first name for God among the Hebrews. See also note 134.

137. *man's habits, like the leaves upon the branch:* This image has its source in the *Ars poetica* of Horace (60–63). This is the only simile we find in Adam's speech to the Pilgrim. And it is indeed an effective one with its overtones of the Earthly Paradise and the generations of mankind.

139–42. *Atop that mountain highest from the sea:* The answer to the Pilgrim's second question (how long was Adam in the Garden of Eden?) is now given: six hours, from sunrise (6:00 A.M.) to 1:00 P.M. This is close to the view of Petrus Comestor (cf. *Par.* XII, 134), found in *Hist. schol.*, *Liber Genesis XXIV:* "Some hold that they were in the Garden for seven hours." For an interesting discussion of the relationship between the hour which Original Sin was committed and the hour of Christ's death on the Cross, see Nardi (311–40). See Sayers (p. 290), who points out that Dante also spent only six hours in the Earthly Paradise, as well as in the eighth heaven.

CANTO XXVII

ALL THE SOULS of the Blest sing "Gloria" to the Trinity with such sweetness that the Pilgrim thinks of his experience in terms of the universe smiling. Suddenly the light of St. Peter begins to take on a reddish glow; the moment the souls have stopped their singing, he begins a bitter invective against his successors and the corruption of the Church. Now all the souls, including Beatrice, have turned red, and Dante compares the change to the eclipse that took place at the death of Christ. St. Peter closes his invective with a vague prediction of a coming reform and invites Dante to reveal all he has heard once he has returned to earth. All the souls in the sphere of the fixed stars now ascend to the Empyrean; the Pilgrim watches them until they are out of sight. Beatrice instructs her ward to look down and through all the space he has travelled. Then, once again, he looks back to Beatrice whose miraculous eyes transport him to the ninth sphere of the Primum Mobile. Beatrice explains the function of this sphere, which is moved directly by God and which gives all the other spheres their movement. She then proceeds to lament the greed of mankind and blames the general disorder of things on earth on the fact that there is no one to govern below, concluding with an announcement that it will not be long before mankind changes its course.

"To Father and to Son and Holy Spirit,"
   all Heaven with one voice cried, "Glory be!"
   inebriating me with such sweet sound.   3

I seemed to see all of the universe
   turn to a smile; thus, through my eyes and ears
   I drank into divine inebriation.   6

O joy! O ecstasy ineffable!
   O life complete, perfect in love and peace!
   O wealth unfailing, that can never want!   9

Before my eyes those four torches kept blazing;
   and then the first light who had come to me
   started to grow more brilliant than the rest,   12

and he took on the glow which Jupiter
    would take, if he and Mars were like two birds
    that could exchange their feathers with each other.   15

That Providence assigning Heaven's souls
    each to his turn and function now imposed
    silence on all the choirs of the blessèd,   18

and I heard: "Do not marvel at my change
    of color, for you are about to see
    all of these souls change color as I speak.   21

He who on earth usurps that place of mine,
    that place of mine, that place of mine which now
    stands vacant in the eyes of Christ, God's Son,   24

has turned my sepulchre into a sewer
    of blood and filth, at which the Evil One
    who fell from here takes great delight down there."   27

The color which paints clouds at break of day,
    or in the evening when they face the sun—
    that same tint I saw spread throughout that Heaven.   30

And as a modest lady, self-secure
    in her own virtue, will at the mere mention
    of someone else's failings blush with shame,   33

so did the face of Beatrice change—
    the heavens saw the same eclipse, I think,
    when the Almighty suffered for our sins.   36

Then he continued speaking, but the tone
    his voice now had was no more different
    than was the difference in the way he looked: 39

"The bride of Christ was not nourished on blood
    that came from me, from Linus and from Cletus,
    only that she be wooed for love of gold;   42

it was for love of this delightful life
    that Sixtus, Pius, Calixtus, and Urban,
    after the tears of torment, spilled their blood.   45

Never did we intend for Christendom
    to be divided, some to take their stand
    on this side or on that of our successors,   48

not that the keys which were consigned to me
  become the emblem for a battleflag
  warring against the baptized of the land,   51

nor that my head become the seal to stamp
  those lying privileges bought and sold.
  I burn with rage and shame to think of it!   54

From here we see down there in all your fields
  rapacious wolves who dress in shepherd's clothes.
  O power of God, why do You still hold back?   57

Sons of Cahors and Gascony prepare
  to drink our blood: O sanctified beginning,
  to what foul ending are you doomed to sink!   60

But that high Providence which saved for Rome
  the glory of the world through Scipio's hand,
  will once again, and soon, lend aid, I know;   63

and you, my son, whose mortal weight must bring
  you back to earth again, open your mouth down there
  and do not hide what I hide not from you!"   66

As frozen vapors flake and start to snow
  down through our air during the time of year
  the horn of heaven's goat touches the sun,   69

so I saw all of Heaven's ether glow
  with rising snowflakes of triumphant souls
  of all those who had sojourned with us there.   72

My eyes followed their shapes up into space
  and I kept watching them until the height
  was too much for my eyes to penetrate.   75

My lady then, who saw that I was freed
  from gazing upward, said, "Lower your sight,
  look down and see how far you have revolved."   78

Since the last time that I had looked below
  I saw that I had moved through the whole arc
  which the first climate makes from mid to end: 81

I saw beyond Cadiz to the mad route
  Ulysses took, and nearly to the shore
  Europa left as a sweet godly burden.   84

More of this puny threshing-ground of ours
    I would have seen, had not the sun moved on
    beneath my feet a sign and more away.   87

My mind in love, yearning eternally
    to court its lady, now was burning more
    than ever to behold the sight of her.   90

And all that art and nature can contrive
    to lure the eye and thus possess the mind,
    be it in living flesh or portraiture   93

combined, would seem like nothing when compared
    to the Divine delight with which I glowed
    when once more I beheld her smiling face.   96

The power which her gaze bestowed on me
    snatched me from Leda's lovely nest, and up
    it thrust me into Heaven's swiftest sphere.   99

The parts of this, the quickest, highest heaven,
    are all so equal that I cannot tell
    where Beatrice chose for me to stay,   102

but she, who knew my wish, began to speak,
    such happiness reflecting in her smile,
    the joy of God, it seemed, was on her face: 105

"The nature of the universe, which stills
    its center while it makes all else revolve,
    moves from this heaven as from its starting-point; 108

no other 'Where' than in the Mind of God
    contains this heaven, because in that Mind burns
    the love that turns it and the power it rains.   111

By circling light and love it is contained
    as it contains the rest; and only He
    Who bound them comprehends how they were bound.   114

It takes its motion from no other sphere,
    and all the others measure theirs by this,
    as ten is product of the two and five.   117

How time can hide its roots in this sphere's vase
    and show its leaves stemming through all the rest,
    should now be clear to your intelligence.   120

O Greed, so quick to plunge the human race
    into your depths that no man has the strength
    to keep his head above your raging waters!   *123*

The blossom of man's will is always good,
    but then the drenchings of incessant rain
    turn sound plums into weak and rotten ones.   *126*

Only in little children can we find
    true innocence and faith, and both are gone
    before their cheeks show the first signs of hair.   *129*

While still a lisper, one observes fast-days,
    but once he's free to speak, he stuffs his mouth
    with all he can at any time of year;   *132*

one still in lisping childhood loves and heeds
    his mother's words, but soon in grown-up language,
    he'd rather like to see her dead and buried;   *135*

thus, the white skin of innocence turns black
    at first exposure to the tempting daughter
    of him who brings the morn and leaves the night.   *138*

My words should not surprise you when you think
    there is no one on earth to govern you
    and so the human family goes astray.   *141*

Before all January is unwintered—
    because of every hundred years' odd day
    which men neglect—these lofty spheres shall shine   *144*

a light that brings the long-awaited storm
    to whirl the fleet about from prow to stern,
    and set it sailing a straight course again.   *147*

Then from the blossom shall good fruit come forth."

NOTES

1–3. *To Father and to Son and Holy Spirit:* The souls in the
eighth sphere burst into a hymn of praise, the liturgical *Gloria
Patri,* now that the Pilgrim has successfully completed the third
and last of his examinations, and is ready to travel through the
Primum Mobile to the Empyrean, his ultimate destination and
God's home. Momigliano is right in saying that this canto begins

with a "fortissimo." I would add that the cry of "Glory be!" in verse 2, put into relief by the break in the natural continuity of the hymn in the opening verse, is proof enough. This outburst of joy on the part of the Blest is the first of three in this powerful canto. The remaining two, however, are not born of joy but rather of indignance.

4–6. *I seemed to see all of the universe:* The beauty of the souls' expression of joy is transmitted to Dante both visually (the smile, once reserved for Beatrice, now extended to the universe) and aurally (the sweetness of the hymn).

9. *O wealth unfailing, that can never want:* Piccarda's explanation in *Paradise* III, 64–68 is reiterated here, this time by the Pilgrim, who now understands the nature of the joy of the blessed souls.

10. *those four torches:* St. Peter, St. James, St. John, and Adam.

13–15. *he took on the glow which Jupiter / would take:* By means of this unusual simile the light of St. Peter's soul seems to grow brighter than the others around him as it takes on a reddish hue (Jupiter's light is white, and that of Mars red, the basis for the poet's figure of "exchange"). Cf. also Canto XIV, 87 and Canto XVIII, 95. Many of the commentators find this doubly hypothetic image difficult to take: all this convolution to say simply that the light of St. Peter changed from white to red?

19–21. *"Do not marvel at my change:* St. Peter proceeds to explain his change of color as the result of the shame he feels when he considers the degeneracy of the papacy. The other souls in this sphere share in this shame and will blush with St. Peter as he voices his disapproval of Pope Boniface VIII.

22–23. *He who on earth usurps that place of mine:* That is to say, Boniface VIII. The opening of St. Peter's denunciation of him is highly emphatic and indignant in tone, with the repetition of "that place of mine" three times as if it were threatening thunder echoing throughout the spheres.

24. *stands vacant:* The papacy is "vacant" only in the sense that it is corrupt and not because, as a number of comentators would have it, the election of Boniface to the high office of pope was invalid.

25 – 27. *has turned my sepulchre:* Through the influence of Satan, Rome—the burial place of St. Peter—has become a place of corruption and carnage, a veritable sewer.

28 – 30. *The color which paints clouds:* The entire eighth heaven with all its inhabitants is tinted with the rosy hue of sunrise or sunset. Ovid uses the image to characterize the embarrassment of the goddess Diana when seen naked by Actaeon, grandson of Cadmus: "When she was caught unclad, a blush mantled her cheeks, as bright as when clouds reflect the sun's rays, as bright as rosy dawn" (*Metam.* III, 183 – 84).

31 – 33. *a modest lady . . . blush with shame:* A good many critics understand verse 33, which in the Italian reads: "pur ascoltando, timida si fane," to mean that Beatrice turns pale, and they support their interpretation with verses 35 – 36 concerning the eclipse that took place at Christ's death on the cross. It is my belief that Beatrice's face, like that of all the rest in this sphere, turns red, a red as dark and deep as that which accompanied the eclipse at the Crucifixion (35 – 36). Why have Beatrice's face turn white and all the others red?

36. *when the Almighty suffered for our sins:* "The Almighty" here refers to Christ; the "eclipse in Heaven" (35) to the change in the color of the heavens during the Crucifixion. (See Matt. 27:45.)

37 – 39. *but the tone . . . the way he looked:* In other words, his voice was as changed as his appearance.

42. *from Linus and from Cletus:* St. Linus succeeded Peter as pope in either A.D. 64 or 67. It is said that a certain Saturnius beheaded him in 76 or 79. Then St. Cletus succeeded St. Linus as pope from ca. 79 to ca. 90. He suffered martyrdom under Domitian.

44. *Sixtus, Pius, Calixtus, and Urban:* Sixtus I was pope under Hadrian from ca. 115 – 125. Pius I was bishop of Rome under Emperor Antonius Pius from ca. 140 to ca. 155. Calixtus I was pope from 217 – 222, followed by Urban I from 222 – 230. All were known as early martyrs.

45. *after the tears of torment:* The "tears" are in reference to the persecutions suffered by the church in its early years.

46 – 54. *Never did we intend for Christendom:* The ancient church

had never intended for its followers to fall into conflicting (pro- and anti-papal) camps. The keys referred to here were those entrusted to St. Peter and used as an emblem by Boniface on his papal standard. Even worse, St. Peter's very countenance appeared on the papal seal for indulgences and for reinstatement after excommunication, "those lying privileges" (53).

57. *O power of God, why do You still hold back:* Though the Poet did not doubt the ways of Divine Wisdom, he did not hesitate to express his anguish and frustration at God's apparent unwillingness to intervene in certain situations. (See Ps. 43:23–24; also *Purg.* VI, 118–20.)

58. *Sons of Cahors and Gascony prepare:* John XXII, pope from 1316–1334, was from Cahors, capital of the province of Quercy in southern France. It was reputed to harbor usurers (see *Inf.* XI, 50). John's successor, Clement V, was a native of Gascony, whose inhabitants were reputed to be greedy. During his pontificate the papacy was transferred to Avignon. (See *Inf.* XIX, 82–87; *Purg.* XXXII, 148–60; *Par.* XVII, 82.)

61–66

St. Peter is as certain of God's will or justice as if he could read it in a book—all souls of the Blest possess this kind of knowledge. Here Dante reaffirms his faith in God's providence. God, he knows, will send help in some form or another. Now St. Peter tells the Pilgrim that when he has returned to earth, it is his mission to tell his fellow men what he has learned.

62. *Scipio's hand:* By means of the victory of Scipio Africanus the Elder over Hannibal in the Second Punic War, Rome was saved.

64–66. *and do not hide what I hide not from you!":* It will be the Pilgrim's sacred duty, as St. Peter announces to him here in an intense but affectionate way, to disclose to his fellow mortals all that he has learned from St. Peter.

67–72. *As frozen vapors flake and start to snow:* Like a snowstorm in midwinter, when the sun is in the sign of Capricorn ("the horn of heaven's goat touches the sun," 69), the spirits float away calmly and silently from the Pilgrim, back up to the Empyrean (Dante used a similar image in his *Vita nuova*, XXIII, 25). This simile involves no ordinary snowstorm, however, for the spirits are moving upward, thereby reversing the normal direction of the flakes. The spirits flow toward God from Whose point of view the image is born. This is the beginning of a number of "inversion" images to be found in this and the remaining cantos of the poem. It would seem that the perspective of the Pilgrim-Poet is beginning to change—and this is as it should be, as we shall soon see.

76 – 78. *look down and see how far you have revolved"*: A few cantos back (*Par.* XXII, 127 – 54) the Pilgrim also looked back down to the material universe and earth. He does so again here, for the last time, before he moves into the higher and purely spiritual realm. (It was also in the eighth heaven that Scipio Africanus the Younger had looked down on the universe. See Cicero, *De re publica*.)

79 – 81. *Since the last time that I had looked below:* The Pilgrim looked down for the first time in Canto XXII, 151 – 53. In medieval cartography the habitable earth (the northern hemisphere) was divided into seven "climates" or zones, delineated on maps by a series of circles drawn parallel to the equator. The first climate corresponds to the constellation of Gemini in the heavenly spheres, and it is in this sign that Dante has been revolving while in the eighth heaven. The first climate extended 20 degrees north of the equator, and each climate extended 180 degrees longitudinally; hence, "the whole arc . . . from mid to end" (80 – 81) measures 90 degrees. In terms of time, since this arc stands for one quarter of the revolution of the heavens around the earth (once every 24 hours), Dante must have spent six hours in the eighth sphere.

82 – 83. *I saw beyond Cadiz:* Dante looks westward and sees as far as the Strait of Gibralter (the western extremity of the inhabited world). To the east he can see the coast of Phoenicia. The reference to Ulysses and his "mad route" (82) recalls the description of his journey in *Inferno* XXVI, a journey that ended in failure because it was undertaken with the wrong intentions by one who was deceiving himself. Not so for the Pilgrim, who is soon to pass from the material to the spiritual world, from time to timelessness, to the completion of a successful journey to God.

83 – 84. *the shore / Europa left as a sweet godly burden:* The shore is the Phoenician shore. According to myth (see *Metam.* II, 833

−75), Jupiter, in love with the nymph Europa, transformed himself into a bull. Europa in all innocence ("sweet," 84) mounted his back, and he carried her off to Crete.

85. *this puny threshing-ground of ours:* The same point of view was expressed when Dante looked down on the earth in Canto XXII, 151.

86−87. *the sun moved on / beneath my feet:* See note 80−81 above. The sun was in Aries while Dante was in Gemini (with Taurus in between). As time passes, the sun continues to move.

88−96. *My mind in love:* Though he has been looking down on earth, the Pilgrim's mind is still filled with thoughts of Beatrice and burns with the desire to look upon her once again. When he finally does turn his eyes to her, he finds her more inexpressibly radiant than ever.

98. *Leda's lovely nest:* This is a reference to the constellation of Gemini. The twins Castor and Pollux were the children of Leda, who was wooed by Jupiter in the form of a swan. When Castor and Pollux died, Jupiter put them in the stars as the constellation Gemini. (Cf. Ovid, *Heroides* XVII, 55−56.)

99. *Heaven's swiftest sphere:* The Primum Mobile, highest and fastest of the revolving spheres.

103. *but she, who knew my wish:* Until this point in the journey Beatrice had always chosen a place for the Pilgrim to stay whenever they entered a new sphere: either the planet contained in each sphere or the constellation (as in the sphere preceding this one). The Pilgrim's wish, here, is to know where he is and the nature of the place.

109−11. *no other 'Where' than in the mind of God:* The Primum Mobile, last of the material heavens, is contained within the Empyrean, highest of the heavens, home of God's mind and an immaterial entity. The Seraphim, the Intelligence of the Primum Mobile, receive their power to move this heaven (and transmit motion to the lower spheres) from God's love in the Empyrean.

112−14. *by circling love and light it is contained:* Just as the Primum Mobile contains all the other lower spheres, so the Empyrean contains it, binding it in love and light. Dante discusses the movement of this sphere in his *Convivio* (II, iii, 8−11).

117. *as ten is product of the two and five:* The eight heavens beneath the Primum Mobile take their revolutions from the speed of the Primum Mobile, just as in mathematics the number ten may be measured by multiplication of its half and its fifty.

118-20. *How time can hide its roots in this sphere's vase:* The starting point of time is in the motion of the Primum Mobile, which cannot be seen, for it has no planet. Its "leaves," however, or the lower spheres, can be perceived by man. This is another of Dante's inverted images (see 67-72 and note; also *Purg.* XXII, 133-34; XXXII, 40-41)—and there are more to come.

121-48

At this point Beatrice's tone changes to one of righteous anger, and she closes the canto with a denunciation of the weaknesses of humanity and its unworthiness to exist in such a well-ordered universe. What St. Peter started earlier in the canto Beatrice now ends, in almost the same number of tercets and certainly in no less of a rage.

124-29. *The blossom of man's will is always good:* Man begins as a good creature but is soon misguided and corrupted as he goes through life. The "incessant rain" (125) is to be understood in the sense of "the influence of corrupt surroundings."

136-38. *Thus, the white skin of innocence turns black:* This is a much-discussed tercet and has been interpreted in a number of different ways. What it seems to convey is the idea that the white skin of the innocent human blackens with corruption and sin as soon as it looks upon worldly goods. "Him who brings the morning and leaves the night" must be the sun; the "tempting daughter" is probably Circe (*Solis filia*) the sorceress who was able to change men into beasts (see *Aeneid* VII, 11). In this context Circe represents worldly goods and temptation to search after them. Continuing, then, the imagery of "change": from childhood to manhood (the preceding three tercets, 127-35), what Beatrice is saying is simply that a child's skin when he is young is white, and then when exposed to the rays of the sun it turns dark—the innocent soul of the child turns black from corruption when he reaches manhood.

141. *and so the human family goes astray:* How many times this point is made in the course of the poem! In verses 22-24 of this canto we were told that the papacy is "vacant"; there is no temporal leader to guide mankind (cf. *Purg.* VI, 76; XVI, 97 – 114; *Par.* XVIII, 125 – 26). Because of all this man is on the wrong path; the right road is lost!

142 – 44. *Before all January is unwintered:* The Julian calendar made the year 365 days and 6 hours long. Due to this inaccuracy the solar year gained one day per century over the regular year. Thus, in less than 90 centuries under this system January would have been shifted into spring. (In 1582, Gregory XIII corrected this error in the calendar.) This certainly is an unusual way to say "action will be taken soon!"

145 – 47. *a light that brings the long-awaited storm:* Here the "human family of verse 141 becomes a "fleet" (146) of ships which, as a result of a "long-awaited storm" caused by a light sent from Heaven—that is to say, the coming of a temporal leader to guide mankind (see also *Inf.* I, 101; *Purg.* XX, 15; XXXIII, 44), is then turned around and made to sail a straight course once more. Dante never lost hope in the eventual coming of Divine intervention.

148. *Then from the blossom shall good fruit come forth:* The canto closes with an abrupt shift in imagery. Dante returns to the image he began in verses 124 – 26: from "rotten plums" (126) to a "fleet" of ships (146) to "good fruit."

CANTO XXVIII

WHEN BEATRICE FINISHES speaking, the Pilgrim notices an unusually bright light reflected in her eyes. He turns around and sees a brilliant point around which are nine glowing circles, all spinning at a rate of speed lesser in proportion to their distance from the central point. Beatrice explains that this point is the source of all the heavens and all of Nature. Puzzled, the Pilgrim wishes to know why the visible order of the universe (the physical picture) does not conform to the order he is presently observing in the model before him (the ideal picture). Beatrice tells him he must not judge by the size of the sphere he sees but rather by the power of the angelic order governing that sphere; since the Seraphic order of the angels who govern the Primum Mobile—the sphere closest to God—is the most powerful order, and since there is perfect correspondence between the heavenly spheres and the angelic orders governing them, the correspondence only *seems* to be in inverse order. (What the Pilgrim is seeing now is the physical universe from the spiritual point of view—from God's eye, as it were—with God at the center.) As the Pilgrim expresses his delight at having understood Beatrice's explanation, the nine fiery circles begin to emit countless singing sparks: the nine orders of angels that govern the nine spheres. Beatrice names the orders of angels, explains their functions, and tells him that Dionysius was right and St. Gregory wrong in his ordering of the angelic hierarchies, and that he should not marvel at the fact that Dionysius was privileged to such secret information since, after all, it was St. Paul in person who told him!

Then once the adverse truth of mankind's present
   miserable state was clearly brought to light
   by her who holds my mind imparadised,   *3*

as one who in a mirror catches sight
   of candlelight aglow behind his back
   before he sees it or expects to see it,   *6*

and, turning from the looking-glass to test
   the truth of it, he sees that glass and flame
   are in accord as notes to music's beat;   *9*

just so do I remember doing then,
    as I stood gazing at the lovely eyes,
    those lures which Love had used to capture me,   *12*

for, when I turned around, my eyes were met
    by what takes place here in this whirling sphere
    whenever one looks deep into its motion.   *15*

I saw a point that radiated light
    so piercing that the eyes its brightness strikes
    are forced to shut from such intensity.   *18*

That star which seems the smallest seen from here
    if set beside that point, like star by star
    appearing in the heavens, would seem a moon.   *21*

Perhaps the distance of a halo's glow
    around the brilliant source that colors it
    when vapors hold it in their density,   *24*

as close as that a ring of fire whirled
    around this point at speed that would surpass
    the sphere that spins the swiftest round the world;   *27*

this one was circled by a second one,
    second by third, and third by yet a fourth,
    the fifth the fourth, and then the sixth the fifth;   *30*

the seventh followed spreading out so wide
    that Juno's messenger, if made complete,
    could not contain it in her circle-bow.   *33*

So came the eighth, the ninth; and each of them
    revolved more slowly according as it was
    in number farther from the central one   *36*

whose radiance was clearest of them all
    for, circling nearest the Pure Spark of Being,
    I think it shares the fullest in Its Truth.   *39*

My lady, who observed my eagerness
    and my bewilderment, said: "On that Point
    depend all nature and all of the heavens.   *42*

Observe the circle nearest it, and know
    the reason for its spinning at such speed
    is that Love's fire burns it into motion."   *45*

And I to her: "If all the universe
    were ordered in the way these wheels are here,
    I would be satisfied with what I see,   48

but from our world of sense we can observe
    the turning of the spheres are more God's own,
    the further from its center they revolve.   51

Now, if my wish to know is to be granted
    here in this wondrous and angelic shrine,
    whose only boundaries are love and light,   54

it still has to be made clear to me why
    the model and the copy are at odds,
    for on my own I fail to understand."   57

"If your weak fingers find it difficult
    to loosen such a knot, it is no wonder,
    for it is tight from never being tried!"   60

So spoke my lady. Then she said: "If you
    wish to be satisfied, listen to what
    I tell you, then, sharpen your wits on it.   63

The course of the material spheres is wide
    or narrow in accord with more or less
    of virtue that infuses each throughout.   66

The greater goodness makes for greater bliss;
    a greater bliss calls for a greater body,
    if it is perfect in all of its parts;   69

therefore, this sphere which sweeps all of the world
    along with it must correspond to this,
    the inner ring, that loves and knows the most.   72

And so, if you will take your measurements
    not by circumference but by the power
    inherent in these beings that look like rings,   75

you will observe a marvelous congruence
    of greater power to more, lesser to small,
    in every heaven with its Intelligence."   78

As splendid clearness and tranquillity
    will overcome the airy hemisphere
    when Boreas blows from his milder cheek   81

a breeze which purifies the air and clears
   all the obscuring mist so heaven smiles
   its loveliness from all its dioceses,   *84*

so was my mind, as soon as I received
   my lady's brilliant answer, and I saw
   the truth shine like a clear star in the heavens.   *87*

When she had spoken her last word, there came
   showers of light from all the fiery rings,
   like molten iron in fire spurting sparks,   *90*

and each spark kept to its own ring of fire—
   the number of them thousand into more
   than any doubling of the chessboard yields.   *93*

I heard them sing "Hosanna," choir on choir,
   to the Fixed Point that holds each to his *ubi*,
   the place they were and will forever be.   *96*

And she, who looked into my mind and saw
   I was confused, told me: "The first two rings
   show you the Seraphim and Cherubim.   *99*

They spin so swiftly speeding in their bonds
   to grow as much like that Point as they can,
   and they can in proportion to their sight.   *102*

Those loves that circle round the other two
   are called the Thrones of the Eternal Aspect;
   they close the first triad of God's own world;   *105*

And know that all of them delight in bliss
   according to how deep their vision delves
   into the Truth in which all minds find rest.   *108*

And so, you understand, their state of bliss
   is based upon the act of seeing God,
   not loving Him which is the second step.   *111*

The measure of their vision is their worth,
   born of His grace and of their own good will:
   for this their ranks proceed from grade to grade.   *114*

The second triad in full blossom here
   in this spring of eternity whose buds
   no nightly frost of Aries can despoil,   *117*

warbling 'Hosanna!' sempiternally,
    sing winter out in threefold melody,
    that sounds through triple ranks of trinity.   120

This hierarchy of divinities
    consists of the Dominions first, and next
    the Virtues, and the third are called the Powers.   123

In the next to last of the last dancing trio
    whirl Principalities, and then Archangels;
    the festive Angels fill the last with play.   126

And all of the angelic ranks gaze upward,
    as downward they prevail upon the rest,
    so while each draws the next, all draw toward God.   129

Dionysius set his mind to contemplate
    these ranks with so much holy zeal for truth,
    he named and ordered them the way I do;   132

Gregory, later, disagreed with him,
    but when he died to waken in this heaven
    he saw the truth, and laughed at his mistake.   135

And that such secrets were revealed by one
    still living on the earth, you need not wonder:
    the one who saw it here told him this truth   138

and many other truths about these rings."

NOTES

1–21

Looking into Beatrice's eyes, as he had once before in the
Earthly Paradise (*Purg.* XXXI, 118–23) when he saw the double
nature of the Incarnate Love reflected therein, first in the Divine
form then in the human, Dante now sees reflected a small but
very intense light, which is the light of God shining down from
the Empyrean. It is a symbolic picture of God, not of His Divine
Essence, but in His relationship to the orders of angels that
govern the spheres. The Pilgrim, then, turns to look directly at
the light of God and the angels.

3. *who holds my mind imparadised:* The word "imparadised" is
my translation for Dante's *'mparadisa*, a verb he invented for the

occasion. There are a number of such inventions in this canto as well as in other parts of the *Paradise*. For a discussion of the style and language of this canto see Contini.

9. *are in accord as notes to music's beat:* The light and its reflection in the mirror are brought together as one in the eyes of the beholder just as singing and musical accompaniment become one in the rhythm.

12. *those lures which Love had used to capture me:* The reference is to the moment in Dante's life (see *Vita nuova*, II) when he first beheld Beatrice and fell in love with her when the god of love acted upon him through the eyes of Beatrice. Here, her eyes perform a very different function: as reflectors of God's love, they are sacred and exalted.

15. *whenever one looks deep into its motion:* All of the critics are puzzled by this verse. Singleton, however, gives a clear explanation (p. 447):

> Apparently whenever someone gazes intently upon this heaven one sees the astounding vision which is now presented (vvs. 16−39). This can only mean a gazing in absorbed contemplation, of course, and points to the basic allegory through the *Paradiso*, which is that of rising in contemplation, by the "ladder" which reaches all the way to the Empyrean (*Par*. XXI, 29; XXII, 68). In climbing this ladder, the verse is implying, one would always come upon such a vision in the ninth heaven, acknowledged heaven of the angels.

16. *I saw a point:* The point is God, an infinitesimal yet brilliant point of light representing the indivisible center of all of Heaven's brightness (cf. *Conv.* II, xii, 27).

19. *from here:* On earth, where the Poet is writing.

22. *a halo's glow:* That is, the kind of misty light that at times is seen surrounding the moon or the sun.

27. *the sphere that spins the swiftest:* This is the ninth heaven, or the Primum Mobile, where the Pilgrim is at present. Dante goes on in the verses that follow to enumerate the other spheres.

31−33. *the seventh followed:* The heaven of Saturn is so great that an expanse of rainbow ("Juno's messenger," Iris) if made into a complete circle would be too small to contain it.

34 – 36. *each of them / revolved more slowly:* Counting from the center, each sphere revolves more slowly than its predecessor.

41 – 42. *"On that Point:* All of creation depends on the First (unmoved) Mover for locomotion and change. The principle is an Aristotelian one and can be found in the Latin translation with which Aquinas was familiar (see *Metaphys.* XII, 7, 1072b).

43. *Observe the circle nearest it:* This is the Primum Mobile, the circle governed by the order of the Seraphim, highest of the angelic orders.

49 – 51. *but from our world of sense we can observe:* Dante has viewed the heavens as most mortals have: from earth. From this point of view the furthest of the spheres (from earth, that is) is most Divine. From his present vantage point, however, the Pilgrim sees that the furthest sphere (from the Empyrean) is least Divine.

55 – 57. *the model and the copy are at odds:* The "model" is the symbolic vision of the spheres now beheld by Dante, in which the central point is the light of God. The "copy" or material universe has the earth as its center surrounded by nine spheres.

58 – 60. *"If your weak fingers find it difficult:* The question of the relation of the physical and spiritual worlds is not easily ⁓nswered, particularly by the unenlightened mind.

64 – 72

Each sphere is imbued with Divine power in proportion to its expanse or width. Accordingly, the larger the sphere or heaven, the stronger its beneficent influence on the parts of the universe below it. It can be said that the larger heavens enjoy a greater capacity of goodness.

70. *this sphere:* The Primum Mobile, which gives motion to all the other spheres.

72. *the inner ring, that loves and knows the most:* This is the circle of fire closest to God containing the Seraphim, the highest order of angels, who love Him the most and know Him best.

76 – 78. *you will observe a marvelous congruence:* Dante is urged to consider the relation of speed and size to excellence, thereby tying together all of Beatrice's remarks on the rings representing

the spheres and the angelic orders. It should be clear now to the Pilgrim that each sphere is controlled by the angelic order best suited to it; that the speed and brightness of each sphere represent the excellence of the angelic order; that the size of the circle represents the excellence of the sphere. God is the center of all the circles and embraces them all.

80. *the airy hemisphere:* That is, the air that surrounds the earth, or the atmosphere.

81. *Boreas:* Early maps frequently personified the winds, showing them as winged heads with inflated cheeks emitting puffs of air. Each wind-god blew a threefold blast: one from the middle of the mouth and one from each of the two corners. Thus Boreas, the north wind, could blow from due north, the northwest, or the northeast. Here Dante refers to the latter, which was known to be the gentlest of the north winds and which clears the skies of clouds.

84. *from all its dioceses:* That is, from all its regions.

88–90. *showers of light:* The sparks of light that Dante sees within each ring of fire represent the individual members of the angelic orders. Each spark is a separate, distinct entity, and yet it fits into the larger scheme of its order and finally into the totality of the nine orders. (For a similar image of sparks in molten iron, cf. *Par.* I, 59–60.)

92. *the number of them thousand into more:* The poet invents the verb *s'inmilla* ("thousand themselves") based on the numeral (see also *Par.* IX, 40, and XIII, 57, for similar inventions).

93. *than any doubling of the chessboard yields:* Considered all together the angels in the nine spheres are so numerous as to be uncountable. The reference to the chessboard comes from an ancient Oriental legend: a Brahmin presented to the King of Persia the game of chess. The king was so pleased by the gift that he promised the Brahmin anything he wanted in return. The Brahmin requested a grain of wheat doubled as many times as there were squares on the chessboard. With the successive doublings the total would have reached many millions—approximately eighteen and one half million million million.

95. *the Fixed Point that holds each to his* ubi: God keeps every angel to its appointed place in the circles of the angelic orders.

Ubi is the Latin adverb for "where" (see *Par.* XXIX, 12 where the word is used again).

98. *I was confused:* The Pilgrim wonders about the orders of the angels.

100–102. *They spin so swiftly . . . to grow as much like that Point:* The extent of their vision of God determines the extent of their desire to resemble God. The speed with which they spin is an indication of their fervor.

103–105. *Those loves that circle:* The Thrones form the bottom of the first triad of the highest set of angelic orders. The term "loves" is used in a similar fashion in Canto XXIX, 18. As for the term "Thrones," Dionysius (see n. 130) claims that they are referred to in this way because of their remoteness from earthly things: they are close to the highest orders, they receive Divine Love, carry God, and are worthy of Divine offices (see *De caelesti hierarchia,* VII).

109–11. *their state of bliss / is based:* Vision belongs to the intellect, which precedes love, which is an act of the will. The question of which comes first, knowledge of God or love of Him, was much discussed by the theologians of Dante's day. Dante's viewpoint is that of Thomas Aquinas, Albertus Magnus, and the Dominicans. The Augustinian-Franciscan school generally held for the other side in favor of primacy of the will.

112–14. *The measure of their vision is their worth:* It is according to their merit that they are able to see God. Merit is bestowed by grace.

115–20

In these two tercets describing the second of the three triads of the hierarchy of angels, the image of the flower in eternal spring is introduced. It will become dominant in the succeeding cantos as the figure of the Celestial Rose, the final image, develops. By positing the idea of "this spring of eternity" and then alluding to autumn in the following verse (117), the poet is able to use the strange verb *sberna* ("to sing winter out" as birds do in the spring) in the next tercet (see note to 118–20).

117. *no nightly frost of Aries can despoil:* On earth, a frosty April

night can ruin the spring blossoms; there is no danger of that in heaven's eternal springtime.

118–20. *warbling 'Hosanna!' sempiternally:* This magnificent tercet in the original reads:

> perpetüalemente *'Osanna'* sberna
> con tre melode, che suonano in tree
> ordini di letizia, onde s' interna.

Dante has structured this tercet to convey the ideas of circularity (eternity) and trinity (God). There are places in the poem where Dante will take pains to use only three words to fill out one verse: so it is here in verse 118 which, incidentally, can be read, making perfect sense, both forward and backward creating the idea of circularity. And the enjambement of *tree / ordini* in verses 119–20 serves the same purpose. But here he goes even further in order to stress the concept of trinity: he manages to use a variation of the word "three" three times in the second and third verses of this tercet (twice in 119: *tre* and *tree;* and once in 120: *s' interna*). In fact, in order to get his last 3 into the tercet he invents the word *s' interna* (from *in* and *terno,* which is similar to his invention of *s' intrea* in *Par.* XIII, 57), and brings the tercet to a close leaving the reader with a sense of "perpetual trinity." While this tercet, then, on a literal level is about the three orders that form the second hierarchy of angels, on another level—the poetic level of language imitating action—it is also a verbal picture of God.

126. *the festive Angels fill the last with play:* The joyful last order of angels completes the hierarchy, which is as follows:

Heavenly Sphere	Angelic Order
9. Primum Mobile	Seraphim
8. Fixed Stars	Cherubim
7. Saturn	Thrones
6. Jupiter	Dominions
5. Mars	Virtues
4. Sun	Powers
3. Venus	Principalities
2. Mercury	Archangels
1. Moon	Angels

127–29. *so while each draws the next, all draw toward God:* In a kind of reciprocal action, as each order focuses its sight upward toward God, so does it pass its influence and knowledge (received from God) downward to the spheres and orders below (128). The entire hierarchical system is pulling toward God.

130. *Dionysius:* Dionysius the Areopagite (mentioned in *Par.* X, 116–17) was a famous Athenian who was converted to Christianity by the preaching of Paul (see Acts 17:34). He is believed to have been the first bishop of Athens, and was martyred there ca. A.D. 95. Medieval scholars ascribed to him a number of works on Divine names, mystic theology, and ecclesiastical and celestial hierarchy. (These works now carry the name Pseudo-Dionysius, and are credited to fifth-to-sixth century neo-Platonists.) *De Caelesti Hierarchia,* which was translated into Latin by Johannes Scotus Erigena in the ninth century, was the medieval textbook of celestial lore. It presents the hierarchy of angels in the same order as Dante, through Beatrice, does here.

133. *Gregory:* Pope Gregory I, "the Great" (590–604) discussed the angelic orders in his *Homilies on the Gospel* (XXIII, 48). He structured the hierarchy as follows: Seraphim; Cherubim; Powers; Principalities; Virtues; Dominions; Thrones; Archangels; Angels. Dante followed this order in the *Convivio* (II, vi). Here he corrects his earlier belief, now accepting the hierarchy held by Thomas Aquinas and others.

135. *he saw the truth and laughed at his mistake:* This is a nice touch on the part of Beatrice, who has until now filled the ears of the Pilgrim with beautifully phrased but very heavy angelology.

136–39. *such secrets were revealed by one:* This is Dionysius, who received the truth from St. Paul ("the one who saw it here"). Cf. *Inf.* II, 28.

CANTO XXIX

AFTER A BRIEF silence Beatrice sees in the mind of God
that the Pilgrim has a question, and so she explains to him that
the creation of the angels by God was an act of pure love that
took place in the Empyrean before time began. She goes on to
explain why some angels rebelled against God and others re-
mained faithful to Him. Since, according to Beatrice, there is so
much confusion on earth concerning the different qualities of the
angels, she wishes to make some further clarifications. Those who
insist that the angels possess memory are wrong. Angels have no
need of memory, because they see everything through God. She
reprehends those men who go around teaching and showing off
new and exotic theories that twist the truth of the ultimate
authority of the Scriptures. Christ, she says, expected his Apos-
tles to spread truth and not garbage. But these ambitious preach-
ers are fattening themselves on the lies they feed their
parishoners. After this digression Beatrice returns to the subject
of angels, explaining that they are so many in number that the
human mind could not possibly think in such terms. The light
of God shines upon this multitude of angels, all of whom receive
His light in as many different ways as there are celestial intelli-
gences. Think, then, how great God is, Who can divide His
light among all these loving and reflecting angelic mirrors and
remain Himself forever One and Whole!

When the twin children of Latona share
    the belt of the horizon and are crowned
    one by the Ram, the other by the Scales,   3

no longer than the zenith holds them poised
    in balance till their weights begin to shift,
    as each moves to a different hemisphere,   6

for just so long, her face a radiant smile,
    was Beatrice silent, her eyes fixed
    upon the Point whose light I could not bear.   9

She said: "I tell you, without asking you,
    what you would hear, for I see your desire
    where every *where* and every *when* is centered.   12

Not to increase His good, which cannot be,
    but rather that His own reflected glory
    in its resplendence might proclaim *I am*   15

in His eternity, beyond all time,
    beyond all comprehension, as pleased Him,
    new loves blossomed from the Eternal Love.   18

Nor did He lie in idleness before,
    for neither 'after' nor 'before' preceded
    the going forth of God upon these waters.   21

Pure form, pure matter, form and matter mixed
    came forth into a perfect state of being
    shot like three arrows from a three-stringed bow.   24

As in crystal or in amber or in glass
    a shaft of light diffuses through the whole,
    its ray reflected instantaneously,   27

so the threefold creation of the Lord
    was rayed into existence all at once,
    without beginning, with no interval.   30

With every essence there was co-created
    its order: at the summit of the world
    the ones created of pure act were set;   33

and pure potential held the lowest place;
    and in between, potential-to-act was tied
    so tight that they can never be untied.   36

Jerome left word with you about the stretch
    of centuries that angels had existed
    before the rest of God's world came to be,   39

but this truth is declared in many texts
    by writers of the Holy Spirit's word,
    and you will find it if you look with care;   42

reason itself can almost understand:
    it could not grant that the angelic powers
    remain short of perfection for so long.   45

So now you know the where and when and how
    these loves came into being, and so already
    three flames of your desire are now quenched.   *48*

Nor could you count from one as high as twenty
    faster than part of the angelic group
    shook the foundation of your elements.   *51*

The rest remained and started practicing
    their art, as you can see, with such delight
    they take no time to pause, but whirl forever.   *54*

The reason for the Fall was the accursed
    presumption of the one you saw below
    crushed by the weight of all the universe.   *57*

These others you see here were humbly prompt
    to recognize their great intelligence
    as coming from the Goodness of their Lord,   *60*

whereby their vision was raised to such heights
    by God's enlightening grace and their own worth
    that now their will was steadfast and entire;   *63*

and should you doubt, I would have you believe
    that the receipt of grace implies one's worth
    in measure as love opens up to it.   *66*

By now, if you have understood my words,
    you should be able to conclude much more
    about this sacred place without more help.   *69*

But since on earth you still teach in your schools
    that the angelic nature is possessed
    of understanding, memory, and will,   *72*

I shall say more and show you the pure truth
    of what on earth has now become confused
    by equivocations in their arguments.   *75*

From the first moment these beings found their bliss
    within God's face in which all is revealed,
    they never turned their eyes away from It;   *78*

hence, no new object interrupts their sight
    and hence, they have no need of memory
    since they do not possess divided thought;   *81*

and so on earth men dream their waking dreams,
  some speaking in good faith, some unbelieving—
  to these belong the greater guilt and shame.   84

You mortals do not keep to one true path
  philosophizing: so carried away
  you are by putting on a show of wits!   87

Yet even this provokes the wrath of Heaven
  far less than when the Holy Word of God
  is set aside or misconstrued by you   90

Men do not care what blood it cost to sow
  the Word throughout the land, nor how pleasing
  he is who humbly takes Scripture to heart.   93

To make a good impression they contrive
  their own unfounded truths which then are furbished
  by preachers—of the Gospel not a word!   96

Some say that during Christ's Passion the moon
  reversed its course intruding on the sun
  whose light, then, could not reach as far as earth—   99

such preachers lie! For that light hid itself,
  and men in Spain as well as India
  shared this eclipse the same time as the Jew.   102

Fables like these are shouted right and left,
  pouring from pulpits—more in just one year
  than all the Lapi and Bindi found in Florence!   105

So the poor sheep, who know no better, come
  from pasture fed on air—the fact that they
  are ignorant does not excuse their guilt.   108

Christ did not say to his first company:
  'Go forth and preach garbage unto the world,'
  but gave them, rather, truth to build upon.   111

With only His word sounding on their lips
  they went to war to keep the faith aflame;
  the Gospel was their only sword and shield.   114

Now men go forth to preach wisecracks and jokes,
  and just so long as they can get a laugh
  to puff their cowls with pride—that's all they want;   117

But if the crowd could see the bird that nestles
in tips of hoods like these, they soon would see
what kind of pardons they are trusting in.   *120*

What folly in mankind's credulity:
no need of proof or testimonials,
men rush at any promise just the same!   *123*

On this Saint Anthony fattens his pig,
and bigger pigs than his get fatter too,
paying their bills with forged indulgences.   *126*

We have digressed enough. Turn your mind's eye
back to the road of truth; we must adjust
discussion to what time is left us here.   *129*

The angelic nature goes so far beyond
the scale of mortal numbers that there is
no word or concept that can reach that far.   *132*

Look in the Book of Daniel; you will see
that when he speaks of thousands of these beings,
no fixed or finite number is revealed.   *135*

The primal Light shines down through all of them
and penetrates them in as many ways
as there are splendors with which It may mate.   *138*

And since the visual act always precedes
the act of loving, bliss of love in each
burns differently: some glow while others blaze.   *141*

And now you see the height, you see the breadth
of Eternal Goodness that divides Itself
into these countless mirrors that reflect   *144*

Itself, remaining One, as It was always."

NOTES

1–9

Beatrice gazes upon God's light ("the Point," 9) for as long
a time as exists between the moment that the horizon crosses the
middle of the moon and the sun (when at the vernal equinox they
are opposite each other at dawn and sunset) and the moment that

the horizon ceases to touch either body; that is, for a brief period: perhaps a minute, as some critics would have it, or a brief instant, as others prefer to see it. But these three tercets certainly do more than convey the amount of time that Beatrice remained silent between cantos; they give the picture of a giant scales at the instant of perfect balance supported from above by the invisible hand of the Creator. This grandiose opening of three tercets to describe an instant in time is an anticipation of Beatrice's discussion of the act of creation, and it is matched by the equally grandiose closing of three tercets telling of the greatness of God.

1. *the twin children of Latona:* Apollo and Diana, the sun and the moon.

3. *one by the Ram, the other by the Scales:* That is to say, when the sun is in Aries and the moon in Libra.

10–12. *where every* where *and every* when *is centered:* Beatrice reads Dante's thoughts as she looks upon God (reflected in God Who is in the Empyrean), the center of all space and time and Who reflects all things.

13–18. *Not to increase His good:* God creates other beings not to augment His own goodness (this is impossible, for He is all goodness), but rather that those creatures might participate and share in His goodness. Thus, God's creation is an extension of His love. The "new loves" (18) are the angels, the first created beings. (Cf. Aquinas, *Summa theol.* I, q. 1, a.1.)

19–21. *Nor did He lie in idleness before:* It is impossible to consider time with reference to God and His creation, for God is timeless; thus, it cannot be said that He was idle before creation.

22. *Pure form, pure matter, form and matter mixed:* Pure form is immaterial spirit (the angels). Pure matter is matter without spirit (the substance of the earth), while form and matter mixed produce the heavens. Aristotle makes this distinction in his *De anima* (II, 2, 414ᵃ).

23. *came forth into a perfect state of being:* The result of the threefold creation was a state of perfection.

24. *shot like three arrows:* The threefold creation came from the triune God with express purpose.

25–27. *As in crystal or in amber or in glass:* A principle of

Aristotelian physics is that light was diffused instantaneously through a translucent medium.

31 – 34. *With every essence there was co-created:* Order came about the same moment the angels were created. These were God's highest created beings, consisting of "pure act" or form as opposed to primal matter or "pure potential."

35 – 36. *and in between, potential-to-act was tied:* The material heavens (spheres, stars, planets), coming between the Empyrean and the earth, were created by God as a mixture of pure act and pure potency, or spirit and matter.

37 – 42. *Jerome left word with you:* St. Jerome (A.D. 340 – 420) wrote a Latin version of the Old Testament, referred to as the Vulgate. Following Thomas Aquinas, Dante takes issue with St. Jerome's view that the angels were created long before the rest of the universe. Dante cites the Scriptures as supporting evidence (Gen. 1:1; Eccles. 18:1). "This truth" (40) is the truth Beatrice is putting forth to the Pilgrim.

43 – 45. *reason itself can almost understand:* Revelation in the form of the Scriptures has been called upon to refute St. Jerome. In addition, Beatrice cites the argument of reason, which holds that the angels are movers, and for them to have been created and then relegated to idleness would have been a paradox.

46 – 48. *So now you know the where and when and how:* In summary, Beatrice has explained (1) that the angels were created in the Empyrean, (2) that they were created at the same moment that time and the universe came into being, and (3) that they were created as perfect beings. These are the "three flames" of the Pilgrim's desire to know that have now been "quenched."

49 – 51. *Nor could you count from one as high as twenty:* The rebellion of a certain group of angels took place over a very brief period of time (less than a minute). In their fall Lucifer and his followers caused the earth to quake (see *Inf.* XXXIV, 121 – 26).

52 – 53. *The rest remained . . . practicing / their art:* Cf. *Inf.* III, 37 – 41, where Dante mentions a group of angels who were in between the rebels and the faithful: they did not rebel against God, and yet they were not true to Him. Consequently, they were scorned from Heaven as well as from the deep reaches of Hell, and were thus relegated to the Vestibule of Hell (see *Inf.*

III, 37–41). At this moment of the poem Dante seems to have changed his view of the angels, excluding, as he does, the "neutral" group altogether.

By "practicing their art" Dante means their contemplation of God as they whirl around the Fixed Point (see also *Par.* XXVIII, 25–36).

55–57. *The reason for the Fall:* Cf again *Inf.* XXXIV and also *Par.* XIX, 46–48.

58–60. *These others you see here were humbly prompt:* The angels were created by God with a vision and an understanding of Him. The angels faithful to God realized that their very being came from God and that they were privileged intelligences. They are called *modesti* (humble) in contrast to Lucifer who was all pride and who because of that pride, which made him want to be like his creator, did not wait for God's "enlightening grace" (see following note 61–63) to be bestowed upon him.

61–63. *whereby their vision was raised to such heights:* These angels who were so "humbly prompt" (58) to recognize their dependence on the Creator were rewarded with God's "enlightening grace" (62), or the light of glory, the light by which God sees Himself and by which the creature may have direct vision of God; they were also rewarded ("raised to such heights," 61) through "their own worth" (62), that is to say, through their humility in waiting for the Creator to bestow His enlightening grace on them. And having received such grace they became bound to loving God and fixed in doing the good, forever wanting whatever He wants. (See Aquinas, *Summa theol.* I, q. 62, a.8.)

65–66. *the receipt of grace implies one's worth:* The ability to open up to receive grace is a function of the capacity to love, or merit, which itself is predetermined.

70–72. *But since on earth you still teach in your schools:* Beatrice condemns as false doctrine the idea that the angels possess memory. (They do, however, possess intelligence and will.) This is the beginning of what Beatrice in verse 127 will call a digression.

73–75. *I shall say more:* Beatrice will now go on with her digressive remarks on erroneous beliefs.

76–78. *they never turned their eyes away from It:* The angels enjoy direct vision of God, and in their total satisfaction with this vision, they have no reason to look elsewhere.

79–81. *hence, no new object interrupts their sight:* Since the concentration of the angels is always on God, they are never interrupted and thereby have no need for memory.

84. *to these belong the greater guilt and shame:* Those who preach what they themselves do not believe are worthy of contempt.

85–126

Beatrice's digression now takes her further away from the subject of the angels. Indignantly she turns her attention to delivering a denunciation of men who distort eternal truths and who care only for their earthly glory.

92–93. *how pleasing / he is:* That is, pleasing in the eyes of God.

97–102. *Some say . . .:* St. Matthew makes reference to the darkness that fell during the Crucifixion: "Now from the sixth hour there was darkness over all the land unto the ninth hour" (Matt. 27:45). St. Luke (23:44) concurs. The preachers whom Beatrice condemns are those who try to explain the phenomenon as an eclipse of the moon. The truth is not what they preach, but rather what the Bible tells us: that the darkness that came over the land when Christ died on the Cross was a miraculous and spontaneous event.

105. *than all the Lapi and Bindi found in Florence:* Lapo and Bindo (diminutives of Iacopo and Ildobrando) were very common boys' names in Florence.

106–108. *so the poor sheep, who know no better:* The followers of these false preachings, ignorant as they are, sustained by empty words, are just as much at fault as those who lead them. They should know the basis of Christian doctrine and be able to discern falsehood instead of taking delight in amusing stories told by the preachers.

110. *'Go forth and preach garbage unto the world':* This is a parody of Christ's words to His Apostles (cf. Mark 16:15): "Go throughout the world and preach the gospel to every creature."

113–14. *they went to war:* The Apostles went forth to fight for

His truth, armed with their faith as a shield of defense and the word of God as a sword of attack (cf. Eph. 6:16 – 17).

117. *to puff their cowls:* That is, when the preacher gets a good response from his congregation, he is so pleased with his own performance that, figuratively speaking, his cowl becomes inflated with his pride; and this approval from his audience is all he is interested in achieving ("—that's all they want," 117).

118 – 19. *But if the crowd could see the bird that nestles:* This is the Devil, in the Middle Ages often depicted as a black bird with the wings of a fallen angel.

120. *what kind of pardons they are trusting in:* I.e., absolution and indulgences in general.

124. *Saint Anthony:* St. Anthony the Great, the hermit of Egypt (not St. Anthony of Padua), was born ca. 250 and lived to be 105. He is considered the founder of monasticism, as those disciples who followed him into the desert drew together and formed an order of sorts. His emblem is a hog (symbolizing the temptations of the Devil), generally represented lying at his feet (to show Anthony's domination of evil). The monks of his order kept herds of swine which ran free through the towns and which the people fed and fattened because of religious superstition. When Dante says in this verse: "On this Saint Anthony fattens his pig," he means that these preachers now make money by playing on the credulity of the people (121), just as the order of St. Anthony long ago fattened their pigs by allowing their parishioners to feed them.

125 – 26. *bigger pigs than his get fatter too:* Concubines and illegitimate children of such preachers also benefit from the sale of false indulgences ("paying their bills with forged indulgences," 126).

127 – 29. *We have digressed enough:* Beatrice now makes an abrupt return to her original topic: the angelic nature. She will now make two further points on the subject, and the tone of her language will change. Beatrice has used rather strong words in talking about the evils of the preachers, calling some of them liars and connecting others with pigs and concubines. Beatrice herself admits that she has digressed.

130 – 35. *The angelic nature goes so far beyond:* Beatrice's first

point is that the number of angelic beings is infinite. She alludes to the Book of Daniel where it is written: "Thousands of thousands ministered to Him, and ten thousand times a hundred thousand stood before Him." (Dan. 7:10).

136–38. *The primal Light shines down through all of them:* The other point made by Beatrice about angelic nature has to do with the diversity that exists within angelic ranks. The light of God, One and indivisible in Itself, shines down into these beings and is received by each of the angels in a different way.

139–41. *And since the visual act always precedes:* Just as God's light is received differently by each angelic being, so each angel displays a different capacity to love based on its vision of God (see *Par.* XXVIII, 109–11).

142–45. *And now you see the height, you see the breadth:* The "height" is the hierarchy of the angelic orders, while the "breadth" refers to their uncountable number. Each angel is a mirror reflecting God's immeasurable, indivisible light. In *Paradise* XIII, 60, Dante expresses the same idea in another of his special three-word verses: "eternalmente rimanendosi una."

CANTO XXX

THE NINE CIRCLES with their central point of light slowly
fade from sight and the Pilgrim looks again at Beatrice, whose
beauty he can no longer find words to describe. Beatrice tells the
Pilgrim that they are now in the Empyrean, and he finds himself
wrapped in a veil of intense light that momentarily blinds him,
but then he feels his powers of sight grow stronger. He sees a
river of light flowing between two banks laden with flowers and
an exchange of countless sparks between the river and the flowers.
Beatrice tells him to keep his eyes fixed on the river, warning
him, however, that what he sees is only a preface to the truth. As
the Pilgrim bends down and takes the river in with his eyes, its
linear form becomes round like a vast lake of light, and what had
appeared to be flowers are now the souls of the Elect, seated in
tiers of petals that grow in circumference the higher they rise,
opening up like an immense rose, all parts of which are equally
clear to the Pilgrim since the laws of nature do not apply here.
The sparks, meanwhile, have taken the shape of angels ceaselessly
flying between God and the Elect. Beatrice leads the Pilgrim
into the center of the Rose, and after showing him how few seats
still remain to be filled, she points to the one soon to be occupied
by the soul of Henry VII who will have tried, but in vain, to
help cure Italy of its ills, and blames Henry's failure on the Pope
(Clement V) who she predicts will be damned to Hell, stuffing
his predecessor (Boniface VIII) deeper down into his hole of
simony.

About six thousand miles away high noon
   is blazing, and the shadow of our world
   already slopes into a level bed,   3

when in the midst of heaven, so deep above,
   a change begins, and one star here and there
   starts fading from our sight at such a depth;   6

and as the brightest handmaid of the sun
   comes closer, and the heavens start to close
   light after light, until the fairest fades,   9

just so the Triumph that forever plays
    its round around the Point of dazzling light
    that seems contained by what Itself contains,   12

little by little faded from my sight;
    and seeing it no more, my love constrained
    my eyes to look again at Beatrice.   15

If all I said of her up to this time
    were gathered in a single poem of praise,
    it would be but a scanty comment now.   18

The beauty I saw there goes far beyond
    all mortal reach; I think that only He
    Who made it knows the full joy of its being.   21

At this point I admit to my defeat:
    no poet, comic or tragic, ever was
    more outdone by his theme than I am now;   24

for, as sunlight does to the weakest eyes,
    so did the mere thought of her lovely smile
    strike every recognition from my mind.   27

From the first day that I beheld her face
    in this life till the vision of her now,
    I could trust in my poems to sing her praise,   30

but now I must stop trying to pursue
    her beauty in my verse, for I have done
    as much as any artist at his best.   33

As such I leave her to the heralding
    of greater clarion than mine, which starts
    to draw its arduous theme now to a close.   36

She, with the tone and gesture of a guide
    whose task is done, said: "We have gone beyond—
    from greatest sphere to heaven of pure light,   39

light of the intellect, light full of love,
    love of the true good, full of ecstasy,
    ecstasy that transcends the sweetest joy.   42

Here you shall see the twofold soldiery
    of Paradise, and one host you will see
    as you will see them on the Final Day."   45

Just as a sudden flash of lightning strikes
   the visual spirits and so stuns the eyes,
   that even the clearest object fades from sight,   *48*

so glorious living light encompassed me,
   enfolding me so tightly in its veil
   of luminence that I saw only light.   *51*

"The Love that calms this heaven forever greets
   all those who enter with such salutation,
   so is the candle for Its flame prepared."   *54*

No sooner had these brief, assuring words
   entered my ears than I was full aware
   my senses now were raised beyond their powers;   *57*

the power of new sight lit up my eyes
   so that no light, however bright it were,
   would be too brilliant for my eyes to bear.   *60*

And I saw light that was a flowing stream,
   blazing in splendid sparks between two banks
   painted by spring in miracles of color.   *63*

Out of this stream the sparks of living light
   were shooting up and settling on the flowers:
   they looked like rubies set in rings of gold;   *66*

then as if all that fragrance made them drunk,
   they poured back into that miraculous flood,
   and as one plunged, another took to flight.   *69*

"The deep desire burning, urging you
   to seek the answers to what you have seen,
   pleases me more, the more I see it surge;   *72*

but you must first drink of these waters here
   before such thirst as yours is satisfied,"
   —so did she speak, that sunlight of my eyes;   *75*

and then she said: "The stream, the jewels you see
   leap in and out of it, the smiling blooms,
   are all prefigurations of their truth.   *78*

These things are not imperfect in themselves;
   the defect, rather, lies within your sight,
   as yet not strong enough to reach such heights."   *81*

No baby, having slept too long, and now
  awakened late, could rush to turn his face
  more eagerly to seek his mother's milk   84

than I bent down my face to make my eyes
  more lucid mirrors there within that stream
  which pours its light for their embetterment;   87

no sooner had the eaves of my eyes drunk
  within those waters, than the river turned
  from its straight course to a circumference.   90

And then, as people at a masquerade
  take off the masks which have until that time
  been hiding their true selves—so, then and there, 93

before my eyes the sparks and flowers changed
  into a greater festival: I saw
  both courts of Heaven in their reality.   96

O splendid grace of God through which I saw
  the one true kingdom's triumph, grant me now
  the power to find the words for what I saw!   99

There is a light above whose glory makes
  Creator visible to his creations
  whose only peace is in beholding Him;   102

in figure of a circle this light spreads,
  and is so vast that its circumference
  would be too loose a belt to bind the sun.   105

And its expanse comes from a single ray
  striking the summit of the First Moved Sphere
  from which it takes its vital force and power.   108

And as a hillside rich in grass and flowers
  looks down into a lake as if it were
  admiring the reflection of its wealth,   111

so, mirrored, tier on tier, within that light,
  more than a thousand were reflected there,
  I saw all those of us who won return.   114

And if the lowest tier alone can hold
  so great a brilliance, then how vast the space
  of this Rose to its outer petals' reach!   117

And yet, by such enormous breadth and height
    my eyes were not confused; they took in all
    in number and in quality of bliss.   120

There, near and far nor adds nor takes away,
    for where God rules directly without agents,
    the laws of Nature in no way apply.   123

Into the gold of the eternal Rose,
    whose ranks of petals fragrantly unfold
    praise to the Sun of everlasting spring,   126

in silence—though I longed to speak—was I
    taken by Beatrice who said: "Look
    how vast is our white-robed consistory.   129

Look at our city, see its vast expanse.
    You see our seats so filled, only a few
    remain for souls that Heaven still desires.   132

In that great chair, already set with crown
    above it and which draws your eyes to it,
    before your summons to this nuptial feast,   135

shall sit the soul, predestined emperor,
    of that Great Henry who one day will come
    to set straight Italy before her time.   138

You are bewitched by blind cupidity
    that makes you starve to death like a poor child
    who has a nurse but pushes her away.   141

And at that time the prefect of God's Court
    will be a man who publicly agrees
    to tread his path, but not so secretly.   144

But God will not permit him to stay long
    in Holy Office: he shall be thrust down,
    where Simon Magus pays his guilt, and he   147

shall stuff the Alagnese deeper down!"

NOTES

1 – 15

    Just as revelation comes gradually, so the Pilgrim's entry
into the Empyrean happens in stages. The imagery of the opening

of this canto emphasizes the notion of slow progression: as dawn approaches the sky begins to brighten, and one by one the stars fade into the total light of day. In the same way, the Point that is the light of God, once beheld as a distinct entity, now is seen to encompass everything, thus containing and representing all of the light the Pilgrim has encountered up to this point in his journey.

1 – 3. *about six thousand miles away:* As the sun rises, the conical shadow of the earth falls toward the horizon. Noon and sunrise are separated by some six hours. This separation can also be measured spatially in the following manner: the earth's circumference was estimated to be 20,400 miles. From sunrise to noon the earth revolves a quarter of its circumference, or 5,100 miles. Thus, if the sun is still 6,000 miles away from high noon, it must be about one hour (or 900 miles) before dawn.

6. *at such a depth:* That is, as seen from the earth.

7. *the brightest handmaid of the sun:* This is Aurora, the dawn (cf. *Purg.* XII, 81 and XXII, 118).

9. *until the fairest fades:* Venus is the brightest planet toward dawn.

10. *the Triumph:* In *Par.* XXVIII, 22 – 39, the Pilgrim saw the nine orders of angels in the form of nine circles of light spinning around the brilliant point of God's light at the center.

16 – 18. *If all I said of her up to this time:* If all that the Poet had written about Beatrice (in all his previous words) up until now, this point in the *Comedy,* were collected into a single poem, it would not be enough to do her beauty justice.

22 – 36

The theme of ineffability, of the Poet's inability to grasp and then render into words the beauty which strikes him with awe, is a recurrent one in the *Paradise.* Here, especially in these verses, the futility of Dante's attempt to describe what he sees is keenly felt and emphatically expressed. For similar moments, cf. Cantos XIV, 79 – 81; XVIII, 8 – 12; XXIII, 22 – 24; 55 – 63.

23. *comic or tragic:* A "comic" poet was one who wrote in the familiar style (hence, Dante's *Comedy*); a "tragic" poet composed

in an exalted, lofty style. (See *De vulg. eloqu.* II, 4; also *Inf.* XVI, 128, and XXX, 113.)

28—33. *From the first day that I beheld her face:* Dante first saw Beatrice, he tells us in his *Vita nuova* (II), when he was nine years old. Since that day he has dedicated many of his verses to her. Now, he has exhausted his abilities in singing her praises and can offer nothing greater.

34—36. *As such I leave her to the heralding:* It is clear now that Dante is moving toward the end of his poem as he tells his reader that he leaves the praising of Beatrice to a greater poet than himself ("a greater clarion"), for he no longer has the words to go on praising her great beauty.

37—39. *"We have gone beyond:* Beatrice's role as guide is now finished; she has passed with the Pilgrim from the Primum Mobile ("greatest sphere" in the sense of size and circumference) to the Empyrean, a purely spiritual heaven outside the realm of time and space. It is pure light, the mind of God. This tercet and the following two are similar in tone and function to Virgil's farewell tercets in the *Purgatory* as they sum up as well as indicate what awaits the Pilgrim just beyond this point (cf. *Purg.* XXVII, 127—42).

40—42. *light of the intellect, light full of love:* The definition of the nature of the Empyrean is based on the workings of trinity: light (vision of the intellect), then love (action of the will, which follows seeing), and finally ecstasy (the joy that comes from the fulfillment of vision and love). The tercet is certainly one of Dante's most successful attempts at imitating action through language. By taking three of the most significant words in the *Paradise*—light, love, and ecstasy—and making them mirror themselves three times in a type of *capfinidas* technique, starting off with the last word, "light" (*luce*) of the preceding verse, the Poet celebrates his entrance into the Empyrean, the realm of no beginning or end. It is all pure light. And he seals the tercet with the word "sweetness," which is used only once. This magnificent tercet with the preceding verse that sets the mechanism in motion is as follows in the original:

. . . al ciel ch'è pura luce:

> luce intellettüal, piena d'amore;
> amor di vero ben, pien di letizia;
> letizia che trascende ogni dolzore.

43–45. *Here you shall see the twofold soldiery:* In Canto XXII (58–68) the Pilgrim was told that he would eventually enjoy the privilege of seeing the souls of the Elect restored to their glorified bodies after the Final Judgment. At this moment he is very close to such a vision. The "twofold soldiery" refers to the Blest along with the host of angels.

46–51. *Just as a sudden flash of lightning strikes:* The light that dazzles the Pilgrim's eyes recalls St. Paul's experience recounted in Acts 22:6–11: "And it came to pass, as I made my journey and was come high unto Damascus about noon, suddenly there shone from Heaven a great light round about me. . . . And when I could not see for the glory of that light, being led by the hand of them that were with me, I came into Damascus." St. Paul's companions also saw the light but did not hear the voice of God as he did. Thus, they did not share the divinely bestowed privilege of his rapture. That the Pilgrim experiences a vision similar to St. Paul's is no coincidence; it is rather a clear sign that he is to be granted the same privilege as St. Paul.

52–54. *"The Love that calms this heaven:* The soul rises from Purgatory through the heavens and finally reaches the Empyrean where it joins the company of the Elect and is ready to receive the greeting and the warmth of Divine Love. In the same way the Pilgrim has been prepared to receive this welcome which amounts to a glorious flash of light surrounding him. All this is preparation for the final vision: "so is the candle for its flame prepared" (54).

57. *my senses now were raised beyond their powers:* The Pilgrim now begins to experience the rapture that is reserved for the immortal souls of the Elect. That a mortal man should be granted such a privilege is truly extraordinary. Cf. Cantos XI, 18; XVIII, 55.

61–69. *And I saw light that was a flowing stream:* Cf. Dan. 7:10: "A swift stream of fire issued forth from before him"; and Rev. 22:1: "And he showed me a river of the water of life, clear as crystal coming forth from the throne of God and of the Lamb." Cf. also Isa. 66:12.

The elements of this vision represent the basic aspects of the Empyrean. The river pouring forth from eternity represents the action of Divine Grace as it flows into God's creation. The flowers that bloom on the banks of the river are the souls of the Blest which receive Divine Grace and Love from God's agents (the angels) represented by the sparks. The movement of the sparks is not unlike that of the bees that draw nectar from and pollinate flowers. The color of the sparks is ruby red, symbolic of God's love. As the Pilgrim "drinks in" this scene with his eyes, he, too, shares in divine Grace. The plastic elements of the description recall the Poet's evocation of the Earthly Paradise (see *Purg.* XXVII), but here all these elements are seen in a more surrealistic light.

75. *so did she speak, that sunlight of my eyes:* Cf. *Par.* III, 1, where Beatrice is compared to the sun. Here the same epithet is used but with emphasis on vision, which is what the canto is all about.

76–78. *The stream, the jewels you see:* Beatrice draws the Pilgrim's attention to the symbolic nature of the things he now sees (see above, note 61–69).

79–81. *the defect, rather, lies within your sight:* See above, note 52–54 concerning the metaphor of the candle.

82–90

Up until this point the light of God has been reflected in Beatrice's eyes, and it is there that the Pilgrim has viewed it (see *Purg.* XXXI, 109–23). Now the Pilgrim's own eyes become mirrors capable of receiving and reflecting Divine Light. The transformation recalls an earlier stage of the journey at which point a similar change occurs: *Par.* I, 67–71 with the reference to Glaucus and the use of the newly coined verb *trasumanar.*

The act of drinking (although here it is the Pilgrim's eyes that do this) recalls the drinking of the waters of the River Lethe in Purgatory (see *Purg.* XXVIII, 130–33; and XXXI, 100–102). At this stage the river of light from which he drinks takes on a different appearance; ceasing its linear flow (symbolizing time), it becomes circular, like a vast lake (symbolizing eternity).

82–87. *No baby, having slept too long:* This image has not pleased all of Dante's critics (see for example Momigliano, p. 819). Perhaps they dislike the fact that while the baby most likely turns his head upward or to the side to reach his mother's breast, the Poet tells us that the Pilgrim bends his face downward

("I bent down my face," 85). I do not find the image disturbing, especially in this canto, where things are not always what they appear to be and where up can often mean down, a river can turn from a straight course into a circumference (cf. 90), and there are a number of other strange happenings. In verse 87 Dante coins the verb "embetterment" (s' *immegli*) for the occasion.

95, 97, 99. *I saw . . . I saw . . . I saw:* The key word in the canto, "saw" (*vidi*), is used three times, always at the end of the verse. The emphatic tone created by the repetition underlines the real (rather than symbolic) aspect of Dante's vision of Heaven.

96. *both courts of Heaven:* The "twofold soldiery" (see vs. 43 above), or the angels and the human souls.

97—99. *O splendid grace of God:* The Poet now, on this special occasion, invokes God's assistance for the completion of his poem rather than that of the Muses or Apollo or his own constellation, as he has done before (see *Par.* I, 13—36; also *Inf.* II, 7 and XXXII, 10).

100—102. *There is a light above whose glory:* As the glory of God shines in the light of heaven, those beings who enjoy beatitude (i.e., the angels and the souls of the Elect) are granted the ability to see Him through His light.

103—105. *in figure of a circle this light spreads:* The light of God is reflected perpetually upward from the convex surface of the Primum Mobile; thus, to the eyes of the Pilgrim it appears to be all around, as if in a circle. It is this same circle of light that forms the gold of the Celestial Rose. The circle, of course, is the symbol of perfection.

106—108. *And its expanse comes from a single ray:* As was just stated (n. 103—105), the light of God streams downward where it strikes the "First Moved Sphere" or the Primum Mobile. Since the surface of this sphere is convex, it reflects the light which it receives into a circular sea of light that surrounds the souls in the Empyrean. From the ray of Divine Light which strikes it, the Primum Mobile receives its motion and the power which it then transmits to the spheres below. (See *Par.* II, 112—23; XXVII, 106—14.)

109—14. *And as a hillside rich in grass and flowers:* Just as a lush hillside is reflected in a lake at the foot of the hill, so do the souls of the Elect appear to Dante in reflection. It is interesting to note that an important element of the simile states that the hillside admires its own reflection; perhaps the Pilgrim marvels at the reflection of the Blest knowing that one day he will join them. The "tiers" suggest the configuration of an amphitheater, which turns out to be the case. So then, in a certain sense, the Pilgrim looks down in order to see up (see n. 82 – 87). The stress is on reflected light.

115 – 17. *And if the lowest tier alone:* Now we are told that it is only the lowest tier of that amphitheater that is greater than the circumference of the sphere of the sun. So imagine the vastness of "its outer petals' reach" (117). And with this verse the amphitheater turns quietly into a rose.

119 – 20. *they took in all / in number:* The Pilgrim now views the entire scene, with all the souls, directly.

122 – 23. *for where God rules directly, without agents:* The Pilgrim has risen beyond the point where space and time apply; thus, distance is meaningless. Moreover, God reigns directly here and not through secondary causes ("Nature") or angelic orders ("agents").

124 – 26. *Into the gold of the eternal Rose:* The golden part of the Celestial Rose is its center or the sea of light referred to earlier (see 89 – 90). The "ranks of petals" are the souls of the Blest (see 112 – 14) which blossom forth in everlasting praise of God, the "Sun" from which they draw life.

129. *how vast is our white-robed consistory:* See Rev. 3:4 – 5: "Thou hast a few names even in Sardis which have not defiled their garments; and they shall walk with me in white, for they are worthy. He that overcometh, the same shall be clothed in white raiment. . . ." See also Rev. 7:13 – 14: "And one of the elders answered, saying unto me, What are these which are arrayed in white robes? and whence came they? And I said unto him, Sir, thou knowest. And he said to me, These are they which came out of great tribulation and have washed their robes and made them white in the blood of the Lamb." Cf. also *Par.* XXV, 88 – 96.

131 – 32. *You see our seats so filled, only a few / remain:* As the reader will soon discover, the celestial assembly is divided in half,

one part being filled with souls who lived before the time of Christ and the other part with souls from after. Following the Harrowing of Hell, the B.C. section was filled. The only spaces that remain, then, are in the A.D. section of the rose, and those places are limited in number, perhaps because, as Dante says in *Conv.* II, xiv, 13: "We are already in the final age of the world."

135. *before your summons to this nuptial feast:* A clear indication that Dante is saving himself a seat in the amphitheater of the Elect.

136-37. *shall sit the soul . . . of that Great Henry:* This is Henry, Count of Luxembourg (b. ca. 1275), who became Emperor Henry VII. He was elected emperor on November 27, 1308, and was supported by Pope Clement V in opposition to Charles of Valois, the candidate supported by the French king, Philip the Fair. Henry was crowned at Aix-la-Chapelle on January 6, 1309. In 1310 he entered Italy to a mixed reception. After a tumultuous three years he became ill and died near Siena on August 24, 1313, and thus never fulfilled the hopes of partisans like Dante to set Italy right once again.

139-41. *You are bewitched by blind cupidity:* Those Italians who oppose Henry are being led astray to their own demise. See Dante's *Epistle* VI, 12, where he exclaims in reference to the Florentines: "Oh, harmonious in ill, oh, blinded by wondrous greed," and in VI, 22: "Nor in your blindness do you perceive the lust that hath sway over you, lulling you with poisonous whisper."

142-44. *the prefect of God's Court:* Clement V was pope (or "prefect") at the time of Henry's death. At first Clement supported Henry's arrival into Italy out of fear of France's extension of her power in Italy, but later on, in fear of the King of France, he changed his position to one of opposition to Henry. Clement's treachery is referred to in Canto XVII, 82, and Dante has already condemned him to Hell where he appears with the simonists (see *Inf.* XIX, 82-87).

145-48. *But God will not permit him to stay long:* Clement outlived Henry by less than a year. In the third *bolgia* of the eighth circle of Hell the simonists are stuck upside down, the soles of their feet aflame. In the hole reserved for popes each new arrival pushes his papal predecessor further down.

147. *Simon Magus:* See *Inf.* XIX, 1 and note.

148. *the Alagnese:* The town of Alagna, or Alagni, was the birthplace of Clement's predecessor in simony, Boniface VIII, Dante's personal archenemy. Beatrice here confirms the prophecy made in *Inf.* XIX, 73–75. These are her last words in the *Comedy,* and as such they emphasize the idea of a final look toward the earth and a last denunciation of the cupidity which beleaguers it. The reader will notice that Beatrice does not mention the name Boniface here; she refers to him merely as "the Alagnese." His name has no place in Paradise, so angry was Dante with the cupidity of the Church and so great his personal hatred for Boniface VIII in particular! Beatrice's last words in the Poem, which bring to a close one of the most mystically lyrical of its hundred cantos, are not sweet ones. They are memorable for their harshness.

CANTO XXXI

THE PILGRIM BEHOLDS the Elect in the form of a pure white rose and the angels like bees continuously flying from God to the Elect and back, transporting His love. Never, however, in spite of their countless numbers, do they block the Divine Light from the Pilgrim's sight. He compares his amazement to that of a barbarian from the far north seeing the splendors of Rome for the first time, and his joy to that of a pilgrim who has reached his final goal. After examining the general formation of Paradise he turns to ask Beatrice a question but finds that a venerable old man has taken her place. The old man explains that Beatrice has asked him to lead her ward to his final goal, and he points to where she is seated in the third from the highest tier of the Rose. The Pilgrim, looking up, sees his lady clearly and offers up to her a tender prayer of gratitude for all she has done on his behalf, expressing his hope that with her help he may someday return to her there as pure as he is at that moment. Beatrice smiles at him and then returns her gaze to God. The old man reveals himself as St. Bernard and urges the Pilgrim to shift his focus even higher to the Virgin Mary on whom his spiritual progress now depends.

So now, appearing to me in the form
  of a white rose was Heaven's sacred host,
  those whom with His own blood Christ made His bride,   3

while the other host—that soaring see and sing
  the glory of the One who stirs their love,
  the goodness which made them great as they are,   6

like bees that in a single motion swarm
  and dip into the flowers, then return
  to heaven's hive where their toil turns to joy—   9

descended all at once on that great bloom
  of precious petals, and then flew back up
  to where its source of love forever dwells.   12

Their faces showed the glow of living flame,
  their wings of gold, and all the rest of them
  whiter than any snow that falls to earth.   15

As they entered the flower, tier to tier,
  each spread the peace and ardor of the love
  they gathered with their wings in flight to Him.   18

Nor did this screen of flying plenitude
  between the flower and what reigned above
  impede the vision of His glorious light;   21

for God's light penetrates the universe
  according to the merits of each part,
  and there is nothing that can block its way.   24

This unimperiled kingdom of all joy
  abounding with those saints, both old and new,
  had look and love fixed all upon one goal.   27

O Triune Light which sparkles in one star
  upon their sight, Fulfiller of full joy!
  look down upon us in our tempest here!   30

If the barbarians (coming from such parts
  as every day are spanned by Helice,
  travelling the sky with her belovèd son)   33

when they saw Rome, her mighty monuments
  (the days the Lateran, built high, outsoared
  all mortal art), were so struck with amazement,   36

then I—coming to Heaven from mortal earth,
  from man's time to Divine eternity,
  from Florence to a people just and sane—   39

with what amazement must I have been struck!
  Truly, between my stupor and my joy,
  it was a pleasure not to hear or speak.   42

And as a pilgrim now refreshed with joy
  surveys the temple of his vow, and wonders
  how to describe it when he is back home,   45

so through the living light I let my eyes
  go wandering among the ranks of Blest,
  now up, now down, now searching all around.   48

I saw love-dedicated faces there,
  adorned in borrowed light and by their smiles
  and gestures graced with chastest dignity.   51

By now, my eyes had quickly taken in
   a general plan of all of Paradise
   but had not fixed themselves on any part;   54

and with new-kindled eagerness to know,
   I turned around to ask my lady things
   that to my mind were still not clear enough.   57

What I expected was not what I saw!
   I thought to see Beatrice there but saw
   an elder in the robes of Heaven's saints.   60

His eyes, his cheeks, were filled with the divine
   joy of the blest, his attitude with love
   that every tender-hearted father knows.   63

And "She, where is she?" instantly I asked.
   He answered: "I was urged by Beatrice
   to leave my place and end all your desire;   66

you will behold her, if you raise your eyes
   to the third circle from the highest tier,
   enthroned where her own merit destined her."   69

I did not say a word but raised my eyes
   and saw her there in all her glory crowned
   by the reflections of eternal light   72

Not from that place where highest thunder roars
   down to the very bottom of the sea,
   is any mortal's sight so far away   75

as my eyes were from Beatrice there;
   but distance made no difference, for her image
   came down to me unblurred by anything.   78

"O lady in whom all my hope takes strength,
   and who for my salvation did endure
   to leave her footprints on the floor of Hell,   81

through your own power, through your own excellence
   I recognize the grace and the effect
   of all those things I have seen with my eyes.   84

From bondage into freedom you led me
   by all those paths, by using all those means
   which were within the limits of your power.   87

Preserve in me your great munificence,
  so that my soul which you have healed may be
  pleasing to you when it slips from the flesh." 90

Such was my prayer. And she, so far away,
  or so it seemed, looked down at me and smiled;
  then to Eternal Light she turned once more. 93

The holy elder spoke: "That you may reach
  your journey's perfect consummation now,
  I have been sent by sacred love and prayer; 96

fly through this heavenly garden with your eyes,
  for gazing at it will prepare your sight
  to rise into the vision of God's Ray. 99

The Queen of Heaven, for whom I constantly
  burn with love's fire, will grant us every grace,
  because I am her faithful one, Bernard." 102

As one who comes from someplace like Croatia—
  to gaze on our Veronica, so long
  craved for, he now cannot look long enough, 105

and while it is displayed, he says in thought:
  "O Jesus Christ, my Lord, the One true God,
  is this what your face truly looked like then?"— 108

just so did I while gazing at the living
  love of the one who living in the world,
  through contemplation, tasted of that peace. 111

"My son of grace," he spoke again, "this state
  of blissful being will not be known to you
  as long as you keep your eyes fixed down here; 114

look up into the circles, to the highest
  until your eyes behold, enthroned, the Queen
  who holds as subject this devoted realm." 117

I raised my eyes. And as at break of day
  the eastern parts of the horizon shine
  brighter than at the point the sun goes down, 120

so I saw, as my eyes still climbed from vale
  to mountain-top, there at the highest point,
  a light outshining all that splendorous rim. 123

And as our sky, where we expect to see
　　the ill-starred shaft of Phaëthon's chariot,
　　burns brightest dimming all the light around,　　　　　126

so there, on high, that oriflame of peace
　　lit up its center while on either side
　　its glow was equally diminishing;　　　　　　　　　129

and all around that center, wings outstretched,
　　I saw more than a thousand festive angels,
　　each one distinct in brilliance and in art.　　　　　132

And there, smiling upon their games and song
　　I saw a beauty that reflected bliss
　　within the eyes of all the other saints;　　　　　135

and even if I were as rich in words
　　as in remembering, I would not dare
　　describe the least part of such beauty's bliss.　　　138

Bernard, when he saw that my eyes were fixed
　　devotedly upon his passion's passion,
　　his own he turned to her with so much love　　　141

that he made mine more ardent in their gaze.

NOTES

2. *a white rose:* While the rose was a symbol of earthly love in
the literature of medieval western Europe (see the Old French
Roman de la Rose, for example), Dante's "white rose" carries pre-
cisely the opposite connotation: it represents Divine love. His
vision of the magnificent rose as "amphitheater" of the Elect is
the highest privilege that could be accorded mortal man. The
rose is also associated with the Passion (the pope blesses a golden
rose on the fourth Sunday of Lent) and with Mary (who presides
over the "sacred host" beheld by the Pilgrim). See Albertus Mag-
nus (*De laud, b. Mariae Virginis,* XII, iv, 33): "And note that
Christ is a rose, Mary is a rose, the Church is a rose, the faithful
soul is a rose."

2–4. *Heaven's sacred host:* The host consists of two groups:
first, the souls of all the Blest, the saints of the Church Trium-
phant (see *Par.* XXX, 43); and second, the angels.

The magnificence of the Pilgrim's vision here is couched in simple terms. With the ordinary simile of bees to the flower, Dante juxtaposes the awesome with the familiar. The idea of dipping in and out of the flower seems to have originated from verses 76 – 78 of the preceding canto.

12. *to where its source of love forever dwells:* That is, to God, still seen by the Pilgrim as reflected light. He will not be granted true or direct vision of God until the end of the Poem.

13 – 15. *Their faces showed:* These angels with their flaming red faces, golden wings, "and all the rest of them / whiter than any snow" bear triumphant colors (red, white and gold). Commentators have given different symbolic meanings to these colors, but no symbolic significance at all seems to be called for at this point. These are probably the most colorful angels in the Poem (in *Purg.* VIII, we saw angels with green wings), and the red and gold color is born of the Pilgrim's vision (as it changes) in the preceding canto (*Par.* XXX, 66).

19 – 21. *Nor did this screen of flying plenitude:* The light of God is not obstructed from the sight of the Blest in the Rose by the flying movement of the angels. Angels are diaphanous (see *Conv.* III, vii, 5).

22 – 24. *for God's light penetrates the universe:* These verses, like so many others in the *Paradise*, call the reader's attention back to the opening verses of this canticle as well as to verses 112 – 48 of Canto II.

26. *abounding with those saints, both old and new:* That is, of the Hebrew ("old") and Christian ("new") Church.

27. *had look and love fixed all upon one goal:* The functions of the intellect ("look") and of the will ("love") are fixed directly on God ("one goal").

28 – 30. *O Triune Light which sparkles in one star:* The invocation is to God in His threefold nature for His light to be shed upon the earth in all its turmoil.

31 – 42

Dante compares his reaction to what he sees before him to the astonishment the barbarians must have felt upon beholding the splendors of ancient Rome for the first time.

32. *Helice:* Also known as Callisto, she was one of Diana's nymphs, who was banished after she had been seduced by Jupiter and had borne him a son, Arcas. Jupiter had Helice transformed into the constellation of the Great Bear (Ursa Major, the Big Dipper) and her son into the Little Bear (Ursa Minor, the Little Dipper). See Ovid (*Metam.* II, 496—530). The geographical indication here is an indefinite one but does emphasize a far northern location.

35. *Lateran:* In Dante's time the Lateran palace in Rome was the residence of the pope. In earlier times it had been an imperial residence donated by Constantine to Pope Sylvester. The original building was destroyed by fire in 1308 and was rebuilt ca. 1586. The original palace was said to have belonged to a family by the name of Laterani.

43—45. *as a pilgrim now refreshed with joy:* Like the earthly pilgrim who takes a holy vow to visit a sacred shrine and then wonders how to document his experience, Dante considers how he will ever continue to describe the marvels of the heavenly shrine which he has been so privileged to see. Once again the theme of ineffability comes into play, as Dante reminds himself of the extreme difficulty of his task.

49—50. *faces there, / adorned in borrowed light:* The "borrowed light" is the light of God reflected in the faces of the Elect.

56. *I turned around to ask my lady:* At the top of the mountain of Purgatory the Pilgrim had turned to Virgil, his guide up to that point in the journey, in order to speak to him and discovered that Virgil was no longer with him (see *Purg.* XXX, 40—54). In the same way Dante turns at this moment to Beatrice, only to find another soul in her place.

60. *an elder in the robes of Heaven's saints:* As we are told in verse 102, this is St. Bernard of Clairvaux. His identity is withheld temporarily so that the Pilgrim may bid a proper farewell to his beloved guide, Beatrice. We have already been told (*Par.* XXX, 129) that the saints are clad in white robes. St. Bernard (1091—1153) was Abbot of Clairvaux and the force behind the Second Crusade. The replacement of Beatrice with St. Bernard suggests that for the ultimate vision of Heaven the Pilgrim requires the guidance of one steeped in mystical contemplation. In his many epistles, sermons, and treatises Bernard's devotion to the Virgin

Mary clearly stands out. Beatrice, in her role of Divine Revelation, is not enough to elevate the soul to the final vision of God; this can be achieved only through mystical contemplation. It is for St. Bernard, who himself was said to have had a mystical vision of God in his first life, to intervene with the Virgin on behalf of the Pilgrim so that he too may enjoy such vision. Dante was quite familiar with Bernard's writings, especially his sermons and his *De consideratione*, to which he refers in one of his letters (*Epist.* XIII, 80).

66. *to leave my place and end all your desire:* St. Bernard has moved from his position in the Celestial Rose to Dante the Pilgrim's side in order to assist him in the final phase of his journey toward God.

69. *enthroned where her own merit destined her":* The first row in the amphitheater of the Rose is that of Mary, the second is Eve's, and the third is Rachel's. Beside Rachel sits Beatrice. Thus, Contemplation (Rachel) and Revelation (Beatrice) are side by side. Beatrice's position in the Rose is a matter of preordained grace bestowed upon her by God when He breathed life into her soul.

70–72. *I . . . saw her there in all her glory crowned:* The Pilgrim still cannot see God directly. He must still behold Divine Light in reflection, in this case, as he looks at Beatrice.

78. *her image I came down to me:* In this, the highest spiritual heaven, there is no air to obstruct vision (see *Par.* XXX, 121–23).

79–87

The Pilgrim's final words to Beatrice are words of tribute and of thanks in which a brief summary of her role in the *Comedy* starting with *Inferno* II is found. It is interesting to note that in the Italian Dante shifts his form of address from the formal *voi* to the familiar *tu* when addressing Beatrice at this point. This change is a surprising one and must be seen in the light of Beatrice's change of status or role in the narrative of the Poem: she is no longer the Pilgrim's guide, no longer playing her allegorical role. She is, once more, the Poet's beloved, and he sees her here for the last time as the blessed soul of a real person, the lady he loved in the earthly realm.

80–81. *to leave her footprints on the floor of Hell:* Beatrice had descended to Limbo in order to invoke the help of Virgil for the Pilgrim who was stranded in the dark wood (see *Inf.* II, 52–108). In this sense Beatrice can be compared to Christ at the time of the Harrowing of Hell (see *Inf.* IV, 52–63). See also *Purgatory* XXIX–XXX for the continuation of this parallel.

85. *From bondage into freedom you led me:* The freedom to which Dante refers is the total release from evil and sin into knowledge of God's justice (see *Summa theol.* II–II, q. 183, a.4, resp.). See also *Purg.* XVI, 79–81. The main action or purpose of the entire *Comedy* rests in this verse.

91–92. *And she . . . looked down at me and smiled:* Beatrice's smile has fortified the Pilgrim all through his journey; it is fitting, therefore, that she should smile upon him one last time, at this moment, in final reassurance.

93. *then to Eternal Light she turned once more:* This solemn verse, the last one in the Poem dedicated to Beatrice (though her name will be mentioned once more in passing in the final canto, vs. 38), is also one dedicated to God. Beatrice is not the final goal of the Pilgrim's journey. God is. And as the Pilgrim looks at Beatrice for the last time, fulfilling the promise he had made in the last chapter of his *Vita nuova* (XLII, 2)—to say of this lady what had never been said of any other lady before—he pictures her as looking in the direction of the True Goal of the Pilgrim's journey: toward the "Eternal Light" of glory, toward the vision which the Pilgrim is about to experience for himself.

94. *The holy elder spoke:* St. Bernard now undertakes to prepare the Pilgrim for the final stage of his journey.

99. *to rise into the vision of God's Ray:* The culmination of the Pilgrim's ascent will occur in the final canto (XXXIII). At this point in the journey he still must see God's light in reflection, even though he views the Rose directly.

100. *The Queen of Heaven:* The Virgin Mary.

102. *I am her faithful one, Bernard":* Not until this verse does Bernard identify himself. See note to verse 60.

103–108. *As one who comes from someplace like Croatia:* That is to say, like that pilgrim who comes from a faraway land in order to look upon the Veronica (*vera icon*), the true image of Christ that was left on a cloth that was used to wipe blood and sweat from His brow and face as He passed by on his way to Calvary. On certain days this holy object was displayed at St. Peter's in Rome for public and pilgrims to view. The image here is similar in tone to the one used earlier in the canto (31–36) treating the amazement of the barbarians.

109–111. *just so did I:* The Pilgrim's awe in encountering St. Bernard arises from his adherence to the belief that Bernard, indeed, "tasted of that peace" of Heaven while still a mortal man.

112. *"My son of grace":* It is most fitting that Bernard at this point address the Pilgrim in terms of grace. It was through the chain of grace (see *Inf.* II) that the journey began, and it was with Mary, who interceded with God on the Pilgrim's behalf, that this special grace originated. The Pilgrim is truly the "son of grace," since it was grace that gave birth to his salvation.

114. *as long as you keep your eyes fixed down here:* The Pilgrim is looking at St. Bernard and not upward toward the Light of God.

115–20. *Look up into the circles:* Bernard tells the Pilgrim to start his examination of the Rose at its highest point where Mary sits. She is Queen of this realm and sits at its highest point beneath God. Again there are resonances of the courtly imagery of Canto II of the *Inferno* as the *Comedy* in this canto, again, starts to come full circle.

123. *a light outshining all that splendorous rim:* Dante's survey of the amphitheater of the Blest begins with Mary, who sits on the highest rim and who is introduced with the splendorous image of the dawn (118–20). And this is as it should be, because it was through her intervention that the Pilgrim was lifted from the dark wood to this realm. Her seat is to the East where the sun rises and in which direction the faithful pray. Medieval cathedrals had this orientation, and medieval cartography placed east, rather than north, as "up."

124–26. *our sky, where we expect to see:* This is the highest area of the horizon where the axle of Phaëthon's chariot broke, that chariot being the sun. The result was that Phaëthon's horse ran wild, and the sun passed so close to the earth that it was almost consumed by the sun's fire. Dante makes frequent use of the

Phaëthon image in the *Comedy* (see *Inf*. XVII, 106–108; *Purg*. XXIX, 118–20; *Par*. XVII, 3).

127. *that oriflame of peace:* This was the standard supposedly given to the kings of France by the Angel Gabriel. It had a flame represented on a golden background. Mary is the bright flame, with the angels in homage to her on either side. Only the color is stressed in the word "oriflame"; and connotations of war are negated by the words that follow it: "of peace."

132. *each one distinct in brilliance and in art:* Each angel in itself represents a separate species or type with a unique ministry. (See *Par*. XXIX, 136–38.)

133–35. *I saw a beauty that reflected bliss:* The smile and beauty of Mary surpass anything Dante has witnessed heretofore, and yet they recall a similar reaction in less lofty spheres to Beatrice. Mary, like Christ, is in her glorified body. They are the only human creatures who enjoy this special state before the Last Judgment.

136–38. *as rich in words / as in remembering:* Here Dante the Poet is speaking. Even if, the Poet says, he could find the proper words and could remember exactly how beautiful Mary was, he would not attempt to describe her. In fact the Poet never will give a description of the Virgin's beauty, which is an act of great reverence on his part.

139–42. *Bernard, when he saw my eyes were fixed:* The ardor of Bernard's gaze guides, directs, and fortifies that of the Pilgrim. What is stressed in these closing four verses is the intensity of vision and warmth of love.

CANTO XXXII

ST. BERNARD NOW reveals the order of the division of the arena of the Rose. A line of souls bisects the Rose vertically, separating those who believed in Christ before His coming from those who believed afterwards. The Virgin is in the highest seat and heads the half of the line containing Hebrew women (Christ to come); St. John the Baptist heads the half comprised of male saints (Christ already come). When St. Bernard instructs the Pilgrim to focus his gaze on the Virgin in order to acquire sufficient strength to contemplate Christ, he sees the angel Gabriel hail her with outspread wings, and all the souls respond with song. Then St. Bernard points out the position of other prominent souls: Adam and Moses; St. Peter and St. John the Evangelist; St. Anne, the mother of the Virgin; and St. Lucy, who, by inviting Beatrice to come to the aid of her lover, set the *Divine Comedy* in motion. Having indicated that little time remains to complete the journey, St. Bernard instructs the Pilgrim to direct his sight to God, and begins his prayer to the Virgin that she may provide the grace necessary to complete the final stage of the journey.

Rapt in love's Bliss, that contemplative soul
　　generously assumed the role of guide
　　as he began to speak these holy words:　　　　　　3

"The wound which Mary was to close and heal
　　she there, who sits so lovely at her feet,
　　would open wider then and prick the flesh.　　　　6

And sitting there directly under her
　　among the thrones of the third tier is Rachel,
　　and, there, see Beatrice by her side.　　　　　　9

Sarah, Rebecca, Judith, and then she,
　　who was the great-grandmother of the singer
　　who cried for his sin: '*Miserere mei,*'　　　　　12

you see them all as I go down from tier
　　to tier and name them in their order,
　　petal by petal, downward through the Rose.　　　15

Down from the seventh row, as up to it,
  was a descending line of Hebrew women
  that parted all the petals of the Rose;   18

according to the ways in which the faith
  viewed Christ, these women constitute the wall
  dividing these ranks down the sacred stairs.   21

On this side where the flower is full bloomed
  to its last petal, sit the souls of those
  who placed their faith upon Christ yet to come;   24

on that side where all of the semi-circles
  are broken by the empty seats, sit those
  who turned their face to Christ already come.   27

And just as on this side the glorious throne
  of Heaven's lady with the other seats
  below it form this great dividing wall,   30

so, facing her, the throne of the great John
  who, ever holy, suffered through the desert,
  and martyrdom, then Hell for two more years,   33

and under him, chosen to mark the line,
  Francis, Benedict, Augustine and others
  descend from round to round as far as here.   36

Now marvel at the greatness of God's plan:
  this garden shall be full in equal number
  of this and that aspect of the one faith.   39

And know that downward from the center row
  which cuts the two dividing walls midway,
  no soul through his own merit earned his seat,   42

but through another's, under fixed conditions,
  for all these spirits were absolved of sin
  before they reached the age to make free choice.   45

You need only to look upon their faces
  and listen to the young sound of their voices
  to see and hear this clearly for yourself.   48

But you have doubts, doubts you do not reveal,
  so now I will untie the tangled knot
  in which your searching thoughts have bound you tight.   51

Within the vastness of this great domain
　　no particle of chance can find a place—
　　no more than sorrow, thirst, or hunger can—　　　　54

for all that you see here has been ordained
　　by the eternal law with such precision
　　that ring and finger are a perfect fit.　　　　57

And, therefore, all these souls of hurried comers
　　to the true life are not ranked *sine causa*
　　some high, some low, according to their merit.　　　　60

The King, through whom this kingdom is at rest
　　in so much love and in so much delight
　　that no will dares to wish for any more,　　　　63

creating all minds in His own mind's bliss,
　　endows each with as much grace as He wishes,
　　at His own pleasure—let this fact suffice.　　　　66

And Holy Scriptures set this down for you
　　clear and expressly, speaking of those twins
　　whose anger flared while in their mother's womb;　　　　69

so, it is fitting that God's lofty light
　　crown them with grace, as much as each one merits,
　　according to the color of their hair.　　　　72

Thus, through no merit of their own good works
　　are they ranked differently; the difference is
　　only in God's gift of original grace.　　　　75

During mankind's first centuries on earth
　　for innocent children to achieve salvation,
　　only the faith of parents was required;　　　　78

but then, when man's first age came to an end,
　　all males had to be circumcised to give
　　innocent wings the strength to fly to Heaven;　　　　81

but when the age of grace came down to man,
　　then, without perfect baptism in Christ,
　　such innocence to Limbo was confined.　　　　84

Now look at that face which resembles Christ
　　the most, for only in its radiance
　　will you be made ready to look at Christ."　　　　87

I saw such bliss rain down upon her face,
  bestowed on it by all those sacred minds
  created to fly through those holy heights,   90

that of all things I witnessed to this point
  nothing had held me more spellbound than this,
  nor shown a greater likeness unto God;   93

and that love which had once before descended
  now sang, *Ave, Maria, gratïa plena*,
  before her presence there with wings spread wide.   96

Response came to this holy prayer of praise
  from all directions of the Court of Bliss
  and every face grew brighter with that joy.   99

"O holy father, who for my sake deigns
  to stand down here, so far from the sweet throne
  destined for you throughout eternity,   102

who is that angel who so joyously
  looks straight into the eyes of Heaven's Queen,
  so much in love he seems to burn like fire?"   105

Thus, I turned for instruction once again
  to that one who in Mary's beauty glowed
  as does the morning star in fresh sunlight.   108

And he: "All loving pride and gracious joy,
  as much as soul or angel can possess,
  is all in him, and we would have it so,   111

for he it is who bore the palm below
  to Mary when the Son of God had willed
  to bear the weight of man's flesh on Himself.   114

Now let your eyes follow my words as I
  explain to you, and note the great patricians
  of this most just and pious of all realms   117

Those two who sit most blest in their high thrones
  because they are the closest to the Empress
  are, as it were, the two roots of our Rose: 120

he, sitting on her left side, is that father,
  the one through whose presumptuous appetite
  mankind still tastes the bitterness of shame;   123

and on her right, you see the venerable
   Father of Holy Church to whom Christ gave
   the keys to this beautiful Rose of joy.   *126*

And he who prophesied before he died
   the sad days destined for the lovely Bride
   whom Christ won for himself with lance and nails   *129*

sits at his side. Beside the other sits
   the leader of those nurtured on God's manna,
   who were a fickle, ingrate, stubborn lot.   *132*

Across from Peter, see there, Anna sits,
   so happy to be looking at her daughter,
   she does not move an eye singing Hosanna;   *135*

facing the head of mankind's family
   sits Lucy, who first sent your lady to you
   when you were bent, headlong, on your own ruin.   *138*

But since the time left for your journey's vision
   grows short, let us stop here—like the good tailor
   who cuts the gown according to his cloth,   *141*

and turn our eyes upon the Primal Love
   so that, looking toward Him, you penetrate
   His radiance as deep as possible.   *144*

But lest you fall backwards beating your wings,
   believing to ascend on your own power,
   we must offer a prayer requesting grace,   *147*

grace from the one who has power to help you.
   Now, follow me, with all of your devotion,
   and do not let your heart stray from my words."   *150*

And he began to say this holy prayer:

NOTES

1. *Rapt in love's Bliss:* Bernard is engrossed in the bliss of his
great love for the Blessed Virgin Mary.

4–6. *"The wound which Mary was to close and heal:* When Mary
gave birth to Christ she provided the means of healing the wound
of original sin. She "who sits so lovely at her feet" (5) is Eve, who

disobeyed God and surrendered to the serpent ("open wider then") after convincing Adam to join her in sin ("and prick the flesh," 6). It is interesting to note, as Buti does in his commentary, that Dante uses the rhetorical device of *hysteron proteron* in this tercet. (See also *Par*. II, 23–24; *Par*. XXII, 109–110). What happens here is that Mary closes the wound inflicted by Eve before she heals it (4) and Eve opens up the wound of original sin before she "prick[s] the flesh" (6).

8. *Rachel:* Counting from the outer rim, or top, of the amphitheater down to the third horizontal row, we find Rachel, who was the seond wife of the Patriarch Jacob and mother of Benjamin and Joseph (see Gen. 29:9–35 and 30:1–24). In *Inf*. IV, 60 we learn that she was among the souls released from Limbo at the time of Christ's descent into Hell. She also appears to the Pilgrim in a dream (see *Purg*. XXVI, 100–108) where she represents the contemplative life. Beatrice's position to Rachel's right is an honored one. See Figure 10.

10. *Sarah, Rebecca, Judith:* Sarah was Abraham's wife and the mother of Isaac. Rebecca was the daughter of Bethuel and the sister of Laban. She was married to Isaac and bore Esau and Jacob (see 67–69). Judith was the daughter of Meraris. She murdered Holofernes (Nebuchadnezzar's general) while he slept and thus saved Bethulia, which was under siege by the Assyrians. After the Assyrians fled the city Judith was celebrated by the Jews as their deliverer.

11–12. *the great-grandmother of the singer:* Ruth was the wife of Boaz and great-grandmother of David, author of the psalm of penitence, the *Miserere mei* ("have mercy on me," Psalm 51). David is also referred to in *Inf*. IV, 58; *Purg*. X, 65, and *Par*. XX, 37. David's sin was his adultery with Bathsheba, wife of Uriah. Bathsheba contrived to have her husband killed in battle and then married David. The offspring of this union was Solomon.

15. *petal by petal:* I.e., seat by seat or soul by soul.

16–18. *Down from the seventh row, as up to it:* The line of seats in the Celestial amphitheater descending from Mary's seat is filled by Hebrew women. St. Bernard has already named Mary, Eve, Rachel, Sarah, Rebecca, Judith, and Ruth. Their line of seats,

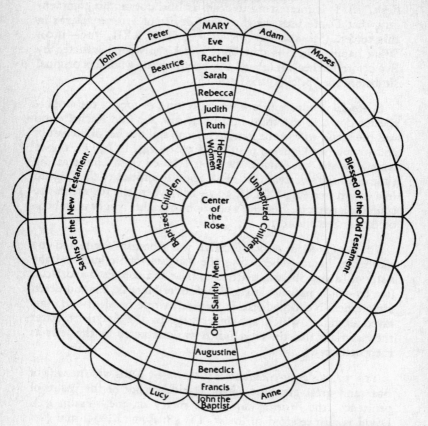

(adapted from Sayers, 1962)

along with the line directly across from them, divides all the seats virtually into two equal parts.

19–21. *according to the ways:* The distinction here is according to the saints of the Old and the New Testament, the former believing in Christ to come and the latter in Christ already come. The women who form the line of demarcation between the two groups also represent the link between B.C. time and A.D. time, particularly the Virgin Mary, who lived between both periods and held both points of view. (Cf. *Par.* XIX, 103–105, and XX, 103–105.)

22–24. On this side where the flower is full bloomed: The B.C. half of the amphitheater is full: not one seat remains in this, the Old Testament section.

25–27. on that side where all of the semi-circles: On the A.D. or New Testament side of the amphitheater there remain a few open seats. When all these seats are filled the process of salvation will end and with it the world. (Cf. *Par.* XXX, 131–32.)

31–33. so, facing her, the throne of the great John: Across from Mary's vertical row in the amphitheater is that headed by John the Baptist, who like the Virgin lived in both eras. He was beheaded two years before the Crucifixion and was in Limbo until Christ descended to free him (see *Inf.* IV, 52–63).

34–36. and under him chosen to mark the line: Only three saints from A.D. time are mentioned as seated beneath the great John the Baptist, while six Hebrew women were mentioned seated below the Virgin who directly faces John. They are St. Francis (see *Par.* XI, 43–117 and note); St. Benedict (see *Par.* XXII, 28–98 and note), whom the Pilgrim had yearned to see in the body (cf. *Par.* XXII, 58–63); and St. Augustine, who was referred to earlier in passing in connection with Orosius and was conspicuously absent from the double garland of Church fathers in the fourth heaven of the sun (see *Par.* X, 120 and note).

St. Augustine was born at Tagaste in Numidia in 354. Though he was raised as an unbaptized Christian by his mother, he soon fell away from her influence and began to lead a dissolute life. He studied at Carthage where for a period of time he was a member of the Manichaean sect. At the age of thirty he was invited to teach rhetoric in Milan, where he met St. Ambrose, bishop of Milan, who converted and baptized him in 387. Later he went to Hippo where he was ordained and finally became bishop in 396. He died there during the siege of the town by the Vandals on August 28, 430. Though he wrote numerous volumes, he is best known for his *Confessions* (written about 400 shortly after he became bishop) and the *City of God* (written between 413 and 427). Dante cites his works frequently in his *Convivio, De monarchia,* and *Epistles.*

Concerning the descending line of order in the Rose from John the Baptist to St. Francis to St. Benedict with St. Augustine coming fourth, Gardner says:

> St. Francis, in whose person the memory of Christ's passion was renewed, and who represents the renovation of the life of evangelical perfection, is opposite to Eve, restored to the beauty that was hers before the fall; St. Benedict, the great contemplative, is opposite to Rachel, the type of contemplation, or "reason illumined by divine revelation"; while the position of St. Augustine corresponds with that of Sarah. Now there is a certain tendency among mediaeval writers to take Sarah as a type of the official Latin Church, and the place of St. Augustine opposite her seems, therefore, to mark him (as in the *De monarchia*) as a doctor of the Church, an official exponent of her theology. Dante's idea, then, in the relative order of these three saints, may well be that, while theology is a sacred thing, contemplation is higher, and the perfect imitation of Christ, represented by St. Francis, is higher still.

37–39. *Now marvel at the greatness of God's plan:* God has ordained that there be as many seats in Heaven for those who lived before as for those who lived after the coming of Christ. We know that there are not many vacant seats left on the A.D. side of the amphitheater (see *Par.* XXX, 132); Dante probably believed that the end of the world was not far off. I doubt he would have divided the amphitheater into two equal halves for symmetrical reasons only.

40–45. *And know that downward from the center row:* The line to which St. Bernard is now referring is a horizontal one which divides the amphitheater into upper and lower halves. In the lower section are the souls of children who died before they reached the age of reason and could exercise their free will.

49–51. *But you have doubts, doubts you do not reveal:* The Pilgrim is wondering to himself why some children have higher seats in the amphitheater than others, since none of them had free will before they died, and thus were not able to gain merit through their actions. The answer to this question is that the degree of beatitude (loftiness in their position in the Rose) is a matter of predestination.

52–57. *Within the vastness of this great domain:* Chance has no place in Heaven, as everything in the celestial realm is preordained. God's will is the force that moves all things here and that determines their place. Just as a ring fits perfectly on a finger (57), so the relationship between a soul's merit and God's grace is a precise one.

59. *sine causa:* "Without cause," a Latin legal expression, used appropriately in this context of Divine Justice.

64—66. *creating all minds . . . let this fact suffice:* The conferring of grace upon a soul is a matter that lies essentially beyond the grasp of the mortal mind, as the reader has been told on a number of occasions in the Poem (cf. *Purg.* III, 37; *Par.* XX, 130—35, and XXI, 91—99).

68—69. *speaking of those twins:* Jacob and Esau were the twin sons of Rebecca and Isaac (see Gen. 25:21—34). St. Bernard mentions them as an example of the mystery of Divine Grace: "And not she only, but also Rebecca, who conceived by one man, Isaac our father; for before the child had yet been born or had done aught of good or evil, in order that the selective purpose of God might stand, depending not on deeds, but on him who calls, it was said to her: 'The elder shall serve the younger'; as it is written, 'Jacob I have loved, but Esau I have hated.' What then shall we say? Is there injustice with God? By no means! For he says to Moses, 'I will have mercy on whom I have mercy' " (Rom. 9:10—15).

72. *according to the color of their hair:* The souls in the heavenly congregation are crowned with Divine Light in proportion to the grace which was bestowed by God on them at birth. The metaphor of hair color may have been suggested to Dante by the fact that Esau had red hair and did not resemble Jacob (see Gen. 25:25).

75. *only in God's gift of original grace:* The capacity for grace which is spiritual vision and understanding of Divine Love is bestowed upon the soul by God when He creates it.

76—84

In the earliest ages of the world up until the time of Abraham, parents' faith in the coming of the Messiah sufficed to save their children. After that time, up until the birth of Christ, circumcision was required. After the Crucifixion innocent, unbaptized children were relegated to Limbo (see *Inf.* IV, 30, 34—36).

79. *when man's first age came to an end:* After the time of Abraham until the birth of Christ.

80. *all males had to be circumcised:* It was believed that the guilt of original sin was transmitted through the male (see *Summa theol.* I – II, q. 81, a.5, resp.).

83. *perfect baptism in Christ:* Circumcision is considered as imperfect baptism and prefigures the sacrament of baptism (cf. *Summa theol.* III, q. 70, a.2). When the word "Christ" appears in end rhyme position in the *Comedy,* it rhymes only with Itself. This is the last of the four instances of this type in the Poem. (See *Par.* XII, 71 – 75; XIV, 104 – 108; XIX, 104 – 108.)

85 – 87. *Now look at that face which resembles Christ:* St. Bernard urges the Pilgrim to return his gaze to Mary. In so doing the Pilgrim completes his circular tour of the Celestial Rose (St. Bernard had begun the circuit with Mary). The brilliance of Mary further prepares the Pilgrim for the vision to come, that of Christ. However, he is not yet aware that Christ will appear to him in a form other than human. His countenance will not be marked by recognizably human features, as is Mary's

88 – 90. *I saw such bliss rain down upon her face:* The "sacred minds" (89) who minister to Mary are the angels. These angelic intelligences of pure spirit fly throughout Heaven. (The Pilgrim saw them as sparks in *Par.* XXX, 64 – 69.)

94 – 96. *and that love which had once before descended:* The angel Gabriel came down to Mary for the Annunciation (see Luke 1:26 – 35), and once before, earlier in the Poem, he was seen symbolically as a light that descended upon Mary and circled her (*Par.* XXIII, 106 – 108).

97 – 99. *Response came to this holy prayer:* The population of the Celestial Rose probably responds by completing the prayer.

108. *the morning star:* Venus. Reference to the morning star is made in the litany to the Blessed Virgin.

109. *loving pride and gracious joy:* The Italian for this is "baldezza e leggiadria," words used frequently in the courtly love lyrics of the times with particular reference to earthly love. Dante transfers them to Paradise, purifying them at the court of the Virgin Mary.

110. *as much as soul or angel can possess:* No creature, either human or angelic, with the exception of Mary, can surpass Gabriel's exalted position.

111. *and we would have it so:* It is God's will that Gabriel be raised to so high a level; therefore it is the will of all the Blest (cf. *Par.* III, 70–78).

112–14. *for he it is who bore the palm below:* In scenes depicting the Annunciation Gabriel was often shown holding palm leaves as a symbol of the Immaculate Conception.

116–17. *the great patricians:* The language of the court continues as Bernard invites the Pilgrim to view the nobles of God's empire of which Mary is Queen (see also the following tercet). Language of this sort was in evidence in Canto XXV at the court of Sts. Peter, James, and John when the Pilgrim was examined on the virtues of Faith, Hope, and Charity.

118. *Those two:* The two highest seats after Mary's are assigned to St. Peter and to Adam.

119. *Empress:* Mary is now referred to in courtly terms (Dante uses the word *Augusta* for "Empress." (See n. 116–17; also *Par.* XXXI, 1–12; cf. also *Inf.* II.)

120. *the two roots of our Rose:* Adam is one root of the Rose because from him sprung those who believed in Christ to come; St. Peter is the other because from him sprung those who believed in Christ who had already come. Both will be called "father" in the following two tercets.

124–25. *and on her right:* St. Peter sits to the right of Mary on the A.D. side of the Rose. His is the highest seat of honor after Mary's.

126. *the keys to this beautiful Rose of joy:* These keys have been mentioned before in the Poem (see *Inf.* XIX, 91–92; XXVII, 124; *Purg.* IX, 117–20, and *Par.* XXIV, 35–36.)

127–30. *And he who prophesied before he died:* St. John the Evangelist, author of the *Apocalypse*, foretold the adversity that would befall the Church. (Cf. *Purg.* XXIX, 143–44.) The "lance and nails" (129) refers to the Crucifixion.

130. *Beside the other:* That is, next to Adam.

131–32. *the leader:* Moses led the Israelites through the desert, and they proved to be a difficult and disloyal group (see Exod. 16:14–35).

133–35. *Across from Peter, see there, Anna sits:* St. Anne was the mother of the Virgin Mary. Her place in the Rose is directly opposite St. Peter and to the right of John the Baptist. She is the only soul in the great amphitheater who is not looking up (directly) at God. Her gaze remains fixed on her daughter across the way. It is a surprisingly human attitude and a very beautiful touch on the part of the Poet: the mother of Mary who is the mother of Christ gazing on the source, as it were, of Christ Himself.

137–38. *Lucy:* She sits directly across from Adam and to the immediate right of John the Baptist. St. Lucy has already come twice to the Pilgrim's aid: first in the action of grace that occurred in Heaven (Beatrice recounts this in Limbo, as Virgil informs the Pilgrim in Canto II, 97–108 of the *Inferno*), and next in her act, which takes place symbolically in the Pilgrim's first dream in the *Purgatory* (IX, 52–63), of carrying the Pilgrim up the mountain to the gate of Purgatory. Verse 138 ("when you were bent, headlong, on your own ruin") brings the reader back to the very beginning of the poem (*Inf.* I, 55–60) when the Pilgrim was forced down the slope into the valley of sin by the relentless she-wolf.

139. *your journey's vision:* This verse has been interpreted in various ways because of the ambiguity of the word *t'assonna*, which I take to mean "journey's vision" (see Barbi, pp. 294–95, and Singleton, pp. 554–56). The journey must not be understood as a dream; on the contrary, throughout the Poem the Pilgrim's experience is purported to be real, in spite of the fact that at various points in the narrative Dante will evoke the notion of the fragility and the ineffability of a dream to suggest just how extraordinary and transcendental an experience he has been granted as a mortal man.

140–41. *like the good tailor:* The Poet has Bernard use a very humble, earthly comparison in an exalted, unearthly context: since the Pilgrim has so little time left before his journey ends, he should make good use of it, like a skillful tailor who knows how to get the most out of a limited amount of cloth. Bernard will stop pointing out the many other souls yet unnamed in the rose and invite the Pilgrim to turn his eyes directly toward God. Some commentators find this image of the tailor too "bourgeois" (see, for example, Porena, p. 317). I feel, however, it is appropriate for the imagery to become more humble the closer the Pilgrim gets to the final vision of God.

142−44. *turn our eyes upon the Primal Love:* The Pilgrim has at last reached the point in his journey where he is ready to raise his eyes and look directly upon God, perceiving him to the extent that Divine Grace has made him capable and worthy ("as deep as possible," 144).

145−48. *lest you fall backwards beating your wings:* The Pilgrim's beatific vision is not guaranteed; he must make an effort, through prayer, to continue his upward progress. Only with the Virgin Mary's aid can the Pilgrim complete his journey. The image of wings is one that has recurred frequently throughout the Poem.

151. *And he began to say this holy prayer:* The 99th canto of the *Comedy* ends very humbly with the word "prayer" and flows naturally into the final canto of the Poem, which opens with that very prayer. There is no break between these cantos; in fact, there are no two cantos in the Poem more unified than these. Dante, "like the good tailor / who cuts the gown according to his cloth" (140−41), at this point in the journey does not (in a sense) begin again but rather continues on.

CANTO XXXIII

ST. BERNARD LOVINGLY praises the Virgin Mary and then recounts the Pilgrim's journey through Hell, Purgatory, and the celestial spheres, entreating the Virgin to clear away the obstacles from the Pilgrim's eyes so that he may behold God's glory. Bernard then signals the Pilgrim to look upward, but he has already done so, spurred on by his clearer sight. He sees the multiform world bound in a single unity with love. Then, as he gazes into the Divine Light, he sees three rings of three different colors all of which share and are bound by one and the same circumference. The first ring of color reflects the second; both reflect the third: the miracle of the Trinity. Again the poet's words begin to fail him. He fixes his eyes on the second ring of reflected light and perceives God in the image of man, but he is·unable to grasp how the forms coincide. Then with a sudden flash the Pilgrim's mind is illuminated by the Truth and he feels, now that the ultimate vision has been granted him, his desire and will turning in harmony with Divine Love, "the Love that moves the sun and the other stars."

"Oh Virgin Mother, daughter of your son,
   most humble, most exalted of all creatures
   chosen of God in His eternal plan, 3

you are the one who ennobled human nature
   to the extent that He did not disdain,
   Who was its Maker, to make Himself man. 6

Within your womb rekindled was the love
   that gave the warmth that did allow this flower
   to come to bloom within this timeless peace. 9

For all up here you are the noonday torch
   of charity, and down on earth, for men,
   the living spring of their eternal hope. 12

Lady, you are so great, so powerful,
   that who seeks grace without recourse to you
   would have his wish fly upward without wings. 15

Not only does your loving kindness rush
   to those who ask for it, but often times
   it flows spontaneously before the plea.   *18*

In you is tenderness, in you is pity,
   in you munificence—in you unites
   all that is good in God's created beings.   *21*

This is a man who from the deepest pit
   of all the universe up to this height
   has witnessed, one by one, the lives of souls,   *24*

who begs you that you grant him through your grace
   the power to raise his vision higher still
   to penetrate the final blessedness.   *27*

And I who never burned for my own vision
   more than I burn for his, with all my prayers
   I pray you—and I pray they are enough—   *30*

that you through your own prayers dispel the mist
   of his mortality, that he may have
   the Sum of Joy revealed before his eyes.   *33*

I pray you also, Queen who can achieve
   your every wish, keep his affections sound
   once he has had the vision and returns.   *36*

Protect him from the stirrings of the flesh:
   you see, with Beatrice, all the Blest,
   hands clasped in prayer, are praying for my prayer."   *39*

Those eyes so loved and reverenced by God,
   now fixed on him who prayed, made clear to us
   how precious true devotion is to her;   *42*

then she looked into the Eternal Light,
   into whose being, we must believe, no eyes
   of other creatures pierce with such insight.   *45*

And I who was approaching now the end
   of all man's yearning, strained with all the force
   in me to raise my burning longing high.   *48*

Bernard then gestured to me with a smile
   that I look up, but I already was
   instinctively what he would have me be: *51*

for now my vision as it grew more clear
    was penetrating more and more the Ray
    of that exalted Light of Truth Itself.   *54*

And from then on my vision rose to heights
    higher than words, which fail before such sight,
    and memory fails, too, at such extremes.   *57*

As he who sees things in a dream and wakes
    to feel the passion of the dream still there
    although no part of it remains in mind,   *60*

just such am I: my vision fades and all
    but ceases, yet the sweetness born of it
    I still can feel distilling in my heart: *63*

so imprints on the snow fade in the sun,
    and thus the Sibyl's oracle of leaves
    was swept away and lost into the wind.   *66*

O Light Supreme, so far beyond the reach
    of mortal understanding, to my mind
    relend now some small part of Your own Self,   *69*

and give to my tongue eloquence enough
    to capture just one spark of all Your glory
    that I may leave for future generations;   *72*

for, by returning briefly to my mind
    and sounding, even faintly, in my verse,
    more of Your might will be revealed to men.   *75*

If I had turned my eyes away, I think,
    from the sharp brilliance of the living Ray
    which they endured, I would have lost my senses.   *78*

And this, as I recall, gave me more strength
    to keep on gazing till I could unite
    my vision with the Infinite Worth I saw.   *81*

O grace abounding and allowing me to dare
    to fix my gaze on the Eternal Light,
    so deep my vision was consumed in It!   *84*

I saw how it contains within its depths
    all things bound in a single book by love
    of which creation is the scattered leaves: *87*

how substance, accident, and their relation
  were fused in such a way that what I now
  describe is but a glimmer of that Light.   90

I know I saw the universal form,
  the fusion of all things, for I can feel,
  while speaking now, my heart leap up in joy.   93

One instant brings me more forgetfulness
  than five and twenty centuries brought the quest
  that stunned Neptune when he saw Argo's keel.   96

And so my mind was totally entranced
  in gazing deeply, motionless, intent;
  the more it saw the more it burned to see.   99

And one is so transformed within that Light
  that it would be impossible to think
  of ever turning one's eyes from that sight,   102

because the good which is the goal of will
  is all collected there, and outside it
  all is defective that is perfect there.   105

Now, even in the things I do recall
  my words have no more strength than does a babe
  wetting its tongue, still at its mother's breast.   108

Not that within the Living Light there was
  more than a sole aspect of the Divine
  which always is what It has always been,   111

yet as I learned to see more, and the power
  of vision grew in me, that single aspect
  as I changed, seemed to me to change Itself.   114

Within Its depthless clarity of substance
  I saw the Great Light shine into three circles
  in three clear colors bound in one same space;   117

the first seemed to reflect the next like rainbow
  on rainbow, and the third was like a flame
  equally breathed forth by the other two.   120

How my weak words fall short of my conception,
  which is itself so far from what I saw
  that "weak" is much too weak a word to use!   123

O Light Eternal fixed in Self alone,
   known only to Yourself, and knowing Self,
   You love and glow, knowing and being known!   *126*

That circling which, as I conceived it, shone
   in You as Your own first reflected light
   when I had looked deep into It a while,   *129*

seemed in Itself and in Its own Self-color
   to be depicted with man's very image.
   My eyes were totally absorbed in It.   *132*

As the geometer who tries so hard
   to square the circle, but cannot discover,
   think as he may, the principle involved,   *135*

so did I strive with this new mystery:
   I yearned to know how could our image fit
   into that circle, how could it conform;   *138*

but my own wings could not take me so high—
   then a great flash of understanding struck
   my mind, and suddenly its wish was granted.   *141*

At this point power failed high fantasy
   but, like a wheel in perfect balance turning,
   I felt my will and my desire impelled   *144*

by the Love that moves the sun and the other stars.

NOTES

1 – 39

The preceding canto announced St. Bernard's prayer to the
Virgin on behalf of the Pilgrim that he be accorded the grace to
see God. As this canto opens, the prayer begins. St. Bernard also
asks Mary's assistance so that, after his vision of God, Dante can
continue to lead a life of righteousness. With its liturgical style
(especially with the use of antithesis in the opening two verses)
the prayer is also a hymn in praise of the Virgin Mary.

7 – 9. *Within your womb rekindled was the Love:* The origin of the
Celestial Rose is the same as that of Christ: the womb of the
Blessed Virgin. At the same time, it was Christ that gave true
life to the flower.

10 – 12. *For all up here you are the noonday torch:* Mary was seen earlier as a rising sun (*Par.* XXXI, 118); now she is compared to the sun in full glory at its height. In Heaven Mary inspires love (there is no need for faith and hope; all here is love); on earth, however, she is a vigorous source of hope.

14 – 15. *would have his wish fly upward without wings:* It has always been the teaching of the Roman Catholic Church that the Blessed Virgin acts as the channel through which God grants favors to man.

16 – 18. *Not only does your loving kindness rush:* It is possible for the Virgin Mary to intercede on behalf of a sinner without her aid having been sought. This was the case with the Pilgrim at the beginning of the *Comedy* (see *Inf.* II, 94 – 99).

19 – 21. *In you . . . in you . . . :* This tercet is the high point of the prayer to the Virgin. The reader must feel the crescendo of praise ("tenderness . . . pity . . . munificence . . . all that is good") concentrated in this tercet structured with the fourfold repetition of "in you." This simple yet powerful tercet in the original reads:

In te misericordia, in te pietate,
in te magnificenza, in te s'aduna
quantunque in creatura è di bontate.

The highest praise of all is contained herein: in Mary is found the highest possible good in any creature.

22 – 24. *This is a man:* St. Bernard now introduces, as it were, Dante the Pilgrim to the Blessed Virgin Mary by giving a brief summary of his voyage from Hell to Paradise.

35 – 36. *keep his affections sound:* Bernard prays for the Virgin's aid once the Pilgrim has returned to earth, thus making her intervention total and cyclical: from earth to God's realm and back to earth again. In his final words to Beatrice (*Par.* XXXI, 88 – 90), the Pilgrim made a similar request of her. St. Bernard now makes the same request of the Virgin, and, in so doing, returns the chain of grace, which began the main action of the Poem in the *Inferno*, back to its source: the Virgin in Paradise.

37. *Protect him from the stirrings of the flesh:* St. Bernard's final request of the Virgin on behalf of the Pilgrim is that she protect

him after the final vision from all human passions (from sin in general) when he returns to the world of the living. Pertile, who interprets verses 34–39 in a different way, takes Bernard's words as a request for protection of the Pilgrim's senses (sight, feeling, and memory) while he is having the final vision so that he will be able to return to earth safe and sound to write the *Comedy*— the final goal of the journey.

38–39. *you see, with Beatrice, all the Blest:* This is the last time the name of Beatrice is mentioned in the Poem. Our final glimpse of her is an impressive one, as she with all the blessed souls of God's Rose join St. Bernard in his prayer to the Virgin on behalf of one mortal man.

40–42. *Those eyes so loved:* Mary's eyes, held in reverence by God and by His Son, are now turned on St. Bernard to show her pleasure at receiving his prayer. Notice that Mary neither gestures nor smiles. Only Beatrice and the Blest smile. Mary expresses her delight only with her look. This clearly puts the Virgin at a higher level of beatitude.

44–45. *into whose being:* Mary, too, must look up to perceive the Light of God. She, however, enjoys a kind of vision that no other human being possesses. In verse 45 Dante coins the verb *s'invii* (from the Latin *inire,* to enter), which I have translated as "insight."

50–51. *but I already was:* St. Bernard withdraws now from the scene, leaving the Pilgrim alone to contemplate God.

55–57. *from then on my vision rose to heights:* The Poet returns to the present to remind the reader that he has returned to earth and that he is recounting his experience within the limits imposed by mortal memory and verbal articulation.

58–60. *As he who sees things in a dream and wakes:* It must be remembered that Dante is not the one doing the dreaming. See the preceding canto (*Par.* XXXII, 139 and note).

61. *just such am I: my vision fades:* This phrase with its verb in the present tense clearly indicates that it is the Poet who speaks now from his vantage point on earth. When the Poet says his vision fades, he is referring *now,*—as he is writing the *Comedy,*— to the vision he had of God *then* in the narrative time of the Poem. The idea of struggling to reach the vision *then* and the

difficulty of recalling and describing it to his reader *now* is the basic structure upon which this canto is built and its imagery developed.

64–66. *so imprints on the snow fade in the sun:* The difficulty of grasping and describing such a marvelous experience is evoked once again through simile: as the snow melts under the sun's rays, and as the Sibyl or prophetess of Cumae wrote her prophecies on leaves that were scattered by the wind, so is Dante's experience in heaven an impressive but ephemeral one. (For the Sibyl see Virgil's *Aeneid* III, 441–51 and VI, 74ff.)

67–75

In this, the final invocation of the Poem, Dante addresses not the Muses and not Apollo, but God Himself. This is only fitting, as the Pilgrim has finally arrived at the point where he is face to face with his Maker. He begs God that he be allowed to recapture "just one spark" of all His glory (71).

76. *If I had turned my eyes away:* The Poet now returns to his narrative, to the time of Dante the Pilgrim in the Poem.

80–81. *I could unite / my vision with the Infinite Worth:* Now the Pilgrim's eyes finally fix themselves on God.

85–90. *I saw how it contains within its depths:* Dante makes his first great effort to describe what he saw in two different images: first the highly poetic image of "all things bound in a single book by love" (85–87) where the universe is seen as a book, contained in God and bound by His love; second a philosophical or scholastic idea of "substance" and "accident" (88–90). "Substance" is a thing existing in itself (a person or angel, for example) while "accident" is a quality residing in a substance (Dante talks about this in his *Vita nuova,* chapter XXV). In God these two elements are joined so as to be inseparable and indistinguishable. The eyes of the Pilgrim are beginning to penetrate more deeply the mystery of God's light.

91–93. *I know I saw the universal form:* The conjoining of substance and accident in God and the union of the temporal and the eternal is what Dante saw at that moment.

94–96. *One instant brings me more forgetfulness:* Returning again to the present time on earth, the voice of Dante the Poet refers once more to the difficulty of recalling and explaining what he has experienced. With this image, which constitutes one of the most surrealistic tercets in the *Comedy*, the theme of ineffability clearly reaches its high point. And how appropriate that this be done in a journey image, the image with which the *Comedy* opens: "Midway along the journey of our life"—the circle of the Poem continues to come full round.

The *Argo* was the first ship ever to sail. On its way to Colchis (during Jason's quest for the Golden Fleece) its shadow passed over the sea-god Neptune, who was stunned by its presence, since he had never seen such a thing on his ocean before. Dante places this event twenty-five centuries before his own time, or at about 1200 B.C., and uses this time reference to convey to his reader how remote his experience seemed in time even a moment after it happened. In other words, the journey of the *Argo* 2,500 years ago is more easily remembered today than is his moment of vision when he had it then. What makes this image such a felicitous one to my mind is the picture the reader is left with: the great sea-god's amazement as he looks up at this strange invader of his realm. The connotations of this image expand through the great sea of the Paradise (and the 2,500 years of time past help to give it that vastness) as Dante, who at the beginning of the *Paradise* had associated himself with Glaucus (see *Par.* I, 67 – 69) a minor sea-god, now suggests an association with the Lord of the Sea. The image is a grandiose one indeed.

97 – 99. *And so my mind was totally entranced:* The Poet now shifts back to the time of the narrative, which is, of course, always in the past tense. Note how this tercet carries overtones of the preceding one: the amazement of Neptune. Longen attempts to connect this tercet to the preceding one and concludes that "verses 94 – 99 represent a syntactical tour de force in which Dante indicates, as a distinct aspect of the mystical event he is literally describing, an apotheosis in himself that is, in fact, beyond the possibility of words to express" (p. 213).

103 – 105. *because the good which is the goal of will:* The will's object is good, just as the intellect's object is vision or knowledge. All good is contained in God (anything not contained in Him is not good), and turning away from this, the end of all desire, would be impossible.

107 – 108. *my words have no more strength than does a babe:* This is another image of the "ineffable," but of the more humble sort.

112 – 14. *yet as I learned to see more:* As the Pilgrim's ability to see increases, he has the impression that the object of his vision is changing. This is a false impression, however, as he knows that God is unchanging in His triunity (109 – 11). The "aspect" of God that he sees "seemed" to change, but it was in truth the Poet himself who was changing as "the power of vision grew" stronger in him.

115 – 20. *Within Its depthless clarity of substance:* The triune aspect of God is now clearly visible to the Pilgrim, and in these two tercets he attempts to describe it: what he sees in the Divine Light is three circles of three different colors all contained distinctly in one and the same circumference. The Father begets the Son, just as a rainbow was thought capable of producing a second (cf. *Par.* XII, 10 – 15). The Holy Ghost then issues from the Father and Son (see *Par.* X, 1 – 2).

121 – 23. *How my weak words fall short:* The inexpressible quality of the Poet's experience is once again emphasized, this time in the "weakest" of all the images of "ineffability."

124 – 26. *O Light Eternal fixed in Self alone:* This extraordinary tercet conveys the oneness of God through its very syntax, which seems to turn everything inward toward "Self." This circular movement is also present in the original, which reads:

O luce etterna che sola in te sidi,
   sola t'intendi, e da te intelletta
   e intendente te ami e arridi!

127 – 32. *That circling:* Within the circle of light the Pilgrim perceives the features of Christ, which, after he has "looked deep into it awhile" (129) become the image of man. The Pilgrim is witnessing the mystery of the Word Incarnate.

133 – 35. *As the geometer:* The Greeks posited the problem of squaring a circle, which was finally proved impossible to solve. The message of the simile is that God is indescribable in human terms, just as a circle cannot be measured in terms of a square.

138. *how could it conform:* For the word "conform" Dante coins the word *s'indova* (from the adverb *dove*)—the last of his word inventions in the poem.

139. *but my own wings could not take me so high:* For the last time

the metaphor of "wings" is used by Dante to represent his upward striving for understanding. This is the culmination of the wings image in the poem.

140–41. *then a great flash of understanding struck:* By sudden insight and the grace of God Dante comprehends how the two natures, the human and the Divine, are united in God. Such is the essence of God, and it is visible to all the souls of the Elect.

142. *At this point power failed high fantasy:* The instant that his mind receives understanding of the dual nature of God, the Pilgrim loses his ability to carry on with his description of the event. By "fantasy" Dante means the capacity to take in images; he has reached his limit, and his vision (and hence, his poem) must end.

143–45. *but, as a wheel in perfect balance turning:* So, by Grace from above, a "great flash of understanding" is briefly given the Pilgrim and he is allowed to enjoy what all the souls of the Blest enjoy throughout eternity. The Pilgrim's will and desire are in perfect conformity with the will of God (see *Summa theol.* I–II, q. 3, a.4: "The essence of happiness consists in an act of the intellect, but the delight that results from happiness pertains to the will"), and it is God, Who is Love, that holds and guides his will and his desire, which are now turning like a perfectly balanced wheel (one in which all points on the wheel are moving at the same speed and with the same rhythm).

The last verse of the poem, a periphrasis of God ("the Love that moves the sun and the other stars") brings the circle around not only to the opening verse of the *Paradise*—"The glory of the One Who moves all things"—but, with the mention of the "sun," to the very beginning of the *Comedy*, and we are reminded of verses 16–18 of the first canto of the *Inferno:*

> I raised my head and saw the hilltop shawled
> in morning rays of light sent from the planet
> that leads men straight ahead on every road.

Like the *Inferno* and *Purgatory*, the *Paradise* ends with the word "stars" (see note to *Inf.* XXXIV, 139). At the end of each canticle the Pilgrim's eyes are fixed upon the stars. Everyone should have his eyes fixed on God's stars, for there is his happiness, and all men desire to be happy.

GLOSSARY AND INDEX
OF PERSONS AND PLACES

Persons and places mentioned by name in the text of the *Paradise* are listed here, with references to the cantos and lines in which they are found, and with references to any notes that mention them. References found within parentheses indicate the passages in the text where the person or place is mentioned. If persons or places have already been cited in *Vol. I: Inferno* or *Vol. II: Purgatory,* canto, line, and note references to those volumes are also given. If sufficient information has been given in my notes and commentary, then only the reference is given here; otherwise, a brief description or explanation is included.

ACONE: a small town in Val di Sieve, Tuscany. See note *Par.* XVI, 65 (XVI, 65).

ACQUASPARTA: a town in Umbria. See note *Par.* XII, 125 (XII, 125).

ADAM: father of mankind. See notes *Purg.* XI, 44, XXXII, 37–42; *Par.* VII, 145–8, XIII, 37, XXVI, 85–96, 109–42, XXXII, 120, 130 (*Inf.* III, 115, IV, 55; *Purg.* IX, 10, XI, 44, XXIX, 86, XXXII, 37; *Par.* VII, 148, XIII, 37, XXVI, 81–142, XXXII, 121–23, 130, 136).

ADIGE: a river of NE Italy. See notes *Inf.* XII, 4–10; *Purg.* XVI, 115; *Par.* IX, 43–48 (*Inf.* XII, 6; *Purg.* XVI, 115; *Par.* IX, 44).

ADIMARI: name of a Florentine family. See note *Par.* XVI, 115–20 (XVI, 115–20).

AENEAS: Trojan prince, son of Anchises by the goddess Venus. Hero of Virgil's *Aeneid.* When Troy falls, he escapes with his father, son, and a number of followers, and after many wanderings unites the Latin and Trojan lines by marrying Lavinia, which opens the way for the founding of Rome. See notes *Inf.* II, 10–48, IV, 122, XXVI, 92–93; *Purg.* XVIII, 136–38; *Par.* VI, 3, XV, 25–27 (*Inf.* II, 32, IV, 122, XXVI, 93; *Purg.* XVIII, 137; *Par.* VI, 3, XV, 27).

AGAPETUS I: pope 535–536. Erroneously believed by medieval historians to have convinced Justinian of the error of his heretical belief that there was but one nature in Christ. See note *Par.* VI, 14-15 (VI, 16).

AGOSTINO, FRA': see Augustine.

AGUGLIONE, BALDO D': prominent Guelf leader. See note *Par.* XVI, 56 (XVI, 56).

AHASUERUS: king of Persia, thought to be identical with Xerxes (q.v.).

ALAGNA (ALAGNI): a town in Latium, about 40 miles SE of Rome. See notes *Purg.* XX, 87; *Par.* XXX, 148 (*Purg.* XX, 86; *Par.* XXX, 148).

ALBA (ALBA LONGA): the most ancient town in Latium, built according to tradition by Ascanius, son of Aeneas (q.v.). See note *Par.* VI, 37-39 (VI, 38).

ALBERICHI: name of an ancient noble family of Florence mentioned by Cacciaguida as being already in decline in his day. See note *Par.* XVI, 88-93 (XVI, 89).

ALBERT I OF AUSTRIA: emperor. See notes *Purg.* VI, 97; *Par.* XIX 115-17 (*Purg.* VI, 97; *Par.* XIX, 115).

ALBERT OF COLOGNE (ALBERTUS MAGNUS): named the "Universal Doctor" on account of his vast learning. His soul is pointed out to Dante as being among the great theologians and others who loved wisdom and truth. See note *Par.* X, 98 (X, 98).

ALCIDES: see Hercules.

ALCMEON: son of Amphiaraus. See notes *Purg.* XII, 50; *Par.* IV, 103-105 (*Purg.* XII, 50; *Par.* IV, 103).

ALIGHIERO: son of Cacciaguida (q.v.). See note *Par.* XV, 91-92 (XV, 91-92).

ALVERNIA, MT.: a mountain in the Casentino, east of Florence. See note *Par.* XI, 106-108 (XI, 106).

AMIDEI: noble Florentine family. See note *Par.* XVI, 136-37 (XVI, 136).

AMYCLAS: a poor fisherman. See note *Par.* XI, 67-69 (XI, 68).

ANANIAS: "the disciple of Damascus"; healed St. Paul's blindness. See note *Par.* XXVI, 10-12 (XXVI, 12).

ANCHISES: father of Aeneas (q.v.) See notes *Par.* XV, 25-27, XIX, 132 (*Inf.* I, 74; *Purg.* XVIII, 137; *Par.* XV, 25, XIX, 132).

ANGELS: the lowest order in the celestial hierarchies, ranking last in the third hierarchy. They preside over the Heaven of the Moon. See note *Par.* XXVIII, 126 (XXVIII, 126).

ANNA, ST.: mother of the Virgin. See note *Par.* XXXII, 133-35 (XXXII, 133).

ANSELM: archbishop of Canterbury. See note *Par.* XII, 137-38 (XII, 137).

ANTANDROS: a city of Great Mysia on the Adranythian Gulf, at the foot of Mt. Ida. See note *Par.* VI, 67 (VI, 67).

ANTHONY, ST.: the Egyptian hermit (251-356) See note *Par.* XXIX, 124 (XXIX, 124).

APOLLO: son of Jupiter and Latona, who gave birth to him and his twin sister, Diana, on the island of Delos. God of song and leader of the Muses. He was god of the sun, Diana being goddess of the moon. See notes *Par.* I, 13-36, 15, 16-17, 20-21, 25, 28-33, 33, 36, XIII, 25-27, XXIX, 1 (I, 13, 33; XIII, 25; XXIX, 1).

AQUINAS, ST. THOMAS (TOMMASO D'AQUINO): (c. 1225/7-1274) the greatest of the scholastic theologians, the "Common Doctor" whose reconciliation of the Christian doctrine with the writings of Aristotle dominated medieval thought. Dante studied the works of St. Thomas closely, and the theological structure of the *Comedy* owes more to him than to any other theologian. Thomas is placed in the sphere of the sun among the Doctors of the Church. See cantos X–XII and notes, and *Purg.* XX, 69 (*Purg.* XX, 69).

ARCA, DELL': name of an ancient noble family of Florence. See note *Par.* XVI, 88-93 (XVI, 92).

ARCHANGELS: lowest order but one in the celestial hierarchies. They preside over the Heaven of Mercury. See note *Par.* XXVIII, 126 (XXVIII, 125).

ARDINGHI: name of an ancient noble family of Florence. See note *Par.* XVI, 88-93 (XVI, 93).

ARGO: the ship *Argo,* built by Argus, son of Phrixius, in which the Argonauts sailed (see under Jason). See note *Par.* XXXIII, 94-96 (XXXIII, 96).

ARIADNE: daughter of Minos and Pasiphaë. See notes *Inf.* XII, 12-21; *Par.* XIII, 13-15 (*Inf.* XII, 20; *Par.* XIII, 14).

ARISTOTLE: the great Athenian philosopher. Plato's most brilliant pupil, but later diverged from his master's teaching. Enormously influential in scholastic philosophy (Dante himself calling him *il maestro di color che sanno*), his work was reconciled to Christian doctrine by Thomas Aquinas, and Dante was well acquainted with Latin translations of his works. See note *Inf.* IV, 131, XI, 79-84, 101-105; *Purg.* III, 37-45; *Par.* XXIV, 130-47, XXVI, 37-39 (*Inf.* IV, 131, XI, 79, 101; *Purg.* III, 43; *Par.* XXIV, 133-35, XXVI, 37-39).

ARIUS: (d. A.D. 336) presbytor of Alexandria. See note *Par.* XIII, 127 (XIII, 127).

ARNO: a river of Italy that runs through Florence. See notes *Inf.* XIII, 143-50, XXX, 64-66; *Purg.* XIV, 17, 31; *Par.* XI, 106-108 (*Inf.* XIII, 146, XV, 113, XXIII, 95, XXX, 65, XXXIII, 83; *Purg.* V, 126, XIV, 17; *Par.* XI, 106).

ARRIO: see Arius.

ARRIGUCCI: name of an ancient noble family of Florence. See note *Par.* XVI, 106-108 (XVI, 107).

ASSISI (ASCESI): a town in Umbria, birthplace of St. Francis (q.v.). See note *Par.* XI, 43-48 (XI, 43-48).

ATHENS: a city of Greece. See notes *Purg.* VI, 139, XV, 97; *Par.* XVII, 46-48 (*Purg.* VI, 139, XV, 97; *Par.* XVII, 46).

AUGUSTINE (FRA' AGOSTINO): one of the earliest followers of St. Francis (q.v.) whom he joined in 1210. See note *Par.* XII, 130 (XII, 130).

AUGUSTINE, ST.: (354-430) father of the Latin Church. See notes *Par.* X, 120, XXXII, 34-36 (X, 120, XXXII, 35).

AUSONIA'S HORN: the southern part of Italy, of which the curve was thought to resemble a horn. See note *Par.* VIII, 61-63 (VIII, 61).

AVELLANA, FONTE: Benedictine hermitage on the NE slope of Mt. Catria. See note *Par.* XXI, 110 (XXI, 110).

BABYLON: a city in Egypt. See note *Par.* XXIII, 135 (XXIII, 135).

BACCHUS: in Greek mythology, the god of wine. See note *Par.* XIII, 25-27 (*Inf.* XX, 59; *Par.* XIII, 25).

BAGNOREGIO (BAGNOREA): a village in Tuscany; birthplace of St. Bonaventura (q.v.) (XII, 128).

BARI: a town of S. Italy on the Adriatic coast. See note *Par.* VIII, 61-63 (VIII, 62).

BARTOLOMEI, ENRICO: see Enrico da Susa.

BARTOMEO DELLA SCALA: see Scala, Bartolomeo della.

BARUCCI: name of an ancient Ghibelline family of Florence. See note *Par.* XVI, 103-104 (XVI, 104).

BEARS: the constellations of the Great Bear (also called the Wain, the Plough, or Ursa Major) and of the Little Bear (Areas, Bootes, or Ursa Minor), which contains the Pole Star. See notes *Inf.* XI, 113-15; *Purg.* XXX, 1; *Par.* II, 8-9, XIII, 7, XXXI, 32 (*Inf.* XI, 114; *Purg.* I, 30, IV, 65, XXX, 1; *Par.* II, 9, XIII, 7, XXXI, 32-33).

BEATRICE: (1266-1290) daughter of Folco Portinari. In the *Vita nuova* Dante says that he first saw and fell in love with her when she was eight years and five months old, and when he was nearly nine. Takes over from Virgil as Dante's guide in *Purg.* XXX.

BEDE: the Venerable Bede, Anglo-Saxon monk and celebrated historian. See note *Par.* X, 131 (X, 131).

BELISARIUS: famous general of the Emperor Justinian (q.v.). See note *Par.* VI, 25 (VI, 25).

BELLA, DELLA: Florentine family. See note *Par.* XVI, 127-32 (XVI, 127-32).

BELLINCION BERTI: Florentine of the ancient Ravignani family. See note *Par.* XV, 112 (XV, 112).

BELUS: king of Tyre, father of Dido (*Par.* IX, 97).

BENEDICT, ST.: founder of the Benedictine Order and of the Monastery of Monte Cassino. See notes *Par.* XXII, 28, XXXII, 34-36 (XXII, 28, XXXII, 35).

BERENGER, RAYMOND: count of Provence. See note *Par.* VI, 128 (VI, 133).

BERNARD OF CLAIRVAUX, ST.: famous abbot of the Benedictine Order. See notes *Par.* XXXI, 60, and notes to XXXII and XXXIII (XXXI, 60ff).

BERNARDO DA QUINTAVALLE: first follower of St. Francis. See note *Par.* XI, 79-81 (XI, 79).

BERNARDO, PIETRO: father of St. Francis. See notes *Par.* XI, 61–63, 88, 90 (XI, 61, 89).

BOETHIUS: Roman statesman and philosopher. See note *Par.* X, 125–29 (X, 124–29).

BONAVENTURE, ST. (BONAVENTURA): general of the Franciscan Order and bishop of Albano. See note *Par.* XII, 29 (XII, 29ff).

BONIFACE VIII (BENEDICT CAIETAN): (c.1217–1303) pope 1294–1303. See notes *Inf.* XIX, 53, XV, 112–14, XXVII, 67–71, 85–90; *Purg.* XX, 87; *Par.* IX, 126, XII, 88–90, XXVII, 19–21, 22–23, 24, XXX, 148 (*Inf.* XIX, 53; *Purg.* XX, 87; *Par.* IX, 126, XII, 90, XXVII, 22, XXX, 148).

BOREAS: the north wind. See note *Par.* XXVIII, 81 (XXVIII, 81).

BOSTICHI: name of an ancient noble Florentine family, mentioned by Cacciaguida as having been prominent in his day. They are said to have been Guelfs and to have fled with the rest of the party from Florence after the battle of Montaperti in 1260. See note *Par.* XVI, 88–93 (XVI, 93).

BOUGIE: a city on the coast of Africa. See note *Par.* IX, 91–93 (IX, 92).

BRENNUS: leader of the Senonian Gauls. See note *Par.* VI, 43–45 (VI, 44).

BRENTA: a river of Italy. See note *Inf.* XV, 7; *Par.* IX, 25–27 (*Inf.* XV, 7; *Par.* IX, 27).

BRUTUS (MARCUS JUNIUS): (85–42 B.C.) Roman statesman. Pardoned by Julius Caesar after he had fought on Pompey's side in the Civil War. He was persuaded by Cassius to take part in the conspiracy to murder Caesar in the hope of reestablishing the Republic. In 42 B.C. their united forces were defeated by Octavian (later Augustus) Caesar and Mark Antony at the Battle of Philippi, and Brutus committed suicide. See notes *Inf.* XXXIV, 65; *Par.* VI, 73–75 (*Inf.* XXXIV, 65; *Par.* VI, 74).

BRYSON: Greek philosopher. See note *Par.* XIII, 125 (XIII, 125).

BUONDELMONTI: leaders of the Guelf party in Florence. See notes *Par.* XVI, 66, 133–35 (XVI, 66, 135).

CACCIAGUIDA: great-great-grandfather of Dante. Nothing is known of his life apart from what Dante writes in the Heaven of Mars, although his existence is attested by a document which refers to his two sons. He was born in Florence in the Sesto di Porta San Piero about the year 1090. His wife came from the valley of the Po and from her the name of Alighieri descended. He was killed in the Second Crusade about 1147. See notes *Par.* XV, 25–27ff, XVI, XVII (XV, 31ff, XVI, XVII).

CADIZ: a seaport on the SW coast of Spain, regarded in Dante's time as the western limit of the inhabitable globe, the mouth of the Ganges River being the eastern limit. See note *Par.* XXVII, 82–83 (XXVII, 82).

CAESAR (CAIUS JULIUS): (100–44 B.C.) dictator of Rome. A brilliant general, he was made consul in 59 B.C., and his conquest of Gaul made him the idol of the people and the army. His rival, Pompey, jealous of his rising power, headed an armed opposition against him. Caesar decisively overthrew Pompey and won the power struggle at the battle of

Pharsalia in 48 B.C. He was made dictator and subsequently offered the kingship, which he refused for fear of offending the people. On the Ides of March, 44 B.C., he was assassinated in the Capitol by a band of conspirators led by Brutus and Cassius. His successor Augustus was the first Roman emperor, and the name Caesar became part of the imperial title. See notes *Inf.* I, 62, IV, 123, XXVIII, 79–102; *Purg.* XVIII, 101, XXVI, 78; *Par.* VI, 58–60, 61–63, 64–66, XI, 67–69 (*Inf.* I, 70, IV, 123, XXVIII, 97; *Purg.* XVIII, 101, XXVI, 77; *Par.* VI, 57, XI, 68–69).

CAESAR, THE THIRD (TIBERIUS CLAUDIUS NERO): adopted son and successor of Augustus, Roman emperor (A.D. 14–37). Dante, regarding Julius Caesar as the first emperor, speaks of Tiberius as the third Caesar. See note *Par.* VI, 87–90 (*Par.* VI, 87).

CAESAR AUGUSTUS (CAIUS JULIUS CAESAR OCTAVIANUS): (63 B.C.–A.D. 14) first Roman emperor; great-nephew of Julius Caesar and adopted by him as heir. After the assassination of Julius, he assumed the name of Caesar and with Lepidus and Mark Antony became one of the triumvirs who took over the government of the Republic. He gradually gathered all the great offices of state into his own hands; in 32 B.C. he accepted the title of Imperator. The defeat of Antony at Actium (31 B.C.) and the death of Lepidus (12 B.C.) left him sole master of the Roman Empire. The epithet Augustus was conferred on him by the Senate in 67 B.C. and was borne by his successors as part of the imperial title. See notes *Purg.* VII, 6, XXIX, 115; *Par.* VI, 73–75, 76–78, 79–81 (*Purg.* VII, 6, XXIX, 115; *Par.* VI, 73–81).

CAGNANO: a river of Italy. See note *Par.* IX, 49 (IX, 49).

CAIETA: see Gaeta.

CAIN: son of Adam, killer of his brother, Abel. See notes *Inf.* XX, 124–26; *Purg.* XIV, 133; *Par.* II, 49–51 (*Inf.* XX, 124; *Purg.* XIV, 133; *Par.* II, 51).

CALAROGA: a city of Castile. See note *Par.* XII, 52–54 (XII, 52).

CALFUCCI: name of an ancient noble family of Florence. See note *Par.* XVI, 106–108 (XVI, 106).

CALIXTUS: pope 217–222. See note *Par.* XXVII, 44 (XXVII, 44).

CAMPI: a small town near Florence. See note *Par.* XVI, 50 (XVI, 50).

CAN GRANDE DELLA SCALA: see Scala, della, Can Grande.

CAPONSACCHI: name of an old Florentine noble family. See note *Par.* XVI, 121 (XVI, 121).

CASAL: a town in Piedmont. See note *Par.* XII, 125 (XII, 125).

CASSINO: the monastery of Monte Cassino, founded by St. Benedict in the year 529, situated in the north of Campania, a few miles from Aquino. See note *Par.* XXII, 37–39 (XXII, 38).

CASSIUS (CAIUS CASSIUS LONGINUS): Roman statesman and general. Pardoned by Julius Caesar after he had fought on Pompey's side in the Civil

War, he was made praetor and was promised the governorship of Syria. However, he headed a conspiracy to assassinate Caesar, persuading Brutus to join it. Defeated with Brutus by Augustus and Mark Antony at Philippi, he committed suicide. See notes *Inf.* XXXIV, 67; *Par.* VI, 73-75 (*Inf.* XXXIV, 67; Par. VI, 74).

CATELLINI: name of an old Florentine family. See note *Par.* XVI, 88-93 (XVI, 88).

CATONA: a town in Calabria, a few miles north of Reggio. See note *Par.* VIII, 61-63 (VIII, 62).

CATRIA: one of the highest peaks in the Apennines. See note *Par.* XXI, 107 (XXI, 109).

CERCHI: name of a wealthy Florentine family of low origin who came from Acone. When Florence was split into Guelf and Ghibelline factions (1215) the Cerchi sided with the former; when the Guelf party itself was split into Bianchi (Whites) and Neri (Blacks), the Cerchi, who by this time had become very wealthy and powerful through commerce, became the leaders of the Whites. See note *Par.* XVI, 65 (XVI, 65).

CERTALDO: small town between Florence and Siena. See note *Par.* XVI, 50 (XVI, 50).

CHARLEMAGNE: (742-814) emperor of the West, son of Pepin le Bref, king of the Franks. He received the imperial crown from Pope Leo III on Christmas day in 800. His wars against heretics and infidels and his twelve peers, of whom his nephew Roland and his friend Oliver are best known, became legendary and were celebrated in the early *Chansons de Geste* and many later epics. See notes *Inf.* XXXI, 16-18; *Par.* VI, 94-96, XVIII, 43 (*Inf.* XXXI, 16; *Par.* VI, 96, XVIII, 43).

CHARLES I OF ANJOU: (1226-1285) king of Naples and Sicily, count of Anjou and Provence, son of Louis VIII and Blanche of Castile. See notes *Inf.* XIX, 98-99, XXVIII, 15-18; *Purg.* VII, 113, XI, 137, XX, 67-68; *Par.* VIII, 72 (Inf. XIX, 99; *Purg.* VII, 113, XI, 137, XX, 67; *Par.* VIII, 72).

CHARLES (CARLO): (1248-1309) king of Naples, count of Anjou and Provence, son of Charles I of Anjou and Beatrix of Provence. See notes *Purg.* V, 68-69, XX, 79; *Par.* VI, 106, XIX, 127-29 (*Purg.* V, 69, XX, 79; *Par.* VI, 106, XIX, 128).

CHARLES MARTEL: (1271-1295) titular king of Hungary. See note *Par.* VIII, 32-84ff, IX, 1 (VIII, 31-147, IX, 1).

CHERUBIM: the highest order but one in the celestial hierarchies. They preside over the eighth sphere (the Fixed Stars). See note *Par.* XI, 37-42, XXVIII, 126 (XI, 39, XXVIII, 99).

CHIANA: a river in Tuscany. See note *Inf.* XXIV, 47-49 (under "Valdichiana"); *Par.* XIII, 24 (*Inf.* XXIX, 47; *Par.* XIII, 24).

CHIARMONTESI: name of an old Florentine noble family. See notes *Purg.* XII, 105; *Par.* XVI, 105 (*Purg.* XII, 105; *Par.* XVI, 105).

CHIUSI (CLUSIUM): one of the twelve ancient Etruscan cities. See note *Par.* XVI, 75 (XVI, 75).

CHRIST: the name of Christ is mentioned thirty-nine times in the *Comedy:* five times in the *Purgatory* and thirty-four times in the *Paradise.* It is not once mentioned in the *Inferno,* though Christ is referred to there by various paraphrases (see *Inf.* and *Purg.* glossaries under Christ). When the name of Christ occurs at the end of a line, Dante does not rhyme with it, but repeats the name itself. There are four instances of this in the *Paradise:* XII, 71-75, XIV, 104-108, XIX, 104-108, XXXII, 83-87. The other twenty-two mentions of his name in the *Paradise* are VI, 14, IX, 120, XI, 72-102, 107, XII, 37, XVII, 51, XIX, 72, XX, 48, XXIII, 20, 72, XXV, 15, XXVI, 53, XXVII, 40, XXIX, 97, 109, XXXI, 3, 107, XXXII, 20, 24, 27, 125.

Other references: as Son of God, VII, 119, X, 1; as Son of God and Mary, XXIII, 136-37, as Son of Mary, XXIII, 106; as Lamb of God, XVII, 32, XXIV, 2; as our Lord, XXIV, 35; as the Redeemer, XIII, 40-42 (see note to 40); as the Bridegroom of Poverty, XI, 31-33, 64, 70-72; as Bridegroom of the Church, XII, 43; as the Bridegroom, III, 107, X, 141; as the Word, VII, 30, XXII, 41, XXIII, 73; as Wisdom, XXIII, 37; as Power, XXIII, 37; as the Almighty, XXVII, 36; as "my Lord, the One True God," XXXI, 107; as "our High Bliss," XIII, 111; as "Him who lifts the weight of every wrong man suffers," XVIII, 5-6; as "Him who had the power to save," XX, 114; as the Son, XXIII, 29, 72; as "our Desire," XXIII, 105; as "our own Pelican," XXV, 113.

Christ's twofold nature as God and Man is referred to in II, 41-42, VI, 13-21, VII, 35-36, XIII, 27, XXIII, 136-37, XXXIII, 4-6; as the second person of the Trinity he is referred to in *Par.* VII, 31-33, X, 1, 51, XXIII, 136-37, XXVII, 24.

CHRYSOSTOM, ST. JOHN: (c. 347-407) Greek father of the Church. See note *Par.* XII, 137-38 (XII, 137).

CIANGHELLA: Florentine woman of ill repute. See note *Par.* XV, 127-29 (XV, 127).

CINCINNATUS (LUCIUS QUINTIUS CINCINNATUS): dictator of Rome (458 B.C.). See note *Par.* XV, 127-29 (XV, 129).

CLEMENCE: daughter of the Emperor Rudolph and widow of Charles Martel; however, the reference could be to her daughter, also called Clemence. See note *Par.* IX, 1 (IX, 1).

CLEMENT V (BERTRAND DE GOTT): pope (1305-1314). It was he who, under pressure from Philip the Fair, transferred the Holy See to Avignon, where it remained from 1309 to 1377. See notes *Par.* XVII, 82, XXVII, 58, XXX, 142-44, 145-48 (XVIII, 82, XXVII, 58, XXX, 142-48).

CLEOPATRA: (69-30 B.C.) queen of Egypt. Mistress of Julius Caesar and Mark Antony. When Antony's defeat by Octavius (Augustus) Caesar was followed by his suicide, she killed herself by the bite of an asp. See notes *Inf.* V, 63; *Par.* VI, 76–78 (*Inf.* V, 63; *Par.* VI, 76).

CLETUS (ANACLETUS): bishop of Rome in the first century (76 or 78 to 88 or 90). See note *Par.* XXVII, 41 (XXVII, 41).

CLYMENE: mother of Phaëton by Apollo. See note XVII, 1 (XVII, 1).

COLCHIS: country of Asia Minor, famous as the land to which Jason and the Argonauts sailed in search of the Golden Fleece. See note *Par.* II, 16–18 (II, 16).

CONRAD III (c. 1093–1152): king of Saxony and uncrowned Holy Roman emperor, the first of the Hohenstaufen. Some have maintained that the reference is to Conrad II, the Salico, but this is unlikely, though it is possible that the two became confused in Dante's memory. See note *Par.* XV, 139 (XV, 139).

CONSTANCE (COSTANZA): empress, mother of Frederick II. See notes *Purg.* III, 143; *Par.* III, 109, 118 (*Purg.* III, 113; *Par.* III, 108–20, IV, 97).

CONSTANTINE THE GREAT: emperor of Rome (306–337) son of the Emperor Constantinus Chlorus. First Christian Roman emperor. See notes *Inf.* XIX, 115–17; *Par.* VI, 1, XX, 55–60 (*Inf.* XIX, 115, XXVII, 94; *Par.* VI, 1, XX, 55–60).

CORNELIA: daughter of Scipio Africanus Major, wife of Tiberius Sempronius Gracchus, and mother of the two famous tribunes, Tiberius and Caius. She is celebrated as a model Roman mother of the old school, who brought up her sons in the utmost rectitude; after her death the people of Rome erected a statue to her inscribed "The mother of the Gracchi." See notes *Inf.* IV, 127–29; *Par.* XV, 127–29 (*Inf.* IV, 128; *Par.* XV, 129).

COSTANZA: see Constance.

CREUSA: daughter of Priam and Hecuba, wife of Aeneas (q.v.). See note *Par.* IX, 97–98 (IX, 98).

CROATIA: a country SW of Hungary between the Sava and the Adriatic. See note XXXI, 103–108 (XXXI, 103).

CUNIZZA: sister of Ezzelino III da Romano. See notes *Par.* IX (IX, 19–66).

CUPID: god of love, son of Venus. See notes *Purg.* XXVIII, 64; *Par.* VIII, 8 (*Purg.* XXVIII, 65; *Par.* VIII, 8).

CYPRIAN: epithet of Venus, goddess of love, the planet Venus. See note *Par.* VIII, 1–2 (VIII, 1–3).

CYRRHA: a town in Phocis, about fifteen miles SW of Delphi where Apollo had his temple and oracle. The name was also applied to one of the peaks of Mt. Parnassus. See note *Par.* I, 36 (I, 36).

DAEDALUS: the cunning artificer who in classical legend lived in Crete and created for Pasiphaë a wooden cow; he also fashioned the labyrinth in which Minos kept the Minotaur, and wings for himself and his son Icarus. See notes *Inf.* XII, 12–21, XVII, 109–11; *Par.* VIII, 126 (*Inf.* XVII, 111, XXIX, 116; *Par.* VIII, 125–26).

D'AGUGLIO, BALDO: see Aguglione.

DAMIAN, PETER: see Peter Damian.

DANIEL: prophet of the Jews. See notes *Purg.* XXII, 146–47; *Par.* IV, 13; XXIX, 130–35 (*Purg.* XXII, 146; *Par.* IV, 13, XXIX, 133).

DANUBE: a river of Europe. See note *Par.* VIII, 65 (*Inf.* XXXII, 25; *Par.* VIII, 65).

DAVID: king of Israel. See notes *Inf.* XXVIII, 137–38; *Purg.* X, 66; *Par.* XX, 37–39, 40–42 (*Inf.* IV, 58, XXVIII, 138; *Purg.* X, 65; *Par.* XX, 37–42).

DECII: famous Roman family. See note *Par.* VI, 47 (VI, 47).

DEMOPHOÖN: son of Theseus and Phaedra. See note *Par.* IX, 100–102 (IX, 101).

DEVIL: see under Lucifer in *Inferno* glossary; see notes *Inf.* VII, 1, XI, 65, XXXI, 19–127, XXXIV, 1, 18, 20, 38–45, 46, 61–63, 79–81, 112–15, 127–32; *Par.* IX, 127–29, XIX, 46–51, XXIX, 55–57 (*Inf.* VII, 1, XI, 65, XXXI, 143, XXXIV, 89; *Purg.* VIII, 131, XII, 24–5; *Par.* IX, 127, 129, XIX, 46–48, XXVII, 26–27, XXIX, 55–57).

DIDO: queen of Carthage. See notes *Inf.* 61–62; *Par.* IX, 97–98 (*Inf.* V, 61, 85; *Par.* IX, 97).

DIONE: mother of Venus. See note *Par.* VIII, 7, XXII, 144 (VIII, 7, XXII, 144).

DIONYSIUS THE AREOPAGITE: Athenian whose conversion to Christianity by St. Paul is mentioned in Acts 18:34. See notes *Par.* X, 115–17, XXVIII, 130, 136–39 (X, 115–17, XXVIII, 130, 138).

DIONYSIUS (DIONYSIUS AGRICOLA): (1279–1325) king of Portugal, son of Alphonso III and Beatrice, daughter of Alphonso X of Castile; he married Isabella, daughter of Pedro III of Aragon. See note *Par.* XIX, 139 (XIX, 139).

DOMINIC, ST.: (1170–1221) founder of the Dominican order. See notes *Par.* XI, 28–36, 37–42, XII, 32ff (X, 95, XI, 35, 38, XII, 31–105).

DOMINIONS: fourth order of angels in the celestial hierarchies, ranking first in the second hierarchy. See note *Par.* XXVIII, 126 (XXVIII, 122).

DONATI, PICCARDA: see Piccarda Donati.

DONATI, UBERTIN: one of the Donati family of Florence who married a daughter of Bellincion Berti. See note *Par.* XVI, 115–20 (XVI, 119).

DONATUS (AELIUS DONATUS): celebrated fourth-century grammarian. See note *Par.* XII, 137–38 (XII, 137).

DYRRACHIUM (DURAZZO): the ancient Epidaninius, a town in Greek Illyria. See note *Par.* VI, 64–66 (VI, 65).

EARTHLY PARADISE: see Eden.

EBRO: a river of Spain. See note *Par.* IX, 89–90 (*Purg.* XXVII, 3; *Par.* IX, 89).

EDEN, GARDEN OF: Earthly Paradise. See notes *Par.* VII, 86–87, XXVI, 109–42, 139–42 (VII, 87, XXVI, 110, 139).

EGIDIO, ST.: see Giles.

EGYPT: symbol of life on earth. Note *Par.* XXV, 56 (XXV, 56).

ELISEO: brother of Cacciaguida. See note *Par.* XV, 136 (XV, 136).

ELYSIUM: abode of the Blessed in classical mythology. See note *Par.* XV, 25-27 (XV, 27).

EMA: a river in Tuscany. See note *Par.* XVI, 142-44 (XVI, 143).

EMPYREAN: the highest sphere, abode of the Deity. See notes *Par.* XXII, 61-65 (XXII, 61-69).

ENGLAND: see note *Par.* XIX, 121-23 (XIX, 122).

ENRICO DA SUSA (ENRICO BARTOLOMEI): (d. 1271) cardinal of Ostia (1261). See note *Par.* XII, 83 (XII, 83).

ESAU: eldest son of Isaac and Rebecca; twin brother of Jacob. See notes *Par.* VIII, 130-32, XXXII, 68-69 (XXXII, 68-69).

EUROPA: daughter of Agenor, mother of Minos, Rhadamanthus, and Sarpedon by Jupiter. See note *Par.* XXVII, 83-84 (XXVII, 84).

EVE: mother of mankind. See notes *Purg.* VIII, 99, XII, 70-77, XXIX, 26; *Par.* VII, 145-48, XIII, 39, XXXII, 4-6 (*Purg.* VIII, 99, XI, 63, XII, 71, XXIX, 24, XXX, 53; *Par.* VII, 148, XIII, 139, XXXII, 5).

FABII: ancient patrician family of Rome that claimed descent from Hercules and from the Arcadian Evander. Produced a long line of distinguished men. See note *Par.* VI, 47 (VI, 47).

FAMAGOSTA: a town in Cyprus. As a seaport it was of considerable importance in the Middle Ages. See note *Par.* XIX, 145-48 (XIX, 146).

FAZIO DA SIGNA. Florentine lawyer. See note *Par.* XVI, 56 (XVI, 56).

FELIX (DON FELIX GUZMÁN): father of St. Dominic. See note XII, 79-81 (XII, 79).

FELTRE: a town in Venetia, on the road between Bassano and Belluno. In Dante's day it was under the lordship of its own bishops. See note *Par.* IX, 52 (IX, 52).

FERDINAND IV: king of Castile and Leon (1295-1312). Some commentators think the reference is to Ferdinand's grandfather Alphonso X. See note *Par.* XIX, 125 (XIX, 125).

FERRARA: a city of Italy in the NE of Emilia. Probably the city where Cacciaguida's wife came from. See notes *Par.* IX, 56, XV, 137 (IX, 56, XV, 137).

FIESOLE: a town near Florence. See notes *Inf.* XV, 61-78; *Par.* XV, 126, XVI, 121 (*Inf.* XV, 62; *Purg.* XV, 126, XVI, 122).

FIFANTI: Ghibelline family expelled from Florence in 1258. See note *Par.* XVI, 103-104 (XVI, 104).

FIGHINE (FIGLINE): a village near Florence. See note *Par.* XVI, 50 (XVI, 50).

FILIPPI: old Florentine noble family. See note *Par.* XVI, 88-93 (XVI, 89).

FLORENCE: in Italy, on the River Arno, chief city of Tuscany and Dante's birthplace. See notes *Inf.* VI, 50, 65-75, 73, X, 88-93, XIII, 143-50, 151, XVI, 73-75, XXIV, 143-50, XXVI, 1-6, 7-9; *Purg.* XIV, 43; *Par.* IX,

127-32, XV, 100-105, 109-11, 118-20, 127-29, XVI, 25ff (*Inf.* VI, 49ff, X, 92, XIII, 143, XVI, 75, XXIV, 144, XXXVI, 1; *Purg.* VI, 127ff, XIV, 51, XX, 75, XXIII, 100; *Par.* IX, 127, XV, 97-129, XVI, 25-154, XXXI, 39).

FOLQUET (FOLCO) OF MARSEILLES: (fl. 1180-1195) troubadour poet. See notes *Par.* IX, 67-68ff (IX, 67-142).

FRANCIS, ST., OF ASSISI: (1182-1226) founder of the Franciscan Order, the Frati Minori. See notes *Par.* XI, 49-54, XIII, 32, XXXII, 34-36 (*Inf.* XXVII, 112; *Par.* XI, 38-117, XIII, 33, XXII, 90, XXXII, 35).

FREDERICK II: (1194-1250) emperor of the Hohenstaufen dynasty. Born at Sesi near Ancona, called "Stupor Mundi" (the "Wonder of the World") by his contemporaries for his multifarious and eccentric brilliance. See notes to *Inf.* X, 119-20, XIII, 58-78, 68-72, XXIII, 64-66; *Par.* III, 119-20 (*Inf.* X, 119, XIII, 59, XXIII, 66; *Par.*, III, 120).

FREDERICK II: (1272-1337) king of Sicily (1296-1337); third son of Peter III of Aragon. On the death of Alfonso II in 1291, James, the second brother, succeeded to the throne of Aragon, leaving Sicily to Frederick, the youngest, but a few years later, ignoring this arrangement, he tried (at the instigation of Pope Boniface VIII) to hand Sicily over to Charles II (of Anjou), king of Naples. The Sicilians rose in protest, renounced their allegiance to James, and offered the Crown to Frederick, who succeeded in holding it against all comers. Frederick seems to have been an excellent and well-loved ruler. He assisted the Emperor Henry VII against Robert of Naples, but after Henry's death, ceased to interest himself in Italian affairs, devoting himself exclusively to the defense of Sicily. See notes *Purg.* VII, 119; *Par.* XIX, 131 (*Purg.* VII, 119; *Par.* XIX, 130-35).

GABRIEL: archangel; the angel of the Annunciation. See notes *Purg.* X, 34-45; *Par.* IX, 137-38, XIV, 36, XXIII, 94-96, XXXII, 94-96, 110, 111, 112-14 (*Purg.* X, 34-45; *Par.* IV, 47, IX, 138, XIV, 36, XXIII, 94-108, XXXII, 103-14).

GAETA: a town in southern Italy in the north of Campania, situated on a promontory at the head of the Gulf of Gaeta. See notes *Inf.* XXVI, 92-93; *Par.* VIII, 61-63 (*Inf.* XXVI, 92; *Par.* VIII, 62).

GALICIA: a province in Spain. See note *Par.* XXV, 17-18 (XXV, 18).

GALIGAIO: member of an old Florentine family. See note *Par.* XVI, 101, 103-104 (XVI, 101).

GALLI: an old Ghibelline family of Florence. See note *Par.* XVI, 103-104 (XVI, 103).

GALLUZZO: a borough of Florence. See note *Par.* XVI, 54 (XVI, 54).

GANGALANDI: one of the Florentine families who received knighthood from Hugh Brandenburg. See note *Par.* XVI, 127-32 (XII, 127-32).

GANGES: a river of India regarded as eastern limit of horizon, reckoned from the meridian of Jerusalem. See notes *Purg.* II, 1-6, XXVII, 1-6 (*Purg.* II, 5, XXVII, 4; *Par.* XI, 51).

GEMINI: constellation of the Twins (sun in Gemini mid-May to mid-June). See notes *Purg.* IV, 61; *Par.* XXII, 112-23, 113-14, 115-16 (*Purg.* IV, 61; *Par.* XXII, 112-23).

GENOA/GENOESE: a city on the northern coast of Italy (*Par.* IX, 90).

GIANDONATI: one of the Florentine families who received knighthood from Hugh of Brandenburg (q.v.). See note *Par.* XVI, 127-32 (XVI, 127-32).

GIANO DELLA BELLA: famous Florentine tribune who, though of noble birth, brought into effect the "Ordinamenti di Giustizia" (Ordinances of Justice) restricting the power of the nobles in Florence. See note *Par.* XVI, 127-32 (XVI, 131-32).

GILES, ST. (EGIDIO) OF ASSISI: one of the three earliest followers of St. Francis. See note *Par.* XI, 83 (XI, 83).

GIOVANNA: mother of St. Dominic. See note *Par.* XII, 79-81 (XII, 80).

GIUDI: old Florentine family. See note *Par.* XVI, 122-23 (XVI, 122).

GIUOCHI: Ghibelline family who held office in Florence in the twelfth century. See note *Par.* XVI, 103-104 (XVI, 104).

GLAUCUS: fisherman of Anthedon in Boeotia. See note *Par.* I, 67-69 (I, 68).

GOAT: constellation of Capricorn (sun in Capricorn mid-December to mid-January). See note *Purg.* XXVII, 69 (*Purg.* IV, 56; *Par.* XXVII, 69).

GODFREY (GOTTIFREDI): duke, leader of the First Crusade. See note *Par.* XVIII, 47 (XVIII, 47).

GRATIAN (FRANCISCUS GRATIANUS): founder of the science of canon law. See note *Par.* X, 103-105 (X, 103).

GRECI: old noble family of Florence. See note *Par.* XVI, 88-93, (XVI, 89).

GREGORY, ST. (GREGORY I, THE GREAT): (c. 540-604) pope. Educated for law and was prefect of Rome for three years, but on his father's death he retired from public life and devoted his fortune to founding monasteries and charitable institutions, eventually becoming a monk in the Order of St. Benedict. About 579 he was made abbot and in 590 he was elected pope. He was an active and rigorous pontiff, checking the Lombard aggressions, lightening up ecclesiastical discipline in France and Italy, and constantly fighting paganism and heresy. His writings include the *Moralia* (a commentary on Job), *Homilies* (on Ezekiel and the Gospels), the *Dialogues,* and *Letters.* See notes *Purg.* X, 75; *Par.* XVIII, 133 (*Purg.* X, 75; *Par.* XXVIII, 133).

GUALDO: a town near Perugia. See note *Par.* XI, 43-48 (XI, 47).

GUALTEROTTI: Florentine noble Guelf family. See note *Par.* XVI, 133-35 (XVI, 133).

GUGLIELMO: see William.

GUIDI: a great Lombard family, with possessions in Tuscany and Romagna; their castle was in Romena. Dante mentions several of them in the *Inferno.* See note *Par.* XVI, 64 (XVI, 64).

GUINEVERE: wife of king Arthur. See note *Par.* XVI, 13-15 (XVI, 15).

HAAKON: king of Norway (1299-1319). See note XIX, 139 (XIX, 139).

HANNIBAL: (c. 247-183 B.C.) Carthaginian general. Son of Hamilcar Barca; the great adversary of Rome. Having overrun Spain, he entered Italy and, in the second Punic War, defeated the Romans at the battles of Lake Trasimeno (217 B.C.) and Cannae (216 B.C.). Eventually defeated by Scipio Africanus Major, he killed himself to avoid capture. See notes *Inf.* XXVIII, 7-12, XXXI, 123; *Par.* VI, 50, (*Inf.* XXXI, 117; *Par.* VI, 50).

HEBREWS (JEWS): see notes *Par.* V, 49-51, VII, 47 (*Purg.* IV, 84; *Par.* V, 49, VII, 47, XXIX, 102).

HECTOR: son of King Priam of Troy. Chief of the Trojan heroes in the *Iliad*, he was killed by Achilles. See notes *Inf.* IV, 122; *Par.* VI, 68 (*Inf.* IV, 122; *Par.* VI, 68).

HELICE (CALLISTO): mother of Arras, the Little Bear. See note *Par.* XXXI, 32 (XXXI, 32).

HENRY II OF LUSIGNAN: king of Cyprus. See note *Par.* XIX, 145-48 (XIX, 147-48).

HENRY VII: (1268-1313) emperor. Elected as Henry VII in 1308 at the insistence of Pope Clement V in opposition to the French candidate, Charles of Valois: crowned at Aix, 1309. The following year he sent ambassadors to Florence announcing that he intended to come to Italy to receive the imperial crown. This had been neglected for sixty years. He was a prince of great parts and piety, eager to heal the internecine feuds which devastated Italy, and to unite the empire under a just rule. Because of opposition and the withdrawal of the pope's support he was unsuccessful. He died at Buonconvento near Siena on August 24, 1313. See note *Par.* XVII, 82, XXX, 136-37 (XVII, 82, XXX, 137).

HERCULES (HERACLES): in classical mythology, a demigod renowned for his enormous strength; the son of Zeus by Alcmene, the wife of Amphitryon. Of his famous twelve labors, two are mentioned in the *Inferno* (see Hercules in *Inferno* glossary). See notes *Inf.* XII, 67-69, XXV, 25-33, XXVI, 108, XXXI, 131-32; *Par.* IX, 100-102 (*Inf.* XXV, 32, XXVI, 108, XXXI, 132; *Par.* IX, 101).

HEZEKIAH: king of Judah. See note *Par.* XX, 49-54 (XX, 49-54).

HIPPOLYTUS (IPPOLITO): son of Theseus and Hippolyte, queen of the Amazons. See note *Par.* XVII, 46-48 (XVII, 46).

HUGH OF BRANDENBURG (UGO DI BRANDENBORGO): marquis and vicar of Emperor Otto III. Said to have conferred knighthoods on six Florentine families. See note to *Par.* XVI, 127-32 (XVI, 127-32).

HUGH OF ST. VICTOR (UGO DI SAN VITTORE): mystic and theologian of the twelfth century. See note *Par.* XII, 133 (XII, 133).

HUNGARY: In Dante's day and for two centuries after his death, Hungary was an independent kingdom. The first king was St. Stephen (1000-1038), and the last king of his line, Andrew III (1290-1301), was on the throne at the assumed date of the action of the *Comedy*. Charles Martel, the friend of Dante, on the death of his mother's brother, Ladislas, became titular king of Hungary and was crowned at Naples, but never reigned, the kingdom being seized by Andrew III, first cousin of his mother's father. The crown, however, eventually came to the son of Charles Martel (Charles Robert), who reigned 1308-1342. See note *Par.* XIX, 142-43 (XIX, 142).

HYPERION: father of Helios. See note *Par.* XXII, 142-43 (XXII, 142).

ICARUS: son of Daedalus. See note *Par.* VIII, 126 (VIII, 126).

ILLUMINATO, DA RIETI: one of St. Francis's earliest followers. See note *Par.* XII, 130 (XII, 130).

IMPORTUNI: old Florentine noble family. See note *Par.* XVI, 133-35 (XVI, 133).

INFANGATI: Florentine family. See note *Par.* XVI, 122-23 (XVI, 123).

INNOCENT III: pope. See note *Par.* XI, 92 (XI, 92).

IPHIGENIA: daughter of Agamemnon and Clytemnestra. See note *Par.* V, 69-72 (V, 70).

IPPOLITO: see Hippolytus.

IRIS: daughter of Thaumas and Electra, originally the personification of the rainbow, she was regarded as the messenger of the gods (among later writers) and of Juno in particular. See notes *Purg.* XXI, 50; *Par.* XII, 12, XXVIII, 31-33 (*Purg.* XXI, 50; *Par.* XII, 12, XXVIII, 32).

ISAIAH: Old Testament prophet. See note *Par.* XXV, 91-93 (XXV, 91).

ISÈRE (ISARA): a river of France. See note *Par.* VI, 58-60 (VI, 59).

ISIDORE, ST., OF SEVILLE (ISIDORUS HISPALENSIS): distinguished ecclesiastic. See note *Par.* X, 131 (X, 131).

JACOB (ISRAEL): the Patriarch, twin brother of Esau. See notes *Par.* VIII, 130-32, XXII, 70-72, XXXII, 68-69 (*Inf.* IV, 59; *Par.* VIII, 130, XXII, 70, XXXII, 68-69).

JAMES: king of the Balearic Islands, youngest son of James I of Aragon and brother of Peter III. Referred to as uncle of Frederick of Aragon. See note *Par.* XIX, 137 (XIX, 137).

JAMES II: king of Sicily and later of Aragon, second son of Peter III of Aragon. On Peter's death in 1285 his eldest son, Alfonso, succeeded to the crown of Aragon and James to that of Sicily. When Alfonso died in 1291, James succeeded to Aragon, leaving the government of Sicily in the hands of the youngest brother, who became King Frederick II. James died at Barcelona in 1327. See notes *Purg.* VII, 119; *Par.* XIX, 137 (*Purg.* VII, 119; *Par.* XIX, 137).

JAMES, ST: the Apostle. See notes *Purg.* XXXII, 43-84; *Par.* XXV, 17-18, 28-33, 33, 38, 53-54, 76, 76-78, 81, 82-84, XXVII, 10 (*Purg.* XXXII, 76; *Par.* XXV, 17-99, XXVII, 1-75).

JANUS: an ancient Roman deity. See note *Par.* VI, 79-81 (VI, 79-81).

JASON: Greek hero who led the Argonauts to fetch the Golden Fleece. See notes *Inf.* XVIII, 86-96; *Par.* II, 16-18 (*Inf.* XVIII, 86; *Par.* II, 17).

JEPHTHAH: the Gileadite, judge of Israel. See note *Par.* V, 66 (V, 66).

JEROME, ST.: father of the Latin Church. See note *Par.* XXIX, 37-42 (XXIX, 37).

JERUSALEM: see note *Par.* XXV, 56 (*Purg.* IV, 68; *Par.* XXV, 56).

JESUS CHRIST: see Christ.

JEWS: see Hebrews.

JOACHIM OF FLORA: abbot of Calabria. See note *Par.* XII, 140 (XII, 140).

JOHN, ST.: the Apostle and Evangelist. See notes *Purg.* XXIX, 150, XXXII, 73-84; *Par.* IV, 29-30, XXIV, 125-26, XXV, 100-102, 112-13, 114, 112-29, XXVI, 1-81, 19, 44, XXXII, 127-30. Reference to Revelations (Dante would have regarded him as the author) XXV, 94-6 (*Purg.* XXIX, 105, XXXII, 76; *Par.* IV, 29, XXIV, 126, XXV, 100-129, XXVI, 1-69, XXXII, 127-29, XXV, 94).

JOHN THE BAPTIST, ST.: forerunner of Christ; patron saint of Florence. See notes *Inf.* XIII, 143-50, XXX, 61-75; *Purg.* XXII, 151, 154; *Par.* IV, 29-30, XVI, 25, XXXII, 31-33 (*Inf.* XIII, 143, XXX, 74; *Purg.* XXII, 152; *Par.* IV, 29, XVI, 25, XXXII, 31).

JOHN THE BAPTIST, ST., BAPTISTRY OF: in Florence. See notes *Par.* XVI, 47-8, XXV, 7-9 (XV, 134, XVI, 47, XXV, 9).

JOHN XXII (JACQUES DUESE): (1244-1334) pope, born at Cahors in Guienne. Succeeded Clement V (after a vacancy of more than two years) in August 1316; died at Avignon. See note *Par.* XXVII, 58 (XXVII, 58).

JORDAN: a river of Palestine. See notes *Purg.* XVIII, 133-35; *Par.* XXII, 94-96 (*Purg.* XVIII, 135; *Par.* XXII, 94).

JOSHUA: son of Nun. See notes *Purg.* XX, 109; *Par.* IX, 125, XVIII, 37 (*Purg.* XX, 110; *Par.* IX, 125, XVIII, 37).

JOVE (JUPITER): the Roman deity; identified with the Greek Zeus, the son of Cronos and Rhea, "father of the gods and men," and chief of the Olympian deities. His spouse was Juno (Greek Hera) and his weapon the thunderbolt. See notes *Purg.* XXIX, 118, XXXII, 109-17; *Par.* XIV, 51-60, XXXI, 19-127, 44-45, 77, 124. (*Inf.* XIV, 52, XXX, 45, 92; *Purg.* XXIX, 120, XXXII, 112; *Par.* IV, 63 (for planet and sphere bearing his name, see Jupiter).

JUBA: son of Hiempsal, king of Numidiah; he supported Pompey against Caesar. After the death of Pompey he joined Marcus Porcius Cato and Metellus Scipio. When the latter was defeated by Caesar and Thapsus, he committed suicide (46 B.C.). See note *Par.* VI, 70-72 (VI, 70).

JUDITH: heroine of the Book of Judith in the Apocrypha. See note *Par.* XXXII, 10 (XXXII, 10).

JULIUS CAESAR: see Caesar (Caius Julius).

JUNO (HERA): goddess, wife of Jove. See notes *Inf.* XXX, 1-12; *Par.* XII, 12 (*Inf.* XXX, 1; *Par.* XII, 12).

JUPITER: Roman deity; see Jove.

JUPITER: planet; sixth in order from the earth, between Mars and Saturn. See notes *Par.* XVIII, 64-66, 68-69, 70, 95-96, 115, 116-17, XX, 17, XXII,

145-47, XXVII, 13-15 (XVIII, 68, 70, 95, 115, 116-17, XX, 17, XXII, 145-47, XXVII, 13-15).

JUPITER, SPHERE OF: *Par.* XVIII-XX, and notes.

JUSTINIAN: surnamed the "Great" Emperor of Constantinople, 527-565. Chiefly renowned for his great codification of the Roman law. His *Corpus Juris Civilis* makes up the "Roman law" as received in Europe. See notes *Purg.* VI, 88; *Par.* VI, 10, 12, 14-15, 19-21, 25, 28 (*Purg.* VI, 88; *Par.* V, 115-39, VI, 1ff).

LA MALTA: see Malta.

LAMBERTI: Florentine family. See note *Par.* XVI, 110-11 (XVI, 110-11).

LAPO SALTERELLO: Florentine lawyer and judge. See note *Par.* XV, 127-29 (XV, 127).

LATERAN: palace that in Dante's time was the residence of the pope. See note *Par.* XXXI, 35 (XXXI, 35).

LATONA (LETO): mother of Apollo and Diana by Jove. See notes *Purg.* XX, 130; *Par.* X, 67-69, XXII, 139-41, XXIX, 1 (*Purg.* XX, 130; *Par.* X, 67, XXII, 139, XXIX, 1).

LAVINIA: daughter of Latinus and wife of Aeneas. See notes *Inf.* IV, 124-26; *Purg.* XVII, 35; *Par.* VI, 3 (*Inf.* IV, 126; *Purg.* XVII, 34-37; *Par.* VI, 3).

LAWRENCE, ST.: martyr. See note *Par.* IV, 83 (IV, 83).

LEDA: daughter of Thestius, wife of Tyndareus, king of Sparta, and mother by Jove of Castor and Pollux and Helen. See note *Par.* XXVII, 98 (XXVII, 98).

LINUS: second pope. See note *Par.* XXVII, 41 (XXVII, 41).

LOIRE: a river of France. The Italian original is Era, which some have taken to be the Saône, from the Latin Arar. See note *Par.* VI, 58-60 (VI, 59).

LOMBARD, PETER: see Peter Lombard.

LUCIA (ST. LUCY): traditionally associated with the special gifts of the Holy Ghost, along with Mary and Beatrice. Together they may indicate an analogue of the Holy Trinity, Father, Son, and Spirit, or in St. Hilary's phrase, Basis, Image, and Gift: Mary the absolute Theotokos, the basis; Beatrice the derived God-bearer, the image; Lucia the messenger, the Gift. Also associated with illuminating grace. See note *Inf.* II, 49-142; *Purg.* IX, 55; *Par.* XXXII, 137-38 (*Inf.* II, 97; *Purg.* IX, 55, 88; *Par.* XXXII, 137).

LUCRETIA: wife of Lucius Tarquinius Collatinus. Having been violated by Tarquin, the son of Tarquinius Superbus, she stabbed herself, calling upon Collatinus to avenge her. See notes *Inf.* IV, 127-29; *Par.* VI, 40-42 (*Inf.* IV, 128; *Par.* VI, 41).

LUNI: an Italian town near Carrara. See note *Inf.* XX, 46-51; *Par.* XVI, 73 (*Inf.* XX, 47; *Par.* XVI, 73).

MACARIUS, ST.: probably St. Macarius the Younger, of Alexandria. See note *Par.* XXII, 49 (XXII, 49).

MACCABEES: Judas Maccabeus, great Jewish warrior whose valor is glorified in the Book of Maccabees (I, III, 3-4). See note *Par.* XVIII, 40 (XVIII, 40).

MAGRA: a small river in Tuscany. See note *Par.* IX, 89-90 (IX, 89).

MAIA: daughter of Atlas and Perone; mother of Mercury by Jove (Jupiter). See note *Par.* XXII, 144 (XXII, 144).

MALEHAUT, DAME DE: one of Queen Guinevere's companions. See note *Par.* XVI, 13-15 (XVI, 14-15).

MALTA: name of ecclesiastical prison, probably on Lake Bolsena. See note *Par.* IX, 53-54 (IX, 53).

MARS: god of war; ancient patron of Florence. See notes *Inf.* XIII, 143-50, XXXI, 49-57; *Par.* IV, 52-63, VIII, 130-32, XVI, 47-48, 145-47 (*Inf.* XIII, 144, XXIV, 145, XXXI, 51; *Purg.* XII, 31; *Par.* IV, 63, VIII, 132, XVI, 47, 146-47).

MARS: fifth planet, according to the Ptolemaic system. See notes *Par.* IV, 52-63, XIV, 97-102, XXII, 145-47, XXVII, 13-15 (*Purg.* II, 14; *Par.* IV, 63, XIV, 100, XXII, 146, XXVII, 14).

MARS, SPHERE OF: See notes *Par.* XIV-XVIII.

MARSYAS: satyr of Phrygia who challenged Apollo to a musical contest. See note *Par.* I, 20-21 (I, 20).

MARY: Blessed Virgin; mother of Christ (see *Purg.* glossary for examples from her life). See notes *Par.* IV, 30, XV, 133, XXIII, 73-75, 88-90, 92, 101, 103-105, 121-26, 128, 139, XXXI, 100, 115-20, 123, 127, 133-35, 136-38, XXXII, 4-6, XXXIII, 1-39 (Prayer of St. Bernard), 40-42, 44-45, IV, 30, XIV, 36, XV, 133, XXI, 122, XXIII, 73-75, 88-111, 118-26, 128, XXXI, 100, 116-42, XXXII, 4, XXXIII, 1-39 (Prayer of St. Bernard), 39-45.

MATTHEW D' ACQUASPARTA: general of the Franciscan order. See note *Par.* XII, 125 (XII, 125).

MEDITERRANEAN: regarded as the largest expanse of water other than the great Ocean. See note *Par.* IX, 84 (VIII, 63, IX, 84).

MELCHIZEDEK: priest and king of Salem (Gen 14:18). See note *Par.* VIII, 124-25 (VIII, 125).

MELISSUS: philosopher of Samos. See note *Par.* XIII, 125 (XIII, 125).

MERCURY: god of commerce; messenger of the gods. See note *Par.* IV, 63 (IV, 63).

MERCURY: second planet from the earth, according to the Ptolemaic system. See notes *Par.* IV, 63, V, 91-93, 94-96, 97-99, VI, 112-14, XXII, 144 (IV, 63, V, 93, VI, 112, XXII, 144).

MERCURY, SPHERE OF: second heaven, presided over by Archangels. See notes *Par.* V, 91-93ff, VII, passim.

MICHAEL, ST.: the Archangel, chief of the Angelic Host. See notes *Inf.* VII, 11-12; *Purg.* XIII, 50-51 (*Inf.* VII, 11; *Purg.* XIII, 51; *Par.* IV, 47).

MILKY WAY: see note *Par.* XIV, 97-102 (XIV, 97).

MINERVA: identified with the Greek Pallas Athena. Patron deity of Athens;

goddess of wisdom. See notes *Purg.* XII, 3; *Par.* II, 8–9 (*Purg.* XII, 31, XXX, 68; *Par.* II, 8).

MINOS: in classical mythology, the legendary king of Crete, who after death became a judge in the underworld. See notes *Inf.* V, 4; *Par.* XIII, 13–15 (*Inf.* V, 4, XX, 36, XXVII, 124, XXIX, 120; *Purg.* I, 77; *Par.* XIII, 14).

MODENA: a town in northern Italy. See note *Par.* VI, 73–75 (VI, 75).

MONTEMURLO: the ancient clivus Cinnae, a hill outside Rome. See note to *Par.* XVI, 64 (XVI, 64).

MOON: the first planet from the earth, according to the Ptolemaic system. See notes *Par.* II, X, 67–69, XVI, 82–4, XXII, 139–41, XXIII, 25–27, XXVIII, 22, XXIX, 1–3, 97–102 (I, 116, II, 25ff, X, 67, XVI, 82, XXII, 139, XXIII, 26, XXVIII, 21, XXIX, 1, 97).

MOON, SPHERE OF THE: first heaven in Dante's conception of Paradise. Presided over by the angels. *Par.* II–IV.

MORONTO: brother of Cacciaguida. See notes *Par.* XV, 136 (XV, 136).

MOSES: lawgiver of Israel. See notes *Par.* XXIV, 135, XXVI, 40–42, XXXII, 131–32 (*Inf.* IV, 57; *Purg.* XXXII, 80; *Par.* IV, 29, XXIV, 136, XXVI, 41, XXXII, 131).

MUCIUS (CAIUS MUCIUS, SCEVOLA): Roman citizen, celebrated for his fortitude. See note *Par.* IV, 84 (IV, 84).

MUSES: the nine Muses, inspirers and patronesses of the arts; dwelt upon Mt. Parnassus, of which, according to Dante, one peak (Nyssa) was dedicated to them, and the other (Cyrrha) to Apollo. They were said to be daughters of Zeus (Jupiter) and Mnemosyne (Memory). See notes *Inf.* II, 7–9, XXXII, 10–12; *Purg.* I, 7–12, XXII, 105, XXIX, 37; *Par.* I, 13–36, 16–17, XVIII, 82, XXIII, 56 (*Inf.* II, 7, XXII, 10; *Purg.* I, 8, XXII, 102, 105, XXIX, 37; *Par.* I, 17, II, 9, XVIII, 82, XXIII, 56).

NATHAN: prophet (II Sam. 12:1–2). See note *Par.* XII, 136 (XII, 136).

NAVARRE: a kingdom in the Pyrenees. See notes *Inf.* XXII, 48–54, 97–132; *Par.* XIX, 143–44 (*Inf.* XXII, 48, 121; *Par.* XIX, 143).

NAZARETH: a village of Galilee. See note *Par.* IX, 137–38 (IX, 137).

NEBUCHADNEZZAR: king of Babylon (605–562 B.C.). See note *Par.* IV, 13 (IV, 13).

NEPTUNE: in Roman mythology, god of the sea. See note *Par.* XXXIII, 94–96 (*Inf.* XXVIII, 83; *Par.* XXXIII, 96).

NERLI: old Florentine noble family. See notes *Par.* XV, 115, XVI, 127–32 (XV, 115, XVI, 127–32).

NICOSIA: a town in Cyprus. See note *Par.* XIX, 145–48 (XIX, 146).

NILE: a river of Egypt. See note *Inf.* XXXIV, 38–45 (*Inf.* XXXIV, 45; *Par.* VI, 66).

NIMROD: biblical king. See notes *Inf.* XXXI, 77; *Par.* XXVI, 124–29 (*Inf.* XXXI, 77; *Par.* XXVI, 126).

NOAH: the Patriarch. See note *Par.* XII, 17–18 (*Inf.* IV, 56; *Par.* XII, 17).

NOCERA: a town near Perugia. See note *Par.* XI, 43–48 (XI, 48).

ORMANNI: old Florentine noble family. See note *Par.* XVI, 88–93 (XVI, 89).

OROSIUS, PAULUS (PAOLO OROSIO): Spanish priest and historian of the fifth century. Dante is indebted to his seven books of *Historiarum adversus Paganos,* usually known as the *Ormista,* for many points such as the story of Semiramis in the *Inferno,* and the character of Alexander the Great. See note *Par.* X, 118–20 (X, 118–20).

OSTIA: see Enrico da Susa.

PACHYMUS: a promontory at the SE extremity of Sicily. See note *Par.* VIII, 67–69 (VIII, 68).

PADUA: a town of Italy in Venetia. See notes *Inf.* XV, 7, XVII, 70; *Par.* IX, 43–48 (*Inf.* XV, 7, XVII, 70; *Par.* IX, 46).

PAEAN: see Apollo.

PALERMO: capital of Sicily. See note *Par.* VIII, 73–75 (VIII, 74).

PALLAS: son of the Trojan Evander. See note *Par.* VI, 36 (VI, 36).

PARMENIDES: Greek philosopher. See note *Par.* XIII, 124 (XIII, 124).

PARNASSUS: mountain of the Muses. See notes *Purg.* XXII, 65; *Par.* I, 16–17 (*Purg.* XXII, 65, XXXI, 140; *Par.* I, 17).

PAUL, ST.: the Apostle. See notes *Inf.* II, 10–48, 28–30; *Par.* XVIII, 133–36, XXIV, 61, 62, 64–66, 67–69, XXVI, 10–12, XXVIII, 136–39 (*Inf.* II, 28, 32; *Par.* XVIII, 131, 136, XXI, 128, XXIV, 61–66, XXVI, 10–12, XXVIII, 138).

PELORUS: a promontory at the NE extremity of Sicily. See notes *Purg.* XIV, 31; *Par.* VIII, 67–69 (*Purg.* XIV, 32; *Par.* VIII, 68).

PENEIAN FROND: the laurel into which Daphne was metamorphosed when pursued by Apollo. See note *Par.* I, 32 (I, 32).

PERA, DELLA: old Florentine noble family. See note *Par.* XVI, 124 (XVI, 126).

PERUGIA: a city of Italy in Umbria. See notes *Par.* VI, 73–75, XI, 43–48 (VI, 75, XI, 46).

PETER, ST.: the Disciple, and according to tradition, the first bishop of Rome. See notes *Inf.* I, 133–35, XIX, 94–96; *Purg.* XIII, 50–51, XIX, 99; *Par.* XVIII, 131–32, 133–36, XXIV, 37–42, 49–51, 52–57, 67–69, 103–105, 115, 125–26, 148–53, XXVII, 19–21, 22–23, 25–27, 46–54, 61–66, XXXII, 124–25, 133–35 (*Inf.* I, 134, II, 24, XIX, 91, 94; *Purg.* IX, 127, XIII, 51, XIX, 99, XXI, 23 (Peter's Vicar), XXI, 63, XXXII, 76; *Par.* IX, 141, XVIII, 131, 136, XXI, 127–29, XXII, 28, XXIV, 19–154, XXVIII, 19–66; XXXII, 125–26, 133).

PETER DAMIAN: a Church Father. See note *Par.* XXI, 121–23 (XXI, 43–135).

PETER LOMBARD: twelfth-century theologian. See note *Par.* X, 106–108 (X, 107).

PETER OF SPAIN: archbishop of Braga, cardinal bishop of Tusculum, and in 1276–1277 pope as John XXI. See note *Par.* XII, 134 (XII, 134).

PETER MANGIADOR: twelfth-century historian and ecclesiastic. See note *Par.* XII, 134 (XII, 134).

PETRUS COMESTOR: see Peter Mangiador.

PETRUS HISPANUS: see Peter of Spain.

PHAEDRA: wife of Theseus, stepmother of Hippolytus. See note *Par.* XVII, 46–48 (XVII, 47).

PHAËTHON: son of Clymene by Apollo. See notes *Inf.* XVII, 106–108; *Purg.* IV, 72, XXIX, 118; *Par.* XVII, 1 (*Inf.* XVII, 106; *Purg.* IV, 72; XXIX, 118; *Par.* XVII, 1).

PHARSALIA: a territory in Thessaly, where Julius Caesar won the decisive battle against Pompey. See note *Par.* VI, 64–66 (VI, 65).

PHILIP IV (THE FAIR): (1268–1314) king of France, second son of Philip III, reigned 1285–1314. His reign was marked by a bitter quarrel with Pope Boniface VIII which arose over the taxations of the clergy. In answer to the pope's declaration that church property was exempt from secular obligations, Philip cut off papal supplies by prohibiting the export of money and valuables from France. Boniface eventually excommunicated Philip, who replied by seizing the pope at Anagni (see notes *Purg.* XX, 87; *Purg.* XX, 86–90). After Boniface's death and the short pontificate of Benedict XI, Clement V, under Philip's influence, succeeded to the papacy, and became a mere tool in Philip's hands. During his pontificate the papal see was transferred to Avignon. See notes *Purg.* VII, 109, XX, 87, 92–93, XXXII, 148–59, 160; *Par.* XIX, 119–20 (*Purg.* VII, 109, XX, 86, XXXII, 152; *Par.* XIX, 119–20).

PICCARDA DONATI: sister of Corso and Forese Donati. See notes *Purg.* XXIV, 10; *Par.* III, 49, 69, 70–78, 85–87, 91–96 (*Purg.* XXIV, 10; *Par.* III, 34–123).

PIETRO BERNARDONE: see Bernardone, Pietro.

PIUS: second bishop of Rome. See note *Par.* XXVII, 44 (XXVII, 44).

PLATO: (c. 428–347 B.C.) the great Greek philosopher, pupil of Socrates and founder of the academic school. Most of his works had not been translated in Dante's time. Dante seems to have read only the *Timaeus,* though some of the Platonic philosophy reached him through St. Augustine. See notes *Inf.* IV, 134; *Purg.* III, 37–45, IV, 1–12; *Par.* IV, 22–24, 49, 52–63 (*Inf.* IV, 134; *Purg.* III, 43, IV, 5–6; *Par.* IV, 24, 49).

PO: a river of northern Italy. See notes *Inf.* XX, 78; *Purg.* XIV, 91, XVI, 115; *Par.* VI, 51, XI, 137 (*Inf.* V, 98, XX, 78; *Purg.* XIV, 91, XVI, 115; *Par.* VI, 51, XV, 137).

POLYHYMNIA: Muse of sacred poetry. See note *Par.* XXIII, 56 (XXIII, 56).

POMPEY (CNEIUS POMPEIUS MAGNUS): (106–48 B.C.) as a young man he was one of Sulla's most successful generals; he lost a struggle for power with Julius Caesar in the Civil War of 49 B.C. See notes *Par.* VI, 53, 64–66 (VI, 53, 72).

POWERS: sixth order of angels in the celestial hierarchies; preside over the Heaven of the Sun. See note *Par.* XXVIII, 126 (XVIII, 123).

PRAGUE: capital of Bohemia. See note *Par.* XIX, 115-17 (XIX, 117).

PRESSA, DELLA: old Ghibelline family. See note *Par.* XVI, 100 (XVI, 100).

PRIMUM MOBILE: ninth heaven in Dante's conception of Paradise. Its existence was first conceived by Pompey to account for the movement of the Heaven of the Fixed Stars. It is the highest of the revolving heavens and imparts motion to all the rest. See notes *Par.* I, 123, II, 112, XXIII, 112-17, XXVII, 99, XXX, 37-39, 106-8 (I, 123, II, 113-14, XIII, 23, XXIII, 112-17, XXVII, 99, XXX, 39, 107).

PRINCIPALITIES: seventh order of angels in the celestial hierarchies; they preside over the sphere of Venus. See notes *Par.* VIII, 35, XXVIII, 126 (VIII, 35, XXVIII, 125).

PROVENÇALS: inhabitants of Provence, former province of France, at one time independent. See note *Par.* VI, 130-32 (VI, 130).

PTOLEMY: king of Egypt. See note *Par.* VI, 69 (VI, 69).

PULCI: Florentine family. See note Par. XVI, 127-32 (XVI, 127-32).

PYRRHUS: king of Epirus. See notes *Inf.* XII, 135; *Par.* VI, 43-45 (*Inf.* XII, 135; *Par.* VI, 44).

QUINTIUS: see Cincinnatus.

RABANUS, MAURUS: archbishop of Mainz. See note *Par.* XII, 139 (XII, 139).

RACHEL: wife of the patriarch Jacob, and mother of Joseph and Benjamin. See notes *Inf.* II, 102; *Purg.* XXVII, 100-108; *Par.* XXXII, 8 (*Inf.* II, 102, IV, 60; *Purg.* XXVII, 104; *Par.* XXXII, 8).

RAHAB: whore of Jericho. See notes *Par.* IX, 115, 116-17 (IX, 115).

RAPHAEL (RAFFAELLO): archangel. See note *Par.* IV, 48 (IV, 48).

RAVENNA: a town near the mouth of the Po. See notes *Inf.* V, 97-99, XXVII, 41-42; *Par.* VI, 61-63 (*Inf.* V, 97, XXVII, 40; *Par.* VI, 61).

RAVIGNANI: old Florentine noble family. See note *Par.* XVI, 97-99 (XVI, 97).

RAYMOND BERENGER: see Berenger, Raymond.

REBECCA: wife of Isaac, mother of Jacob and Esau. See note *Par.* XXXII, 10 (XXXII, 10).

RED SEA: see notes *Inf.* XXIV, 85-90; *Purg.* XVIII, 133-35; *Par.* VI, 79-81, XXII, 94-96 (*Inf.* XXIV, 90; *Purg.* XVIII, 134; *Par.* VI, 79, XXII, 95).

RENOUARD: legendary Saracen convert. See note *Par.* XVIII, 46 (XVIII, 46).

RHINE: a river of Germany. See note *Par.* VI, 58-60 (VI, 58).

RIPHEUS: Trojan hero. See notes *Par.* XX, 68, 82, 122-23, 128, 130-32 (XX, 68, 100, 118-29).

RHODOPE: a mountain in Thrace. "She of Rhodope" is Phyllis, daughter of Sithon, king of Thrace. See note *Par.* IX, 100-102 (IX, 100).

RHONE: river of France. See note *Inf.* IX, 112–117; *Par.* VI 58–60, VIII, 58–60 (*Inf.* IX, 112; *Par.* VI, 60, VIII, 58).

RIALTO: one of the islands on which Venice is built. See note *Par.* IX, 25–27 (IX, 26).

RICHARD OF ST. VICTOR: celebrated mystic, theologian, and scholastic philosopher. See note *Par.* X, 131–32 (X, 131).

ROBERT GUISCARD: duke of Apulia and Calabria. See note *Par.* XVIII, 48 (XVIII, 48).

ROLAND: epic hero, represented in the *Comedy* as nephew of Charlemagne and one of the Twelve Peers. Many legends and poetical traditions have clustered around him. See note *Inf.* XXXI, 16–18; *Par.* XVIII, 43 (*Inf.* XXXI, 18; *Par.* XVIII, 43).

ROME, ROMANS: a city of Italy. See notes *Inf.* II, 15–21, XIV, 94–119, XV, 61–68, XXVI, 56–60, XXXI, 59; *Purg.* XXII, 145, XXXII, 100–108; *Par.* IX, 139–42, XV, 126 (*Inf.* I, 71, II, 21, 27, XIV, 105; XV, 77, XVIII, 28, XXVI, 60, XXXI, 59; *Purg.* VI, 112, XVI, 106, XIX, 107, XXI, 89, XXII, 145, XXXII, 102; *Par.* IX, 140, XV, 126, XIX, 102, XXXI, 34).

ROMUALD: founder of the Order of Reformed Benedictines. See note *Par.* XXII, 49 (XXII, 49).

ROMULUS: founder of Rome. See note *Par.* VIII, 130–32 (VIII, 131).

RUBICON: a river in northern Italy; flows into the Adriatic a few miles north of Rimini. See note *Par.* VI, 61–63 (VI, 62).

RUDOLPH I OF HAPSBURG: (1218–1291) emperor (1272–1291), eldest son of Albert IV, count of Hapsburg, founder of the imperial house of Austria. See notes *Purg.* VII, 94; *Par.* VIII, 72 (*Purg.* VI, 103; VII, 94; *Par.* VIII, 72).

RUTH: great-grandmother of David. See note *Par.* XXXII, 11–12 (XXXII, 11).

SABELLIUS: third-century theologian. See note *Par.* XIII, 127 (XIII, 127).

SACCHETTI: Guelf family of Florence. See note *Par.* XVI, 103–104 (XVI, 104).

SALTERELLO, LAPO: see Lapo Salterello.

SAMUEL: the prophet (*Par.* IV, 29).

SANNELLA, DELLA: noble family of Florence. See note *Par.* XVI, 88–93 (XVI, 92).

SAÔNE: a river of France. See Loire.

SARAH: wife of Abraham. See note *Par.* XXXII, 10 (XXXII, 10).

SARDANAPALUS: king of the Assyrian empire of Ninus. See note *Par.* XV, 107–108 (XV, 107).

SATAN: see Devil.

SATURN: seventh planet from the earth, according to the Ptolemaic system. See notes *Purg.* XIX, 3; *Par.* XXII, 145–47 (*Purg.* XIX, 2; *Par.* XXII, 146).

SATURN, SPHERE OF: seventh sphere in Dante's conception of Paradise. It is presided over by the Thrones. See *Par.* XXI-XXII, 1-99.

SCALA, BARTOLOMMEO: eldest son of Alberto della Scala. See note *Par.* XVII, 70-72 (XVII, 71-72).

SCALA, CAN FRANCESCO DELLA: (1291-1329) commonly called Can Grande; third son of Alberto della Scala. A great Ghibelline prince, a patron of the arts, and a generous friend to the exiled members of his party, including Dante. Many commentators consider him the greyhound of *Inf.* I and the DXV of *Purg.* XXXIII. See note *Par.* XVII, 76-78 (XVII, 76-78).

SCIPIO (PUBLIUS CORNELIUS SCIPIO AFRICANUS MAJOR): (c. 234-183 B.C.) Roman general. See notes *Inf.* XXXI, 115-18; *Purg.* XXIX, 115; *Par.* VI, 53, XXVII, 62 (*Inf.* XXXI, 116; *Purg.* XXIX, 115; *Par.* VI, 53, XXVII, 62).

SCOTLAND: see note *Par.* XIX, 121-23 (XIX, 122).

SEINE: a river of France. See note *Par.* VI, 58-60 (VI, 58).

SEMIFONTE: a fortress in the Valdelsa SW of Florence. See note *Par.* XVI, 61-63 (XVI, 62).

SEMELE: daughter of Cadmus, king of Thebes; mother of Bacchus by Jupiter. See notes *Inf.* XXX, 1-12; *Par.* XXI, 5 (*Inf.* XXX, 1-2; *Par.* XXI, 5).

SERAPHIM: highest order of angels in the celestial hierarchies. They preside over the Primum Mobile. See notes *Par.* IX, 77-78, XI, 37-42, XXVIII, 126 (IV, 28, IX, 77-78, XI, 37, XXVIII, 99).

SICHAEUS: uncle and husband of Dido. See notes *Inf.* V, 61-62; *Par.* IX, 97-98 (*Inf.* V, 62; *Par.* IX, 98).

SICILY: an island in the Mediterranean, divided from Italy by the Straits of Messina. See note *Par.* XIX, 131 (*Purg.* III, 116; *Par.* VIII, 70, XIX, 131).

SIGER OF BRABANT: doctor of philosophy and professor at the University of Paris. See note *Par.* X, 136-38 (X, 136).

SIGNA: see Fazio da Signa.

SILE: a small river of northern Italy in Venetia. See note IX, 49 (IX, 49).

SIMOIS: a river in the Troad. See note VI, 67 (VI, 67).

SIMON MAGUS: magician. See note *Inf.* XIX, 1-6; *Par.* XXX, 147 (*Inf.* XIX, 1; *Par.* XXX, 147).

SINIGAGLIA (SENIGALLIA): a town on the Adriatic NW of Ancona. See note *Par.* XVI, 74 (XVI, 74).

SIROCCO: east or SE wind (*Par.* VIII, 67).

SIXTUS I: third-century bishop of Rome (119-127). See note *Par.* XXVII, 44 (XXVII, 44).

SIZII: noble family of Florence. See note *Par.* XVI, 106-108 (XVI, 108).

SOLDANIERI: noble family of Florence. See note *Par.* XVI, 88-93 (XVI, 93).

SOLOMON: king of Israel. See notes *Par.* X, 109-14, XIII, 93, 97-102 (X, 109-14, XIII, 99-108, XIV, 37-60).

SOLON: Athenian legislator. See note *Par.* VIII, 124-25 (VIII, 124).

SORGUE: a river of France. See note VIII, 58-60 (VIII, 124).

SPAIN: see notes *Purg.* XVIII, 101; *Par.* VI, 64–66 (*Purg.* XVIII, 102; *Par.* VI, 64).

STEPHEN URASH II: king of Rascia (Dalmatia). See note *Par.* XIX, 140 (XIX, 140).

SUBASIO, MT.: a mountain in northern Umbria. See note *Par.* XI, 43–48 (XI, 45).

SULTAN OF EGYPT: see notes *Inf.* XXVII, 85–90; *Par.* XI, 100–105 (*Inf.* XXVII, 90, *Par.* XI, 100).

SUN, SPHERE OF THE: fourth sphere in Dante's conception of Paradise. It is presided over by the Powers. (*Par.* X, 28 to XIV, 81.)

SWABIA: ancient duchy in SW of Germany. See note *Par.* III, 119–20 (III, 119).

SYLVESTER, ST.: one of the earliest followers of St. Francis. See note *Par.* XI, 83 (XI, 83).

TAGLIAMENTO: a river of northern Italy. See note *Par.* IX, 43–48 (IX, 44).

THADDEUS OF ALDEROTTO: thirteenth-century physician. See note *Par.* XII, 83 (XII, 83).

THOMAS AQUINAS, ST.: see Aquinas.

THRONES: third order of angels in the celestial hierarchies. They preside over the sphere of Saturn. See notes *Par.* IX, 61–63, XXVIII, 126 (IX, 61, XXVIII, 104).

TIBER: the river on which Rome stands. See notes *Inf.* XXVII, 29–30; *Purg.* II, 103 (*Inf.* XXVII, 30; *Purg.* II, 103; *Par.* XI, 106).

TIMAEUS: name of a work by Plato. See note *Par.* IV, 49 (IV, 49).

TITUS (FLAVIUS SABINUS VESPASIANUS): Roman emperor. See notes *Purg.* XXI, 82; *Par.* VI, 92–93 (*Purg.* XXI, 82, *Par.* VI, 92).

TOBIT: name given in the English version of the Vulgate to the Jew who was healed of blindness by the archangel Raphael. See note *Par.* IV, 48 (IV, 48).

TOPINE: a stream in Umbria. See note *Par.* XI, 43–48 (XI, 43).

TORQUATUS (TITUS MANLIUS): Roman hero. See note *Par.* VI, 46 (VI, 46).

TOSINGHI: Florentine family. See note *Par.* XVI, 112–14 (XVI, 112–14).

TRAJAN (MARCUS ULPIUS TRAJANUS): (c. 53–117) Roman emperor (98–117). A good commander, victorious in wars against the Dacians and the Parthians, and as a ruler well liked for love of justice and his simple life. See notes *Purg.* X, 73–93, 75; *Par.* XX, 44–48, 103–105, 106, 108, 109, 112–14 (*Purg.* X, 76; *Par.* XX, 44–48, 106–107, 146–48).

TRESPIANO: a borough of Florence. See note *Par.* XVI, 54 (XVI, 54).

TRINACRIA: name used by Virgil and other Latin poets for Sicily.

TRIVIA: name given to Diana (or the moon). See note *Par.* XXIII, 25–27 (XXIII, 26).

TRONTO: a river of central Italy. See note *Par.* VIII, 61–63 (VIII, 63).

TROY (ILIUM, ILION): an ancient coast town in Asia Minor. Troy was taken and sacked by the Greeks under Agamemnon, after ten years' siege for the recovery of Helen. The siege is described in Homer's *Iliad* and the sack in Virgil's *Aeneid*. See notes *Inf.* XXX, 98; *Purg.* XII, 25–63; *Par.* XV, 126 (*Inf.* I, 74, XXX, 22, 98, 114; *Purg.* XII, 61, 62; *Par.* XV, 126).

TUSCANY, TUSCANS: a region of Italy which mostly lies between the Apennines and the Mediterranean, extending roughly from the Gulf of Genoa in the north to Orbitello in the south. The Arno is its major river, and Florence, Dante's birthplace, is its chief city. See notes *Inf.* X, 22–27, XXVIII, 106–108 (*Inf.* X, 22, XXII, 97, XXIII, 76, 91, XXIV, 123, XXVIII, 108, XXXII, 66; *Purg.* XI, 58, 110; XIII, 149; XIV, 16, 103, 124; *Par.* XXII, 117).

TYPHOEUS: hundred-headed monster. See note *Par.* VIII, 70 (VIII, 70).

UBALDO, ST.: bishop of Gubbio. See note *Par.* XI, 43–48 (XI, 44).

UBERTI: famous Ghibelline family of which Farinata (*Inf.* X) was a member. See note *Par.* XVI, 109–10 (XVI, 109–10).

UCCELLATOIO, MT.: a hill outside Florence. See note *Par.* XV, 109–11 (XV, 109).

UGHI: Florentine noble family. See note *Par.* XVI, 88–93 (XVI, 88).

UGO DI BRANDENBORGO: see Hugh of Brandenburg.

UGO DI SAN VITTORE: see Hugh of St. Victor.

ULYSSES (ODYSSEUS): prince of Ithaca; hero of Greek mythology, renowned for his cunning. His exploits at the siege of Troy are recounted in Homer's *Iliad* and his wanderings in the *Odyssey*. See notes *Inf.* XXVI, 55–57; *Purg.* XIX, 22; *Par.* XXVII, 82–83 (*Inf.* XXVI, 55; *Purg.* XIX, 22; *Par.* XXVII, 83).

URBAN I: bishop of Rome (222–230). See note *Par.* XXVII, 44 (XXVII, 44).

URBISAGLIA (URBS SALVIA): once an important town. See note *Par.* XVI, 73 (XVI, 73).

URSA MAJOR, URSA MINOR: see Bears.

VALDIGREVE: a small river in Tuscany. See note *Par.* XVI, 66 (XVI, 66).

VAR: a river of southern France. See note *Par.* VI, 58–60 (VI, 58).

VATICAN: Vatican hill in Rome. See note *Par.* IX, 139–42 (IX, 139).

VECCHIO, DEL: old Florentine noble family. See note *Par.* XV, 115 (XV, 115).

VENUS: goddess of love. See notes *Purg.* XXVIII, 64; *Par.* VIII, 1–2 (*Purg.* XXVIII, 64; *Par.* VIII, 1–2).

VENUS: third planet from the earth according to the Ptolemaic system. See notes *Purg.* I, 13–30, XXV, 130–31, XXVII, 94; *Par.* VIII, 1–2, 12, IX, 33–36, XXII, 144 (*Purg.* I, 19, XXV, 132; XXVII, 94; *Par.* VIII, 2, 11–12, IX, 33, XXII, 144).

VENUS, SPHERE OF: third sphere in Dante's conception of Paradise. It is presided over by the Principalities. *Par.* VIII and IX.

VERDE: a river of Italy, now the Garigliano. See note *Par.* VIII, 61–63 (*Purg.* III, 131; *Par.* VIII, 63).

VERONA: a city of Italy in Venetia. See notes *Inf.* XV, 123–24, XX, 67–69; *Par.* XVII, 70–72 (*Inf.* XV, 122, XX, 68; *Purg.* XVIII, 118; *Par.* XVII, 70).

VERONICA, ST.: reference is made to her veil, believed to bear the impression of Christ's face. See note *Par.* XXXI, 103–108 (XXXI, 104).

VICENZA: a city of Italy in Venetia (*Par.* IX, 47).

VIRGIL (PUBLIUS VERGILIUS MARO): (70–19 B.C.) Roman poet, born near Mantua. Writer of the *Aeneid,* which tells the story of Aeneas and celebrates the origins of the Roman people and empire (see Aeneas). His fourth Eclogue was accepted as a prophecy of Christ's birth. In medieval legend he had the reputation of being a white magician. In the *Comedy* he generally stands for human reason, guiding Dante through Hell and accompanying him through Purgatory. See *Inferno* and *Purgatory.* See note *Par.* XV, 25–28 (XV, 26, XVII, 19, XXVI, 120).

VIRGIN MARY: see Mary.

VIRTUES: the fifth order of angels in the celestial hierarchies. They preside over the Sphere of Mars. See note *Par.* XXVIII, 126 (XXVIII, 123).

VISDOMINI: old Florentine family. See note *Par.* XVI, 112–14 (XVI 112–14).

WAIN: see Bears.

WENCESLAS IV: king of Bohemia (1278–1305). See notes *Purg.* VII, 101; *Par.* XIX, 125 (*Purg.* VII, 101; *Par.* XIX, 125).

WILLIAM: count of Orange; defender of Christendon. See note *Par.* XVIII, 46 (XVIII, 46).

WILLIAM II: king of Sicily and Naples (1166–1189). See note *Par.* XX, 61–62 (XX, 62).

XERXES: king of Persia (485–465 B.C.); the story of his marriage to the Jewess Esther is told in the Bible. See notes *Purg.* XXVIII, 71; *Par.* VIII, 124–25 (*Purg.* XXVIII, 71; *Par.* VIII, 124).

ZEPHYR: the west wind. See note *Par.* XII, 46 (XII, 46).

SELECTED BIBLIOGRAPHY

All classical Greek and Latin texts cited are those of
the Loeb Classical Library unless otherwise stated.

Aglianò, Sebastiano. "Restauro di *Paradiso XVI*, 1 – 15, Note e Discussioni." *La Bibliofilia* 69 (1967): 191 – 223.

Albèrtus Magnus. *Opera omnia*. Edited by Auguste and Emile Borgnet. Paris, 1890 – 99.

Alighieri, Dante. *La Commedia secondo l'antica vulgata*. Edited by Giorgio Petrocchi. Vol I: *Introduzione*. Vol. IV: *Paradiso*. Milan, 1966, 1967.

_____. *Le opere di Dante: Testo critico della Società Dantesca Italiana*. 2nd ed. Florence, 1960.

Anderson, Donald M. *The Art of Written Forms: The Theory and Practice of Calligraphy*. New York, 1969.

Anonimo fiorentino. *Commento alla Divina Commedia d'anonimo fiorentino del secolo XIV*. Edited by Pietro Fanfani. Vol. III, 1874.

Aquinas, Thomas. *Opera omnia*. Parma, 1852 – 73. Photolithographic reimpression, with Introduction by Vernon J. Bourke, New York, 1948 – 50.

_____. *On the Truth of the Catholic Faith, Summa contra Gentiles*. Garden City, N.Y., 1955 – 57.

_____. *Summa theologica*. Translated by Fathers of the English Dominican Province. 3 vols. New York, 1947 – 48.

Aristotle. "Antiqua Translatio." In Thomas Aquinas, *Opera omnia*.

_____. *Meteorologica*. In Thomas Aquinas, *In Aristotelis libros De caelo et mundo, De generatione et corruptione, Meteorologicorum expositio*. Ed. Raimondo M. Spiazzi, O.P. Turin, 1952.

_____. *Nicomachean Ethics*. In Thomas Aquinas, *Commentary on the Nicomachean Ethics*, translated by C.I. Litzinger, O.P. 2 vols. Chicago, 1964.

Auerbach, Eric. "Dante's Addresses to the Reader." *Romance Philology* VII (1954): 268 – 78.

Augustine. *St. Augustine's Confessions*. Translated by William Watts (1631), preface by W.H.D. Rouse. 2 vols. LCL, 1912.

_____. *Ad Marcellinum De civitate Dei contra paganos*. In Migne, *P.L.* XLI.

Baldacci, Osvaldo. "I quattro cerchi e le tre croci in *Par.* I, 38." *Cultura neolatina* 25(1965): 53 – 61.

Beall, Chandler B. "Dante and His Reader." *Forum Italicum* 13(1979): 299–343.

Benvenuto da Imola. *Comentum super Dantis Aldigherij Comoediam*. Edited Giacomo Filippo Lacaita. Vols IV, V. Florence, 1887.

Bergin, Thomas G. *A Diversity of Dante*. Rutgers University Press, 1969.

Bernard of Clairvaux. *De diligendo Deo*. In Migne, *P.L.* CLXXXII.

————. *Meditationes piissimae de cognitione humanae conditionis*. In Migne, *P.L.* CLXXXIV.

————. *Sermones de diversis*. In Migne, *P.L.* CLXXXIII.

————. *Sermones de tempore*. In Migne, *P.L.* CLXXXIII.

————. *Sermones in Cantica Canticorum*. In Migne, *P.L.* CLXXXIII.

Boethius. *The Consolation of Philosophy*. In *The Theological Tractates*, ed. and trans. H. F. Stewart and E. K. Rand; *The Consolation of Philosophy*, trans. "I.T." (1609). Revised by H. F. Stewart, pp. 128–411. LCL, 1962.

————. *De institutione musica*. In *De institutione arithmetica; De institutione musica*, ed. Gottfried Friedlein, pp. 175–371. Leipzig, 1867.

————. *The Theological Tractates; The Consolation of Philosophy*. Edited and translated by H. F. Stewart and E. K. Rand. Cambridge, Mass., 1962.

Bonaventure. *Opera omnia*, ed. PP. Collegii a S. Bonaventura. Quaracchi, 1882–1902:
  Itinerarium mentis in Deum, vol. V
  Legenda sancti Francisci, vol. VIII
  Soliloquium de quatuor mentalibus exercitiis, vol. VIII

Bosco, Umberto and Reggio, Giovanni. *La Divina Commedia: Paradiso*. Le Monnier, 1982.

Busnelli, Giovanni. *Il concetto e l'ordine del 'Paradiso' dantesco. Parte I: Il concetto*. Città di Castello, 1911.

Buti, Francesco da. *Commento di Francesco da Buti sopra la Divina Comedia di Dante Allighieri*. Edited by Crescentino Giannini. Vol. III. Pisa, 1862.

Carroll, John S. *In Patria*. London, 1971.

Casini, T. and Barbi, S. A. *La Divina Commedia di Dante Alighieri*. 6th edition. Florence, 1926.

Chimenz, Siro A. *La Divina Commedia di Dante Alighieri*. Turin, 1968.

Contini, Gianfranco. *Il canto XXVIII del Paradiso*. Florence, 1965.

Corti, Maria. *Dante a un nuovo crocevia*. Florence, 1981.

Curtius, Ernst Robert. *European Literature and the Latin Middle Ages*. Translated by Willard R. Trask. New York, 1953.

Dionysius. *De caelesti ierarchia*. In Migne, *P.L.* CXXII.

Dronke, Peter. "Orizzonti che rischiari: Notes towards an Interpretation of *Paradise XIV*." *Romance Philology* 29(1975): 1 – 19.

Enciclopedia dantesca. Edited by Umberto Bosco. 5 vols. Rome, 1970.

Gaffney, James. "Dante's Blindness in *Paradiso* XXV–XXVI: An Allegorical Interpretation." *DSARDS* 91: 101 – 112.

Galimberti, Cesare. *Il canto VII del Paradiso*. Florence, 1968.

Gardner, Edmund G. *Dante's Ten Heavens*. New York, 1970.

————. *Dante and the Mystics*. London, 1913.

Grandgent, Charles H. *La Divina Commedia*. Revised by C. S. Singleton. Cambridge, Mass., 1972.

Gregory I. *Homiliarum in Ezechielem prophetam libri duo*. In Migne, *P.L.* LXXVI.

Griffin, Mary. "*Paradiso* XXVI, 97." *Modern Language Notes*, 71(1956): 30 – 33.

Guéranger, R. R. Dom Prosper. *The Liturgical Year. Paschal Time*, trans. from the French by the Rev. Dom Laurence Shepherd. 2d ed. Vol I. London, 1888.

Isidore of Seville. *Etymologiarum sive Originum libri XX*. Edited by W.M. Lindsay. Vol. II. Oxford, 1911.

Kantorowicz, Ernst H. *Frederick the Second*. New York, 1957.

Lana, Jacopo della. *Comedia di Dante degli Allagherii col commento di Jacopo della Lana bolognese*. Edited by Luciano Scarabelli. Vol. III. Bologna, 1866.

Landino, Cristoforo. *Dante con l'espositioni di Christoforo Landino et d'Alessandro Vellutello. Sopra la sua Comedia dell'Inferno, del Purgatorio, e del Paradiso*. Venice, 1596.

Latini, Brunetto. *Li livres dou tresor de Brunetto Latini*, ed. Francis J. Carmody. Berkeley, 1948.

Longen, Eugene. "The Grammar of Apotheosis: *Paradiso* XXXIII, 94–99." *Dante Studies* 97(1975): 209–214.

Mattalia, Daniele. *La Divina Commedia*. Vol 2: *Paradiso*. Milan, 1960.

Migne, J. P., ed. *Patrologiae cursus completus: Series Latina*. Paris, 1844–64 (with later printings).

Momigliano, Attilio, ed. *La Divina Commedia di Dante Alighieri*. Vol. III: *Paradiso*. Florence, 1947.

Musa, Mark. *Dante's Inferno*. Bloomington, Ind., 1971.

—————. *Dante's Vita nuova*. Bloomington, Ind., 1973.

—————. *Advent at the Gates: Dante's Comedy*. Bloomington, Ind., 1974.

—————. "Virgil Reads the Pilgrim's Mind." *Dante Studies*, 95 (1977):149–52.

—————. *Dante's Purgatory*. Bloomington, Ind., 1981.

Nardi, Bruno. *Saggi di filosofia dantesca*. Florence, 1967.

—————. "L'averroismo di Sigieri e Dante." *Studi danteschi* 22(1983): 83–113.

Norton, Charles Eliot. *The Divine Comedy of Dante Alighieri*. Revised edition. Vol. III: *Paradise*. Boston, 1902.

L'Ottimo Commento della Divina Commedia. Edited by Alessandro Torri. Vol. III. Pisa, 1829.

d'Ovidio, Francesco. "Il nome di Dio nella lingua d'Adamo." *Ultimo volume dantesco*. Rome, 1926.

Palmieri, Pantaleo. "Pietro Damiano già peccatore in *Pd*. XXI, 122." *Studi e problemi di critica testuale* 15(1977): 62–83.

Pasquazi, Silvio. *All'eterno dal tempo*. Florence, 1966.

Pertile, Lino. " '*Par.*' XXXIII: l'estremo oltraggio." *Filologia Critica*, Jan–April (1981), 1–21.

Peter Lombard. *Sententiarum libri quatuor*. In Migne, *P.L.* CXCII.

Petrus Comestor. *Historia scholastica*. In Migne, *P.L.* CXCVIII.

Pietro di Dante. *Super Dantis ipsius genitoris Comoediam commentarium*. Edited by Vincenzo Nannucci. Florence, 1845.

Porena, Manfredi. *La Divina Commedia*. Vol. III: *Paradiso*. Bologna, 1964.

Richard of St. Victor. *In Cantica Canticorum explicatio*. In Migne, *P.L.* CXCVI.

Sansone, Mario. *Il canto VII del Paradiso*. Florence, 1973.

Sapegno, Natalino. *La Divina Commedia*. Milan, 1957.

Sayers, Dorothy and Reynolds, Barbara. *The Comedy of Dante Alighieri, Cantica III, Paradise*. Penguin Books, 1971.

Scartazzini, G. A. and Vandelli, Giuseppe. *La Divina Commedia. Testo critico della Società Dantesca Italiana*. Commentary by G. A. Scartazzini. 17th edition revised by Giuseppe Vandelli: Milan, 1958.

Seznec, Jean. *The Survival of the Pagan Gods: The Mythological Tradition and Its Place in Renaissance Humanism and Art*. Trans. B. F. Sessions. NY: Harper, 1961.

Sinclair, John D. *The Divine Comedy*. Vol. III. London, 1948.

Singleton, Charles S. trans. *The Divine Comedy*. Vol. III: *Paradiso*, pt. 2: *Commentary*. Princeton, N.J., 1973.

Spitzer, Leo. *Romanische Literaturstudien*, pp. 574 – 95, Tübingen, 1959.

Steiner, Carlo. *La Divina Commedia*. Vol. III: *Paradiso*. Turin, 1942.

Stronski, Stanislaw. *Le Troubador Folquet de Marseille*. Cracow, 1910.

Temple Classics. *A Translation of the Latin Works of Dante Alighieri*. London, 1940.

Toffanin, Giuseppe. *Sette interpretazioni dantesche*. Naples, 1947: 77 – 85.

Torraca, Francesco. *La Divina Commedia*. Vol. III: *Paradiso*. Rome, 1952.

Toynbee, Paget. *A Dictionary of Proper Names and Notable Matters in the Works of Dante*. Revised by C. S. Singleton. Oxford, 1968.

Vernon, William Warren. *Readings on the "Paradiso" of Dante*. 2 vols. London, 1909.

Villani, Giovanni. *Cronica di Giovanni Villani*. Edited by Gherardi Dragomanni. 4 vols. Florence, 1844 – 45.

von Richthofen, Erich. *Veltro und Diana*. Tübingen, 1956.

Wilcox, Ruth Turner. *The Mode in Hats and Headdress*. Scribners, 1945.

FOR THE BEST IN PAPERBACKS, LOOK FOR THE

In every corner of the world, on every subject under the sun, Penguin represents quality and variety—the very best in publishing today.

For complete information about books available from Penguin—including Puffins, Penguin Classics, and Arkana—and how to order them, write to us at the appropriate address below. Please note that for copyright reasons the selection of books varies from country to country.

In the United Kingdom: Please write to *Dept. JC, Penguin Books Ltd, FREEPOST, West Drayton, Middlesex UB7 0BR.*

If you have any difficulty in obtaining a title, please send your order with the correct money, plus ten percent for postage and packaging, to *P.O. Box No. 11, West Drayton, Middlesex UB7 0BR*

In the United States: Please write to *Consumer Sales, Penguin USA, P.O. Box 999, Dept. 17109, Bergenfield, New Jersey 07621-0120.* VISA and MasterCard holders call 1-800-253-6476 to order all Penguin titles

In Canada: Please write to *Penguin Books Canada Ltd, 10 Alcorn Avenue, Suite 300, Toronto, Ontario M4V 3B2*

In Australia: Please write to *Penguin Books Australia Ltd, P.O. Box 257, Ringwood, Victoria 3134*

In New Zealand: Please write to *Penguin Books (NZ) Ltd, Private Bag 102902, North Shore Mail Centre, Auckland 10*

In India: Please write to *Penguin Books India Pvt Ltd, 706 Eros Apartments, 56 Nehru Place, New Delhi 110 019*

In the Netherlands: Please write to *Penguin Books Netherlands bv, Postbus 3507, NL-1001 AH Amsterdam*

In Germany: Please write to *Penguin Books Deutschland GmbH, Metzlerstrasse 26, 60594 Frankfurt am Main*

In Spain: Please write to *Penguin Books S. A., Bravo Murillo 19, 1° B, 28015 Madrid*

In Italy: Please write to *Penguin Italia s.r.l., Via Felice Casati 20, I-20124 Milano*

In France: Please write to *Penguin France S. A., 17 rue Lejeune, F–31000 Toulouse*

In Japan: Please write to *Penguin Books Japan, Ishikiribashi Building, 2–5–4, Suido, Bunkyo-ku, Tokyo 112*

In Greece: Please write to *Penguin Hellas Ltd, Dimocritou 3, GR–106 71 Athens*

In South Africa: Please write to *Longman Penguin Southern Africa (Pty) Ltd, Private Bag X08, Bertsham 2013*